Business and Professional Communication

Fifth Edition

Sara Miller McCune founded SAGE Publishing in 1965 to support the dissemination of usable knowledge and educate a global community. SAGE publishes more than 1,000 journals and over 600 new books each year, spanning a wide range of subject areas. Our growing selection of library products includes archives, data, case studies, and video. SAGE remains majority owned by our founder and after her lifetime will become owned by a charitable trust that secures the company's continued independence.

Los Angeles | London | New Delhi | Singapore | Washington DC | Melbourne

Business and Professional Communication

KEYS for Workplace Excellence

Fifth Edition

Kelly Quintanilla Miller

Texas A&M University

Shawn T. Wahl

Missouri State University

Los Angeles | London | New Delhi
Singapore | Washington DC | Melbourne

FOR INFORMATION:

SAGE Publications, Inc.
2455 Teller Road
Thousand Oaks, California 91320
E-mail: order@sagepub.com

SAGE Publications Ltd.
1 Oliver's Yard
55 City Road
London, EC1Y 1SP
United Kingdom

SAGE Publications India Pvt. Ltd.
B 1/I 1 Mohan Cooperative Industrial Area
Mathura Road, New Delhi 110 044
India

SAGE Publications Asia-Pacific Pte. Ltd.
18 Cross Street #10-10/11/12
China Square Central
Singapore 048423

Printed in the United States of America

Library of Congress Control Number: 2022921907

23 24 25 26 27 10 9 8 7 6 5 4 3 2 1

Acquisitions Editor: Charles Lee

Content Development Editor: Cassie Carey

Production Editor: Astha Jaiswal

Copy Editor: Diane DiMura

Typesetter: diacriTech

Cover Designer: Candice Harman

Marketing Manager: Victoria Velasquez

BRIEF CONTENTS

DETAILED CONTENTS

PREFACE

It is our pleasure to share the fifth edition with you! As instructors, we must answer many questions when planning a business and professional communication course. First, we must address the broader conceptual questions, such as "What do we want our students to learn?" "How can this information be applied to their current and future professional lives?" "How can we make this material meaningful, useful, and interesting to students with a variety of professional goals and interests?" "How can all important information, skills, and competencies relevant to business and professional communication be covered in one term?"

Next, we must address the nuts-and-bolts questions that emerge about how to organize so much information and how to translate it into accessible language for students. Instructors often grapple with questions such as "Should I require both an individual and team presentation?" "How much time should I put in the schedule for mock interviews?" "How much attention should be given to résumé development?" "How can this course be delivered online?"

We considered many of the same questions and challenges as we made decisions about what content to cover in this text. **Our mission** in writing this book was to focus the research and competencies related to business and professional communication so that it can easily be covered in one term across delivery formats (e.g., traditional, online, hybrid). Further, we wanted to provide a book that speaks directly to the student as a developing professional by focusing on the actual experiences—from the job search to developing workplace relations to managing the challenges of coworker bullies, difficult clients, burnout, and the like. We also wanted to provide a text that is adaptable to a variety of instructional needs—for our colleagues who may need the flexibility to emphasize individual presentations and for others who may focus more on team presentations, not include oral communication at all, or deliver the course online. We recognize the diversity from one college or university to the next.

In response to our goal of focusing directly on the individual student experience related to the development of business and professional excellence, we developed an **organizing feature** (the KEYS process described below), which we believe will help instructors guide students and developing professionals in a variety of professional contexts. The KEYS process fosters the primary theme of this text—one that encourages students, regardless of industry or career, to strive for **professional excellence**. In this text, we provide 14 tightly focused chapters in which the best material—drawn from the research bases of communication, business, leadership, psychology, education, and other disciplines—is explored with relevance to the KEYS process. This book doesn't attempt to cover the entire business and professional world—we've made difficult choices regarding the content, based on our years of communication consulting in the business world, teaching communication in higher education, and experimenting with texts written by our friends and colleagues across the nation. What we ended up with represents the cutting-edge work in the field, including research from a variety of methods as well as popular literature, human resources, corporate consulting, and leadership coaching. **Our goal is to connect students across industries and academic disciplines to both theory and practice by applying information regarding business and professional communication directly to professional life *inside* and *outside* the workplace—without overwhelming them.**

We believe that one of the strengths of this text is that it addresses the challenges we face in today's workplace. In addition to our experience as teacher–scholars in communication, we have worked as consultants designing training and development programs for organizations in a variety of industries. While all these organizations face similar communication challenges, other textbooks merely mention the problems and rarely address solutions. *Business and Professional Communication: KEYS for Workplace Excellence* not only examines workplace problems (e.g., difficult people, negative impacts of technology, work–life balance, corporate health); it also provides students with a communication process that helps them solve problems and continue their professional journeys.

ORGANIZING FEATURE: KEYS FOR WORKPLACE EXCELLENCE

We believe that developing an organizing feature lends clarity to a textbook. Further, such a feature helps students apply material directly to their lives. The **organizing feature** running throughout the text is KEYS, a process designed to develop students' critical thinking skills and make them more reflexive communicators with the ability to adapt and continually improve.

The KEYS process includes the following four phases: **K**now yourself, **E**valuate the professional context, **Y**our communication interaction, and **S**tep back and reflect.

> **K**now yourself: Challenging students to actively assess their skills as communicators and then develop strategies to utilize their strengths and develop their weaknesses
>
> **E**valuate the professional context: Teaching students to proactively address the needs of their audience and understand the constraints of the professional communication context, as well as developing their skills for communicating with a variety of audiences and contexts
>
> **Y**our communication interaction: Asking students to monitor their own verbal and nonverbal communication in addition to the audience within each interaction
>
> **S**tep back and reflect: Examining the effectiveness of verbal and nonverbal messages students convey to others and the overall success of various communication interactions and then taking what they've learned and starting the KEYS process again; developing the ability to continually adapt and improve using a personalized communication inventory

OVERVIEW OF THE BOOK: STRATEGIES FOR EXCELLING IN THE WORKPLACE AT EVERY STAGE

The book is organized into five distinct parts. Part I provides an overview of the foundations and key concepts important to the study of business and professional communication and introduces students to central principles related to verbal and nonverbal communication and listening. The next four parts correspond with the stages of experience that come with entering the workplace for the first time, receiving a promotion, or changing careers. **Each chapter includes cutting-edge research, skills, and tips that will help students to advance in the workplace at every stage of their career by honing their communication skills.** Throughout the text, we connect important issues such as cultural diversity, cultural competence, mutual respect, gender, ethnicity and race, religion, people with disabilities, and more to the business and professional context. With each phase of development, students will gain interpersonal competency, enhance their organizational ability, and refine their presentational skills. The final stage of experience, Part V, *Surviving in the Workplace*, encourages students to develop strategies for balancing work and life through communication, a topic not covered in most business and professional communication textbooks.

Features of the Textbook

We provide several unique pedagogical features to help students understand and apply the concepts and theories introduced in the text. The features help reinforce the book's themes and promote critical thinking in readers.

- **Chapter Outlines** detail the organization of each chapter, while **Chapter Objectives** help students prioritize information so that they can learn more efficiently.

- An **opening chapter narrative** connects students to the primary chapter content—a brief example of real-world stories to gain attention from readers as they move into a new topic. In all chapters, opening chapter narratives are ripped-from-the-headlines news stories representing actual events and real experiences across business and professional contexts.

- Themes from the narratives appear throughout each chapter and are applied to and evaluated with the KEYS feature in a summary section, called **KEYS for Excellence in the Workplace**, that appears at the end of each chapter.

- The KEYS organizing theme is also highlighted in four distinct instructional features: **Know Yourself** features self-assessments and inventories for readers to hone their communication skills; **Evaluate the Professional Context** encourages application of knowledge to a variety of professional contexts and situations; **Your Communication Interaction** focuses on making competent communication choices and selecting the appropriate communication channel from calling a face-to-face meeting to using social media and technology; and **Step Back and Reflect** presents challenges and dilemmas in business and professional contexts, promoting analysis of what went wrong in specific business and professional situations. All boxed features contain discussion questions to promote critical thinking and classroom discussion.

- Communication ethics is emphasized in all chapters with a feature called **Ethical Connection**, which connects the topic to an ethical perspective—because it's the foundation of business and professional excellence.

- All chapters also include a feature called **Executive Summary**, designed to promote reading comprehension and serve as a guide to help connect chapter concepts to the chapter objectives.

- We include **Discussion Questions** that instructors may use as a means of generating class discussions about chapter content, as actual assignments, or as thought-provokers for students to consider on their own time.

- Complete **References** to the research base cited within the text appear at the end of the book. Students may find these references useful as they prepare assignments or conduct their own research projects. Instructors may use the references to gather additional material for their own research or to supplement instruction.

- **Tools for Professional Excellence** feature focuses on communication skills development, career tips, and practical strategies for contexts related to business and professional communication, social media, and technology.

- **Action Items** feature encourages students to apply chapter content to business and professional communication skills and contexts.

NEW TO THIS EDITION

- **Updated photo program** in each chapter helps students see themselves in a variety of business of professional contexts.

- **Updated examples** exist throughout the textbook that use the COVID-19 pandemic as an example. This book is not COVID-heavy but does acknowledge how our world of work has changed.

- **The revised "KEYS" feature** connects the reader to a variety of business and professional contexts across industries.

- **Updated Ethical Connection** and **Tools for Professional Excellence** encourage critical thinking and application of content to work life.

DIGITAL RESOURCES

This text includes an array of instructor teaching materials designed to save you time and to help you keep students engaged. To learn more, visit sagepub.com or contact your SAGE representative at sagepub.com/findmyrep.

ACKNOWLEDGMENTS

This project has been both exciting and challenging. Thus, there are many people we would like to acknowledge. The authors wish to thank the team at SAGE, with whom it's been a pleasure to work, including Terri Accomazzo, Jennifer Jovin, and Sarah Wilson, who all offered great assistance, feedback, and encouragement.

We are grateful to our colleagues and friends in the field of communication whose advice and encouragement helped inform our decisions during the review process of this text. We would like to thank all reviewers who worked on this project for all past editions.

We'd like to thank the reviewers of this edition:

Sara Baker Bailey, *Southern CT State University*
Jennifer Keohane, *University of Baltimore*
Brandi A. Quesenberry, *Virginia Tech University*
Susan Tomasovic, *George Mason University*

In addition, we would also like to thank the reviewers who provided in depth chapter feedback centered around insuring the quality of diversity, equity, and inclusion materials:

Adrianne Ford, *University of St. Mary*
Keith Hearit, *Western Michigan University*
Melissa Hernández-Katz, *University of Texas at Dallas*
Jie Ke, *Jackson State University*
Sharon Storch, *University of Nebraska Omaha*
Joseph Velasco, *Sul Ross State University*
Megan Young, *Stetson University*

Reviewers for the third edition:

Valerie Arias, *Loyola Marymount University*
David M. Bollinger, *University of North Carolina Wilmington*
Dan Carrison, *University of La Verne*
Bruce A. Crawley, *Western Kentucky University*
Karyn Friesen, *Lone Star College—Montgomery Speech Department*
Jennifer Millspaugh, *Richland College*
Mark Zampino, *University of Hartford*

Reviewers for the second edition:

Diane L. Carter, *University of Idaho*
Katherine M. Castle, *University of Nebraska–Lincoln*
Jennifer Karchmer, *Western Washington University*

Alison McCrowell Lietzenmayer, *Old Dominion University*
Amanda Retberg, *Wisconsin Lutheran College*
Astrid Sheil, *California State University, San Bernardino*
Scott Wilson, *Central Ohio Technical College*

Reviewers for the first edition:

Karla Mason Bergen, *College of Saint Mary, Omaha*
Nicholas F. Burnett, *California State University, Sacramento*
Carolyn Clark, *Salt Lake Community College*
Dale Cyphert, *University of Northern Iowa*
Dale Davis, *University of Texas at San Antonio*
Kristina Drumheller, *West Texas A&M University*
Randy Duncan, *Henderson State University*
Leonard M. Edmonds, *Arizona State University*
Michele Foss-Snowden, *California State University, Sacramento*
Jeffrey Dale Hobbs, *University of Texas at Tyler*
Melody A. Hubbard, *Northwest Missouri State University*
William W. Kenner, *University of Michigan–Flint*
Erika L. Kirby, *Creighton University*
John Ludlum, *Otterbein College*
Marie A. Mater, *Houston Baptist University*
M. Chad McBride, *Creighton University*
Aysel Morin, *East Carolina University*
Laura Umphrey, *Northern Arizona University*
Denise Vrchota, *Iowa State University*

Thanks also to our colleagues, friends, and students at Texas A&M University–Corpus Christi and Missouri State University. We are especially grateful to Garrett Ruzika for his contributions to the research-gathering process, photographic selections, permissions, and instructional supplements.

Kelly thanks her mother, Barbara Miller, for always being there for her and her daughter, Logan, for being the most wonderful blessing anyone could ever receive. She would also like to thank her coauthor Shawn for his incredible friendship. Shawn would first like to thank his friend and collaborator Kelly Miller for her continued commitment to this project. He would like to thank his colleagues, friends, and students in the Reynolds College of Arts and Letters at Missouri State University. Finally, Shawn thanks his family and friends for their support and belief in this book and his passion for teaching and studying communication. Thanks to my family for believing him; his brothers, Larkin Wahl and Shannon Wahl, for their confidence and support, and his pug dogs, Bentley (B Pug) and "Pete the Almighty" (P Pug) for loving him in every moment. Shawn's mother, Evelyn Klaerner Wahl, passed away in 2019—he dedicates this fifth edition in memory of her.

INTRODUCTION FOR STUDENTS

Let us introduce ourselves as your coauthors. We approach this project with years of experience teaching basic communication courses such as public speaking, business and professional communication, interviewing, teamwork and leadership, organizational communication, and public relations. Balanced with our teaching experience and expert knowledge in the communication field are years of professional consulting and real-world experience in a variety of industries, including retail, manufacturing, shipping, health care, government, education, and more. We know firsthand the communication challenges you will face and the communication skills you will need to succeed. Based on our teaching and professional experience, we wrote this book for you, the student as a developing professional.

When designing this text, we talked to professors and students alike, trying to get a sense of their needs. Two themes emerged from those conversations. First, instructors and professors are frustrated because students do not read their books. As a result, class discussions, exam scores, and student learning suffer. On the flip side, students are frustrated because they find most books extremely expensive and full of information they deem unimportant. Repeatedly, students asked, "Why can't professors just put the stuff I need to know on a PowerPoint slide?" Our goal when writing this text is to address both problems and needs. We have tried to develop a text that speaks directly to you as a student who desires success after graduation. We realize that those of you taking this class and reading this text are interested in different professions and are in different stages of your professional lives. Given the array of professional journeys taking place in the lives of you, the readers, we have included topics that will be valuable to everyone. The topic areas of the text will focus on *beginning communication principles, entering the workplace, developing in the workplace, excelling in the workplace, presenting in the workplace*, and *surviving in the workplace*. We explore the experiences you will face as you transition from student to professional and, eventually, to leader. You will come to understand the role of communication in successfully handling situations such as interviewing for jobs, providing feedback to supervisors, and working in teams. As an additional feature, this text not only discusses the greatest challenges we all face in the modern workplace but also provides communication strategies for overcoming those challenges. Issues such as excelling under the pressure of increasingly competitive customer service demands, managing emotions when dealing with irate customers, overcoming stress and burnout, and managing difficult people are just a few of the topics covered. We hope that this approach will engage you as both a student and a reader.

When you hear the word *professional*, who or what comes to mind? Do a suit and a tie equate to professional excellence, or is it something more?

iStockphoto/laflor

WHAT IS BUSINESS AND PROFESSIONAL COMMUNICATION?

Although many of these subjects will be expanded upon in later chapters, these are some of the core principles that will set the foundation for your study of business and professional communication.

Interviewing

Obviously, your first step into the business world will involve landing a job. *Interviewing* is the process of making yourself available to employers in a formal setting and in the best possible light. Although the main goal of interviewing is to get a job, it also gives you the opportunity to determine whether the particular job is right for you. Interviewing is a two-way street; you should also use this time to make sure that an organization meets your needs as a professional and that the organizational culture will allow you to thrive. Knowing how to prepare for an interview, anticipating questions, dressing appropriately, providing credible and effective answers, and following up after an interview are all critical aspects of being a competent interview participant.

Relational Communication

Although you may be an effective communicator in interpersonal settings, you need to know how to apply relational communication to the business and professional world. Communication initiation, maintenance, and even disengagement are all necessary skills to possess for workplace relationships. You will be tasked with forming effective relationships with your coworkers, supervisors, customers, vendors, and subordinates. Much of your communication will challenge you to balance small talk, self-disclosure, task delegation, and many other functions that are essential in the workplace. Also, when business relationships turn sour or costly, you must know how to end the relationship with minimal tension and negative consequences.

Mediated Communication

The new media have opened numerous new channels for communication professionals. Computer-mediated communication offers convenience and timely access to pertinent information, and it connects communicators across the globe via screen taps and mouse clicks. However, as a communication professional, you must be aware of the inherent drawbacks of mediated communication. Be aware that traditional public speaking skills don't always translate as effectively (e.g., video or telephone conferences) and must be altered to fit the situation at hand.

Presentational Speaking

Public speaking is one of the most feared—but also most important—functions of business and professional communication. This textbook will introduce you to various types of business presentations, including informative, persuasive, and public presentations. You will learn how to research and prepare your presentation, how to analyze your audience (as well as who your *target* audience should be), and how to create memorable and effective introductions and conclusions that will stick in the mind of your audience. You will learn about the balance of having excellent content while also delivering it to the audience in an engaging way. Also, you will learn about many of the multimedia presentation aids available to you, as well as when (and if) visual aids are appropriate for your presentation.

Written Documents

Effective professional communication asks you to be not only a great communicator and speaker, but also an effective writer. Although the type of written communication you engage in can vary greatly depending on your profession, there are certain universal skills you should always have. You must know how to structure the information; select the right style, tone, and language; and determine what length is appropriate to cover all the important information while also being short enough to keep the readers' attention. You must learn how to cultivate and maintain credibility, and use appropriate grammar and punctuation to emphasize professionalism. This may seem like a daunting to-do list, but through study and practice you will be able to create professional, engaging, and effective written communication for your business or organization.

BUSINESS AND PROFESSIONAL EXCELLENCE IN CONTEXT

The text's driving theme is **professional excellence**. To demonstrate excellence as a professional, you must demonstrate excellence as a communicator. Excellence does not equate to merely communicating a message effectively or simply demonstrating communication competencies. Professional excellence means being recognized for your skills as a communicator and serving as a role model to others. Before you begin your journey with this important topic, it is important to understand some fundamental areas of communication, such as verbal communication, nonverbal communication, and listening. Additionally, it's important to understand the business and professional contexts that will receive specific attention in this book. The business and professional contexts you will explore are beginning communication principles (i.e., verbal and nonverbal communication, listening), the job-seeking process, workplace culture and diversity, interpersonal communication, team communication, communication and technology, written communication, leadership, presenting as a professional, and work–life balance. These are the contexts that will no doubt shape your experience as a professional. Keep in mind that communication is at the core of the business and professional contexts you will study in this course. Let's take a look at each one in more detail.

Verbal and Nonverbal Communication

Chapter 2 explores the importance of verbal and nonverbal communication as the foundation of beginning principles needed to guide your study of business and professional communication across contexts. Verbal communication is both our words and our verbal fillers (e.g., *um, like*). Verbal messages are created through language. Effective communication involves accurate interpretations of others' verbal messages as meaning is cocreated. Further, nonverbal communication (sometimes referred to as body language) includes all those ways we communicate without words.

The handshake is an important example of nonverbal communication experienced in many business and professional situations.

iStockphoto/PeopleImages

Listening

Chapter 3 connects listening to your study of business and professional communication. Effective listening is central to fostering interpersonal relationships with coworkers, leaders, and clients. Effective listening can impact one's relationship satisfaction and can be a determining factor in whether someone is an effective communicator. Listening, in addition to other communication abilities, is a likely predictor of who gets promoted or who receives other relevant rewards such as status and power. In all, listening is a beginning communication skill or basic principle important to your study of business and professional communication. You will learn the importance of listening across business and professional contexts using the KEYS process.

Résumés, Interviews, and Negotiation

The context you will study in Chapter 4 is job seeking. Our approach is to provide the information you'll need to conduct a comprehensive job search and know yourself in terms of professional goals and the type of work environment you desire. Job seeking is one context in which business and professional excellence is critical to your success.

Getting to Know Your Diverse Workplace

Once you've landed the job, you'll enter a diverse workplace context. You will no doubt have coworkers whose views of the world and ways of living are different from yours. Further, it can take time to learn the organizational culture in terms of your role and how you fit in. As Chapter 5 explores, getting to know your diverse workplace goes beyond new employee orientation. The diverse workplace context requires professional excellence fostered by cultural competence, perception checking, and mutual respect.

Interpersonal Communication at Work

Central to your personal and professional growth in any career are the relationships and overall rapport you'll have with your boss, coworkers, and clients. Chapter 6 reviews the importance of **interpersonal communication** in common business and professional encounters. Interpersonal communication (also referred to as people skills) helps you build relationships in your personal and professional life, but these skills also can help you to survive many challenges (e.g., conflict, difficult coworkers and clients).

Where would you begin to search for jobs in the industry or profession in which you're interested?
iStockphoto/gilaxia

Strengthening Teams and Conducting Meetings

Another common experience for professionals across industries is working in a team context. You've probably heard other people use terms such as *team player, team skills*, and *team building* in reference to job performance. Working in a team context can be both a rewarding and an exhausting experience for any professional. Chapter 7 pays specific attention to the team context you'll likely encounter in your professional life, as well as strategies that foster professional excellence in team communication. This chapter also focuses on the skills needed to run effective meetings, a primary tool for team communication.

Technology in the Workplace

Technology in business and professional contexts is central to communication, planning, marketing, networking, organization, research, and the like. Technology allows you to communicate faster than in years past with the use of email, personal digital assistants, and a host of other devices designed to make the exchange of information in business instant rather than delayed. Chapter 8 examines the impact of communication and technology on business and professional contexts, including the role of social media as a professional tool and a professional barrier. As technology enables you to excel at work with faster information exchange and interaction, it's important to be aware of the problems and misunderstandings that can occur as the result of various technology-based communication channels.

Business and Professional Writing

Chapter 9 examines written communication as it connects to professional excellence. As you enter business and professional contexts that require you to use written communication, it is important for you to make decisions that will ensure professional excellence. Written communication can challenge professionals in a variety of contexts. How do I select the correct format to get the message out? Is it appropriate for me to send this document via email? What tone should

As much as anyone wants to be successful professionally, it's important to think about personal and family life, too. Unfortunately, maintaining balance can be difficult.

iStockphoto/Kerkez

I strive for in this message? These are only a few of the questions about written communication that you may encounter in your career.

Leadership and Conflict Management

Chapter 10 reviews the role of leadership in business and professional contexts. In order to excel as a leader, you must understand what leadership is and get to know what style of leader you are and if your style works best in the business and professional context in which you're working. Further, this chapter explores the challenges leaders experience, as well as strategies for leading difficult people and managing workplace conflict.

Presentations

As a professional, you will enter situations that require you to give presentations. The presentation context arises in many forms (e.g., informative, persuasive, motivational, team). Chapters 11, 12, and 13 explore the presentation skills essential to your professional success. When you're faced with an opportunity to give a formal presentation, pitch a product, present research findings, run a meeting, conduct a morning huddle, acknowledge outstanding employees, or motivate your team in difficult times, view that speaking situation as a chance to communicate professional excellence.

Work–Life Balance

Chapter 14 looks at how the various experiences in your professional and personal life can be in conflict with one another. This tension can present quite a challenge, which can lead to stress and burnout. We emphasize the importance of work–life balance, explore the triggers that cause imbalance, and present communication strategies that enable you to sustain professional excellence and foster meaningful and successful relationships in your personal life.

Present in each of these contexts is the KEYS process.

BEGINNING COMMUNICATION PRINCIPLES

iStockphoto/NicolasMcComber

1

BUSINESS AND PROFESSIONAL EXCELLENCE IN THE WORKPLACE

After studying this chapter, you should be able to

1.1   Identify key areas of human communication within business and professional contexts

1.2   Explain the components of the communication model

1.3   Identify the types and causes of communication apprehension

1.4   Discuss communication and professional excellence from an ethical perspective

1.5   Identify the four KEYS to communication in the workplace

Communication has increasingly become a cornerstone of professional excellence in the workplace. As an employer, Twitter embodies both communication and professional excellence; its entire platform relies on the drive for communication while requiring a level of professionalism to make the company profitable. Below we take a look at how Twitter incorporates these two ideals:

- *What it does:* Twitter is a global online information network that allows users to share content and conversations in real time. The company has more than 217 million monthly active users who create approximately 500 million tweets every day (Aslam, 2022). This amount of traffic requires an effective and motivated team of employees to manage.

- *Challenges:* An anonymous survey conducted by Great Rated! indicated that 87% of employees reported that the company often or almost always provided training, fair promotions, and personally challenging work; and 88% of employees felt that Twitter offered more than just a job, but also the opportunity to develop a worldwide forum of communication that creates special meaning.

- *Atmosphere:* The majority of Twitter employees report enjoying their colleagues and find the workplace to be cooperative and fun. Professional excellence requires employees to work fluidly with one another, thus minimizing miscommunication and conflict.

- *Rewards:* 85% of employees reported that Twitter supports their work–life balance and compensates them fairly. Feeling essential to company success is a great motivator to encourage employees to strive for professional excellence.

Reading about employee feedback concerning Twitter may have you motivated to find a career devoted to such positive professional excellence. However, successfully applying to and being accepted at such an organization is no easy feat. You may ask yourself, "Will I be able to get an interview? Will I be considered for a promotion at work? Will I fit in at my new job? What's the best way to run a meeting? What are the qualities of a professional presentation? How should I respond to negative coworkers?" The preceding questions are commonly asked by people entering the workplace for the first time, as well as by people changing job titles, duties, or careers. It seems that regardless of the position or the industry in which you desire to work, there is one thing that will make or break the experience: communication. So welcome to the world of business and professional communication. As you study business and professional communication over the course of this semester, we encourage you, regardless of your major, to take these principles and objectives to heart. After all, communication is the key to professional excellence, and professional excellence is the key to success.

UNDERSTANDING THE IMPORTANCE OF HUMAN COMMUNICATION IN BUSINESS AND PROFESSIONAL CONTEXTS

As you begin your study, it's important to define what communication means. Communication has been defined in many ways, but here's the definition we prefer: Human communication is the process of understanding our experiences and the experiences of others through the use of verbal and nonverbal messages (Edwards et al., 2019; Ivy & Wahl, 2019; Regenbogen et al., 2012). People come to understand that communication in everyday experiences is the essential process and skill that helps them make sense of things in both personal and professional contexts.

Even if you have some reservations about your communication skills, you probably consider yourself to be a good communicator and good listener. Most people do. After all, it's difficult to admit being bad at something you do all day, every day, for your entire life. Because communication is so much a part of our everyday lives, we think of communication as a simple process. Communicating comes so naturally to us that we rarely feel the need to give communication a second thought. When was the last time you really stopped and examined your communication skills? Do you stop and examine your communication regularly? Most people don't.

In some cases, people who fail to reflect on their communication skills trudge through life thinking they are great communicators when they are, in actuality, dreadful communicators. They exemplify a behavior called communication bravado—perceiving their communication as effective, while those around them perceive it as ineffective (Quintanilla & Mallard, 2008). Ineffective communicators view communication as simply talking—but truly effective communicators know it is far more complicated than that.

Do you take your communication skills for granted? Are you suffering from communication bravado? Let us assure you that you do indeed have some weaknesses in your communication and listening, simply because everyone does. However, understanding why communication is important and how the communication process works is the first step in overcoming those weaknesses and starting on the road to professional excellence (see Table 1.1).

In addition, there are several important ways in which the key areas of human communication as a whole influence and are essential for effective communication in the workplace.

Role-Taking

The critical functions of human communication (sending and receiving messages, offering feedback, identifying the "role" of different communicators) must also be applied to the context of business communication. For example, car salespeople must basically give sales "presentations" to any potential buyers who visit their car lot. Much of their success is determined by how well they can tailor their message depending on the individual needs of many different customers. If customers give verbal or nonverbal cues expressing concern about the fuel efficiency of their prospective vehicle, the salesperson must modify the message to emphasize each car's gas mileage as a major selling point. This dynamic aspect of role-taking and feedback keeps the transaction flowing.

Previous Communication Experiences

The way people respond initially to new business transactions depends greatly on their previous communication experiences in similar situations. Using the previous example, have you experienced buying a new vehicle or making another major purchase (house, major appliance, business)? Depending on whether that experience was positive or negative, it helps form the basis for how you communicate in similar transactions in the future. Therefore, from a business standpoint, your initial communication impression is of critical importance.

Communication Channels

Depending on your physical location, your communication approach can alter significantly (Ivy & Wahl, 2019). For example, your communication with a classmate will likely be much more informal than your communication with a professor. Similarly, the channel of communication can also affect communication. Many people feel comfortable taking a more aggressive or assertive tone when using email than when engaging in face-to-face communication.

TABLE 1.1 ■ Action Items. Communication Excellence in the Workplace		
Sales	Allow online shopping for customers.	Retail outlet Target allows customers to order in-store items from home for added convenience. More and more retailers are also offering curbside pickup options for customers who order items online.
Customer service	Use social media to reach out directly to consumers.	Electronics retailer Best Buy responds directly to customer concerns and complaints via its Facebook and Twitter pages.
Public relations	Use nontraditional media platforms to reach the target audience.	After a TikTok creator jokingly made low-quality redesigns of major company logos, various companies—such as Nascar, Tinder, and Tampax—changed their TikTok profile photos to the creator's redeisgns (Press-Reynolds, 2021).

Cultural Influences

The way we communicate, with whom we communicate, and what we communicate are almost always influenced by culture (Wahl & Simmons, 2018). Culture is an ongoing social institution that has its own set of behavioral rules. For our discussion, *organizational culture* influences how we (as members of a business or professional organization) frame our communication with others both within and outside that organization. For example, the communication that takes place in a board meeting of lawyers will feature a different set of decorum, rules, and *norms* when compared with a brainstorming session among creative writers for a small company. To be a competent communicator in your organization, you must be dynamic in adhering to the rules and norms of different communication situations.

Communication Relationships

The perceived social hierarchy between communicators, whether they be strangers or intimates, significantly influences the nature of the communication interaction. The way you communicate with a customer would differ from the way you communicate with a coworker, which would also differ from how you communicate with your supervisor. Organizational structures require that you be fluid in switching your communication strategies depending on your relationship with the other communicator(s). This includes not only your initial communication, but also the type of feedback you give and the amount of appropriate self-disclosure the sender and receiver provide one another.

Regardless of your major or the career path you eventually follow, effective communication will be essential to your success in the workplace (Gray, 2010). For instance, effective communication has been shown to affect employee engagement and workplace relationships (Karanges et al., 2015). Employers understand the value and importance of communication in their employees; in Monster's (2021) *The Future of Work* report, they found teamwork and collaboration to be the second-most important skill employers look for in potential employees. Further support for the importance of communication in your professional careers comes from business and industry focus groups. You'll notice that all the competencies listed in the "Tools for Professional Excellence" box are connected to your study of business and professional communication in this course.

STEP BACK AND REFLECT
ETHICAL CONSIDERATIONS

Throughout this text, you will be given opportunities to step back and reflect on other people's communication interactions. But in this first exercise, we would like you to step back and reflect on your own communication. Read the questions below. When it comes to both your written and your verbal communication, can you always answer yes to these questions? Can you think of examples for which you could not answer yes?

Lying: Are you telling the truth?

Secrets: Are you respecting the boundary placed around information by avoiding disclosure to others?

Integrity: Are you discerning right from wrong and explaining your reasoning for your decision? In other words, are you vocal about the ethics driving your decision (e.g., care and love, financial, respect for individual rights, equal for all)?

Aggressive communication: Are you communicating with others without aggression and abuse of power? Are you communicating with others in a dignified and respectful manner? Are you communicating with mutual respect and open dialogue?

Plagiarism (cheating): Are you communicating information that is authentic and not plagiarized? Is the source of information being credited appropriately?

Step Back and Reflect

1. Have you ever taken part in any of these communication behaviors?

2. If so, did you consider them unethical? Why or why not?

3. Did you consider them unprofessional? Why or why not?

COMMUNICATION: A COMPLEX PROCESS

Communication is a complex process that consists of a number of elements, all of which are in play every time you communicate (see Figure 1.1). Those who demonstrate professional excellence consider these elements every time they communicate. By the end of this course, so will you. Let's examine each of these elements in more detail.

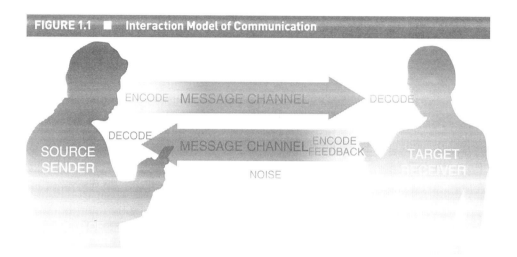

FIGURE 1.1 ■ Interaction Model of Communication

ENCODE   MESSAGE CHANNEL   DECODE

DECODE   MESSAGE CHANNEL   ENCODE
FEEDBACK

SOURCE
SENDER

NOISE

TARGET
RECEIVER

Sender and Receiver

We stated earlier that, speaking practically, communication involves sending and receiving messages. So it should be no surprise that you take on the roles of sender and receiver when you communicate. When you are acting as the sender, you encode your messages with verbal and nonverbal cues to help others understand what you mean. When the receivers of your messages respond or decode your message, you find out if your message was successfully transferred. In one sense, this exchange of message and response is a cocreation of meaning, in that both parties play a role in cocreating a meaningful exchange. Although the person initiating the exchange (the sender) can't control how the listener (or receiver) interprets the message, the goal is for the listener to understand the meaning of the message as the sender intended it.

The respective roles of sender and receiver in communication seem fairly clear-cut, but in truth, communication is experienced in a more holistic manner—not as senders and receivers but as communicators. Consider an example: You run into a friend, Pat, while walking to class. Pat says, "Hey, how's it going?" You return the greeting and begin to tell Pat about your plans for the weekend (you are attending a cousin's wedding). At some point during the story you are telling (how your cousin met her fiancé), you notice Pat checking their wristwatch. You cut off your story and say goodbye, and each of you walks to class. In one view of this example, you and Pat switch off as senders and receivers: Pat sends you a greeting, which you receive; you send Pat an explanation of your weekend plans and a story, which Pat receives; then Pat sends you a non-verbal cue that time is short, which you receive by ending the encounter. In another view of this example, you and Pat are both communicators, as you simultaneously send and receive messages (see Table 1.2).

TABLE 1.2 ■ Tools for Professional Excellence Skills You Need for Your Career

When thinking about your future career path, consider these eight behavioral skills often needed in the workplace:

Type of skill	What that skill looks like in the workplace
Technical skills	● Gaining technical skills ● Maintaining these technical skills ● Developing these technical skills relevant to your work
Critical thinking skills	● Strategic thinking ● Analytical skills ● Quantitative analysis ● Problem-solving skills
Persuasive communication skills	● Speaking ● Listening ● Writing ● Fluency in digital communications ● Presenting ● Personal branding ● Body language (i.e., nonverbal communication) ● Emotional intelligence
Personal organization skills	● Time management ● Prioritization and organization ● Multitasking
Manageability skills	● Taking direction ● Listening ● Implementation
Teamwork skills	● Working for the good of the team to support team goals
Leadership skills	● Leading by example ● Being a power for good ● Working toward desirable outcomes
Creativity skills	● When the above skills are developed and practiced, creativity is likely to occur and come together into a successful action plan

Source: Yate, M. (2020, September 22). 8 behavioral skills for increased job security. *Society of Human Resources Management.* Retrieved from https://www.shrm.org/resourcesandtools/hr-topics/organizational-and-employee-development/career-advice/pages/8-behavioral-skills-for-increased-job-security.aspx

Message and Feedback

Implicit in the preceding discussion of senders and receivers is that a message is communicated. One principle from the field of communication suggests that you cannot *not* communicate.

To say that you cannot *not* communicate is *not* to say that everything is communication. Rather, it means that messages have both a verbal and a nonverbal component. In the previous example, Pat did not say anything verbally, but he did send a message nonverbally when he checked his watch. What was his message? That is not clear. He may have been giving a nonverbal cue that your wedding story was too long. He may have had an appointment and needed to be on his way. Only Pat knows for sure. The point is, regardless of whether or not Pat intended to provide a message, he did, and you responded in accordance with the meaning you took from that message.

Also included in the communication model is feedback. In the model, you will see that feedback is sent from the receiver to the sender. However, since the distinction between sender and receiver is in many ways arbitrary, feedback is the same as the message. The notion of feedback reminds us, as communicators, to look for cues from the other person or persons with whom we are communicating.

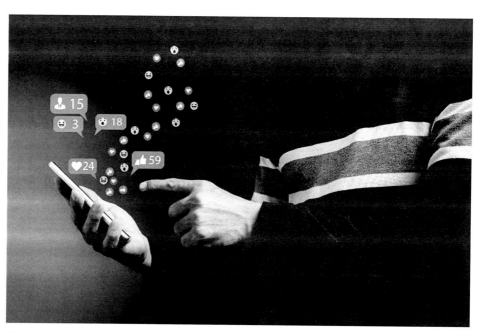

With instant messaging tools such as Slack and Microsoft Teams increasingly becoming the norm in workplaces, feedback often takes the nonverbal form of a thumbs up or an emoji reaction.

iStockphoto/Umnat Seebuaphan

Channel

The channel is simply the method by which you send your message. With all the technology available today, deciding which channel to use can be a daunting task. When you advance in your career and move into a leadership position, you'll have to evaluate the merits of various communication channels daily. Given the message, should you meet with members of your team one on one or call a meeting? Is it better to send an instant message or an email? Should you call, or should you text? Each communication channel brings with it a variety of strengths and weaknesses that will be discussed in a later chapter.

Context

Always and everywhere, communication is contextual. Context refers to the location, time, and occasion where communication occurs. Developing **professional excellence** means beginning to assess your communication context and use that information when developing your message. For instance, consider the context of the business and professional communication course. Virtually everyone in the course is there because they have to be. As a result, if you give a speech in this course, your audience may not be interested in or knowledgeable about the topic you select; you might need to educate them and take conscious steps to capture their interest. However, if you are giving a speech to a group of employees about their cost-of-living and merit raises, they will be hanging on your every word.

Noise

Noise is part of the communication context. Noise can be either external or internal. External noise includes distractions such as audible talking during a meeting, ruffling of papers, or a Zoom call taking place in the next cubicle. For our purposes, the definition of external noise is extended to include any external factor that could interfere with a communicator's ability to focus on the message. In a meeting, external noise might also include a team member sending text messages with the sound on or whispering while your boss is talking.

Internal noise encompasses any internal condition or state that interferes with the communicator's ability to focus on the message. If your meeting starts at 11:00 a.m., your team members may be looking forward to lunch; if you hold an emergency meeting at 6:00 a.m., your team may be tired. Being hungry or tired creates internal noise. Developing professional excellence includes learning to consider things such as context and noise when making decisions about your communication interactions. Remember that both internal and external noise are doing more than just preventing you from focusing on the message. That is, both types of noise can interfere with your understanding of the message. You can be focused on a message and still not understand.

YOUR COMMUNICATION INTERACTION
ANNOYING COWORKERS

As you read the passage below, consider what would be a more effective communication strategy in this situation.

Nina just began a new job at a software company. She loves her new workplace, except for a few obnoxious coworkers. These particular coworkers continually leave food and trash lying around, play loud music in the middle of the workday, and tell inappropriate jokes in front of the other employees, all to the point that Nina's ability to get work done has deteriorated. Nina has tried asking the employees to quiet down, to no avail, and is now considering bringing her concerns to the head of the company, who is rarely in the office. Nina decides to send the head of the company an email in which she lets out all of her frustration.

Questions to Consider

1. Was sending an email the best way for Nina to express her feelings about her coworkers, or could she have used a different communication channel?
2. What are some things Nina should keep in mind the next time she communicates in the workplace using email?
3. What are some situations where email is the ideal form of communication?

COMMUNICATION APPREHENSION

Effective communication skills are essential if you want to excel in leadership. Put simply, to move up the ladder of success, you must develop your communication skills. Unfortunately, communication apprehension is a very real problem that stops many talented individuals from achieving professional excellence. What is communication apprehension?

Types of Communication Apprehension

According to James C. McCroskey (1982), one of the leading researchers in the communication discipline, communication apprehension is "an individual's level of fear or anxiety associated with either real or anticipated communication with another person or persons". You can understand your own communication apprehension by thinking about your communication in particular situations. What types of communication situations increase your apprehension? According to McCroskey (1984), there are at least four types of communication apprehension:

- _____ means that one possesses a "shy trait." In general, shy people tend not to raise their hands in class a lot, avoid certain social situations, and feel extremely anxious about giving a professional presentation.

- _____ describes a fear of communicating in certain contexts. A fear of public speaking is a great example of context communication apprehension. For example, a student may not be nervous about meeting new people or participating in small groups, but presenting a speech in front of the class promotes a high degree of apprehension.

- Audience-based communication apprehension explains a person's fear of speaking to certain people or groups. For example, a person may feel comfortable speaking in front of friends in their social circle, but speaking in front of colleagues at work makes them extremely nervous.

- Situational communication apprehension refers to apprehension to communicate in specific sets of circumstances; everyone at some point in their lives is going to feel apprehensive about communicating something. Think of a person you might want to impress, such as a boss or an interviewer. In general, you are an outgoing person and don't mind presenting in front of people, but someone you want to impress may promote an uneasy or anxious feeling.

Causes of Communication Apprehension

Now that we've reviewed the different types of communication apprehension, let's take a look at some of the causes. Communication scholar Michael Beatty (1988) lists eight causes of communication apprehension. Review the list that follows to see if any of the causes resonate with you personally:

- _Novelty:_ If the type of communication situation, such as giving a speech or running a meeting, is not something you do every day, it can create apprehension until you become familiar with this task or situation.

- _Formality:_ Preparing and organizing something to be in the spotlight can promote the feeling of formality that makes you nervous or apprehensive.

- *Subordinate status:* If someone in charge of you, such as a manager at work, is evaluating your presentation, their higher status and evaluation can cause anxiety.

- *Peer evaluation:* "How are my coworkers going to respond to me?" This question addresses concerns you may have about your peers evaluating you. These concerns can in turn cause apprehension.

- *Dissimilarity:* Sometimes you may feel different from the audience. Having nothing in common with the audience causes anxiety.

- *Conspicuousness:* Feeling as though you are in the spotlight and all eyes are on you can certainly cause anxiety.

- *Lack of attention:* When you feel as though a listener or the audience is bored and uninterested in your message or presentation, you may begin to feel apprehension.

- *Prior history:* Many people have had a bad experience during a communication interaction, such as an interview, a presentation, or a meeting. This negative experience can create anxiety the next time you find yourself in a similar situation.

As you can see, there are many different types and causes of communication apprehension. Identifying the types and causes of your communication apprehension is important, but not nearly as important as learning the skills that will reduce those fears.

Know Yourself

Personal Report of Communication Apprehension

As you read the index below and answer the questions, think about how this knowledge can help you be a better communicator.

Personal Report of Communication Apprehension (PRCA-24)

The PRCA-24 is the instrument most widely used to measure communication apprehension. The measure permits one to obtain subscores on the contexts of public speaking, dyadic interaction, small groups, and large groups.

This instrument is composed of 24 statements concerning feelings about communicating with others. Please indicate the degree to which each statement applies to you by marking whether you *strongly disagree* = 1; *disagree* = 2; are *neutral* = 3; *agree* = 4; or *strongly agree* = 5.

_____ 1. I dislike participating in group discussions.
_____ 2. Generally, I am comfortable while participating in group discussions.
_____ 3. I am tense and nervous while participating in group discussions.
_____ 4. I like to get involved in group discussions.
_____ 5. Engaging in a group discussion with new people makes me tense and nervous.
_____ 6. I am calm and relaxed while participating in group discussions.
_____ 7. Generally, I am nervous when I have to participate in a meeting.
_____ 8. Usually, I am comfortable when I have to participate in a meeting.
_____ 9. I am very calm and relaxed when I am called on to express an opinion at a meeting.
_____ 10. I am afraid to express myself at meetings.
_____ 11. Communicating at meetings usually makes me uncomfortable.

_____ **12.** I am very relaxed when answering questions at a meeting.

_____ **13.** While participating in a conversation with a new acquaintance, I feel very nervous.

_____ **14.** I have no fear of speaking up in conversations.

_____ **15.** Ordinarily, I am very tense and nervous in conversations.

_____ **16.** Ordinarily, I am very calm and relaxed in conversations.

_____ **17.** While conversing with a new acquaintance, I feel very relaxed.

_____ **18.** I'm afraid to speak up in conversations.

_____ **19.** I have no fear of giving a speech.

_____ **20.** Certain parts of my body feel very tense and rigid while giving a speech.

_____ **21.** I feel relaxed while giving a speech.

_____ **22.** My thoughts become confused and jumbled when I am giving a speech.

_____ **23.** I face the prospect of giving a speech with confidence.

_____ **24.** While giving a speech, I get so nervous I forget facts I really know.

Scoring

Group discussion: 18 – (scores for Items 2, 4, and 6) + (scores for Items 1, 3, and 5)

Meetings: 18 – (scores for Items 8, 9, and 12) + (scores for Items 7, 10, and 11)

Interpersonal: 18 – (scores for Items 14, 16, and 17) + (scores for Items 13, 15, and 18)

Public speaking: 18 – (scores for Items 19, 21, and 23) + (scores for Items 20, 22, and 24)

Group discussion score:_____

Meetings score:_____

Interpersonal score:_____

Public speaking score:_____

To obtain your total score for the PRCA, simply add your subscores together:_____

Scores can range from 24 to 120. Scores below 51 represent people who have very low communication apprehension. Scores between 51 and 80 represent people with average communication apprehension. Scores above 80 represent people who have high levels of trait communication apprehension.

COMMUNICATION ETHICS

With professional excellence as our goal, we believe that ethical behavior must serve as a foundation for people to be treated with fairness, dignity, and respect. Central to professional excellence is communication ethics. Ethics is the general term for the discussion, determination, and deliberation processes that attempt to decide what is right or wrong, what others should or should not do, and what is considered appropriate in our individual, communal, and professional lives (By et al., 2012; Japp et al, 2005; Johannesen et al., 2008). What considerations or factors help shape our ethical decisions as professionals? Ethical considerations are the variety of factors important for us to consider in any scenario in which we're making a decision, conducting an evaluation, or making a selection (Bok, 1989, 1999; Carter, 1996; Japp et al., 2005; Mathenge, 2011; Tannen, 1998). Ethical considerations vary from person to person, and it is not always as simple as the black-and-white world of right and wrong. For example, you may experience ethical dilemmas, situations that do not seem to present clear choices between right and wrong or good and evil.

If you are asked to do something illegal, then it may be easy to make a decision. "No, I will not do something illegal." But what if it is not illegal? What if everyone else does it? What if it is just bending the rules a little bit? The questions in the "Step Back and Reflect" box are ones that ethical communicators must always consider.

Many ethical considerations are connected to our values and virtues. Values are moral principles or rules that determine ethical behaviors. Values are often articulated in *should* or *should-not* statements. Sometimes values are presented as statements of what a group believes or as lists of rules people intend to honor. Many readers of this text will take jobs in industries that ask all employees to support organizational values, specific principles or guidelines such as safety, teamwork, integrity, or ownership that are typically outlined in support of any given organizational mission or goal. For example, some health care systems and private education institutions ask employees to support certain religious values. Regardless of industry, organizational values address both the experience of the people working for the company and the experience of customers with service and product quality. To minimize ethical dilemmas in your professional career, seek employment with organizations that share your values.

In 2021, Facebook employee Frances Haugen shared internal documents with Congress and with the press that she claimed show how Facebook made unethical decisions to incentivize profits over its users' well-being. Her actions, while risky, received bipartisan support from members of Congress and renewed calls for social media regulation (Zakrzewski & Albergotti, 2021).

iStockphoto/Wachiwit

Once you've been promoted or elected into a particular position of leadership, you may think, "That's it—job over; I've arrived." We emphasize that leadership is a skill, one that needs to be developed and maintained throughout life. Think about the qualities of excellent leaders. Ethics should be among those qualities. And like all other leadership skills, your ethics must be developed and continually maintained. Although not every reader of this book is currently in a leadership position, has the goal of becoming a CEO, or even wants to become a leader, the KEYS process with communication ethics at the foundation drives excellence in professional situations.

KEYS FOR EXCELLENCE IN THE WORKPLACE

We opened this chapter with attention to how Twitter embodies communication and professional excellence by considering employees' feedback about their experiences at work. We defined human communication and provided a practical communication model. We defined professional excellence: being recognized for your skills as a communicator, serving as a role model to those around you, recognizing your strengths and developing your weaknesses, being audience centered, understanding the context, and possessing the ability to adapt and continually improve.

Next, we situated our topic of study within the workplace as a communication context and discussed communication apprehension as a common obstacle for professionals. We introduced the KEYS process as a way for professionals to develop their communication. *Know yourself* means actively assessing your skills as a communicator and then developing strategies to utilize your strengths and develop your weaknesses. *Evaluate the professional context* entails proactively addressing the needs of your audience and understanding the constraints of the communication situation, as well as developing your skills for communicating with a variety of audiences and situations. *Your communication interaction* requires you to monitor your own verbal and nonverbal cues, in addition to the cues from the audience within each communication interaction. *Step back and reflect* encourages you to examine the effectiveness of verbal and nonverbal messages you convey to others and the overall success of various communication interactions and then take what you've learned and start the process again, developing the ability to adapt and improve continually.

ETHICAL CONNECTION
TOM'S LACK OF COMMUNICATION

As you read this passage and answer the questions, consider how the way you communicate has an ethical dimension.

Tom is a recent college graduate who landed a job as an information technology manager at a computer manufacturing plant. Tom never really enjoyed talking to new people, so he made sure his degree involved working with computers so he could minimize his interactions with coworkers. However, once he began his new job, it became obvious that a great deal of his work involved interacting with other people. Because Tom disliked communicating with his coworkers, they often perceived Tom as grumpy and unfriendly. Management made several attempts to coach Tom on his communication skills, but he refused to make any effort to work well with others. His lack of communication led to technical problems going unaddressed and sabotaged the company's team-based working environment. Tom was eventually fired from his position and attempted to find another job that did not require him to interact with other employees.

Questions to Consider

1. What is the ethical issue with Tom refusing to communicate with his coworkers?
2. Is Tom wrong to assume that there are many jobs out there that do not require communication skills?
3. What could Tom have done differently to save his job at that particular company?
4. How could Tom use the KEYS process to train himself to be a better communicator?

This introductory chapter has provided you with an understanding of some of the basic terminology and the importance of communication excellence. In the second chapter, we explore some of the most important verbal and nonverbal skills needed to enter the workplace or, put simply, how to put the KEYS process into action (see Figure 1.2).

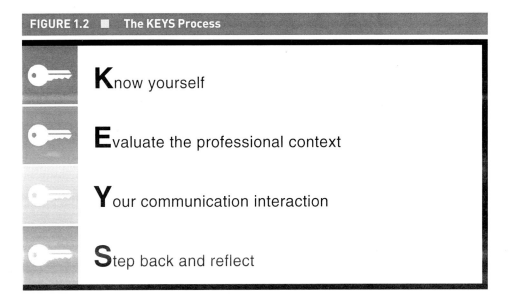

FIGURE 1.2 ■ The KEYS Process

Know yourself

Evaluate the professional context

Your communication interaction

Step back and reflect

EXECUTIVE SUMMARY

Now that you have finished reading this chapter, you should be able to

Discuss the importance of human communication in business and professional contexts:

- Role-taking and feedback are critical to the success of business and professional communication.

- Communicators are affected by their previous communication experiences.

- Physical surroundings and communication channels influence communicators.

- Communication is altered by cultural influences.

- Communicators are influenced by the perceived relationship between them.

Explain the components of the communication model:

- The person initiating the exchange is the sender, while the person listening to the exchange is the receiver.

- Generally speaking, the process of sending and receiving communication is that a message is communicated.

- When you are acting as the sender, you encode your messages with verbal and nonverbal cues to help others understand what you mean.

- When the receiver of your message responds or decodes your message, you find out if your message was successfully transferred.

- Feedback is communication sent from the receiver back to the sender.

- The channel is the method by which you send your message (e.g., voice, phone, email).

- Context refers to the location, time, and occasion where communication occurs.

- Noise can be either external or internal. External noise includes distractions such as audible talking during a meeting, ruffling of papers, or a cell phone going off in the next cubicle. Internal noise encompasses any internal condition or state that interferes with the communicator's ability to focus on the message.

Identify the types and causes of communication apprehension:

- Trait communication apprehension means that one possesses a "shy trait." In general, shy people tend not to raise their hands in class a lot, avoid certain social situations, and feel extremely anxious about giving a professional presentation.

- Context-based communication apprehension describes a fear of communicating in certain contexts.

- Audience-based communication apprehension explains a person's fear of speaking to certain people or groups.

- Situational communication apprehension refers to apprehension to communicate in specific sets of circumstances; everyone at some point in their lives is going to feel apprehensive about communicating something.

- Causes of communication apprehension include novelty (when the type of communication is not something you do every day), formality (when a communication is being prepared that will be in the spotlight), peer evaluation (when concerns arise about how coworkers will respond), and prior history (when a prior bad experience in a communication interaction causes anxiety in similar situations), among others.

Discuss communication and professional excellence from an ethical perspective:

- *Ethics* is the general term for the discussion, determination, and deliberation processes that attempt to decide what is right or wrong, what others should or should not do, and what is considered appropriate in our individual, communal, and professional lives.

- Ethical considerations are the variety of factors important for us to consider in any scenario in which we're making a decision, conducting an evaluation, or making a selection.

- Ethical dilemmas are situations that do not seem to present clear choices between right and wrong or good and evil.

Identify the four KEYS to communication in the workplace:

- *Know yourself:* challenging people to assess their skills as communicators actively and then develop strategies to utilize their strengths and develop their weaknesses.

- *Evaluate the professional context:* teaching people to address the needs of their audience proactively and understand the constraints of the professional communication context, as well as developing their skills for communicating with a variety of audiences and contexts.

- *Your communication interaction:* asking people to monitor their own verbal and nonverbal cues in addition to the cues of the audience within each communication interaction.

- *Step back and reflect:* examining the effectiveness of verbal and nonverbal messages we convey to others and the overall success of various communication interactions and then taking what we've learned and starting the process again; developing the ability to adapt and improve continually.

EXPLORE

1. Visit any of the websites for major social media companies (Facebook, Twitter, LinkedIn, etc.). Under the "About Us" section, read the company mission statement and goals for the organization. Do you believe the company communicates professional excellence to its audience? Write a brief statement either agreeing or disagreeing with this question.

2. Break into small groups and create a bulleted list of what your team believes embodies professional excellence in communication. Compare your list with those of other groups in the class. Are there any practices that are universal across all groups?

3. Select any company or organization, and write a brief summary of its best communication practices. How can you apply these practices to your study of communication and to your professional career?

REVIEW

1. Define *human communication*.

2. Perceiving your communication as effective while those around you perceive it as ineffective is known as _____.

3. Identify the four steps of the KEYS process.

4. The _____ is the method by which you send your message.

5. _____ refers to the location, time, and occasion where communication occurs.

6. Define *communication apprehension*.

7. _____ is the general term for the discussion, determination, and deliberation processes that attempt to decide what is right or wrong, what others should or should not do, and what is considered appropriate in our individual, communal, and professional lives.

8. _____ are principles or guidelines that support an organizational mission or goal.

DISCUSSION QUESTIONS

1. What are the contexts for business and professional excellence?

2. Why is it important to study communication?

3. Why must a speaker consider all the elements in the communication model for communication with excellence?

4. Discuss the KEYS process introduced in this chapter. What are the four KEYS features?

5. Work through a personal example—something you either encountered in the past or are presently experiencing—to help you make sense of the KEYS process. Does it help you get more familiar with the situation? Are there changes you need to make considering this particular situation?

TERMS TO REMEMBER

audience-based communication apprehension
    (p. 12)

channel (p. 10)

communication apprehension (p. 12)

communication bravado (p. 5)

context (p. 11)

context-based communication apprehension
    (p. 12)

decode (p. 8)

encode (p. 8)

ethical considerations (p. 14)

ethical dilemmas (p. 15)

ethics (p. 14)

external noise (p. 11)

feedback (p. 10)

human communication (p. 5)

internal noise (p. 11)

message (p. 10)

noise (p. 11)

organizational values (p. 15)

professional excellence (p. 4)

receiver (p. 8)

sender (p. 8)

situational communication apprehension
    (p. 12)

trait communication apprehension (p. 12)

values (p. 15)

2   VERBAL AND NONVERBAL COMMUNICATION

CHAPTER OBJECTIVES

After studying this chapter, you should be able to

2.1   Define verbal communication

2.2   Define nonverbal communication

2.3   Identify and define the codes of nonverbal communication

2.4   Discuss examples of how verbal and nonverbal communication are related

2.5   Apply the KEYS approach to conduct yourself with professional excellence through verbal and nonverbal communication in the workplace

Verbal and nonverbal communication have increasingly taken place in a digital environment. The use of emojis has long since been popular on social media, but their use has also started to become a common way to give feedback even in professional environments; for example, Zoom allows users to share various emojis such as clapping hands and thumbs up during a video conference. Today, you will look at emojis, memes, and GIFs and try to deduce if they are worth being a part of your social media marketing efforts as well as teach you a thing or two that will help you use these graphics without embarrassing yourself. We have seen a significant rise in their usage for marketing purposes only in the last couple of years. The main reason for that is actually quite simple; brands and businesses noticed that emojis are a great way to connect and engage with millennials and Generation Z. Additionally, these graphics are a form of visual content, and social media craves visual content (Supan, 2017). As you read this chapter, remember to reflect on how the internet and social media have altered the way you communicate both verbally and nonverbally in the social and professional environments.

VERBAL COMMUNICATION

What is verbal communication? **Verbal communication** encompasses both our words and our verbal fillers (e.g., *um, like*). Verbal messages are created through language. Effective communication involves accurate interpretations of others' verbal messages as meaning is cocreated. Otherwise, the meanings of the words you communicate will not be understood. As a professional, you must make effective use of your language skills and improve your abilities to interpret other people's messages. Robinson and Robinson (1982) concluded that if speakers are to be consistently efficient at conveying verbally their intended meanings to listeners, they must understand that intended meanings may not be fully conveyed by a message and that many factors can lead to a listener's failure to understand what a speaker means.

The symbols communicators use are abstract, vague, and sometimes arbitrary. Because symbols can make things a bit off or fuzzy, we have to interpret the meaning. So we construct meanings as we interact with other people and by processing the information in our own heads (Duck, 1994; Keyton & Beck, 2010). This process of meaning construction is also symbolic, because we use words to think about what things mean (Keyton & Beck, 2010; Wood, 2009). In a series of growth models, words had a stronger effect on engagement skills whereas early gesture use predicted later development of social-emotional concepts. Therefore, even in early development, symbols serve as both communication tools and mental tools to construct understanding of the social-emotional world (Vallotton & Ayoub, 2009).

"You're on mute!" Verbal communication in collaborative work groups is essential in both face-to-face and medi-ated contexts, but when verbally communicating over video conferencing tools such as Zoom, technology sometimes becomes an unexpected barrier.

iStockphoto/Drazen_

When you really think about it, it is an absolute miracle that we can communicate with one another at all. Really, think about it for a moment. We have selected a bunch of arbitrary symbols we call words and gestures to represent "things." These can be things we have never seen or never can see, such as feelings. Nevertheless, we use those symbols to express our thoughts, desires, and emotions, and somehow communication does occur. Because of the need for interpretation of meaning, being an audience-centered communicator is a must for professional excellence. It is obvious that communication affects how we are perceived by our audience(s). Still today, some people believe that communication works like a pipeline (i.e., if you send a message, the target will no doubt be reached); if you said something and another person heard it, then effective communication occurred. We should know from experience that this simply is not the way it works. With little effort, you could give a dozen examples of times when you said something and the listener completely misunderstood the message.

Let's look at an example from the retail industry to illustrate the point. A customer comes into a grocery store and asks for green beans. Trying to provide good customer service, a manager explains, "The green beans are on Aisle 8." Twenty minutes later, the customer is still wandering around the store frustrated. Why? Because canned green beans are on Aisle 8, fresh green beans are on Aisle 1, frozen green beans are on Aisle 14, and the prepared green beans she wanted are in the deli across from Aisle 10. "Green beans" is an arbitrary symbol with various interpretations of meaning.

Verbal communication concerns communication rules—shared understanding of what communication means and what constitutes appropriate communication given the context. Two kinds of rules guide communication (Pearce et al., 1979). Regulative rules describe when, how, where, and with whom to talk about certain things. These same rules also dictate appropriateness. For instance, it might be appropriate for your boss to call you at home after hours, but would it be appropriate for you to do the same if you had a concern about your travel schedule?

What's appropriate for the person with power or control may not be appropriate for those serving in a subordinate role. To demonstrate professional and workplace excellence, you must be able to monitor your own appropriateness when communicating. In addition, constitutive rules define what communication means by prompting us to count certain kinds of communication. In other words, we learn what counts as paying attention (e.g., eye contact) and showing affection (e.g., kissing, hugging), as well as what counts as being inappropriate (e.g., interrupting conversations, rolling one's eyes; Duck, 2007; Wood, 2009).

Being aware of yourself can make the difference between losing your job and nurturing a promising career. We see examples of this in the news headlines and front-page stories of our favorite magazines and newspapers. In 2021, *Jeopardy!* executive producer and host Mike Richards stepped down as host after only hosting five episodes; he stepped down due to backlash after his past offensive remarks about women, Jewish individuals, and Haiti resurfaced. Two weeks later, *Jeopardy!* permanently severed ties with Richards (Yahr, 2021). What are the ethical considerations in this situation? What might you take from this story when considering your verbal communication in the workplace? Undoubtedly, the words we say are extremely important. Yet, of equal importance is what we communicate without words.

STEP BACK AND REFLECT
CONFIDENT CONNIE

As you read this passage and answer the questions, step back and reflect on what went wrong in this professional situation.

Connie works in the accounting department of a manufacturing company. She often complains to her family and friends that her coworkers do not like her and treat her differently than they do the other staff. She is not invited to lunch outings, and she notices that people walk away when she approaches. She considers herself a friendly, outgoing person and cannot figure out what she is doing wrong. Connie believes her coworkers may resent her because she is able to work well with all her clients and is skilled in accounts reconciliations, resulting in company savings of thousands of dollars each month. She is confident in her abilities and speaks proudly in meetings, providing guidance to her teammates about work issues. She enjoys sharing her success stories and has no apprehension about asking questions in meetings. She has been with the company longer than everyone, including her boss, and she often reminds him of the history of why things are done a certain way. Connie is confident that even if her coworkers are jealous of her abilities, her boss recognizes her value as an employee. However, when she receives her performance review, she is shocked by her supervisor's comments:

"Feedback has been shared with Connie several times on her engagement in team meetings. Connie constantly repeats points discussed and closed in meetings, which is a distraction for several analysts. It is evident that Connie is having a hard time following along in meetings, as points and topics are constantly being repeated for her to understand. Feedback has been shared with Connie on staying on point and not drifting off to other tangents. At times, Connie's body language, comments, and tone of voice during meetings seem aggressive and indicate that she disagrees with her manager. This has been shared with Connie and she has been asked to improve."

Step Back and Reflect

1. What went wrong?

2. How could Connie use the KEYS approach to improve her communication interaction?

3. How can the KEYS process be a reflexive exercise for both Connie and her manager?

NONVERBAL COMMUNICATION

What is nonverbal communication? Put simply, nonverbal communication (also referred to as body language) includes all those ways we communicate without words. A more technical definition for nonverbal communication is communication other than spoken or written language that creates meaning for someone (Ivy & Wahl, 2019).

The literature provides considerable support for the effectiveness of nonverbal communication as a tool for conveying thoughts, attitudes, perceptions, and meaning. Research indicates that about 55% of interpersonal messages are conveyed nonverbally (Lavan, 2002). This seems logical, because most human beings are visually dominant and live in a society dominated by visual images and are thus more inclined to believe the evidence of the eyes than that of the other senses (Sampson, 1995). In fact, a widely held viewpoint among scholars is that communication is optimized when verbal and nonverbal elements operate in an integrated fashion, producing a coordinated and synchronized effect (Jones & LeBaron, 2002; Laplante & Ambady, 2003). R. Harrison and Crouch (1975) suggested that verbal communication is only the tip of the communication iceberg and that "nonverbal communication precedes and perhaps structures all subsequent communication."

Nonverbal symbols are everywhere, even though we tend to use verbal forms for our most formal communications. In fact, the nonverbal system accounts for 65% to 93% of the total meaning of communication (Birdwhistell, 1970; Mehrabian, 1981). Nolan (1975) concluded that the many theories of language evolution had one important argument in common: "Nonverbal behavior precedes verbal behavior in the evolution of communication."

ETHICAL CONNECTION
TAKING THE SPOTLIGHT

As you read this passage and answer the questions, consider how the way you communicate has an ethical dimension.

Sheila and David work for an advertising firm and are partners assigned to work on a major advertising campaign. Sheila is a seasoned account manager, while David is a recent college graduate hired as a junior account executive. He is very enthusiastic and has several ideas that he shares excitedly with Sheila via email. Sheila never responds to the email. In a meeting with management to propose their ideas, however, Sheila takes the lead on presenting; as a result of her nonverbal and verbal communication, management concludes that she was responsible for the work. In fact, when commended on the ideas, she accepts the praise and makes no reference to David. David, by contrast, is afraid to say anything, and his bosses have no clue that the majority of the ideas were his.

Questions to Consider

1. What are the ethical considerations and dilemmas in this scenario?
2. What did Sheila communicate or not communicate during her presentation, and how?
3. How could David use his verbal and nonverbal skills in the future to keep this situation from happening?
4. What do you believe should be the appropriate, professional response in this situation?
5. Does communicator intent affect the ethics in situations such as this?
6. Do you believe the outcome of this situation would have changed if David had talked directly to Sheila instead of using email?

What kinds of behavior are included in the term *nonverbal communication*? Your "walk, stance, posture, and footsteps are a form of nonverbal communication. What you wear and how you look, move, and gesture, as well as your facial and eye expressions all count as nonverbal communication" (Ivy & Wahl, 2019). What are the purposes of nonverbal communication? Why is nonverbal communication important?

Argyle (1988) suggested that nonverbal behavior serves four purposes. The first function is to express emotion. Consider a moment when you may have had a conflict with a friend or family member. When that person asked you what was wrong, you probably responded, "Nothing," but you could not control your facial expressions, which indicated otherwise. Displaying appropriate emotion is vital to professional excellence. One should show passion and drive but also demonstrate resilience and be able to triumph over day-to-day disappointments in the workplace. Could you imagine a classroom environment where students displayed extreme emotion each time they received a grade that was lower than expected? How do you think your productivity would be affected?

Does it ever feel like you spend forever choosing the right emoji when messaging somebody? Emojis can be an effective tool in nonverbal communication because they communicate attitudes and tone which can be difficult to convey through writing.

iStockphoto/canbedone

The second function of nonverbal communication is to convey interpersonal attitudes. Being skilled in observing and interpreting the nonverbal behavior of others will give you an edge over other professionals. For example, a young woman competing for a promotion with another employee noticed that her coworker would always approach their boss with issues first thing in the morning. The coworker would then complain that he had to repeat himself and that their supervisor seemed to forget what he had been told. The young woman observed that her supervisor always seemed rushed and distracted until he had his coffee and had checked and responded to pressing emails. She made sure always to approach him when he seemed more relaxed and focused. When he offered her the promotion, her supervisor said he appreciated her timing and how she always kept him in the loop.

The third function is to present one's personality, such as character, disposition, or temperament. Think about the different work environments you frequent during your week—the bank, the school library, restaurants, and so on. What are the character traits of employees at each of these establishments? Do you expect that the librarian will be as outgoing as a server in a crowded bar? Make a list of the top five jobs you have considered, and write down some of the personality traits that might be expected. How might your verbal and nonverbal communication vary between the positions?

Finally, the fourth purpose of nonverbal communication is to accompany verbal communication. Ekman (1965) specified the important ways that verbal and nonverbal behaviors interrelate during human communication. Nonverbal communication can simply *repeat* what is said verbally. It can also *conflict* with what is being said. Verbal and nonverbal communication can be incongruous, or in disagreement. Think of a time at home, work, or school when you experienced someone saying he or she was being truthful yet could not look you in the eye. Did you assume that person was being deceptive? Or think of a time when a loved one said, with a raised voice and tear-filled eyes, that nothing was bothering him or her. When verbal communication carries one message and body language a conflicting message, the result is likely to be communication failure (Jones & LeBaron, 2002; Laplante & Ambady, 2003).

Ekman (1965) also found that nonverbal communication can *complement* or accent a specific part of the verbal message. This can include placing emphasis on certain words by slowing down your speech or changing your tone. Nonverbal behavior can also be a *substitute* for a word or phrase within a verbal message. How many of you have ever nodded instead of saying yes when your professor asked you if you understood the curriculum? Or perhaps you have looked away to avoid eye contact instead of saying that you do not want to be called on to answer the question being asked.

Nonverbal communication may also *accent* (amplify) or *moderate* (tone down) parts of the verbal message. As well, nonverbal communication is distinct in its ability to *regulate* verbal behaviors by coordinating our verbal and nonverbal behavior in the production of our messages or those of our communication partner (Ekman, 1965). Imagine the last time you had a conversation with a roommate or friend. How did you determine whose turn it was to speak? Did you use eye contact to end the conversation or to let the other person know you were listening? What hand gestures or sounds might you have made to show your partner that you wanted to speak?

Recall the definition of human communication as presented earlier in the text: the process of understanding our experiences and the experiences of others through the use of verbal and nonverbal messages. In fact, in an effort to categorize the meaning associated with nonverbal behavior, Mehrabian (1981) identified three dimensions that indicate how we use nonverbal communication to make sense of things in both personal and professional contexts:

- *Immediacy:* We react to things by evaluating them as positive or negative, good or bad.

- *Status:* We perceive behaviors that indicate various aspects of status to us—for example, rich or poor, strong or weak, superior or subordinate.

- *Responsiveness:* We perceive activity as being active or passive. This signals the intensity of our feelings about a person or subject.

Remember that our cultural backgrounds can determine how physically close we get to others and how close we let others get to us.

iStockphoto/Atstock Productions

Knapp and Hall (2009) proposed that these three dimensions are basic responses to our environment and are reflected in the way we assign meaning to both verbal and nonverbal behavior.

Now that we have explored the value and importance of nonverbal communication and how we assign meaning, it is crucial that we examine the *components* of nonverbal communication to understand it on a deeper level. Although we focus on these nonverbal communication codes in Western culture, remember that perceptions or reactions to nonverbal communication can vary in other cultures.

CODES OF NONVERBAL COMMUNICATION

The primary categories or codes of nonverbal communication include vocal expression; space, environment, and territory; physical appearance; body movement, gestures, and posture; facial and eye expressions; and touch (see Table 2.1; Ivy & Wahl, 2019).

Vocal Expression

Vocalics, sometimes referred to as paralanguage, refers to how people use their voices to communicate and express themselves (Foley & Gentile, 2010; Ivy & Wahl, 2019). Vocalic cues include tone (quality) of voice, volume, articulation, pitch (highness or lowness), rate of speech, and use of silence. The voice reveals our emotions, our thoughts, and the relationships we have with others. A growing body of evidence from multidisciplinary research in acoustics, engineering, linguistics, phonetics, and psychology suggests that an authoritative, expressive voice can make a big difference in one's professional career. Scientific studies show that someone with authority characteristically speaks low, slow, and with vocal intonation (Louët, 2012). Vocalics provide information about our self-confidence and knowledge and influence how we are perceived by others (Hinkle, 2001). Think about the direct impact that tone of voice can have in a professional setting. What does your voice say about you to others?

TABLE 2.1 ■ Nonverbal Communication Codes: Consider the Professional Context	
Nonverbal Code	Consider the Professional Context
Kinesics (body movement, gestures, and posture)	How do you think gestures and body movement impact professional contexts?
Facial/eye behavior	Can you think of some examples of professional face and eye behavior? How can face and eye behavior lead to negative perceptions?
Vocalics (paralanguage)	What vocal qualities do you perceive as professional? Unprofessional?
Space/territory	How can space and territorial violations impact business and professional contexts?
Touch	Can you think of positive ways to use touch in professional contexts? In contrast, can you think of some negative uses of touch?
Environment	What are the qualities of a professional environment?
Physical appearance	In what ways does physical appearance impact business and professional communication?

Space

The impact of space on communication is called proxemics, or how people create and use space and distance, as well as how they behave to protect and defend that space (Foley & Gentile, 2010; Hall, 1959, 1966; Ivy & Wahl, 2019). Violations of territory and our personal space can be detrimental in business and professional settings.

Have you ever been on a crowded elevator and been uncomfortable because it seemed as though people were invading your personal space? When you go to the library, how many of you place your backpacks on the table or chair next to you to claim your space? What would happen if someone sat down in that chair anyway? Violations can be alarming, possibly even threatening. Our relationships with others, power and status, and our cultural backgrounds determine how physically close we get to others and how close we let others get to us (Burgoon & Jones, 1976).

What preferences do you have related to space and distance? Edward T. Hall (1963) identified four zones of space in middle-class U.S. culture. The first is the *intimate zone* (0 to 18 inches). This is usually reserved for our significant others, family members, and closest friends. It is rare that a stranger can enter this space without making us feel violated. These interactions mostly occur in private and signify a high level of connection, trust, and affection. The *personal zone* (18 inches to about 4 feet) is reserved for personal relationships with casual acquaintances and friends. The *social zone* (4 to 12 feet) is the distance at which we usually talk to strangers or conduct business. If you went to your professor's office to discuss a grade, for example, you would most likely remain at a distance of 4 to 12 feet. The *public zone* (more than 12 feet) refers to the distance typical of large, formal, public events. In large lecture classrooms, campaign rallies, or public speeches, the distance between speaker and audience is usually more than 12 feet. Understanding these spatial zones is important to your everyday nonverbal communication competency.

People became increasingly aware of space and distance during the COVID-19 pandemic.

iStockphoto/LanaStock

Environment

The constructed or natural surroundings that influence your communicative decisions, attitude, and mood are termed the environment (Foley & Gentile, 2010; Ivy & Wahl, 2019). People are influenced by environmental factors such as architecture, design, doors, windows, color, lighting, smell, seating arrangements, temperature, and cleanliness (P. Harris & Sachau, 2005; Jackson, 2005). Take a moment to think about what preferences would be related to your work environment. How does the environment (e.g., temperature, lighting, color, furniture) impact your communication?

Consider other things in the environment that can serve as nonverbal cues about who you are. These environmental factors you create and control are what serve as nonverbal messages to others who enter the space. As one scholar put it, "People cannot be understood outside of their environmental context" (Peterson, 1992, p. 154). The environments we create for ourselves often speak volumes about those relationships we consider most important (Lohmann et al., 2003). For instance, negative emotions and aggressive behavior of employees are two noticeable reasons for increased organizational costs (e.g., poor productivity, high staff turnover, low organizational commitment; Alarcon, 2011; Banks et al., 2012).

The way we perceive our environment and the environments of others is an important factor in how we respond. Overall, we perceive the environment in six distinct ways (Knapp & Hall, 2006). The first is *formality*, which is an understanding people have of environment that relates to how comfortably they can behave, in light of their expectations. Sometimes it is more about the atmosphere of a certain place than the place itself. The second way we can perceive the environment is *warmth*. This means that the environment gives off a certain sense of warmth, comfort, or a welcoming context based on our past or current experience. Think of a favorite smell from your childhood, for example. Smells in an environment contribute to our perception of warmth.

People are influenced by their environments. What are the nonverbal messages in this professional office environment that could impact communication?

Stockphoto/T_A_P

Privacy is another way the environment can be perceived. Do you prefer a crowded and noisy restaurant or a peaceful and quiet one? Do you choose a seat in the back of a movie theater or in the middle next to many other moviegoers? Another perception we have is *familiarity*, which means that we tend to react cautiously when we meet new people or are confronted with an unfamiliar environment. Not knowing where we are and what to expect makes us feel less comfortable. We like knowing what to expect and how to behave in the environment.

Another perception of environment is that of *constraint*. Think about your living situation. Do you like sharing a room or home with another person? Whenever we feel that our personal space is being invaded, we feel constrained. Most of our perceptions of constraint are shaped by the amount of privacy and space available to us. The final perception of environment is *distance*. Our perceptions of distance in an environment pertain to physical arrangements. We like to know how far away the closest door is or how many people can fit into an elevator. We create distance by avoiding eye contact or taking a longer route to avoid saying hello to a person we find annoying. Review the tips focused on establishing an effective workspace in Tools for Professional Excellence 2.2.

TABLE 2.2 ■ **Tools for Professional Excellence.** Setting Up an Effective Workspace

To set up an effective workspace, take note of these useful tips:

Key Points	Practical Tips
Think beyond the desk.	● Incorporate movement into the office: A workspace that breaks the "bond between user and desk" can bring physical and psychological benefits to its employees.
	● Create work areas where employees can both sit and stand.
	● Bring in different sizes of tables, chairs, and even sofas for meetings or lunch breaks.

(Continued)

TABLE 2.2 ■ Tools for Professional Excellence (*Continued*)	
To set up an effective workspace, take note of these useful tips:	
Key Points	**Practical Tips**
Your office is an extension of your culture and brand.	● Consider what you want your workspace to say about the culture of your company, which can help foster a sense of belonging in employees. ● Think carefully about what furnishings and décor items are used in the workspace. ● Don't be afraid of color: A workspace that is all white or gray can have negative health effects on employees, while a workspace that incorporates colors like blue or red can help keep employees productive and motivated.
Include an area for meaningful play.	● Incorporate a play area to help employees break free from the monotony of email and phone calls. ● While something as simple as a couch or two will do, don't be afraid to get creative and incorporate games, such as ping-pong, into the play area. ● "Play means connection": Play areas can help employees build bonds with one another and fosters communication and success.
Allow employees to design their own workspace.	● Let employees have a say in the design process, especially when it comes to expressing who they are; doing so can boost employee morale, which further improves the company's productivity. ● Give employees some control in how the workspace should look by letting them pick the color, allowing them to personally decorate their section of the workspace, or inviting them to bring in their pets.

Source: Vozza, S. (2013, March 11). Rethink your office design: Designing a more effective workspace. *Entrepreneur.* Retrieved and adapted from www.entrepreneur.com/article/226034

Physical Appearance

Physical appearance refers to the way our bodies and overall appearance nonverbally communicate to others and impact how we view of ourselves in everyday life (Ivy & Wahl, 2019). Physical appearance plays an important role in communication. Making the connection between physical appearance and nonverbal communication is important for two reasons: (1) The way we represent ourselves and our physical appearance reveal a lot about who we are, and (2) the physical appearance of other people influences our perception of them, how we talk to them, how approachable they are, how attractive or unattractive we think they are, and so on. Clothing is also a part of our physical appearance that is often critical to professional situations. Clothing helps you convey a sense of professionalism. Clothing and other appearance aspects, termed artifacts (e.g., jewelry, tattoos, piercings, makeup, cologne, eyeglasses), send nonverbal messages and help others form perceptions of us, both good and bad (Okoro & Washington, 2011; Roach, 1997). The nonverbal message sent by your clothing is a powerful part of professional excellence. Appearance is extremely important in our society. In fact, according to Armour (2005), employers also agree that physical appearance matters. An intranet software firm in the Northeast requires formal business attire on the job. Men must wear ties, cannot have beards, and cannot wear their hair past shoulder length. "Clients like to see a workforce that looks conservative," says the chief operating officer. That being said, many workplaces have embraced less formal dress codes after having their employees return to the office during the COVID-19 pandemic (Hartmans, 2021). If you are unsure about how to dress for your workplace, it is usually best to err on the conservative side and dress more formally. Although the criteria for what is acceptable in each environment might vary, physical appearance undoubtedly can affect one's perceived professional excellence.

When a large portion of the workforce started working from home due to the COVID-19 pandemic, many organizations' dress codes became less formal.

iStockphoto/visualspace

Body Movement

Kinesics is a general term for the study of human movement, gestures, and posture (Birdwhistell, 1970; Foley & Gentile, 2010; Ivy & Wahl, 2019). Kinesics provides valuable information about a person to others. Have you ever heard someone make reference to how a certain person carries themselves? Have you ever talked about a person who has a certain presence in the room? Perhaps you have said, "They walk like a leader." Some people carry themselves in ways that convey pride and confidence, while others have poor posture and seem to lack confidence. Ekman and Friesen (1969b) classified movement and gestures according to how they function in human interaction. The five categories of kinesics are emblems, illustrators, affect displays, regulators, and adapters.

Emblems are specific, widely understood meanings in a given culture that can actually substitute for a word or phrase. An example of this would be placing your pointer finger in front of your lips to indicate to someone to be quiet. Illustrators are gestures that complement, enhance, or substitute for the verbal message. If you were describing the length of the biggest fish you ever caught, you might use your hands to illustrate the size. Or when you are giving directions, you might point to show which way to go. Affect displays are facial expressions and gestures that display emotion. A smile can be an affect display for happiness, while a scowl can display frustration. Regulators are gestures used to control the turn-taking in conversations. For example, you might make a hand motion to encourage someone or raise your own hand to get a turn at speaking. When we are eager to speak, we typically make eye contact, raise our eyebrows, open our mouths, take in a breath, and lean forward slightly. We do the opposite if we do not want to answer. Head nods, vocal expressions (such as *um*), facial expressions, body postures, and eye contact can be seen as connectors that keep the conversation together and make it coherent. When these sorts of nonverbal cues are absent from a conversation, it might trigger a negative reaction, and we could come to believe that our conversational partner is not listening at all. Adapters are gestures we use to release tension. Playing with your hands, poking, picking, fidgeting, scratching, and interacting nonverbally with your environment are all adapters that reveal your attempts to regulate situations and to make yourself feel more at ease and able to function effectively. Adapters can alert us that another person is uncomfortable in some way (Ekman & Friesen, 1969b).

YOUR COMMUNICATION INTERACTION
TO TWEET OR NOT TO TWEET

As you read the passage below, consider what would be a more effective communication strategy in this situation.

Ryan is the new digital media intern at a public relations firm. During one of his first meetings, members of the digital media team outline new hashtags they would like to test on the company's social media accounts, and get consumer feedback. Eager to show off his social media savvy, Ryan immediately logs on to his personal Twitter account and shoots off a series of tweets using the new hashtags. Later that day, Ryan receives an email from the head of the digital media team, reprimanding him for using a personal social media account while on the job.

Questions to Consider

1. Was Ryan justified when he tweeted during the meeting? Why or why not?
2. To promote the company, what other communication channel(s) could Ryan have used instead of his personal Twitter account?
3. When, if ever, is it acceptable to use a personal social media account while on the job?
4. If you were the head of the digital media team, how would you handle Ryan's situation?

Facial Behavior

Facial expressions (including the study of eye behavior, called oculesics) are also critical codes that have been studied by nonverbal communication scholars (Ivy & Wahl, 2019). The face can be considered a gallery for our emotional displays (Gosselin et al., 1995). What does another person's face tell you about them? What emotion is the person expressing? How is the person feeling? Are your coworkers surprised to see you? Did your colleagues find your presentation to be entertaining, or were they disappointed? Your face and eye behavior play a huge role in the messages you send in business and professional contexts.

It is important not only to have a basic understanding of the emotions communicated by the face but also to be aware of how we manage our faces in daily interactions. Social norms and communication expectations in our culture set the rules for what kinds of emotional expressions are appropriate in certain situations. Facial management techniques are categories of behavior studied by Ekman and Friesen (1969a, 1969b) that determine the appropriate facial response for a given situation. The four most common techniques are neutralization, masking, intensification, and deintensification.

The process of using facial expressions to erase how we really feel is called neutralization. People who neutralize their facial expressions are often referred to as having a poker face. Masking means hiding an expression connected to a felt emotion and replacing it with an expression more appropriate to the situation. If we use an expression that exaggerates how we feel about something, it is called intensification. By contrast, if we reduce the intensity of our facial expression connected to a certain emotion, it is called deintensification.

A significant part of facial expressions involves use of the eyes. About 80% of the information in our everyday surroundings is taken in visually (Morris, 1985). Kleinke (1986) purports that eye contact and gaze functions provide information, regulate interaction, express intimacy, exercise social norms, and facilitate personal, situational, and relational goals. Evasive glances and limited-duration eye contact on the part of a communicator tend to reduce compliance with requests (Gueguen & Jacob, 2002). What can people tell about you by looking into your eyes?

Touch

Touch, also called haptics in nonverbal research, is the most powerful form of nonverbal communication. However, it's also the most misunderstood and has the potential for severely negative consequences if not enacted appropriately (Ivy & Wahl, 2019). Several different systems for categorizing touch have been developed to help us better understand this complex code of nonverbal communication. One of the best means of classifying touch behavior was developed by Heslin (1974). The first, functional/professional touch, serves a specific function. These touches typically take place within the context of a professional relationship and are low in intimacy. An example would be the essence of greeting rituals in business situations, the *professional handshake* (Hlemstra, 1999). The handshake is critical to making a good first impression as a professional, although handshakes fell out of favor during the COVID-19 pandemic and were often replaced with elbow bumps to maintain better social distancing. As handshakes have made a return in many parts of the world, think about what you look for in a handshake. What does a professional handshake feel like?

Social/polite touch is connected to cultural norms, such as hugs or pats on the back. Once again, these touches convey relatively low intimacy within a relationship, whereas friendship is the type people use to show their platonic affection toward each other. Hugs and kisses on the cheek might be exchanged between two close friends, for example.

, by contrast, is highly personal and intimate. People communicate strong feelings of affection toward each other with these kinds of touches; in this case, hugs may last longer, and kisses may be on the lips. The last category involves sexual arousal. These touches are extremely intimate.

FORMING RELATIONSHIPS WITH VERBAL AND NONVERBAL COMMUNICATION

Developing interpersonal, verbal, and nonverbal communication skills requires you to differentiate between the content and relational layers of messages. As you communicate with other people, your messages have two layers (Dillard et al., 1999; Watzlawick et al., 1967). The first is the content layer. The content layer consists of the "information being explicitly discussed" (Adler & Proctor, 2007, p. 16). The content layer may include descriptive information such as the time of a meeting, a project due date, or the names of the coworkers assigned to a team. You exchange content with others to function and retrieve basic information.

The second layer is relational. The relational layer reveals "how you feel about the other person; whether you like or dislike the other person, feel in control or subordinate, feel comfortable or anxious, and so on" (Adler & Proctor, 2007, p. 16). The relational layer may be communicated by your choice of words. For example, an executive may call her employees by their first names, while the employees are required to refer to the executive as Mrs. Villarreal. The difference in formality of names signifies a difference in control. The relational level can also be communicated nonverbally through tone of voice, use of space, and eye contact.

For example, Jason is really nervous about making a deadline, but he can't finish until Rachel completes the financial section of the project. Jason could ask Rachel, "What time will you be done with financials?" to retrieve a specific time reference, such as "Sometime this evening." These words reflect the content layer. If Jason wants to send the message that he's annoyed with Rachel, he could add a negative tone: "What *time* will you be done with financials?" If Jason is indeed annoyed, then he has effectively communicated both the content and relational layers of his message. However, if Jason did not intend to express annoyance, then his message is ineffective on the relational level.

There are communicators out there who do not pay attention to the relational layer of their messages. As a result, they don't realize how they're coming across to others. To achieve professional excellence, you must think beyond the content layer of your messages and also assess the relational layer. This can be supported by using the KEYS process.

Verbal and Nonverbal Communication and Their Impact on Professions

In this chapter, we have explored verbal and nonverbal communication—why they are important, their definitions, their principles, and their components. As you consider your professional goals, think about how you will use verbal and nonverbal communication to succeed in your career. We have included the following examples of the importance of verbal and nonverbal communication in a variety of industries. Even if your desired profession is not listed in the sections below, know that developing your professional excellence and communication competence is invaluable no matter what path you may take in life (see Table 2.3).

TABLE 2.3 ■ Action Items. Skills for Observing Nonverbal Communication

Listen	Listen for different verbal inflections and tone of voice.	Watch a political speech and observe the ways that vocalics influence message reception.
Observe	Inspect nonverbal cues to determine how a person responds to verbal communication.	Pay attention to the body language of people as you give them either positive or negative reinforcement.
Understand	Gain data from multiple interactions with different people in an attempt to generalize your findings.	After several communication interactions, step back and reflect on whether there were any nonverbal cues that are reliable across contexts.

The handshake is critical to making a good first impression. During the COVID-19 pandemic, however, many people replaced handshakes with elbow bumps and greetings from afar to help maintain social distancing.

iStockphoto/martin-dm

Customer Service and Sales

Recall the importance of proxemics, or the impact of space on communication. Manning and Reece (1989) found that success in productivity and sales was linked to the distance between sales representatives and prospects, salesperson posture, handshake techniques, facial expressions, arm movements, hand movements, and placement of the legs and feet. Those sales representatives who rely primarily on the spoken word to communicate with prospects may be neglecting an important tool for conveying their ideas. In addition, Leigh and Summers (2002) conducted an investigation that examined the effectiveness of nonverbal communication in a sales context. Using recorded presentations, they found that nonverbal cues (eye gaze, speech hesitations, gestures, clothing, and posture) influenced the experimental buyers' perceptions of the sales representative and their evaluation of the sales presentation.

Journalism and Television Broadcasting

Those in the public eye must demonstrate effective nonverbal and verbal communication. How many times have you seen a clip of an on-camera flub being played over and over again on TikTok, YouTube, or the local news? In the opinion of some scholars, as well as television commentators, arrogant body language on the part of many journalists in the United States has led to low public respect and esteem for them (Lehrer, 1998).

Public Service

Individuals who work in environments such as libraries or government offices (e.g., Department of Motor Vehicles, utility companies) are sometimes criticized for their communication and viewed as distant and unhelpful. Evidence indicates that individuals who are trained in nonverbal communication can replace negative perceptions of themselves with positive ones (Sampson, 1995).

Hospitality Management

Customer service is especially important in the hotel and restaurant industries. A number of hotel and restaurant managers have improved their organizations' image among guests by providing client services employees (e.g., hosts, servers, desk clerks, bellhops) with training in verbal and nonverbal communication (Jafari & Way, 1994). In restaurants, eye contact, facial expression, body position, and posture of the staff, including servers and cashiers, affect how customers rate the value of the service (W. B. Martin, 1986).

Medical Professions

Many people can probably share a story about an unpleasant experience at the doctor's office. As physicians compete to attract and retain a strong client base, their services can be interpreted positively by potential patients through correct body language on the part of the physicians and their employees. Patients often choose a physician based on their perceived image of the doctor, as revealed by verbal and nonverbal communications (Hill & Garner, 1991).

Teaching Professions

There is evidence that the nonverbal communication of teachers influences the evaluation direction (positive or negative) and level of performance they receive from their students (Babad et al., 2003). Consider the different teaching and communication styles of your current professors. What do you find are the common communication traits of the professors you enjoy most?

Companies within the service and food industries often compete to provide the best products and service to their customers. Chick-fil-A is well known for its focus on customer service. What does good customer service look and sound like?

iStockphoto/ivanastar

Legal Professions

A study has indicated that lawyers can project a favorable impression of themselves and their firms for prospective clients through sustained eye contact and other forms of body language, such as an erect but relaxed sitting position and close proximity to the clients (Clarke, 1989).

Television shows like NBC's *Law and Order* can shape our general perception of various professional roles. In your view, do you think the verbal and communication skills (or a lack of them) portrayed by characters in television shows influence our expectations of medical as well as other professionals?

iStockphoto/MattGush

Accounting and Finance

In the same vein as lawyers, accountants can benefit through the technique of maintained and appropriate eye contact, good posture, and close proximity to clients (Pickholz & Zimmerman, 2002).

Management (Private and Public)

Managers in both business and not-for-profit organizations can more effectively convey ideas to their employees through correct use of nonverbal communication (Hancock, 1999). Further, job evaluations of employees by their supervisors have been found to correlate with smiling, gaze, hand movement, and body orientation (DeGroot & Motowidlo, 1999). In a similar vein, managers can effectively convey impressions of empathy and power through body language (Gabbott & Hogg, 2000).

KEYS TO EXCELLENCE IN VERBAL AND NONVERBAL COMMUNICATION

In the opening of this chapter, we discussed the ways verbal and nonverbal communication can be conveyed in different communication contexts. Do you believe that this also affects your business communication? Think about how using the KEYS strategies can positively affect your nonverbal communication with others. The first step, *know yourself*, asks you to inventory the types of nonverbal cues you display to others. This can be difficult, but try to be aware even of the small, unconscious nonverbal cues you create. Sometimes the worst nonverbal cues we display are the ones we are not even aware of making.

The next step, *evaluate the professional context*, requires that you assess what nonverbal signals are considered acceptable in your workplace. Are your meetings informal, or is there a set decorum on how people interact? Notice how both your coworkers and superiors convey nonverbal cues during workplace interactions, and gauge how your nonverbal cues line up with those of others in your company.

The third step, *your communication interaction*, involves taking an immediate reflexive inventory of both your nonverbal communication and your partner's. How do you react to your partner's nonverbal signals? How do they react to yours? Think about what sets you at ease when communicating with others, and try to accomplish the same goal when talking with customers, employees, or superiors. The more open people feel when talking with you, the more likely they are to disclose information more honestly and comfortably.

The final task, *step back and reflect*, requires you to analyze your communication after the interaction has ended. Did you walk away feeling satisfied with your nonverbal communication? Did your communication partner seem at ease when talking with you? Assess what seemed to be the most effective nonverbal cues and which ones appeared to create a negative perception.

EVALUATE THE PROFESSIONAL CONTEXT
A DAY WITH THE CHIEF

As you evaluate the passage below, consider whether this behavior is appropriate for this professional context.

Mark is a top-performing salesperson at a pharmaceutical supply company. As a reward for his performance, he is treated to a trip to the corporate office in California to meet the CEO, Ms. Mills. Ms. Mills has a reputation for being harsh, stern, and hard to work with. Mark's coworkers warned him about interacting with her, stating that she rarely makes eye contact, never smiles, and dislikes being approached unless she initiates the conversation. Although he is excited to travel, he is also nervous about what he and Ms. Mills might talk about. He prepares by thinking about how he can share his sales strategies and techniques. On the day of the meeting, he waits patiently for Ms. Mills's assistant to call him into her office. When he is escorted in to meet her, he is shocked by welcoming and personable behavior from Ms. Mills. He approaches, shakes her hand, and waits for her permission to sit. Ms. Mills is nothing like her reputation indicated. The meeting is going well and Ms. Mills asks Mark several thoughtful questions about why he is successful, ways the staff can be supported, and how the company fits in with his professional goals. Mark feels more and more comfortable as she leans forward to listen intently to what he is saying. Mark loosens his tie, crosses his legs, and begins sharing stories of how he feels his immediate supervisor has dropped the ball on more than one occasion and that the team would be better if more money were allocated to incentives and bonuses. Mark immediately sees Ms. Mills's eyes begin to squint and her brow furrow. She stands up abruptly and says in a gruff voice that their time is up and that her assistant will show him out.

Questions to Consider

1. Given the professional context, what would you have done the same and/or differently if you were in Mark's position?
2. Do you think Mark accurately evaluated the context? Why or why not?
3. What communication factors led to the change in the CEO's disposition?
4. How could the KEYS process help Mark improve his communication skills?

Much like the relationships between traditional and new media, new venues for business communication can help or hinder your professional career. Remember that nonverbal communication does take place in digital contexts, and learn how to use nonverbal cues appropriately. This can lead to better (and more honest) communication and allow you to practice professional excellence in the workplace.

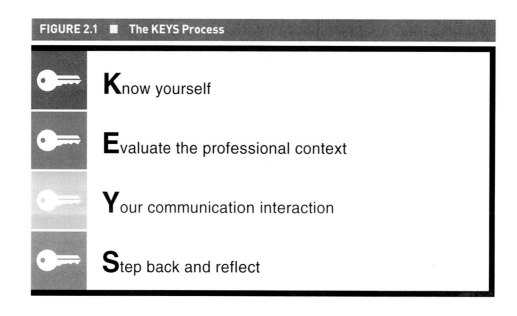

FIGURE 2.1 ■ The KEYS Process

Know yourself

Evaluate the professional context

Your communication interaction

Step back and reflect

EXECUTIVE SUMMARY

Now that you have finished reading this chapter, you should be able to

Define verbal communication:

- Verbal communication is both our words and verbal fillers (e.g., *um, like*). Verbal messages are created through language. Effective communication involves accurate interpretations of others' verbal messages as meaning is cocreated.

Define nonverbal communication:

- Nonverbal communication (also referred to as body language) includes all those ways we communicate without words.

Appraise your verbal and nonverbal communication skills:

- Developing interpersonal, verbal, and nonverbal communication skills requires you to differentiate between the content and relational layers of messages. As you communicate with other people, your messages have two layers.

- The content layer consists of the "information being explicitly discussed" (Adler & Proctor, 2007, p. 16). The content layer may include descriptive information such as the time of a meeting, a project due date, or the names of the coworkers assigned to a team.

- The relational layer reveals "how you feel about the other person; whether you like or dislike the other person, feel in control or subordinate, feel comfortable or anxious, and so on" (Adler & Proctor, 2007, p. 16). The relational layer may be communicated by your choice of words.

Discuss examples of how verbal and nonverbal communication are related:

- Some communicators do not pay attention to the relational layer of their messages. As a result, they don't realize how they're coming across to others. To achieve professional excellence, you must think beyond the content layer of your messages and also assess the relational layer.

Apply the KEYS approach to conduct yourself with professional excellence through verbal and nonverbal communication in the workplace:

- The first step, know yourself, asks you to inventory the types of nonverbal cues you display to others. This can be difficult, but try to be aware even of the small, unconscious nonverbal cues you create. Sometimes the worst nonverbal cues we display are the ones we are not even aware of making.

- The second step, evaluate the professional context, requires that you assess what nonverbal signals are considered acceptable in your workplace. Are your meetings informal, or is there a set decorum for how people interact? Notice how both your coworkers and superiors convey nonverbal cues during workplace interactions, and gauge how your nonverbal cues line up with those of others in your company.

- The third step, your communication interaction, involves taking an immediate reflexive inventory of both your nonverbal communication and your partner's. Think about what sets you at ease when communicating with others, and try to accomplish the same goal when talking with customers, employees, or superiors. The more open people feel when talking with you, the more likely they are to disclose information more honestly and comfortably.

● The final task, step back and reflect, requires you to analyze your communication after the interaction has ended. Did you walk away feeling satisfied with your nonverbal communication? Did your communication partner seem at ease when talking with you? Assess what nonverbal cues seemed the most effective and which ones appeared to create a negative perception.

EXPLORE

1. Write down a few examples of times in which you saw an emoji, GIF, or meme used inappropriately in a professional or academic setting. If you cannot think of any specific examples, identify situations when it would be appropriate and inappropriate to use an emoji, GIF, or meme in professional or academic settings.

2. Observe a social gathering, and compare and contrast the nonverbal displays present versus what you would see in a business or professional setting. Are there significant nonverbal communication differences when people are relaxing or at work? List several examples that support or refute this claim.

3. Watch any video of your choosing that features someone giving a speech or presentation to a group of people. In what ways does the speaker blend verbal and nonverbal communication? Write a brief statement describing how nonverbal cues can both enhance and hurt verbal communication.

REVIEW

1. Define *verbal* and *nonverbal communication*.

2. Explain the difference between regulative rules and constitutive rules.

3. _____ refers to how people use their voices to communicate and express themselves.

4. The impact of space on communication, or how people create and use space and distance, is known as _____.

5. The constructed or natural surroundings that influence your communicative decisions, attitude, and mood refer to _____.

6. List and briefly describe the six different perceptions of environment.

7. The general term for the study of human movement, gestures, and posture is _____.

8. Identify the four facial management techniques that determine the appropriate facial response for a given situation.

DISCUSSION QUESTIONS

1. What two rules guide communication? Why is appropriateness important when communicating? Share an example of a time when you experienced inappropriate communication. Who was the communicator? Why was it inappropriate?

2. Ethical consideration: In a workplace, when, if ever, is it appropriate to verbally communicate something that is not true? Does this apply to your personal relationships? Ask three people this same question, and note their responses.

3. What are the principles of nonverbal communication? Discuss at least two nonverbal communication codes. Which codes discussed in this chapter are the most important to you as a professional?

4. Name three reasons why nonverbal communication is important. Work through a personal example of a time when you needed to improve your verbal or nonverbal communication. What changes would you have made in the situation?

5. Step back and reflect on a time when you received criticism at work or school. How did you respond verbally? How did you respond nonverbally? How did the environment contribute to your communication?

Know Yourself

Nonverbal Communication

As you read the index below and answer the questions, think about how this knowledge can help you be a better communicator.

Nonverbal Immediacy Scale—Observer Report

This measure will allow you to assess your own nonverbal immediacy behaviors.

Directions: The following statements describe the ways some people behave while talking with or to others. Please indicate in the space at the left of each item the degree to which you believe the statement applies to [fill in the target person's name or description]. Please use the following 5-point scale:

1 = *never*; 2 = *rarely*; 3 = *occasionally*; 4 = *often*; 5 = *very often*.

_____ 1. I use my hands and arms to gesture while talking to people.
_____ 2. I touch others on the shoulder or arm while talking to them.
_____ 3. I use a monotone or dull voice while talking to people.
_____ 4. I look over or away from others while talking to them.
_____ 5. I move away from others when they touch me while we are talking.
_____ 6. I have a relaxed body position when I talk to people.
_____ 7. I frown while talking to people.
_____ 8. I avoid eye contact while talking to people.
_____ 9. I have a tense body position while talking to people.
_____ 10. I sit close or stand close to people while talking with them.
_____ 11. My voice is monotonous or dull when I talk to people.
_____ 12. I use a variety of vocal expressions when I talk to people.
_____ 13. I gesture when I talk to people.
_____ 14. I am animated when I talk to people.
_____ 15. I have a bland facial expression when I talk to people.
_____ 16. I move closer to people when I talk to them.
_____ 17. I look directly at people while talking to them.
_____ 18. I am stiff when I talk to people.

_____ **19.** I have a lot of vocal variety when I talk to people.

_____ **20.** I avoid gesturing while I am talking to people.

_____ **21.** I lean toward people when I talk to them.

_____ **22.** I maintain eye contact with people when I talk to them.

_____ **23.** I try not to sit or stand close to people when I talk with them.

_____ **24.** I lean away from people when I talk to them.

_____ **25.** I smile when I talk to people.

_____ **26.** I avoid touching people when I talk to them.

Scoring for Nonverbal Immediacy Scale—Observer Report:

Step 1. *Start with a score of 78. Add the scores from the following items:*
1, 2, 6, 10, 12, 13, 14, 16, 17, 19, 21, 22, and 25.

Step 2. *Add the scores from the following items:*
3, 4, 5, 7, 8, 9, 11, 15, 18, 20, 23, 24, and 26.

Total score = Step 1 *minus* Step 2.

Source: Richmond, V. P., McCroskey, J. C., & Johnson, A. E. (2003). Development of the Nonverbal Immediacy Scale (NIS): Measures of self- and other-perceived nonverbal immediacy. Communication Quarterly, 51, 502–515.

How did you score? What surprised you about your score? You can also try the measure on others. Simply fill out the measure with another person's behaviors in mind. For instance, you might find it interesting to fill out the survey for your least and most favorite professors to determine whether their nonverbal immediacy might play some role in the degree to which you like them. Do you notice differences in their use of nonverbal immediacy behaviors? Did you learn more in one class? What class did you enjoy more?

TERMS TO REMEMBER

adapters (p. 33)

affect displays (p. 33)

artifacts (p. 32)

codes (p. 28)

communication rules (p. 23)

constitutive rules (p. 24)

content layer (p. 35)

deintensification (p. 34)

emblems (p. 33)

environment (p. 30)

friendship/warmth touch (p. 35)

functional/professional touch (p. 35)

haptics (p. 35)

illustrators (p. 33)

intensification (p. 34)

kinesics (p. 33)

love/intimacy touch (p. 35)

masking (p. 34)

neutralization (p. 34)

nonverbal communication (p. 25)

oculesics (p. 34)

physical appearance (p. 32)

proxemics (p. 29)

regulative rules (p. 23)

regulators (p. 33)

relational layer (p. 35)

sexual arousal (p. 35)

social/polite touch (p. 35)

vocalics (p. 28)

3 LISTENING

Apple angered many of its customers back in 2016 when it removed several features from its MacBook Pro models; while these changes helped create a thinner, sleeker design, many people complained about having to purchase expensive ports to use basic features they previously had access to. However, in 2021, many of these features—including the SD card slot and HDMI port—made a return to MacBook Pro models, which led to many people commending Apple for listening to its most loyal customers (Leswing, 2021). Today, companies have a multitude of tools and technologies available to get immediate and effective customer feedback. Whether they have physical locations (Best Buy) or are entirely digital (Amazon), listening to customer feedback is critical to long-term success.

As you study this chapter, think about the variety of methods people can use to listen effectively. From a professional standpoint, critical listening skills are invaluable. However, being an effective listener can benefit your academic, social, and romantic life as well. Use the tools and information gained in this chapter to continually assess the communication around you.

How important is listening in the communication process? What role does listening play in developing professional excellence? According to Crockett (2011), the average person remembers between 25% and 50% of what they hear. That means that when you talk to your boss, colleagues, customers, friends, or family, they are likely to retain less than half of the conversation. Our poor memories are not to blame; rather, most of us simply do not listen well. To compound matters, the diversity and environment of today's workforce makes listening more difficult. In many workplaces, it is not uncommon for work teams to consist of people from several countries or ethnic backgrounds, with varying levels of technological communication knowledge and practice. Even if everyone speaks English, some might use different dialects and speech patterns. Maximizing performance in such a multicultural and highly technological work environment means learning to listen. We will explore the concept of diversity and communication further in Chapter 5 (Getting to Know Your Diverse Workplace). Understanding why listening is important is crucial to help us improve our listening skills overall. The ability to be an effective listener plays a role in one's business and professional communication and is a prerequisite to demonstrating professional excellence. Listening is also vital to the needs of companies of all sizes and dynamics.

According to Stengel et al. (2003), the most basic principle in the consumer products industry is "listen to the customer." Without an intimate knowledge of ever-changing trends and tastes, you are likely to lose out to competitors who are more tuned in. The notion that success also depends on listening to employees might seem just as basic. For instance, when customers perceive a high level of listening behavior by a salesperson, it enhances their trust in the salesperson and leads to greater anticipation of future interaction (Ramsey & Sohi, 1997). Yet this is not as easy as it sounds, and due to poor listening, a company's leaders—regardless of industry—are often oblivious to what employees are concerned about and why. A good example is the Jayson Blair episode at the *New York Times*. Blair fabricated and plagiarized multiple articles. By the time senior leaders got around to listening to their employees' concerns about the reporter's misdeeds, damage had been done to the organization's reputation. The problem of managers not hearing what staffers are saying is common in corporate life (Stengel et al., 2003). But the problem is not necessarily whether managers are hearing their staff. The problem lies in the ability to listen. Listening is a fundamental and complex part of the communication process. Let's explore it in more detail.

HEARING AND LISTENING

In casual conversation, most of us use the words *hearing* and *listening* as if they mean the same thing. However, as a professional striving for communication excellence, it's important for you to have a clear understanding of the difference between these terms. Hearing is your physical ability to detect sounds. It is the physiological process or function of receiving sounds. Your hearing is what gets tested at the doctor's office. Listening, however, is not one's physical ability. Recall the importance of nonverbal communication skills, which help you differentiate between the content and layers of messages. Listening requires you to concentrate on the verbal and non-verbal messages being sent and to determine the meaning of those messages. Effective listening is central to fostering interpersonal relationships with coworkers, leaders, and clients. Effective listening can affect one's relationship satisfaction and can be a determining factor in whether someone is an effective communicator.

The effects of one's listening abilities are far-reaching. Sypher et al. (1989) reported that an individual's listening ability has implications for productivity, teamwork, one's overall organization, and perhaps one's own success. Listening, in addition to other communication abilities, is a likely predictor of who gets promoted or receives other relevant rewards, such as status and power. Sypher et al. found that better listeners hold higher level positions and are promoted more often than those with less developed listening abilities.

Wouldn't life be fantastic if everyone were an excellent listener? Can you imagine an entire career without any misunderstandings? The trouble is, many people make the mistake of thinking excellent hearing equals excellent listening. You have no doubt already experienced communication misunderstandings in the workplace—you know firsthand that excellent hearing does not necessarily equal excellent listening.

Developing excellence as a listener can be difficult, but to achieve professional excellence, you must hone your ability to listen effectively. In fact, Haas and Arnold (1995) state that a growing body of research suggests that listening ability, or the perception of effective listening, is inextricably linked to effective individual performance in organizations. Nichols and Stevens (1957) found that good listeners regularly engage in mental activities while listening. A good listener periodically reviews and mentally summarizes the talking points completed thus far. Throughout the talk, the listener "listens between the lines," in search of meaning that is not necessarily put into spoken words. They pay attention to nonverbal communication (facial expressions, gestures, tone of voice) to see if it adds meaning to the spoken words. The listener may also weigh the evidence used by the talker to support the points they make. It takes a lot of practice to become a good listener, and listening has become a lot more difficult.

Maximizing performance in teams means learning to listen. Careful listening is particularly important in leadership positions because, while leaders generally have access to more lines of communication, information that flows to them can often have key facts omitted so as to give the information a positive spin (Bryant & Sharer, 2021).

iStockphoto/fizkes

So how can you develop your skills as a listener? The first step is to admit that listening is difficult. Don't fall into the trap of assuming that because you have good hearing, you have good listening skills, too. Take Carey, for example. Carey was born deaf, and while she could not physically hear others speak, she was an excellent listener. She used an interpreter, lip reading, and a highly developed ability to read nonverbal cues to make sense of the messages she received. In fact, her inability to hear may have caused her to develop her exceptional listening abilities. Carey outperformed many of her colleagues who did possess perfect hearing. Although they sat beside Carey in meetings, hearing every word, they fell victim to the barriers to listening excellence. These barriers include failing to limit distractions, failing to focus on the message, and failing to be active listeners. In any business and professional situation, you'll encounter some or all of these barriers. An important part of professional excellence is being able to develop your listening skills and overcome the barriers.

STEP BACK AND REFLECT
TROUBLE AT HOME, TROUBLE WITH TRAINING

As you read this passage and answer the questions, step back and reflect on what went wrong in this professional situation.

Jennifer is a recent college graduate who started a new job as a recruiter for a local nonprofit. Her job consists of placing individuals with employment barriers into jobs. She must build relationships with employers, secure job leads, screen candidates, and report her monthly hires and placements. Her position is commission based, which means she must make placements to earn money. While in training, she found herself preoccupied by several things going on at home. She was fighting with her boyfriend and in a conflict with her roommate. Her boyfriend sent her numerous text messages while her new manager explained the job responsibilities to the class of new hires. Between worrying about her relationship and the pressures of learning a new job, she heard the new manager say that she should do anything in her power to get placements, as this was the most important thing to remember of all the training content.

A few weeks into her position, Jennifer found that she felt really lost about how to do her job well. She was not making any placements. Whenever she approached her coworkers, they did not seem to listen to her. They rarely looked up from their computers or phones, and she had to repeat her questions several times before they answered. When they did respond, they answered only parts of her questions. Jennifer was left confused and frustrated. They all said the same thing, however: Getting placements was the most important thing to focus on, no matter how she met her goal. She followed their lead and began claiming credit whenever any of her clients found a job, whether she had assisted them or not. Jennifer was cutting corners to reach her placement outcomes. She had "heard" the message loud and clear. A few months later, Jennifer, her coworkers, and their immediate supervisor were terminated, and the nonprofit was under investigation for fraudulent reporting.

Step Back and Reflect

1. What went wrong?

2. What role did listening play?

3. What are the ethical considerations?

4. What critical listening strategies can Jennifer employ to help her in the workplace?

5. How could Jennifer use the KEYS approach to improve her communication interaction?

BARRIERS TO LISTENING

Failing to Limit Distractions

As we covered in Chapter 1, noise is part of every communication interaction. External noise includes distractions such as audible talking during a meeting, ruffling of papers, or a Zoom meeting happening in the next cubicle. Whenever possible, you should take steps to control the external noise that might interfere with your ability to listen to others, as well as their ability to listen to you. For example, when you are talking to someone on the phone, turn away from your computer if you're distracted by messages in your inbox. If you're running a meeting, begin by asking everyone to turn off or put away their cell phones. If the work environment is such that it's difficult for people to break away from distractions, hold a retreat away from your worksite to maximize the team's ability to listen effectively. For example, Jennifer (in the Step Back and Reflect section) failed to limit her distractions when she did not turn off her cell phone prior to the new-hire training. Instead, she focused on reading the messages from her boyfriend, increasing her inability to listen to the trainer. We must be conscious of the extent to which environmental, physical, psychological, and experiential factors affect the quality of listening (Highet, 1989).

Internal noise encompasses any internal condition or state that interferes with the communicator's ability to focus on the message. Even when we are listening in real time—on a cell phone, for example—listening has become more multilayered. During a cell phone conversation, we expect the speaker to be doing something else. Whether we think about it consciously or not, during the conversation we assess what the speaker is saying as well as what they are *not* saying because of where they are or whom they are with. Technology has changed not only the tools we use to listen but also when and where we use them, and even what we think about as we listen (Jalongo, 2008).

Controlling internal noise in others can be difficult, as it may be hard to predict. Still, you can minimize some internal noise in others. For example, holding long meetings without food or bathroom breaks will guarantee internal noise in your team. Minimize the noise by providing food and giving breaks. Say you are a health care provider who has to deliver bad news. News such as "You have cancer" or "You will need surgery" will create tremendous internal noise. In situations such as these, allow the listener time to deal with the news before giving additional information or instructions they will need to listen to, comprehend, and remember.

Whenever possible, you should take steps to control the external noise that interferes with your ability to listen to others. For example, if you have to be on a video call but are working in a noisy environment, wearing noise-cancelling headphones could help you control some external noise.

iStockphoto/zamrznutitonovi

As for the internal noise within *you*, you must reflect on what is causing your internal noise and address those factors. If you have an urgent matter to deal with, don't try to hold a conversation with someone. You simply won't be able to listen. Tell the other party you will need to reschedule your conversation for a time when you can give your undivided attention. If matters in your personal life are affecting your ability to listen on the job, you must become aware of those issues and address them. For example, Jason has been experiencing a personal conflict with his partner. They both feel he's been spending too much time at work and not enough time at home. Jason's conflict at home serves as internal noise when his coworker, Rachel, tells him she will not have her part of the project to him on time. As she explains how her workload has doubled over the past few weeks due to some vacant positions in her department and she really wants an extension, all Jason can think about is the fact that his part of the project will now have to be completed over the weekend. For Jason, developing professional excellence includes learning to manage his internal noise so he can listen. If Jason had listened to Rachel, he could have supported her desire for an extension, and they could have jointly requested a solution that would benefit them both. Like Jason, Jennifer (from the Step Back and Reflect section) was experiencing internal noise as a result of her relationship conflicts at home. Her failure to limit external distractions and to address the factors leading to internal noise prevented her from developing professional excellence.

Failing to Focus on the Message

In the ever-changing world of social media and emerging technology, we are locked into a mode of continuous partial attention, where we are always scanning our smartphones for the latest update or reading emails while on Zoom calls. Multitasking is the norm, despite some evidence that it prevents us from doing anything to the best of our abilities (Fryer, 2009). In addition to distractions and noise, or maybe because of noise, you may fail to focus on the message being sent. As a result, you are not listening effectively. Beyond noise, some additional factors that may distract your focus on the message include jargon, message overload, receiver apprehension, and bias. Or you may fail to focus on the message because it is difficult to comprehend.

YOUR COMMUNICATION INTERACTION
THE PROMOTION

As you read the passage below, consider what would be a more effective communication strategy in this situation.

Cara has worked at her employer for a few years and considers herself an asset to the company. Her annual review is coming up, and she is debating whether or not to ask her boss for the promotion she feels she deserves. Cara decides to get on her boss's good side in the days before her review, and does so by making coffee runs, taking on extra duties around the office, and even taking him lunch. Feeling confident that she has won him over, Cara casually mentions the promotion, to which her boss responds with a big smile and several head nods. A week later, one of Cara's coworkers excitedly announces that she received the promotion. Feeling hurt and confused, Cara immediately texts her boss and asks him why she did not receive the promotion.

Questions to Consider

1. What could Cara have done differently in the face-to-face interactions with her boss to avoid miscommunication?
2. Was texting the best communication channel for Cara to have used when confronting her boss? Why or why not?
3. If you were Cara, how would you handle the news that you were passed over for the promotion?
4. If you were Cara's boss, how would you respond to her text?

If a speaker uses jargon (technical words used by specialized groups) with which you are not familiar, you may think, "What in the world are they talking about? Why should I even pay attention to this stuff?" and then simply tune out. Jargon is a language of familiarity. It can be a useful tool when everyone has a common understanding of the terms at hand. If there is no common understanding, language can separate, insulate, and intimidate. Good communication is the result of the use of common terms that are clearly understood by both parties (Morasch, 2004).

People are unable to listen when they are experiencing internal noise. Reschedule important conversations if you have an urgent matter to deal with.

iStockphoto/Jay Yuno

Message overload can have the same impact as jargon. Message overload occurs when a speaker includes too many details in a message, making it difficult for the listener to comprehend. As the listener tries to make sense out of the specific details, they lose focus on the primary message. Presenters sometimes make the mistake of including too many graphs and charts during their talks, which leads the audience to message overload. As a listener with professional excellence, you must stay engaged even if the message is difficult to comprehend. Listen for the main points, and request a copy of the notes or PowerPoint slides after the presentation. If the jargon or message overload comes as part of a conversation, not a presentation, engage in active listening.

Have you ever been nervous about listening to a presentation on an unfamiliar subject or about being involved in a conversation with a person you want to impress? You might be listening to someone give you specific directions about a complicated task or sitting in a lecture trying to take notes on classroom material. In any of these cases, you might be apprehensive about listening to the speaker. This feeling is called receiver apprehension. Receiver apprehension refers to "the fear of misinterpreting, inadequately processing, and/or not being able to adjust psychologically to messages sent by others" (Wheeless, 1975, p. 262). This could mean having a fear of coming across new information or of being judged on your ability to remember the information correctly (Wheeless et al., 1997). Research has demonstrated that a person with high receiver apprehension tends to have more problems with information processing and general listening effectiveness (Chesebro & McCroskey, 2001).

We also need to limit our bias in order to be better listeners. Bias is any assumption we make or attitude we have about a person, an issue, or a topic before we have heard all the facts. If you equate a speaker with subject matter or experiences that have made you feel frustrated or angry in the past, chances are good that you will be biased about that person before they give the speech. That bias may prevent you from listening to what that person has to say, and you may miss some important information. Bias is not limited to individuals; it can also apply to groups. For example, if you feel strongly about a particular topic because of your values, you may refuse to listen to any other perspective, no matter whom it comes from. Effective listening requires you to put your biases aside and regard others as having a valid point of view worthy of your time and careful attention. To reduce bias, you need to acknowledge that bias might exist and try to remove it from your evaluation of the message.

A listener with professional excellence stays engaged even if the message is difficult to comprehend.

iStockphoto/izusek

Failing to Be an Active Listener

Just as there is a difference between hearing and listening, there are also differences between various types of listening. In your professional career, you will engage in three types of listening: informational, critical, and empathetic. Informational listening occurs when you focus on the content of the message to acquire knowledge. Part of learning a new position involves listening to information during new-employee orientation and one-on-one training. Critical listening asks you to evaluate the information being sent. For example, Trey has been asked to seek three separate bids from business-development consulting firms. Trey must critically listen and then evaluate the advantages and disadvantages of each proposal. Empathetic listening is listening to understand the speaker's point of view without judgment. If a customer comes to you with a complaint and you listen to them to try to understand the problem from their perspective, without countering, criticizing, or judging, you have engaged in empathetic listening. Research tells us that listening with empathy is the basis for a host of important workplace skills and strategies: assessing situations, making rational decisions, generating connections between theory and practice, arriving at deeper understandings of beliefs, adapting to new perspectives, informing instructional decisions, challenging traditions, improving teaching and learning, and validating ideals (Jalongo, 2008).

Where does active listening fit in? Isn't it a type of listening? No, it is not a type of listening; rather, it is a *way* to listen. Every time you engage as a listener, you must consciously decide if you are going to be an active listener or a passive listener. As a passive listener, you will simply receive a message and make sense out of that message without feedback or verification. For example, watching the news on television is passive listening, because there is no need to provide feedback since a response is not expected. Poorly run meetings often have everyone but the leader acting as passive listeners. In contrast, as an active listener, you are required to make sense out of the message and then verify that your sense making is accurate. In other words, you must verify that you understand the message as the speaker intended. To achieve professional excellence in interpersonal relationships, you must always be an active listener.

An active listener focuses on asking questions and will often listen to the message and then paraphrase it for the sender. Let's say an employee complains to you by saying, "I'm sick of the attitude around here. Some people stroll into work whenever they feel like it, and the customers suffer. The poor customers have to be put on hold forever, and they get really upset." As an active listener, you can summarize that message to check your understanding: "You feel irritated when people are late for work because it means the phones are not covered and we are not providing the best service we are capable of." In some situations, paraphrasing is critically important. At the same time, many professionals view continual paraphrasing as unnatural or mechanical in style. Still, when there's a high likelihood of misunderstanding, a little paraphrasing can make a big difference in the communication interaction.

An active listener makes sense out of the message and then verifies that the sense making is accurate. We often see news anchors and talk show hosts using this listening tactic when interviewing guests.

iStockphoto/Veni

Another technique is reflection. Jalongo (2008) categorizes reflective listening as different from ordinary listening in four important ways. Reflective listening means the listener (1) listens thoughtfully to the meaning of the speaker's words; (2) considers the content of the message, both stated and implied; (3) thinks about the feelings associated with the message, attending to the speaker's verbal and nonverbal cues; and (4) makes every effort to reflect that message accurately. Questions are another tool used by the active listener. By asking questions, you can develop a better understanding of the speaker's message and provide support to the speaker. Tools for Professional Excellence 3.1 provides several tips focused on effective note taking—one more quality of active listening.

Politicians like California Governor Gavin Newsom often make public appearances to give constituents a sense that they are listening to them and their concerns.

iStockphoto/Tommy Wu

Graham et al. (2008) highlight the importance of developing a sense of being "in charge" of the listening process. Being in charge of listening includes both knowing how and knowing when to use which strategies. We have defined listening, discussed why it is important, and revealed the various barriers that may prevent one from listening effectively. Now we will explore in more detail some of the different styles and categories of listening (see Table 3.1).

TABLE 3.1 ■ Tools for Professional Excellence. Effective Note-Taking	
To take effective notes in the workplace, follow these practical tips:	
Key Points	**Practical Tips**
Don't just take notes; read them.	● Simply taking notes in the moment is not enough to recall the information: Rereading what you've written later on is vital.
	● Notes are meant to be used as storage for information that can be accessed at any time, not just once and then forgotten.
Digital or handwritten?	● There are varying opinions on which method is the best when it comes to note-taking: Some people argue that digital note-taking can be a distraction, while others argue that digital note-taking is more efficient and improves information recall.
	● Use whichever method works best for you and provides the most useful set of notes.
Supercharge your notes.	● Notes with hierarchical ordering or numbered sections prove to be the most accurate.
	● Notes that contain some sort of organizational pattern are more useful for information recall than are freestyle notes.
Doodling isn't just for fun.	● Using visual note-taking methods, such as mind-mapping, can enhance the material and improve your ability to recall and present the information.
	● If a piece of information seems important, underline it to make it stand out and help you remember it later.
Take breaks.	● Continuous listening and note-taking can result in fatigue and decrease the effectiveness of the notes.
	● Whenever possible, take short breaks from note-taking: This ensures the quality of future notes, and helps you process those you've already taken.

Source: Codrea-Rado, A. (2013, March 20). The complete guide to taking notes effectively at work. *Quartz.* Retrieved and adapted from qz.com/64539/complete-guide-to-taking-notes-effectively-at-work/

LISTENING STYLES AND CATEGORIES

Barker and Watson (2000) classified four listening preferences or styles. People-oriented listeners are interested in demonstrating concern for others' emotions and interests, finding common ground, and responding. These listeners demonstrate a genuine concern for others' feelings and identify with emotional states of human behavior. This type of listener can become "over-involved with the feelings of others" (Watson & Barker, 1995, p. 3). Action-oriented listeners are interested in direct, concise, error-free communication that is used to negotiate and accomplish a goal; these listeners are easily frustrated by disorganized presentations. Content-oriented listeners are interested in intellectual challenge and complex information; they want to evaluate information carefully before forming judgments and opinions. Time-oriented listeners prefer brief communication; such listeners seek interaction that is concise and to the point, and they want to know the length of time available before the communication begins. What type of listener are you? Do you recognize the styles of your boss, family, or friends?

Listening can also be divided into a variety of categories. Listening in interpersonal situations is usually categorized as either conversational or presentational. When the speaking role shifts from one person to another with some degree of frequency, we call it conversational listening. In a conversational situation, the person who was actively listening one minute can assume the major speaking role the next, while the previous speaker becomes a listener. Conversational listening is an integral part of meaningful one-on-one social relationships and professional interpersonal exchanges. Conversational listening most often emerges in face-to-face situations but may also take place over the telephone or video calls. Presentational listening is a type of listening that takes place in situations where a clear role of speaking and listening functions is prescribed. In presentational listening, roles are usually formal and defined as active speaker and responsive listener. The listening environment is based on the following conditions: mode (conversational or presentational), environment (formal or informal), and relationship (social or business; Nelson & Heeney, 1984).

EVALUATE THE PROFESSIONAL CONTEXT

MIGUEL AND THE MULTITASKING MISHAP

As you evaluate the passage below, consider whether this behavior is appropriate for this professional context.

Miguel had a successful career as an event planner. He started off as an assistant at an agency, but through hard work and consistent results, he had developed his own client list and saved enough money to start a company out of his home. He specialized in weddings and took pride in helping couples plan their dream events. As his client base continued to grow due to word-of-mouth referrals, he struggled to keep up with all the client requests but did not have the funds to hire additional employees. Miguel found himself multitasking on most days, and he was often double booked. The summer months were especially hectic.

One of his repeat clients, Tamara, hired him to plan a 50th anniversary party for her parents, as she had been so pleased with how her wedding turned out. It was an especially important event because Tamara's father had been diagnosed with cancer a few months before. A few weeks before the party, Miguel was meeting with a new client when the phone rang. Tamara was on the phone, extremely upset because they needed to move up the event due to a medical procedure scheduled around the original event date. Miguel took the call while working with the new client. While showing the new client fabric samples and place settings, he listened to Tamara and assured her he would take care of it, and they agreed on an available date.

On the day of the event, Tamara, Miguel, her parents, and their guests arrived at the venue to find that another event had already begun. Miguel was mortified when he realized that he had forgotten to reschedule the event with the venue. Although he attempted to apologize and offered alternatives, the damage was done. The family was extremely upset. Tamara began to cry, called Miguel an insulting name, and told him she would be sure to tell all her friends and acquaintances about the experience.

Questions to Consider

1. What could Miguel have done differently to avoid this situation?
2. Should Tamara have handled the situation differently?
3. How could the KEYS process help Miguel manage his clients' needs and expectations despite his hectic schedule?

IMPROVING YOUR LISTENING

Now that you have an understanding of the types, styles, and categories of listening, we can share additional ways to improve your listening skills. Becoming a better listener takes time and effort. The HURIER model provides a framework for skill-based listening by defining listening as six interrelated components: **H**earing, **U**nderstanding, **R**emembering, **I**nterpreting, **E**valuating, and **R**esponding (Brownell, 1994, 1996).

Hearing refers to concentrating on and attending to the message. The first step toward better listening is making sure you can properly hear the other person. Be sure that you limit any distractions that would prevent you from doing so. Understanding is the process of attaching meaning to the verbal communication, or comprehending the literal meaning of the message. We often do this unconsciously. Understanding a message requires that we first hear the message, but it also includes being able to understand the speaker's use of language and the basic context of the information. Remembering includes recalling the message so that it can be acted on. Listening not only requires us to be present, in the moment, and mindful but also necessitates anticipating future interactions. One way to help yourself remember the message is to create an outline of the main points.

Interpreting is the step where we make sense of the verbal and nonverbal codes to assign meaning to the information received or the sensitivity to nonverbal and contextual aspects of the message (Brownell, 1994). Interpreting is an important part of the collaborative process of communication. Ethically interpreting a message means you are not intentionally letting your own bias or beliefs interfere with your interpretation. Evaluating is the logical assessment of the value of the message (Brownell, 1994). Learning to evaluate a message without bias, distractions, apprehension, or gender or cultural differences takes time and patience.

After interpreting and evaluating the message, you must decide how to reply or respond. Responding is the last step and involves giving some form of *response* to the message, either verbally or nonverbally. Communication would not be collaboration if not for this vital step. Paraphrasing, summarizing, reflecting, and asking questions all demonstrate responsiveness. Using nonverbal cues such as head nods, emotional expressions, or verbal utterances is also a good way to show you are listening. The six-step process, when used in combination with active listening skills and barrier avoidance, will result in development of your professional excellence.

Know Yourself

Listening Anxiety

As you read the index below and answer the questions, think about how this knowledge can help you be a better communicator.

The following statements apply to how various people feel about listening to others. Indicate to what degree these statements apply to how you feel. Please use the following 5-point scale:

5 = strongly agree, *4* = agree, *3* = are undecided, *2* = disagree, or *1* = strongly disagree.

_____ **1.**   While listening, I get nervous when a lot of information is given at once.
_____ **2.**   I get impatient and anxious when listening to someone discuss theoretical, intellectual issues.
_____ **3.**   I have avoided listening to abstract ideas because I was afraid I could not make sense of what was said.

_____ **4.** Many classes are annoying and uncomfortable because the teacher floods you with detailed information in the lectures.

_____ **5.** I feel agitated or uneasy when someone tells me there is not necessarily a clear, concrete way to deal with an important problem.

_____ **6.** While listening, I feel tense when I have to analyze details carefully.

_____ **7.** It is frustrating to listen to people discuss practical problems in philosophical and abstract ways.

_____ **8.** When I hear abstract material, I am afraid I will be unable to remember it very well.

_____ **9.** I experience anxiety when listening to complex ideas others tell me.

_____ **10.** When I listen to complicated information, I often fear that I will misinterpret it.

_____ **11.** I do not feel relaxed and confident while listening, especially when a lot of information is given at once.

_____ **12.** Listening to complex ideas is not a pleasant, enjoyable experience for me.

_____ **13.** When listening, I do not feel relaxed and confident that I can remember abstract ideas that are being explained.

Add all scores together: _____

The higher the score, the higher your listening anxiety.

Source: Adapted from Wheeless, L. R., Preiss, R. W., & Gayle, B. M. (1997). Receiver apprehension, informational receptivity, and cognitive processing. In J. A. Daly, J. C. McCroskey, T. Ayres, T. Hopf, & D. M. Ayers (Eds.), Avoiding communication: Shyness, reticence, and communication apprehension (pp. 151–187). Hampton Press.

Note: This is a modified version of the Listening Anxiety Test.

Research in listening has just begun to explore the many aspects of this complex and central communication process. According to Nixon and West (1989), listening is the most basic communication skill and supersedes all learning processes. Historically, listening has been the most neglected instructional and research area. However, now professional organizations such as the International Listening Association, academic institutions, and others are providing increased training materials devoted to listening research. Through proficient use of listening instruction, people learn listening guidelines and can develop listening skills in ways similar to learning mathematics, physical fitness, reading, and writing (Nixon & West, 1989).

Gibbs et al. (1985) assert that listening awareness and instruction can accomplish four major objectives: (1) increasing understanding of the nature of listening and its importance in the total communication process, (2) diagnosing listening abilities and practices, (3) developing skills and techniques to improve listening effectiveness, and (4) creating awareness of the importance of effective listening to personal and professional success. In schools that have instituted listening instruction, students' listening comprehension has as much as doubled in just a few months. Continuous evaluation of one's own listening abilities and participating in listening instruction or learning measures increases retention, promotes critical thinking, and facilitates learning (see Table 3.2).

Being mindful of your listening effectiveness is valuable in the professional environment. According to Haas and Arnold (1995), listening plays a pivotal role in conceptions of communication competence in coworkers. In other words, your ability or inability to listen

Technology has affected our ability to listen. Limit distractions by silencing your cell phone before a presentation or professional meeting. If you are on a video call, you can limit distractions by muting your computer or tablet's email and instant messaging notifications.

iStockphoto/FG Trade

will directly affect whether your coworkers perceive you as possessing communication competence. In turn, you will also judge your coworkers' abilities to communicate effectively by how well they demonstrate listening skills. Failure to recognize that listening is just as important as verbal communication is inevitably detrimental. In fact, many Fortune 500 companies, as well as several management training programs used across the United States, identify listening as one of the most important communication skills in the workplace (Haas & Arnold, 1995).

Nelson and Heeney (1984) explain that a truly competent listener goes beyond simply hearing; listening includes comprehending meaning, analyzing relationships, interpreting impressions, and evaluating content. The ancient adage still rings true today—the beginning of wisdom is silence. The second stage is listening (Gibbs et al., 1985). Will you value the knowledge gained in this chapter and improve your listening skills to develop professional excellence? How have your listening skills affected your work, school, or home life?

TABLE 3.2 ■ Action Items. Skills for Being an Active Listener		
Skill	**Strategy**	**Application**
Observe	Watch the verbal and nonverbal cues your communication partner is expressing.	Use a debate-style forum that encourages you to focus entirely on the other person before you are allowed to respond.
Focus	Don't do anything else while listening.	Block out all other distractions and give your undivided attention to the other person.

Skill	Strategy	Application
Acknowledge	Acknowledge the message, even if you don't agree with it.	Your acknowledgment can be verbal (*uh huh, yes*) or nonverbal (a head nod).
Respect	Let the speaker finish.	As tempting as it can be to voice your opinion, remember to respect the other person's time first.

KEYS TO LISTENING EXCELLENCE

The opening section of the chapter discussed Apple's ability to listen to its customers. Try to apply Apple's practices to the KEYS strategy. The first step, *know yourself*, allowed Apple to realize there was a better way to deliver the products that the company's customers want (by listening to their complaints).

The second step, *evaluate the professional context*, involved Apple assessing their current offerings compared to the wants and needs of their customers. Apple saw that its customers generally favored features over slim design and so made the decision to implement that feedback.

For the third step, *your communication interaction*, Apple used its "Unleashed" event to communicate the MacBook Pro's changes to the public.

The final strategy, *step back and reflect*, is likely currently in progress at the time of writing. The company may see an increase in market share and an overall more favorable public perception after listening to its customers' concerns.

What listening skills do you use when interacting with others? Can the Apple example be used by other companies to generate both profit and goodwill?

ETHICAL CONNECTION
LISTENING TO EMPLOYEES

As you read this passage and answer the questions, consider how the way you communicate has an ethical dimension.

Amber and Daniel are both personnel managers at a large company. Although both jobs are identical in size and duties, the feedback that Amber and Daniel each receive could not be more different. Daniel's employees feel safe approaching him with new ideas and concerns and are overall satisfied with the feedback they receive. Employees who work for Amber, on the other hand, often complain that talking to her is like talking to a brick wall. They say that their concerns go unaddressed and that when they forward a new idea for the company, their suggestions are shrugged off without any discussion. At a recent supervisor meeting, the company executives discussed the disparity between Amber's and Daniel's employee satisfaction surveys and retention rates. Amber seemed at a loss as to why her department was underperforming in comparison with Daniel's.

Questions to Consider

1. What is the ethical dilemma involved in being a poor listener?

2. Why would employees be happier working in an environment with a manager who effectively listens to their ideas and concerns?

3. Why is it so important that Daniel provides feedback relating to his employees' communication?

4. How can Amber use the KEYS process to become a more effective listener?

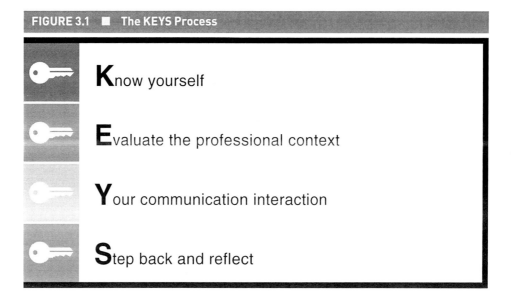

FIGURE 3.1 ■ The KEYS Process

Know yourself

Evaluate the professional context

Your communication interaction

Step back and reflect

EXECUTIVE SUMMARY

Now that you have finished reading this chapter, you should be able to

Explain the difference between hearing and listening:

- Hearing is your physical ability to detect sounds. It is the physiological process or function of receiving sounds.

- Listening requires you to concentrate on the verbal and nonverbal messages being sent and to determine the meaning of those messages. Effective listening is central to fostering interpersonal relationships with coworkers, leaders, and clients.

Discuss the barriers to listening and how to avoid them:

- External noise includes distractions such as audible talking during a meeting, ruffling of papers, or a cell phone going off in the next cubicle. Whenever possible, you should take steps to control the external noise that might interfere with your ability to listen to others, as well as their ability to listen to you.

- Internal noise encompasses any internal condition or state that interferes with the communicator's ability to focus on the message. Controlling internal noise in others can be difficult, as it may be hard to predict. Still, you can minimize some internal noise in others. For example, holding long meetings without food or bathroom breaks will guarantee internal noise in your team. Minimize the noise by providing food and breaks.

- Message overload occurs when a speaker includes too many details in a message, making it difficult for the listener to comprehend. As the listener tries to make sense of the specific details, they lose focus on the primary message. If the jargon or message overload comes as part of a conversation, not a presentation, engage in active listening.

Describe strategies for developing and sustaining professional excellence using active listening skills:

- People-oriented listeners are interested in demonstrating concern for others' emotions and interests, finding common ground, and responding. Action-oriented listeners are interested in direct, concise, error-free communication that is used to negotiate and accomplish a goal. Content-oriented listeners are interested in intellectual challenge and complex information. Time-oriented listeners prefer brief communication.

- An active listener focuses on asking questions and will often listen to the message and then paraphrase it for the sender.

- Another technique is that of reflection. Jalongo (2008) categorizes reflective listening as different from ordinary listening in four important ways. Reflective listening means the listener (1) listens thoughtfully to the meaning of the speaker's words; (2) considers the content of the message, both stated and implied; (3) thinks about the feelings associated with the message, attending to the speaker's verbal and nonverbal cues; and (4) makes every effort to reflect that message accurately.

- Questions are another tool used by the active listener. By asking questions, you can develop a better understanding of the speaker's message and provide support to the speaker.

Define the six-step process of listening:

- The HURIER model refers to a six-step listening process: **H**earing, **U**nderstanding, **R**emembering, **I**nterpreting, **E**valuating, and **R**esponding (Brownell, 1994, 1996). Hearing refers to concentrating on and attending to the message. The first step toward better listening is making sure you can properly hear the other person.

- Understanding is the process of attaching meaning to the verbal communication, or comprehending the literal meaning of the message.

- Remembering includes recalling the message so that it can be acted on. Listening not only requires us to be present, in the moment, and mindful but also necessitates anticipating future interactions.

- Interpreting is the step where we make sense of the verbal and nonverbal codes to assign meaning to the information received or the sensitivity to nonverbal and contextual aspects of the message (Brownell, 1994). Interpreting is an important part of the collaborative process of communication.

- Evaluating is the logical assessment of the value of the message (Brownell, 1994). Learning to evaluate a message without bias, distractions, apprehension, or gender or cultural differences takes time and patience.

- Responding is the last step and involves giving some form of response to the message, either verbally or nonverbally. Communication would not be collaboration if not for this vital step. Paraphrasing, summarizing, reflecting, and asking questions demonstrate responsiveness.

Apply the KEYS approach to conduct yourself with professional excellence while developing your listening skills in the workplace:

- Know yourself. Understand the components of being an active listener and critically apply them to your professional interactions. Realize your strengths and weaknesses as a listener and adapt accordingly.

- Evaluate the professional context. Learn whether your professional environment uses formal or informal communication. Also, pay attention to jargon used at your work. Use active listening to create understanding of words or phrases you are not familiar with.

- Your communication interaction. Take what you have learned from the first two steps and try communicating with fellow business professionals. Are you using the workplace jargon correctly and effectively? Be critical about the responses you receive from your peers.

- Step back and reflect. Ask yourself if you and your communication partner(s) came away from the interaction with mutual understanding. Think about what was effective and what was not. Repeat the process to gain greater and more effective strategies for being a good listener and a good communicator.

EXPLORE

1. Think of a company and look at the company's customer reviews and feedback on Google or another website that posts customer reviews. Do you believe the company does an effective job of listening to its customer base? Are there any improvements you would recommend to make the company a more effective listener?

2. Think about the ways you use the internet and social media to gain knowledge about businesses and products. How important is peer and customer feedback to you in your own purchasing decisions? Write about a time you used either word-of-mouth or online reviews to reach a purchasing decision.

3. Identify a movie or television show in which a character engages in poor listening techniques. What nonverbal cues do they give off that show a lack of interest? What critical listening skills could be used to improve the communication in the given situation?

REVIEW

1. Define *hearing* versus *listening*.

2. Explain the difference between external noise and internal noise.

3. Technical words used by specialized groups are known as _____.

4. _____ is any assumption we make or attitude we have about a person, an issue, or a topic before we have heard all the facts.

5. _____ are interested in demonstrating concern for others' emotions and interests, finding common ground, and responding.

6. Identify the different components of the HURIER model.

7. _____ occurs when a speaker includes too many details in a message, making it difficult for the listener to comprehend.

8. _____ listening asks you to evaluate the information being sent.

DISCUSSION QUESTIONS

1. What is the difference between hearing and listening, and why does it matter?

2. List three barriers to listening. Which barriers most frequently affect your ability to listen? List the steps you will take to improve your ability to avoid these barriers.

3. What is listening bias, and how has it affected your communication interactions in the past? What can you do to avoid it in future interactions?

4. List and define the four listening styles. Which style do you most relate to? Will this change now that you know how listening affects your professional excellence?

5. What is the difference between active and passive listening? Conversational and presentational listening?

TERMS TO REMEMBER

action-oriented listeners (p. 56)
active listener (p. 54)
bias (p. 53)
content-oriented listeners (p. 56)
conversational listening (p. 57)
critical listening (p. 53)
empathetic listening (p. 53)
evaluating (p. 58)
hearing (p. 47)
HURIER model (p. 58)
informational listening (p. 53)
interpreting (p. 58)
jargon (p. 51)

listening (p. 47)
message overload (p. 52)
paraphrase (p. 54)
passive listener (p. 54)
people-oriented listeners (p. 56)
presentational listening (p. 57)
questions (p. 55)
receiver apprehension (p. 52)
reflection (p. 55)
remembering (p. 58)
responding (p. 58)
time-oriented listeners (p. 56)
understanding (p. 58)

ENTERING THE WORKPLACE

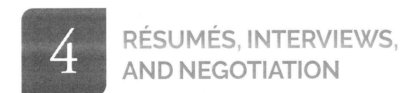

4 RÉSUMÉS, INTERVIEWS, AND NEGOTIATION

CHAPTER OBJECTIVES

After studying this chapter, you should be able to

4.1   Identify the six stages of the job-seeking process

4.2   Explain the important role of exploring in the job-seeking process

4.3   Explain the importance of researching job openings and potential employers

4.4   Develop a customized résumé and cover letter when applying for a job

4.5   Discuss examples of how to interview successfully

4.6   Discuss the importance of following up after an interview

4.7   Explain how to evaluate a job offer and negotiate terms

4.8   Apply the KEYS approach to conduct yourself with professional excellence throughout the job-seeking process

Many job seekers focus so much on answering interview questions that they forget they need to ask questions as well. Don't waste this opportunity. Ask smart questions, not just as a way to show you're a great candidate but also to see if the company is a good fit for you. You're being interviewed, but you're also interviewing the company. Haden (2016) recommends a few example questions:

- **What do you expect me to accomplish in the first 90 days?** If you weren't asked this question, ask it yourself. Great candidates want to hit the ground running. They don't want to spend huge chunks of time in orientation and training but end up with failure.

- **What are the company's highest priority goals this year, and how would my role contribute?** Great candidates want a job with meaning, with a larger purpose, and they want to work with people who approach their jobs the same way.

- **What percentage of employees was brought in by current employees?** Employees who love their jobs naturally recommend their company to their friends and peers. The same is true for people in leadership positions— people naturally try to bring on board talented people they previously worked with. They've built relationships, developed trust, and shown a level of competence that made someone go out of their way to follow them to a new organization. All of that speaks incredibly well to the quality of the workplace and the culture.

As you read this chapter, remember that there is no one-size-fits-all type of résumé, cover letter, or interview strategy. It is important to do your homework on the company and tailor your job-hunting strategy to the goals of the company. After reading this chapter, you should have the tools necessary to make your pre- and post-interview impression stand out with potential employers.

What do you want to be when you grow up? This is a question you have been asked from the time you were old enough to speak. Back then, you probably had no trouble responding. "I want to be an astronaut/a movie star/a doctor." These are all common responses from children and, indeed, all interesting occupations. However, as you aged, most of you probably became less certain about what you wanted to be when you grew up.

This uncertainty makes selecting a major in college a daunting task for many students. Once you *have* selected, the uncertainty remains as you face the plethora of career choices available to every major. For example, communication is a highly sought-after skill but not a job title. So in a way, a degree in communication makes you qualified for nothing and everything all at once. The communication major must explore various areas of the discipline to find their individual focus. Within each of those areas are countless opportunities that can be both exciting and overwhelming.

In a time where most job applications are done online and automatic rejection emails are commonplace, you may at times feel as though you're applying for any job out there. But in reality, the job-seeking process is about finding the position that matches your professional skills and qualifications.

iStockphoto/simpson33

Even seemingly defined majors such as nursing, accounting, and teaching require career exploration. You may want to be a nurse, but what kind of nurse? Do you want to work for a doctor's office, a clinic, or a hospital? With what kind of population do you wish to work? Would you prefer to work with children, women, older adults, people with diabetes, those who have suffered burns, or patients with cancer? The choices are many.

Fortunately, there is no need to fear. Considering that the average person holds numerous jobs in their lifetime, you'll have your entire career to grow, develop, and find your perfect fit. However, getting started on the right path can help maximize success and minimize frustration. By applying KEYS to the job-seeking process, you can start on the right path.

THE JOB-SEEKING PROCESS

What is the job-seeking process? What does it entail? Seeking a job is a multifaceted process that is part research, part performance, and part roller-coaster ride. The job-seeking process involves six stages: exploring, researching, applying, interviewing, following up, and negotiating.

We have integrated the KEYS process into our discussion of the stages of job seeking. By doing this, we hope that you will begin to see how the KEYS process can be applied to this communication situation, as well as to others that we cover in later chapters. Our discussion of the job-seeking process will be skills based. In other words, we are going to focus on communication skills (e.g., writing résumés, being interviewed) that will help you excel in the job-seeking process.

As a student of communication, it's important to realize that the discussion of communication skills is, in fact, the application of communication theory. As you read about the various skills, reflect on the theories and concepts we covered in Chapters 1, 2, and 3. For example, you learned that communication is a transactional process, not a pipeline. In this chapter, you will apply that concept by developing audience-centered messages. You also learned in the opening chapter that the communication context affects messages. Being offered a job changes the context and thereby changes the rules. So the question "What is the salary range and the benefits package?" sends two very different messages depending on when it is asked during the interviewing process. You learned in Chapter 2 that nonverbal communication is a vital component in any message. This chapter shows how the regulative rules for nonverbal communication (e.g., clothing, handshakes, eye contact) matter in the job-seeking process. In Chapter 3, you learned strategies to improve your listening. Excellent listening is a critical first step to successfully answering questions during interviews.

STAGE ONE: EXPLORING

The exploring stage begins with you, the job seeker. During this stage, you will need to explore both yourself and potential careers.

Self-Exploration

The first step in the KEYS approach is *know yourself*, so begin there with self-exploration. Take time to explore your goals and priorities. Here are just a few questions you should consider: What are you best at? What do you enjoy doing the most? What motivates you? What salary range do you need to live the lifestyle you desire? Is a family-friendly career a priority for you? Would you prefer to work in a large or small organization?

Taking time to think about your goals and priorities is an important part of the job-seeking process—it will help you determine what type of career you wish to pursue and what types of organizations you wish to work for.

Career Exploration

Career exploration requires you to research opportunities in your major that correspond with your goals and priorities. Being a foreign correspondent may sound like a wonderful career, but if being a highly involved parent is your top priority, foreign correspondent would not be a wonderful career for you. Instead, you could use that same skill set to work for a local public relations firm, which would not require you to spend long periods of time away from your children.

As you narrow down career opportunities, it's important to develop a clear understanding of what each career entails. When you find a career that seems interesting, you need to do some investigating. Interview several people in that line of work and find out what the job involves. Ask questions that will help you determine if this career lines up with your goals and priorities. If it seems like a good fit, try shadowing someone in the field for a week or two. Then seek an internship that will allow you to develop a clearer understanding of this career choice. To many people, this may seem like an unnecessary step, but the interviewing phase of the job-seeking process isn't about finding the candidate with the most qualifications; it's about finding the person who is the best fit for the job and the company. The more you know about a given occupation, the more effectively you will be able to describe how your skills line up with the position.

Know Yourself

Dominique Explores Her Career

As you read the passage below and answer the questions, think about how this knowledge can help you with your career search.

Dominique was an outstanding student who was driven to succeed. As graduation approached, however, she was shocked to realize she had never clearly defined her goals for her future career or for her life. She had never thought about her priorities as they related to the type of position she wanted after graduation. "I guess I just thought I would graduate and someone would knock on my door and say, 'Come work for us. We have the perfect job for you!'" When she came to the realization that such a knock was never coming, she began with the first step in the KEYS approach to professional excellence, *know yourself.* She determined she wanted a position that gave her autonomy, allowed her to lead groups, would pay for graduate school, and would not make her dress in business attire each day. She also discovered that her interviewing skills needed some polishing. Armed with this insight, Dominique began searching for a position that would meet her criteria, simultaneously practicing her interviewing skills. After a few months of searching and interviewing, Dominique found a position that was the perfect fit. Five years later, she has completed her master of arts degree, received a promotion, and not worn formal business attire since her initial interview. If you find yourself in the same position as Dominique, use the following questions to guide your career exploration.

Questions to Help You Explore Your Career

_____ **1.** What are my greatest strengths?

_____ **2.** What are my greatest weaknesses?

_____ **3.** What kind of organization do I want to work for? What kind of organization do I not want to work for?

_____ **4.** What do I know about this organization?

_____ **5.** Where do I really want to work?

_____ **6.** Why do I want to change jobs?

_____ **7.** What do I expect as far as salary and benefits?

_____ **8.** Where do I see myself going in the next few years?

_____ **9.** What makes me stronger than other applicants?

STAGE TWO: RESEARCHING

The researching stage of the job-seeking process comprises two components: researching openings and researching potential employers.

Researching Openings

Once you have an idea of what you are looking for in theory, you must begin to seek positions that exist in reality. For some students, this can be disappointing. Your dream job may require five years of experience that you do not have. The honest truth is that few students land their dream job right out of college. So become aware of the steps or experiences you'll need to get to your dream job, and begin working your way up the ladder.

When should you start your job search? This is a process that will take months, so plan accordingly. A good rule of thumb is for graduates to allow between three and six months to find that first job after graduation.

Where should you look for a job? The answer is simple: everywhere! Begin by using the resources available at your college or university. Most institutions of higher education have career planning centers. Your center may go by a slightly different name, such as career services, career placements, career development, or career consulting; regardless of the name, these centers are a vital resource in your job search.

Career services centers will often hold job fairs on campus or have information about job fairs in the surrounding community. Find out the dates for these job fairs and come ready to be interviewed. This means you should dress in business attire and have a résumé with you.

Today's job-seeking process may entail a lot of time spent using online employment systems. Recruiters and hiring managers often use applicant tracking systems that search for keywords in your resume that match keywords in their job ad (Ryan, 2021).

iStockphoto/SARINYAPINNGAM

The internet has become an excellent tool for locating employment opportunities. Multiple websites are dedicated to matching employees to jobs, including Monster.com, LinkedIn, Indeed.com, and the like. When job seeking, you should make it a habit to check out employment opportunities in the city or cities that interest you on such websites. In addition to employment-based websites, most organizations now post job openings on their company websites.

Another useful tool for finding openings is word of mouth. Tell everyone you know that you are job searching, making certain to be specific about the kind of job you are looking for. Saying "I am looking for a job in business" is very different from saying "I am looking for a job in hotel management." Whom should you tell? Tell family, friends (your friends and your parents' friends), classmates, professors, former employers, people at church, contacts from your internships—tell anyone who will listen.

One family member you should be certain to contact is your Uncle Sam. Yes, Uncle Sam (aka the U.S. government) can help you find a job. Try searching for jobs on USAJobs.gov to find government employment opportunities.

If you don't wish to work for the federal government, Uncle Sam can still be of help. According to the U.S. Bureau of Labor Statistics' (2010) *Occupational Outlook Handbook,*

> The State employment service, sometimes called the Job Service, operates in coordination with the U.S. Department of Labor's Employment and Training Administration. Local offices, found nationwide, help job seekers to find jobs and help employers to find qualified workers at no cost to either. To find the office nearest you, look in the State government telephone listings under "Job Service" or "Employment."

In addition to state employment agencies, which are run by the government, private agencies, also known as headhunters, can assist you in your job search. Unlike state agencies, private agencies are for-profit organizations that charge a fee for their services. The amount of the fee and who pays it vary.

TABLE 4.1 ■ Tools for Professional Excellence How to Use LinkedIn

To use LinkedIn for your job search and professional networking, follow these useful tips:

Key Points	Practical Tips
Make a findable and visually appealing profile.	● For your profile picture, use a headshot that is as professional looking as possible. ● Write a headline that is sharp and to the point, yet says a lot about who you are. Use the 220 characters to express your creativity and give viewers a clear vision of the kind of person and professional you are. ● Use keywords that relate to your career or field of work, which will make your profile easier to find.
Use your profile to showcase everything that doesn't fit on your résumé.	● Fill out as many of the description areas as possible; this gives viewers even more insight into you as a professional and individual, and it says more about you than your headline gives you the room to do. ● Link to outside sources (i.e., previous employers, examples of previous work) to further highlight your skills and accomplishments. ● The more you develop your profile, the more likely you are to establish new connections.
Strategically connect with others.	● Connect with existing contacts (whether professional or personal) to establish a foundation for forging new relationships. ● If you receive a connection request from someone you don't know, or you wish to connect with someone you don't know, research the person to find out whether it is worth connecting with them.

(Continued)

TABLE 4.1 ■ Tools for Professional Excellence *(Continued)*	
To use LinkedIn for your job search and professional networking, follow these useful tips:	
Key Points	**Practical Tips**
	● When connecting with someone new, craft a personal, detailed message that lets the person know who you are and why you want to connect with them. This will help you get your foot in the door, without scaring off the prospective new connection.
	● If connecting on LinkedIn fails, approach the person about connecting somewhere less formal, such as in person or on another social media site.
Snoop on your valuable network.	● If you're interested in a specific company, or you are hiring for your own company, don't be afraid to look through other users' profiles for any information that could give you a leg up, or help you find the perfect employee.
	● Keeping tabs on the connections you've made can help open doors you may not know existed, or give you the opportunity to help someone else.
Stay active on the site.	● You get the most out of LinkedIn by using it consistently, not just when you need it for a specific purpose.
	● Treat your profile as you would any other social media account by logging in on a consistent basis and keeping your account information current and updated.
	● Staying active on the site will also keep you in the loop of any site changes and help you adapt to these changes.

Source: Shin, L. (2014, June 26). How to use LinkedIn: 5 smart steps to career success. *Forbes.* Retrieved and adapted from www.forbes.com/sites/laurashin/2014/06/26/how-to-use-linkedin-5-smart-steps-to-career-success/

An often overlooked place to find openings is professional associations. Almost every industry has a professional association that sponsors meetings and conferences. Joining the local, regional, or even national chapter of a professional association will greatly enhance your ability to network with other professionals who may be looking to hire. When joining a professional association, be certain to inquire about outlets for job postings as well as student membership fees or dues.

Researching Potential Employers

At this point, it should be clear that job searching is time-consuming. Therefore, you do not want to waste valuable time and energy on positions and organizations that do not fit your desires, goals, and priorities. Think about this stage of the job-seeking process as job researching, not job searching. You are not simply searching for vacant positions. You are researching positions and companies to find the right fit between your skills and desires and their needs and opportunities. (See Table 4.1 Tools for Professional Excellence to explore several best practices for how to use LinkedIn.)

Before applying, take a few moments to research the position and the company. This research not only will help you determine if you truly wish to apply for this position with this organization but also will help you down the line when you customize your résumé and prepare for your interview. Remember, excelling as a communicator means you must be audience centered. You can't be audience centered if you do not know your audience.

Where do you find information on potential employers? You can begin by researching their websites, but remember that the purpose of company websites is to make the organization look appealing, so you do not want to end your research there. If you know anyone who works for the organization in question or has a similar type of position with a different organization, interview them for insights. Other sources of information that may be helpful include the Chamber of Commerce, Better Business Bureau reports, and/or your college's annual placement reports. According to Crosby (2000),

> Public libraries and career centers have valuable information about employers, including companies' annual reports to shareholders, reports kept by local chambers of commerce, trade journals, and business indexes, such as *Hoover's Business Index* and *Dun and Bradstreet.*

(Note: In 2003, Hoover's was acquired by Dun & Bradstreet, and in 2017, the platform began operating as D&B Hoovers.)

STAGE THREE: APPLYING

Once you have researched a place you would like to consider for employment, it's time to turn your attention to résumés and cover letters.

Developing Résumés

A _____ provides a picture of who you are as an employee by highlighting your skill set. An excellent résumé illustrates how you fit this position and this organization and highlights the skills you possess relevant to the skills required by the position for which you are applying.

There is no one standard form for a résumé—it's not one size fits all. When selecting the format for your résumé, select a format that will highlight your strengths and downplay your weaknesses. Regardless of which format you select, whenever possible, you should customize your résumé to each position and organization. Although formats vary, every résumé should be no more than one page and must be visually appealing.

Chances are you'll be applying for multiple positions while you are job seeking. Therefore, it's important to develop a generic résumé that you can use as a starting point for the customized résumé you develop for each position.

When developing your résumé, you will have to determine if you plan to use a chronological, functional, or combination résumé. These résumé types are defined in the sections that follow.

Chronological

This is the most common form and probably the easiest to prepare. The chronological résumé emphasizes employment and/or experience history, listing elements in reverse chronological order (i.e., your most recent experience first). This format is especially useful to new graduates or those with limited work experience.

Functional (Skill Based)

This functional résumé emphasizes skills and attributes that can be applied to a variety of employment situations; your skills are broken down into categories that quickly communicate to employers what you can do for them. This format is useful for candidates without direct employment-related experience or for those who wish to work in fields unrelated to their academic major.

Combination

For many candidates, a combination of elements from the chronological and functional résumé formats works best. Regardless of which résumé type you select, your résumé will include some or all of the following sections.

Contact Information

Begin your generic résumé by listing your contact information (see Figure 4.1). You should include your name, address, phone number, and email address. Believe it or not, many prospective job seekers are taken out of the running due to problems with their contact information. You should make certain the address you provide will be valid throughout your job search. The same holds true for phone numbers and email addresses.

Your résumé is one of the most important factors in the job application process. How might tailoring your résumé change when applying for a job with a large retailer like Amazon compared to applying for a local nonprofit organization?

iStockphoto/4kodiak

When it comes to the telephone, remember that your voicemail greeting will make an impression on prospective employers. If you want to communicate with professional excellence, use a professional message for your voicemail. This same level of professionalism should extend to your email address. An email address such as "partygirl2021" or "mrtequila" is going to land your résumé in the trash. Addresses such as "snugglebear" or "cutiepie" are unprofessional as well. Choose an email address related to your name, and be certain to check your email account regularly.

It's also important to make sure there is nothing online that you would not want your future employer to see. What comes up when you google your name? What information can be found on your social media accounts? If you think prospective employers don't bother to check these sites, you're wrong. Not only do employers use Google to run background checks on potential employees; they also check Facebook, Twitter, and other forms of social media (Finder, 2006; Slovensky & Ross, 2012).

FIGURE 4.1 ■ Generic Résumé

Heather Gutiérrez
3606 Bon Soir Drive   Houston, Texas 78044   361.815.4949
heather.gutierrez@gmail.com

Summary of Qualifications
- Strong interpersonal skills
- Bilingual (Spanish, speak, read and write fluently)
- Conduct audits procedures, create reports and implement corrective/preventive measures
- Perform inventories, create reports and reconcile results
- Expert in Microsoft Office
- Prepared professional presentations
- Ability to manage multiple projects
- Effective problem solving techniques
- Purchases supplies and conduct inventory using on-line procedures
- Skilled in normal administrative processes
- Experience in training staff in software and administrative duties

Education
University of Houston
    Spring 2013 – Expected Graduation Date August 2016
    Bachelor of Arts in Communication
    3.5 GPA

Coursework

Interpersonal Communication	Public Speaking
Business and Professional Communication	Intercultural Communication
Communication Theory	Small-Group Communication
Persuasion	Media and Society
Graphic Design	Research Methods
Digital Journalism	Voice and Diction

Class Project
Coordinator, ABC: Read With Me   October – December 2014
    Duties – Leading team discussions, planning meetings, collaborate with team members, develop and promote campaign, develop relationship with donors, and create data report.

Work Experience
Office Assistant, Texas
University of Houston – Dean's Office   August 2014 – June 2016
    Duties — General Administrative including: answer phone, create correspondence, supply inventory, record retention, and maintain personnel files.

    Other assignments : planned special events, designed web content, developed brochures, flyers, press releases, and presentations, drafted letters, and oversaw two major projects to revamp the personnel files and records retention processes.

Office Administrator, Zales, Inc.   August 2010 – Febuary 2014
    Duties — General Administrative including: answer phone, pay invoices, create correspondence, inventory responsibility, handle money, reconcile statements, conduct inventory, customer service, and inventory audit control.

Student Organizations

Lambda Pi Eta, National Communication Honor Society	Inducted May 2016
Leadership Award Recipient, Communication Club	2015
National Society of Leadership and Success	Inducted February 2015
Student Reading Council	2013 – 2014

References available upon request

Side annotations:
- Your generic résumé should include any and all information you could utilize for constructing a résumé for a prospective job opening.
- Include an email address that is professional and appropriate.
- Include any skills and abilities you have gained.
- If you decide to include your GPA, be certain it will reflect positively.
- Include your assigned duties, as well as other duties and experiences you have had on the job. Always seek opportunities that will expand and utilize the skills you are learning while completing your degree.

Objective and Summary

An objective is a one- or two-sentence declarative statement about your career goals. An example of an objective would be "To obtain a position as a reading specialist with the Altoona Area School District." The benefit of including an objective is debatable. Some people argue it can be beneficial and has been a résumé standard for years. Others argue that since the objective is clear (to obtain the position), there is no need to waste space stating the obvious. Many résumés have moved away from the objective to a **summary** of skills and traits.

Education

If you're a recent college graduate, your education is, in all likelihood, the most important thing you want future employers to consider, so your education section should be displayed prominently. Include the name of any college or university from which you have graduated or that you are currently attending. As a general rule, a college graduate should not list their high school education or high school accomplishments.

List the name of your degree and your major (e.g., bachelor of science in biology). You may also wish to state a minor if you have one. Include the date of graduation (e.g., "Degree conferred December 2021"). If you're in your final semester, you can use something such as "Degree anticipated May 2023."

You may also wish to list some relevant courses. For the purposes of the generic résumé, list all the courses you think may be relevant during your job-seeking process. You can narrow the list during the customizing step.

Students often ask if they should include their grade point average (GPA) on their résumé. The answer is simple—it depends on your GPA. If your GPA is a 3.0 or higher, include it. For some students, the overall GPA is under a 3.0 but the GPA for coursework in their major is much higher. If that's the case, then list your major GPA.

Experience

A section on experience is a standard part of the résumé. As you advance in your career, you will most likely label this section as employment experience, which will take precedence over your education. Yet, for most college graduates, including relevant experience, not just employment experience, is more beneficial. Using the general title "Relevant Experience" allows you to incorporate a broader range of information. In this section, you can list your relevant employment history as well as internships, relevant class projects, relevant work with student organizations, or volunteering. For example, you may be applying for a job that requires leadership and grant-writing experience. During college, you worked as a waitress, but you were also the president of two student organizations, and as part of an English course, you wrote a grant for the local food bank, which was funded. All this information can be included in the "Relevant Experience" section because it's relevant to the position for which you are applying.

Skills

Skills may be incorporated under your experiences or may be a separate category. Some students opt for a résumé format that includes a separate skills section or lists skills rather than integrating them into the "Relevant Experience" section. Which format should you use? The answer is whichever format does a better job of highlighting you.

Employment Experience

If you've been lucky enough to work at a job that's relevant to the position you're seeking, prominently display that experience and your job duties. For most college graduates, however, this will not be the case.

Let's look at a few possible scenarios. In the first scenario, your work history is by and large unrelated to the career you are pursuing, but your work on campus through class projects, internships, and student or volunteer organizations is related. To best showcase your skills in this situation, list the class projects, your internship, and your work with the Sociology Club under "Relevant Experience," as previously discussed. Give some details about each experience. Then you can simply list your places of employment, job titles, and employment dates later in the résumé in a section titled "Employment Experience," "Employment History," or "Work History."

If your work history is not directly related to the position you are pursuing, list the place of employment, job title, employment dates, and some skills you acquired at this job. Even if the job is not directly related to your career, you likely gained or honed some skill(s) that will make you a more appealing applicant. For example, if you worked as a waiter, you have developed your customer service skills, worked both independently and as part of a team, handled difficult situations with professionalism, and demonstrated the ability to multitask.

Awards and Hobbies

Should you include awards and hobbies on your résumé? As always, the answer is it depends. Include an awards and honors section only if you have multiple listings and they are relevant to the position. Academic awards and honors strengthen you as a candidate, but noting that you were on the homecoming court does not. If you have only one award or honor but you think it is relevant, make sure to include it somewhere but do not set aside an entire section of the résumé to highlight it. It may be best to discuss it in your cover letter.

As for hobbies, do not put a hobbies and interests section in your résumé. If you do have a hobby or interest directly relevant to the position, work it into your cover letter or résumé as a skill or experience. Otherwise, leave it out.

References

References should not be listed on your résumé. You can make a note about references at the bottom of the page (e.g., "References available on request"), but the purpose of the résumé is to highlight you, so don't waste space listing references. This is not to imply that securing good references is not an important step in the job-seeking process; references are an extremely important part of the process.

Do not ask your references for generic letters of recommendation. You should submit letters of recommendation only to positions that request such letters. If letters of recommendation are required, then and only then should you solicit them from your references.

Customizing Résumés

The second step in the KEYS model is to *evaluate the professional context*, which includes your audience and the organization. All the research you have gathered during the previous stages of the job-seeking process will enable you to do just that. During the remaining stages of the process, you must take the information you have gathered and apply it to your communication interactions. These interactions include customizing your résumé and cover letter, as well as being interviewed (see Figure 4.3).

Reviewing Your Audience

The research you have done on the organization will give you some insight into the organization's mission and values. In addition, the job posting will tell you exactly what the organization is looking for in terms of this position.

How do you customize your résumé? Begin with the generic résumé you have already developed. Systematically go through the generic résumé, identifying the information that is most relevant to this position. During the first round of cuts, delete all the information that is not relevant to the position. If the remaining information does not fit on one page, go back and eliminate the information that is least relevant to the position. When customizing your résumé, the goal is to include information about yourself that addresses every qualification noted in the job posting without exceeding the one-page limit.

Your first audience may be an employee in the Human Resources (HR) Department whose job is to determine if you meet the minimal qualifications for this position. In some cases, the HR Department may use a computer scanning program that counts the number of key words from the job posting found in each résumé. Because of these types of HR screening processes, you must make certain that the language on your résumé matches the language in the job posting exactly. Once you have determined which information will be included in this customized résumé, go back and customize the language. Let's say, for example, that you have applied for a position that requires "proven leadership experience." You believe your two-year tenure as the president of the Kinesiology Club demonstrates your leadership experience. In your generic résumé, you've listed this experience and included "leadership" as one of your skills—this is not enough. The job posting specifically states "proven leadership experience," so you should not imply or dance around the wording used in the posting. To customize your résumé, change the wording in the skills section from "leadership" to "proven leadership experience."

Creating Visual Appeal

Although résumés can come in a variety of different forms, all résumés should be visually appealing and utilize a parallel structure. In terms of visual appeal, you need to include a balance between text and white space. Too much white space indicates a lack of qualifications. On the flip side, too much information jammed on a page does not make you look more qualified. Instead, it makes your résumé difficult to read, which makes you less appealing. Remember, a résumé is a snapshot. You can't include every detail of your life, so make sure to include the information that is most relevant to this position at this organization.

The font you select for the text of the résumé should be 12 point—no less than 11 point if you need more space—for easy reading. When selecting a font, you want to stick with standard fonts such as Arial, Helvetica, and Times New Roman to ensure easy electronic transfer.

As for parallel structure, decide on a heading system, and keep it consistent throughout the résumé. If your first major heading is bold, 14 point, and all capitals, then all major headings should be bold, 14 point, and all capitals.

The use of a parallel structure can also be applied to your word choices. For example, when listing your duties and work experience, use active verbs (see Figure 4.2). In addition, you may utilize a list of bulleted duties and skills. Whichever format you select, remember to use that format throughout that section of the résumé.

It's also critical to edit résumés, applications, and cover letters carefully. Make it a habit to check, double-check, and triple-check. Spelling errors seem to jump off the page at potential employers. If you want to be considered for an interview, your résumé can contain no spelling errors. Remember, spelling and grammar check catches only misspelled words, not incorrect words. Also, make certain your grammar is correct. For example, when discussing a former job or experience, use past tense; when discussing a current job or experience, use present tense.

Once your résumé and cover letter are complete, you should laser print them onto 8½- by 11-inch bond paper, also known as résumé paper. Pink paper with a spritz of perfume may have

FIGURE 4.2 ■ Résumé Action Words

Achieved	Established	Launched	Produced
Administered	Evaluated	Maintained	Programmed
Analyzed	Examined	Managed	Proposed
Budgeted	Expanded	Mediated	Recommended
Built	Expedited	Motivated	Recruited
Calculated	Explained	Negotiated	Reduced
Composed	Facilitated	Obtained	Reinforced
Conducted	Formulated	Operated	Researched
Created	Generated	Organized	Reviewed
Delivered	Handled	Participated	Scheduled
Demonstrated	Implemented	Performed	Supervised
Developed	Improved	Planned	Translated
Directed	Increased	Presented	Updated
Distributed	Initiated	Processed	Utilized

helped Elle Woods get into Harvard Law School in *Legally Blonde*, but that works only in the movies. Your best bet is to select white or off-white paper—unscented, of course.

Developing Electronic and Scannable Resumes and Online Applications

Back in the day, résumés and cover letters were either mailed or hand-delivered to organizations. Today, organizations are requesting that résumés be submitted electronically or that the information traditionally found in a résumé be submitted via an online application.

When it comes to submitting electronic or scannable résumés, you must be sensitive to the style and formatting of the document. Electronic résumés should be prepared in common programs, such as Microsoft Word. Scannable résumés should be simplistic; so avoid any decorative fonts or graphics.

For electronic applications, you'll most likely be cutting information from your résumé and pasting it into the application. Although this may allow you to include more information than the standard one-page résumé, the information presented should still be concise and relevant.

Developing Cover Letters

Cover letters accompany your résumé and serve to introduce you as a potential employee, highlight your résumé, and demonstrate your writing skills. According to Buzzanell (1999),

> The goal of the cover letter is to get prospective employers to look at your résumé, the goal of a résumé is to get the prospective employer to ask you on an interview, and the goal of the interview is to get you the job.

Begin the cover letter by stating that you're interested in a specific position (state the exact position title). In the next paragraph or two, highlight why you are qualified for this position, making specific reference to the required skills and qualifications noted in the job posting. End the letter by expressing your desire to discuss your qualifications further during an interview. Like the résumé, your cover letter should be concise, no more than one page. Use the same paper and font for both your résumé and your cover letter.

EVALUATE THE PROFESSIONAL CONTEXT

Customizing the Résumé

As you evaluate the passage below, note how effectively Heather adapts her experience for this professional context.

Heather will soon be graduating from college. She has taken time to know herself and has developed clearly defined career goals. She is currently pursuing positions that will allow her to combine her love of communications and campaign development. She has found a position with HDS Life, Inc. (see the job posting below). After doing some research on HDS Life, she is certain she would be a good fit for both the position and the organization. In Figures 4.1 (page 73) and 4.3 (below), you will find (1) her generic résumé, (2) her cover letter, and (3) her customized résumé.

Questions to Consider

1. How does the customized résumé differ from the generic résumé?
2. Has Heather effectively adapted her experience to this professional context?
3. Has she done an effective job in customizing her résumé and cover letter?
4. Do they reflect the information found in the job posting?
5. Are they visually appealing?
6. What advice would you give Heather?

FIGURE 4.3 ■ Customized Cover Letter and Résumé

CUSTOMIZED COVER LETTER AND RÉSUMÉ

Advertisement for Position

HDS Life, Inc. seeks an Assistant Director of Communications

Position Description
The Assistant Director of Communications actively develops and promotes the HDS Life, Inc. narrative to key external and internal audiences and stakeholders. This role works across businesses to help build HDS Life's strategic communications message, and promotes efforts to achieve business goals and growth targets. The Assistant Director of Communications will provide administrative assistance for the Director of Communications, provide high-profile communication support to the HDS Project Management Office and to a variety of stakeholders.

Position Requirements
Proven administrative experience and expertise interacting with Leadership with strong execution and results orientation. Excellent organization and project management skills. Excellent communication (oral, written, and design). Effective problem-solver with expertise at anticipating and resolving issues; solution oriented, proactive and team-spirited. Strong collaborator. Advanced software skills in PowerPoint, Visio, Word, Excel and industry experience preferred. Bachelor's degree required; communication field preferred. Ability to stay up to date on presentation technology and capabilities.

(Continued)

FIGURE 4.3 ■ Customized Cover Letter and Résumé (*Continued*)

(Continued)

CUSTOMIZED COVER LETTER

Be certain to maintain the font and format for both the resume and the cover letter.

Heather Gutiérrez

3606 Bon Soir Drive • Houston, Texas 78044 • 361.815.4949
heather.gutiérrez@gmail.com

July 1, 2016

HDS Life, Inc.
2727 Allen Parkway
Houston, Texas 77019

Attention: Ms. Natalie Contreras

Re: Assistant Director of Communications

Dear Ms. Contreras:

Include which position you are interested in.

I am writing in regard to the job description for the Assistant Director of Communications position. I believe my skills, education, and experience are an excellent match for the job duties and requirements listed. My résumé is attached for your review. The document includes information regarding my Bachelor of Arts degree in Communication and work experience. Also enclosed is a list of references.

Include education.

Use specific language the job posting requires for the candidate.

I have proven success and direct experience in all position requirements. During my time at the University of Houston, I created brochures and other marketing materials; wrote the web content that developed the narratives of the College of Liberal Arts and provided support to senior management and all other stakeholders. I am proficient in Microsoft Office, have experience with event planning, preparing and delivering professional presentations, preparing correspondence, conducting inventories, responding to audits, maintaining accounts payable and receivable, and handling all aspects of customer service.

Include any skills and abilities that qualify you for that particular position.

Strengths I would bring to the Assistant Director of Communications position include my ability to learn quickly, attention to detail, initiative, and strong communication skills. I pride myself on my professional and organizational skills, as well as my strong work ethic. I would appreciate the opportunity to interview for this position.

Express desire to further discuss your qualifications during an interview.

Thank you in advance for your consideration. I look forward to speaking with you.

Cover letter should be limited to one page.

Sincerely,

Heather Gutiérrez

(*Continued*)

FIGURE 4.3 ■ Customized Cover Letter and Résumé (*Continued*)

CUSTOMIZED RÉSUMÉ

Heather Gutiérrez

3606 Bon Soir Drive • Houston, Texas 78044 • 361.815.4949
heather.gutierrez@gmail.com

Summary of Qualifications
- Excellent oral and written skills
- Excellent organization and project management skills
- Proven interpersonal, customer service, and collaborative skills
- Proactive problem solving skills
- Bilingual (Spanish, speak, read and write fluently)
- Advanced software skills including, PowerPoint, Visio, Word, and Excel
- Ability to manage multiple projects
- Highly experienced at developing professional presentations and reports

Education
University of Houston
Bachelor of Arts in Communication,   3.5 GPA
Spring 2013 – Expected Graduation Date August 2016

Relevant Coursework

Interpersonal Communication	Public Speaking
Business and Professional Communication	Intercultural
Communication	

Relevant Experience

Office Assistant, University of Houston   August 2014 – June 2016
Office Administrator, Zales, Inc.   August 2010 – Febuary 2014
Relevant Duties – Provided outstanding customer service, created correspondence, paid invoices, planned event ranging from 10–200 attendees, served as project manager, developed a variety of communication and marketing materials, and designed web content.

Coordinator, ABC: Read With Me   October – December 2014
Duties – Facilitated team discussions, planned meetings, collaborated with team members, developed and promoted public relations campaign, develop relationship with donors, and create data report. Exceeded fundraising goals by 150%.

Student Organizations and Awards

Lambda Pi Eta, National Communication Honor Society	Inducted May 2016
Leadership Award Recipient, Communication Club	Received 2016
National Society of Leadership and Success	Inducted February 2016
Student Reading Council	2013 – 2014

References available upon request

Margin notes: "The most important information that potential employers should remember about you should go in the R-zone" (Diaz, 2013). Be certain to use font that is easily legible. Include an email address that is professional and appropriate. Use specific nouns and keywords to describe job duties and qualifications. If applicable, adjustments should be made to match those specified in the job posting. If you decide to include your GPA, be certain it will reflect positively. Creating distinctive headings and subheadings make a document easier to read. Instead of "Work Experience," it is often better to have "Relevant Experience" as you may include class projects, student organizations, and internships. Provide information that helps describe the nature of your student organization. For example: honors societies, social organizations, and service organizations often are named with Greek letters. Highlight anything that demonstrates your proven leadership skills. Formatting should be consistent through the entirety of the résumé. Balancing white space and margins creates a document that is appealing.

STAGE FOUR: INTERVIEWING

When your average college graduate thinks of the job-seeking process, they often think about the fourth stage, interviewing. But for students such as yourself who wish to achieve professional excellence, the work you have done in the previous stages will benefit you immensely during the interviewing stage. As you prepare for the interview, you already have a clear sense of who your audience is and what they are looking for in a candidate. Furthermore, your first communication interactions with the potential employers (your résumé and cover letter) not only highlighted you as a candidate but also began to demonstrate how you'll fit into their organization.

Although securing an interview is an exciting milestone in the job-seeking process, you're still several steps away from being hired. To land the position, you must do two important tasks: prepare and practice.

Before the Interview

To demonstrate professional excellence, you will need to prepare your message, anticipate the questions, script your answers, practice your answers, prepare your appearance, and reduce your nervousness.

Preparing Your Message

A student once remarked, "Preparing for an interview would be simple if we knew the questions in advance." The bad news is that you do not have a crystal ball that will magically reveal your interview questions, but the good news is that you have something almost as telling. By reviewing your skills, the job posting, and your research, you can determine exactly what information to present during the interview.

Prior to walking into your interview, you should have a clear understanding of the information you plan to present. Begin by looking at the job posting. What qualifications are a must for this position? How do you meet each of these qualifications? For example, if the position states that the candidate must be highly organized, make a list of examples that demonstrate your organizational skills. Review the duties you'll be responsible for in this position. If you'll have to write, make a list of examples that show you are an effective writer. Then gather some samples of your writing to bring along to the interview.

Next, review your résumé and cover letter. Are there areas where you might need to elaborate? What information do you want to restate in the interview? What are some examples or experiences that illustrate the skills highlighted on your résumé? In the end, you should be ready to discuss specific examples, stories, and experiences that are relevant to the position.

Finally, make a list based on important points you learned while doing your research. This list should include things you learned about this company that made it appealing to you and questions you may have about the position or the organization.

Anticipating Questions

Once you have completed your lists and reviewed your research, it's time to practice answering questions. You can never be 100% certain about what's going to be asked during the interview, but you can make some educated guesses.

Begin by imagining yourself as the interviewer. If you were going to hire someone for this position, what questions would you ask? How could you learn more about the interviewee's qualifications and skills? What would you be looking for in their answers? This exercise can help you anticipate possible questions, but it should also help you formulate stronger answers to those questions when the time comes for you to answer them.

Next, check out some resources that include sample interview questions as well as some helpful tips. Books such as *Best Answers to 201 Most Frequently Asked Interview Questions, 301 Smart Answers to Tough Interview Questions*, and *The 250 Job Interview Questions You'll Most Likely Be Asked* provide a variety of possible questions.

Be certain to practice both behavioral questions and traditional questions. Behavioral questions explore how you have handled past situations and ask you to respond to hypothetical situations. For example: "Tell me about a time when you had to meet a very short deadline." or "Give me an example of a time you served as a leader." Traditional questions include some of the old standards listed below:

Tell me a little about yourself.

Why did you apply for this position?

What makes you qualified for this position? Why should we hire you?

What are your strengths? What are your weaknesses?

What would your former employer (professor, friend) say about you?

What are three words that describe you?

What are your short-term goals? What are your long-term goals?

Do you have any questions for us?

Scripting Answers

When it comes time for the interview, remember you are in control of your answers. The interviewer may ask slightly different questions from the ones you've practiced. Yet the information you present during the interview should be the same information you practiced prior to the interview. The purpose of practicing is not to guess the exact questions that will be asked—it's to learn to professionally present important information about your qualifications for the position and your fit in the organization.

If possible, you should prepare by scripting answers that follow a three-part formula. First, directly answer the question. Then, back up your answer with a specific example that supports your answer. Finally, connect the answer back to the company or the position.

Let's say you are applying for a position managing a retail team for Company A. The interviewer asks, "Have you had much experience working with groups?" Begin by answering the question: "Yes, I have had extensive experience working with groups, both as a group member and as a leader." That would be an average answer.

Some interviewers will inquire further about your experience; others may not. You do not want to miss this opportunity to highlight your experience, so extend your answer to include an example:

Yes, I have had extensive experience working in groups, both as a group member and as a leader. For example, last semester, I worked with a group of graduating seniors on a semester-long marketing project. It was a challenging experience, because the majority of the group had senioritis. At first, they didn't care much about the assignment, but I knew I could change that attitude, so I volunteered to be the leader. Once I was elected, I made certain everyone in the group participated when selecting the topic. This helped get everyone involved from the beginning. Then we divided the project into manageable pieces that allowed everyone to have a balanced workload and a sense of ownership. In the end, we received the highest grade in the class.

This is a good answer, but to turn it into an excellent answer, the job seeker needs to take one more step by relating the answer back to the position and the organization:

> In fact, one of the things exciting to me about working for Company A is the opportunity to lead teams. I realize the challenges on the job will be different from what I faced in the classroom, but that is precisely the kind of challenge I am looking for in a position.

When it comes to answering questions, you want to be strategic. Answering strategically means discussing and emphasizing your skills and experiences that relate to this position. It means applying the KEYS of knowing yourself and evaluating your professional context. It does not mean you can lie, exaggerate, or fudge your answers. Lies, even little white lies, are unethical in any interview situation. If you have to lie to get the job, then this is not the right job for you.

How do you answer questions strategically? Let's say that during your research you learned that Company A has won awards for its customer service. During your interview, you might emphasize your desire to work for a company that has been recognized for excellence and highlight your excellent customer service skills—assuming, of course, that both these things are true (see Table 4.2).

TABLE 4.2 ■ Action Items Skills for the Job Interview

Skill	Strategy	Application
Review your résumé/cover letter.	Check to see if your résumé/cover letter fits the job requirements and adjust if necessary.	Align your skills and experience to correlate with requirements listed in the job description.
Understand your personal selling points.	Identify what key skills and experience you can offer to the employer.	Do a self-assessment that highlights your strongest qualities, and intertwine those with your listed professional skills.
Prepare answers to expected questions.	Be prepared to answer what can be expected of you about the job, and identify the key message you want to get across.	Gain feedback from other professionals already in the industry, as well as their own personal job interview experiences.
Practice delivery.	Make sure you can deliver your answers with the utmost confidence.	Practice several times in front of family, friends, or any other willing audiences.

In many interviews, the interviewer will allow some time at the end for you to ask a few questions. Therefore, you should prepare several questions for the employer. Although you would love to ask about salary, benefits, and vacation, this is not the time. That comes after you are offered the job. At this stage in the process, your questions are more about showing your research and interest in the position than about getting additional information. It is an opportunity for you to demonstrate that you have researched this company and will be a valuable asset. So you might ask something like "When researching Company A, I noticed you have a six-month training program. Can you tell me a little more about what that program entails?"

While job interview formats are often one on one be prepared for a variety of formats, including those that involve a committee or technology.

iStockphoto/fizkes

Practicing Answers

Reading questions and thinking through the answers is an effective way to begin practicing, but to be fully prepared, you must take part in mock interviews. Enlist the help of family members and friends to run through questions with you. Have different people take different approaches to the interview. Have some mock interviewers smile and give you a lot of feedback. Have others be stern and cold and provide little feedback.

One of the best tools in improving your skills as an interviewee is the video recorder. On most college campuses, the career services center can help you in this process. Receiving professional feedback from the career services staff will be helpful, but watching yourself in action is the most powerful tool available for improvement. If your campus does not have a career center or if your career center does not tape mock interviews, find someone with a smartphone or tablet and record it yourself.

When practicing, keep in mind that there are a wide variety of interview formats. The good news is, although the settings vary, the basic rules for an effective interview remain the same across situations.

Telephone interviews are often used during the early screening phases of the interview process. When doing a phone interview, remember to block the call-waiting feature if you have it. Also, ensure your cell phone battery is charged. Never chew gum, smoke, eat, drink, or use the bathroom during a phone interview, because the noise will be picked up on the other end. When you have finished delivering your answer, wait for the next question. Even if it takes the interviewer(s) a moment or two to ask the next question, do not try to fill that silence. When being interviewed via videoconference, try to imagine the camera is a person and respond accordingly. This means making eye contact with the camera and smiling.

Face-to-face interviews also come in a variety of formats, which include the standard one-on-one interview, a series of one-on-one interviews, panel interviews, and interviews with multiple interviewees. The same rules that apply in the standard one-on-one interview apply in each of these settings, but keep a few things in mind for each context. If you have a series of one-on-one interviews, you may feel as though you are repeating yourself. But remember, each interviewer is hearing your information for the first time, so not only it is okay to repeat yourself, it is necessary. If you find yourself answering questions for a panel of interviewers, always acknowledge the person who asks the question but address your answer to (and make eye contact with) the entire group when responding. If you find yourself being interviewed with a group of other candidates, always treat your competition with respect and professionalism. The way you treat the other candidates is indeed part of how you will be assessed.

On occasion, your interview may be conducted during a meal. In this context, answering questions, not eating, is your priority. Keeping this in mind, order food that will be easy to eat. This is not the time to order barbequed ribs or crab legs, even if the interviewers order it for themselves. The same goes for alcohol. During the meal, follow all the basic rules of etiquette. If you are not certain of all the rules, review an etiquette book prior to the interview—at the very least, review the different types of silverware. And never talk with your mouth full.

Preparing Your Appearance

For many students, preparing for the interview begins and ends with purchasing a suit. Although presenting a professional image is an important part of your nonverbal communication in the interview, wearing an Armani suit will not land you the job. Your interviewing attire is in a sense a uniform that identifies you as a professional. Many books and articles have weighed in on the subject of appropriate interview attire (Dorio & Axelrod, 2000; Molloy, 1988, 1996; Ruetzler et al., 2012). In the end, these books can be summarized in a few basic rules that job seekers should follow when putting together their interviewing uniform.

For formal interviews, you should elect to wear a tailored dark suit with a light shirt or a tailored dress. Choose a conservative pattern when wearing a tie, and if you elect to wear jewelry, keep it simple so it isn't distracting. Finally, you should wear closed-toe shoes that are dark and polished, and when wearing high heels, the heel should be no higher than 2 inches (Harvard University, 2022).

Interviewers do not expect to see new college graduates in expensive, designer-label suits, nor do they expect to see them in ill-fitting suits. When purchasing your suit, the fit is extremely important. There is nothing professional about sleeves that cover your hands or a too-short skirt. It is worth your money to have your suit professionally altered.

YOUR COMMUNICATION INTERACTION

Mark's Zoom Interview

As you read the passage below, consider what would be a more effective communication strategy in this situation.

Mark is preparing for a Zoom interview with a company to which he has applied. He wants to be comfortable for the interview, so he grabs his laptop, a cup of coffee, and settles into bed in his favorite t-shirt and sweatpants. A few minutes later, his laptop beeps and the Zoom screen pops up with the interviewer. Mark and the interviewer exchange introductions, and the interview begins. A minute later, Mark's dog begins barking loudly down the hall, which causes Mark to yell for it to be quiet. The interviewer then asks Mark a series of questions about why he wants to work for the company, what he enjoys most about the work he does, and so on. Mark suddenly cannot remember any of the answers he had come up with the night before, and when he nervously goes to take a sip of coffee, he spills it all over himself and curses out loud. Toward the end of the interview, Mark's laptop begins beeping loudly, indicating that it is running out of battery power. The interviewer asks what the beeping noise is. Mark replies that he does not hear anything, all while frantically searching for his laptop charger. A few seconds later, the laptop runs out of power, and the screen goes black. Mark stares at the blank screen before pulling the covers over his head and sinking deeper into bed.

Questions to Consider

1. What do you think was Mark's most critical mistake during the interview?
2. What are some things Mark could have done differently when preparing for the interview? What about during the interview?
3. What do you think Mark's next move should be?
4. How are Zoom and video interviews similar to face-to-face interviews? How are they different?

Modern technology has opened the door for video calls hosted by interview committees, which saves company money on travel. How would you prepare for a phone or video interview?

iStockphoto/insta_photos

Men should wear basic black dress shoes. Both men and women need to polish their shoes prior to the interview. Men should wear dark, over-the-calf dress socks that correspond with the outfit. (When you sit down, your pant leg will rise and the interviewer will see if you have on your white running socks!). Men should keep a two-piece rule in mind for jewelry: one watch, as long as it appears professional with the suit, and one ring, such as a wedding band or college class ring.

Both men and women should carry a briefcase, a portfolio, or some sort of professional bag. Under no circumstances is it acceptable to carry your backpack. For women, it is a wise idea to put your essentials in your briefcase and leave your purse at home. Carrying two bags can make you appear cluttered. Your bag must look professional and correspond with your outfit. Inside your bag, you should include extra copies of your résumé, contact information for your references, samples of your work, and mints or a breath freshener. What you should not have in your bag is your cell phone. Nothing will lose you a job faster than your phone going off during the interview. Don't take any chances; leave it in the car.

If you wear polish, it should be a light, neutral color. With the exception of one small pair of earrings,, all other piercings should be removed. In addition, tattoos should be covered. Both men and women should also avoid perfumes and colognes when interviewing. Your interviewer may not like your fragrance or, worse yet, may be allergic to it. If you are a smoker, take extra measures to ensure that you do not smell like smoke. If possible, don't smoke in your suit, wash your hands after smoking, and freshen your breath.

As for your hair, it should be neat and clean. If you have long hair, pull it back. If you wear it short, make sure to schedule a trip to the hairstylist prior to your interview. You don't want to look shaggy. If you have facial hair, ensure it looks trimmed and tidy.

Where do the personal touches fit into the interviewing uniform? They don't fit in anywhere. Putting on the interviewing uniform may make you feel like a bit of a conformist, but in the end, it's your interviewing skills and qualifications that will set you apart as an individual, not your clothes or tattoos.

Reducing Nervousness

For many job seekers, interviewing is an uncomfortable communication interaction for several reasons. First, it is a high-pressure situation in which all eyes are on you. Next, your desire to land the job increases whatever anxiety you might normally feel when communicating with strangers. Finally, many job seekers do not feel comfortable "tooting their own horns." Although you will not be able to eliminate these feelings completely, you can minimize them by practicing. Learning to feel comfortable talking about your skills and accomplishments is a must for successful interviewing. After all, if you don't promote yourself, no one will.

Being at your best mentally and physically reduces nervousness. Preparing and practicing will help you be at your best mentally. But you also need to be at your best physically. This means getting a proper night's sleep before the interview. If you have failed to prepare in advance, staying up all night prior to your interview will only make you look and feel less than your best.

If you have to travel to the interview, it is wise to scout out the location a day or two in advance. Be certain you know the route to the building and the interview location inside the building. Always allow plenty of extra time for unexpected obstacles, such as traffic. If the interview is outside your local region, it's wise to drive or fly there the day before the interview and stay in a hotel or with friends. This will allow you to come to the interview fresh and well rested—as opposed to tired, wrinkled, and sleep deprived, all of which will increase your nervousness (see Table 4.3).

TABLE 4.3 ■ **Tools for Professional Excellence** How to Interview Online	
Nowadays, job interviews using online video communication channels, such as Zoom, are becoming more common. Take note of these practical tips to help you nail the online video interview:	
Interview Stage	**Practical Tips**
Before your interview	<ul><li>Determine the best device to use for the interview (i.e., computer, tablet, cell phone).</li><li>Make sure the interview will be conducted in the proper location:<ul><li>Secluded enough so as to prevent any outside interference or distractions</li><li>With a generic background, such as a plain white wall; keep in mind virtual backgrounds can be distracting to the interviewer and are best avoided unless a plain background is not possible</li><li>With diffused lighting to prevent shadows or glare</li><li>Where you can be seen from the waist up, not just your head</li></ul></li><li>Test all technological devices: Make sure all batteries are charged, internet connections are working, and the volume is at an appropriate level.</li><li>Conduct a mock interview with a friend or family member so that you can practice your interview skills, as well as test the technology.</li><li>Have at least one backup plan in place in case of any technological glitches.</li><li>Prepare for the actual interview by researching the company, preparing any responses to potential questions, and making sure you look professional.</li></ul>
During your interview	<ul><li>Even though it is online, treat the interview as if it were face to face: Use your nonverbal skills (solid eye contact, smiling, hand gestures, good posture) to impress the interviewer.</li><li>Always make direct eye contact with the camera, not the screen.</li><li>Have a series of notes off to the side to aid you in the interview, but don't overuse them or you'll end up looking away from the camera too often.</li><li>Pause before answering any questions to compensate for any blips in the internet signal.</li></ul>
After your interview	<ul><li>As with any type of interview, follow up by sending the interviewer a thank-you letter.</li><li>Follow up occasionally with the interviewer to remind him or her of your interest in working for the company.</li></ul>

Source: Hansen, R. (n.d.). Top tips for how to ace your online video job interview. *Quintessential Careers.* Retrieved from www.quintcareers.com/acing_online_ video_interview.html

During the Interview

Arrive for the interview at least 10 minutes early for a face-to-face interview; for video interviews, it is a best practice to join the meeting a few minutes early to ensure the technology is working correctly. When waiting for your interview to begin, show patience and professionalism. Remember that you are being interviewed during every interaction with the organization, whether you're interacting with the official interviewer or not. So treat everyone from the parking attendant to the receptionist to the CEO with the same level of professionalism and respect.

When you meet the interviewer, look them in the eye and shake their hand. Your handshake should be firm. This means you do not want an overpowering, bone-crushing shake, nor do you want a wimpy, limp-wristed shake (Bass, 2010; Ivy & Wahl, 2019).

First impressions are extremely important when interviewing. Research has found that it takes as much as double the information in the opposite direction to change an interviewer's initial impression of an interviewee (Huffcutt, 2010; Judge et al. 2000). This means if you make a good first impression, you will have to work pretty hard to turn it into a negative impression.

During the interview, try to monitor your nonverbal communication. Sit up straight, maintain eye contact, and avoid speaking too quickly or using vocal fillers. If you are asked a question that you need a moment to think about, take that moment to think. Do not fill the silence with "umms" and "aahs." The bottom line is that nonverbal cues do bias interviewer ratings (Bass, 2010; Dipboye, 1992).

Central to being an excellent interviewee is being an excellent listener. Focus on each question asked. If you are unclear about what the interviewer wants, ask for clarification. If the interviewer asks a question with multiple parts, make a mental note of each part and then begin to answer.

If you have prepared and practiced, you will be ready to answer the questions. Include as much of the information you practiced as possible in your answers. Ask the follow-up questions you prepared. Know that your preparation and practice will help you stand out as a candidate.

Remember to remain positive about your qualifications, your experiences, your former employers, your major or field, the job, and the organization. It's important to remain positive even when discussing weaknesses or failures. This can be accomplished by discussing a weakness or failure that will not affect you in this position (Crosby, 2000; K. Gray, 2011).

Illegal Questions

Ideally, you will never encounter an interviewer who asks illegal questions, but you should prepare in case it happens. What is an illegal question? According to the Civil Rights Act of 1964, Title VII, and subsequent legislation, employers may not consider race, color, religion, sex (including sexual orientation and gender identity), national origin, disability, or age when hiring or promoting employees. Therefore, they legally can't ask questions related to these categories.

When an interviewer said to Yelena, "I see you worked for the Jewish Community Center. Are you Jewish?" she was not sure how to respond. There are several ways Yelena could approach this question. First, she could answer it directly and move on: "Yes, I am Jewish." She could directly answer the question with a follow-up: "Yes, I am Jewish. Why do you ask?" She could use humor to deflect the question: "Is this a test to see if I know which questions are illegal?" Or she could refuse to answer: "I do not see how that question is relevant to my qualifications." What is the correct way to handle this situation? Although many students would prefer to use one of the last three approaches, they often are afraid such an answer will hurt their chances of getting the job. Regardless of how you answer the question, make note of what occurs. If you believe your answer negatively affected your chances of being hired, then you have a discrimination case on your hands. If you are offered the job, you may decide not to take it because this question might be an indicator of a hostile work environment. At the very least, you should report this behavior to someone higher in the organization.

Salary Questions

Although you should never bring up the issue of salary prior to being offered the position, you should be prepared in case the interviewer asks about your salary expectations. To prepare, research the appropriate pay for the position you are seeking. Be sure to examine pay-scale varia-tions related to credentials, experience, and location. If asked, you can give a vague response such as "I expect a salary that is competitive in this market." If the interviewer requests something more specific, give a range starting with the employer's probable salary and ending with a little above what you are willing to accept.

STAGE FIVE: FOLLOWING UP

When the interview ends, be certain to thank your interviewer verbally. Once you return home from the interview, formalize your thank you with a card. A handwritten thank-you card for the interviewer not only demonstrates professional excellence but also guarantees that the inter-viewer will think of you favorably after the interview. If you were interviewed by more than one person, you can either send a thank-you card to everyone who interviewed you or send just one card to your main contact and mention the other parties in the message (Crosby, 2000; Vanevenhoven et al., 2011). If you have been communicating with the interviewer via email, then you can send the thank-you message through email.

Thank-you letters, especially handwritten ones, are an excellent way to follow up after an interview.

iStockphoto/fizkes

If any additional information was requested during the interview, get that information to your potential employer immediately. This will demonstrate your enthusiasm for the position and your attention to detail.

For many, what comes next is the most emotionally draining part of the job-seeking pro-cess—the waiting. It may be days, weeks, or even months until you hear back about the position. Remain patient. Under no circumstances do you want to appear like a stalker, calling or email-ing twice a day to see if a decision has been made.

Use this time to engage in the last of the KEYS, *step back and reflect*. How would you rate your communication interactions? How did you perform during the interview? What did you do well? What can you improve for next time? What have you learned about the job-seeking process? What have you learned about interviewing? What have you learned about yourself?

STAGE SIX: NEGOTIATING

Although it may seem at times that the job-seeking process will never end, it will—and it will end with you accepting an offer. Yet the sixth stage of the job-seeking process involves more than just saying yes.

Once an offer is made, the ball is in your court. This is the time to ask clarifying questions about salary, benefits, work conditions, and the like. This is also the time to negotiate. A negotiation is a discussion between two or more parties to reach an agreement that concludes some matter. In this case, the matter being concluded is the terms of your employment. However, the skills and strategies used to engage in employment negotiations are the same skills and strategies needed to successfully negotiate personnel issues, contracts, legal matters, and other workplace issues.

The first rule to good negotiation is to act with professional excellence. In fact, negotiation experts often stress the need to maintain a polite, collegial, and collaborative tone. During negotiations, both parties should be looking for the best solution to meet the needs of both sides. Using the unite approach, described in detail in Chapter 7, is an excellent strategy for achieving this objective.

You may have to make a difficult decision in the process of negotiating your salary. What are some ways in which you could respond to a salary offer you feel is too low?

iStockphoto/SDI Productions

According to Hansen (n.d., "Salary"), you should let the employer make the first offer, but you should not feel obligated to accept that offer if it is inadequate. How will you know if it is inadequate? You must do your homework and research salary norms, as well as benefits and other perks, for the industry, the region, and this organization. In fact, doing your homework and thoroughly researching the situation is critical for all types of negotiation. You can't negotiate a contract if you have no idea what is acceptable and expected in the industry.

According to Johnson (2012), you must also research your value. Your value is based on factors such as education, length of experience, certifications, and management responsibility. Throughout your career, your value will increase, as will your ability to negotiate better contracts for yourself. In other words, the need to negotiate effectively becomes increasingly important as your career progresses.

One common mistake made during negotiations is failing to negotiate for things other than salary. For example, performance expectations, benefits, moving expenses, equipment, and vacation time are all extremely valuable. It may be beneficial to accept a lower salary if the offer includes a company car and great health benefits. Again, keep in mind that your counteroffer must be reasonable and in line with the research you have done.

To make a counteroffer, you can state something such as "I am very interested in working for your company. Although I would love to be a part of your team, I would like to discuss a few small issues. First, would it be possible to increase the salary offer by $5,000? This would put my starting salary in line with other entry-level salaries for folks with similar education and experience in your organization."

Once you have received the final offer, *step back and reflect*. Take into account all you have learned about the organization and the position during your research and the interviewing process. Compare this information with your goals and priorities. If you believe you are a good fit for the position and the organization and that the organization is a good fit for your goals and priorities, accept the offer. If it's not a good fit, then politely and professionally decline the offer. Declining may be difficult if you do not have another job lined up, but saying yes to the wrong job will be more difficult in the long run.

KEYS TO EXCELLENCE IN THE JOB-SEEKING PROCESS

At the beginning of this chapter, Haden (2016) offered several excellent examples of interview questions to help land a job. When examining the first key, *know yourself*, it is important to know exactly how you want to describe yourself as a valuable asset to an employer. Before you ask any of Haden's sample questions, make sure to do a self-inventory to highlight your unique skills and motivations that set you apart from other applicants.

The next key, *evaluate the professional context*, would be an excellent time to ask Haden's first question: What do you expect me to accomplish in the first 90 days? It gives you an excellent idea of what the employer is specifically looking for while also giving you an in-depth look at the character and context of the organization.

The third key, *your communication interaction*, would be the time to use other intelligent and relevant questions to bolster your interview credentials. Besides Haden's examples, it is a good idea to develop your own thoughtful questions that can pertain specifically to the company or organization to which you are applying.

After the interview has concluded, it is time to *step back and reflect* over how your questions were received. Did the interviewer(s) respond positively to your inquiries? How useful were the answers you were given? Although no one wants to go through numerous interviews, over time this practice can give you some reliable and helpful information as to what companies are looking for. Asking specific questions allows you to show great interest in an organization, indicates that you have already done some work studying the organization, and emphasizes your drive to work there.

STEP BACK AND REFLECT

Trying to Fit In

As you read this passage and answer the questions, step back and reflect on what went wrong in this professional situation.

Malia was excited about the possibility of working as a computer programmer with Company Y. Company Y had a reputation for being an organization with high-quality professionals who enjoyed a laid-back environment. It was not uncommon for these award-winning employees to come to work in shorts and flip-flops. Given their reputation, Malia took a more relaxed approach to her attire when interviewing with Company Y. She wanted to demonstrate that she could fit in at the organization, so she came to the interview dressed in a business-casual outfit (khakis and a blouse). Although her interview went well, Malia was not offered the position.

Step Back and Reflect

1. What went wrong?

2. How should you dress for an interview?

3. Should organizational culture influence interview attire? Why or why not?

4. How could Malia use the KEYS approach to improve her communication?

FIGURE 4.4 ■ The KEYS Process

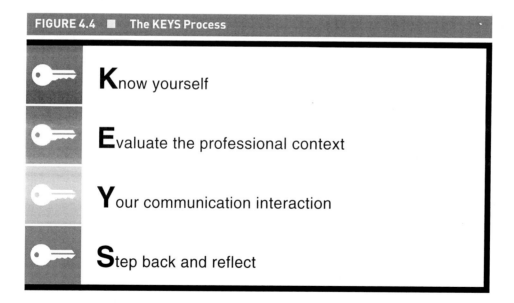

Know yourself

Evaluate the professional context

Your communication interaction

Step back and reflect

EXECUTIVE SUMMARY

Now that you have finished reading this chapter, you should be able to

Identify the six stages of the job-seeking process:

- The exploring stage begins with you, the job seeker. During this stage, you will need to explore both yourself and potential careers.

- The researching stage of the job-seeking process comprises two components: researching openings and researching potential employers.

- Once you have researched a place you would like to consider for employment, it's time to turn your attention to résumés and cover letters in the applying stage.

- The interviewing stage involves using your work from the previous stages to project a professional and competent image of yourself to a potential employer.

- Following up after the interview is the next stage. Delivering a handwritten thank-you card to the interviewer not only demonstrates professional excellence but also guarantees that the interviewer will think about you favorably after the interview.

- Although it may seem at times that the job-seeking process will never end, it will—and it will end with you accepting an offer. Yet the sixth stage of the job-seeking process, negotiating, involves more than just saying yes.

Explain the important role of exploring in the job-seeking process:

- Self-exploration is important; taking time to think about your goals and priorities is an important part of the job-seeking process—it will help you determine what type of career you wish to pursue and what types of organizations you wish to work for.

Explain the importance of researching job openings and potential employers:

- As you narrow down career opportunities, it's important to develop a clear understanding of what each career entails. When you find a career that seems interesting, you need to do some career exploration.

- You do not want to waste your valuable time and energy on positions and organizations that do not fit your desires, goals, and priorities. Think about this stage of the job-seeking process as job researching, not job searching. You are not simply searching for vacant positions; you are researching positions and companies to find the right fit between your skills and desires and their needs and opportunities.

Develop a customized résumé and cover letter when applying for a job:

- There is no one standard form for a résumé—it's not one size fits all. When selecting the format for your résumé, choose one that will highlight your strengths and downplay your weaknesses.

- Cover letters accompany your résumé and serve to introduce you as a potential employee, highlight your résumé, and demonstrate your writing skills.

Discuss examples of how to interview successfully:

- To demonstrate professional excellence, you will need to prepare your message, anticipate the questions, script your answers, practice your answers, prepare your appearance, and reduce your nervousness before the interview.

- During the interview, remember that you are being evaluated during every interaction with the organization, whether you're interacting with the official interviewer or not. So treat everyone from the parking attendant to the receptionist to the CEO with the same level of professionalism and respect.

Explain how to evaluate a job offer and negotiate terms:

- Maintain a polite, collegial, and collaborative tone while negotiating.

- Let the employer make the first offer, but do not feel pressured to accept that offer if it is inadequate.

- Research your value, and remember to negotiate things other than salary as well.

- Compare the offer to your goals and interests.

Apply the KEYS approach to conduct yourself with professional excellence throughout the job-seeking process:

- Know yourself by capitalizing on your strengths and realizing your weaknesses.

- Evaluate the professional context by searching for positions, researching each company, and then customizing your résumé and cover letter for each position.

- Your communication interaction begins when your résumé and cover letter are reviewed, making it important to treat each step with care and diligence.

- Step back and reflect. Your preparation and practice have served you well. If you do not land this position, you will continue to present the same level of professional excellence with other companies until you do land a job.

EXPLORE

1. Visit a business news website (such as *Forbes, Business Insider*, or a similar organization) and identify three types of employment advice it offers that you haven't learned in class. Do you find this advice to be beneficial or possibly effective? How important is it to gain feedback from the business community to supplement your academic knowledge?

2. Watch a YouTube video (or some other type of multimedia example) that shows a realistic mock interview. Put yourself in the place of the interviewee and use the KEYS process to analyze their performance. What (if any) insight did this activity give you?

3. Visit your campus employment aid center. Many colleges and universities will offer to guide you in creating your résumé and cover letter, as well as do mock interviews. Take advantage of the advice they can give you, and also take the opportunity to create a professional connection if you can.

REVIEW

1. Identify the six stages of the job interview process.

2. _____ requires you to research opportunities in your major that correspond with your goals and priorities.

3. A(n) _____ provides a picture of who you are as an employee by highlighting your skill set.

4. A(n) _____ is a one- or two-sentence declarative statement about your career goals.

5. A(n) _____ accompanies your résumé and serves to introduce you as a potential employee, highlight your résumé, and demonstrate your writing skills.

6. _____ explore how you have handled past situations, as well as asking you to respond to hypothetical situations.

7. A(n) _____ is a discussion between two or more parties to reach an agreement that concludes some matter.

8. It is _____ for an interviewer to ask an interviewee questions relating to race, color, religion, sex, national origin, disability, or age.

DISCUSSION QUESTIONS

1. Discuss the experiences you've had interviewing. How did the interviews go? Were you nervous? What will you strive to do differently in preparation for future interviews?

2. Take a moment to reflect on your dream job. Have you conducted an electronic search of the organization? What is it about the organization that makes you want to work there?

3. What are the qualities you're looking for in an employer? Related to some of the information in this chapter, how could you retrieve information to see if those qualities exist?

4. Discuss the resources your campus has in place to support the job-seeking process. Do you plan to use these resources?

5. Take an inventory of your email address and any social networks such as Facebook or Instagram where you have a membership or maintain a profile. Is there any information an employer could retrieve from the internet that may be perceived as negative?

ETHICAL CONNECTION
MAYA'S TWITTER PROBLEM

As you read this passage and answer the questions, consider how the way you communicate has an ethical dimension.

Maya had excellent experience, credible references, and an outstanding grade point average. Nonetheless, she was repeatedly passed over while less qualified friends were interviewed and then hired. Maya could not understand what was going wrong, so she went to her university's career service center for some help. Her counselor commended her on her résumé and cover letter but told her she must do something about her Twitter account. Maya was shocked. She could not believe her private social networking account was being viewed by employers.

Questions to Consider

1. Do you think it's ethical for employers to run background checks using search engines or to evaluate job candidate information posted on social networking sites such as Twitter? Why? Why not?

2. If you were Maya, would you change your Twitter account?

3. What do you believe should be the appropriate, professional response in this situation?

4. Has the visibility and permanence of online disclosure changed the way you portray yourself on social networking sites?

TERMS TO REMEMBER

awards and honors (p. 81)

behavioral questions (p. 88)

career exploration (p. 72)

career planning centers (p. 74)

contact information (p. 78)

cover letters (p. 83)

customized résumé (p. 77)

education (p. 80)

electronic résumés (p. 83)

employment experience (p. 80)

exploring stage (p. 72)

face-to-face interviews (p. 91)

generic résumé (p. 77)

hobbies and interests (p. 81)

illegal questions (p. 95)

internet (p. 74)

internship (p. 73)

job fairs (p. 74)

job seeker (p. 72)

job-seeking process (p. 71)

mock interviews (p. 90)

negotiation (p. 97)

objective (p. 79)

one-on-one interview (p. 91)

online application (p. 83)

panel interview (p. 91)

private employment agencies (p. 75)

professional associations (p. 76)

references (p. 81)

relevant experience (p. 80)

researching stage (p. 73)

résumé (p. 77)

scannable résumés (p. 83)

scripting answers (p. 88)

self-exploration (p. 72)

shadowing (p. 72)

skills (p. 80)

State employment service (p. 75)

telephone interviews (p. 90)

traditional questions (p. 88)

videoconference (p. 90)

white space (p. 82)

word of mouth (p. 75)

5 GETTING TO KNOW YOUR DIVERSE WORKPLACE

CHAPTER OBJECTIVES

After studying this chapter, you should be able to

5.1   Assess the culture in your organization

5.2   Describe each phase of the assimilation process

5.3   Define key concepts related to diversity in the workplace and the important role they play

5.4   Discuss examples of different kinds of diversity that you may encounter as you enter the workplace

5.5   Apply the KEYS approach to conduct yourself with professional excellence as you get to know your diverse workplace

Companies and business leaders are continuing to learn that diversity and inclusion go hand-in-hand with a strong, successful business. *Fortune* magazine regularly identifies the top companies for diversity and inclusion, and it recently used 14 key metrics—including the percentage of underrepresented individuals as board members, the percentage of female employees, the percentage of employees with disabilities, and others—to identify the top companies in these areas. Their results identified Microsoft, Centene, Target, Gap, and Biogen as being the top five Fortune 500 companies for diversity and inclusion based on their 14 key metrics (Quiroz-Gutierrez, 2021). Learning your workplace culture is critical to your success. Cultural competence, perception checking, and mutual respect are necessary for any member of the workforce. As a student, it is important that you begin assessing the culture of your environment now to help you do so again in the workplace. This chapter focuses on aspects of workplace diversity and the methods by which you can analyze, engage, and assimilate to your working environment in a healthy manner.

After weeks, or more likely months, of job seeking, the day you have been waiting for will finally arrive. You will begin your life as a professional. You can step off the emotional roller coaster known as job seeking, but don't unbuckle your safety harness quite yet. Beginning a new job, even if it's a promotion or a different position within the same company, brings with it almost as many emotional ups and downs as job seeking. This chapter explores the importance of getting to know your diverse workplace. As you enter any workplace for the first time, it's critical to get to know not only the organizational or workplace culture but also the array of diverse people with whom you'll be working. While diversity has always been important to discuss and consider, business leaders are rapidly understanding just how important it is; job board website Indeed reported a 56% spike in job listings for diversity, equity, and belonging roles between September 2019 and September of 2020 (Kellogg Murray, 2021).

Microsoft is among the top Fortune 500 companies for diversity and inclusion.

LEARNING YOUR WORKPLACE CULTURE

Just as every other new employee does, you will learn about your workplace's organizational culture through an assimilation process. The assimilation process is really part of a much larger phenomenon known as socialization—the experiences that shape our attitudes, perceptions, emotions, and communication choices (Bremner, 2012; Myers & McPhee, 2006; Wahl & Scholl, 2014). From the day you were born, your parents, your siblings, your relatives, your friends, your teachers, and even strangers have been working to socialize you into the culture or cultures that make up their experiences. So what is a culture? Put simply, culture is the rules of living and functioning in society (Bremner, 2012; Gudykunst, 2004; Samovar et al., 2007). How you talk, behave, dress, and think is heavily influenced by the ways others have socialized you into various cultural groups.

Just as you took part in the assimilation process as a child learning how to function in family and community, you now will undergo an assimilation process on the job, learning how to function in this organization. Every organization has its own organizational culture. Two organizations known for their unique cultures are Zappos and Starbucks (see Figures 5.1 and 5.2). Review the corporate profiles on each organization. Do the organizational cultures of Zappos and Starbucks appeal to you as a customer or employee?

To excel in your new position, you must learn the unique culture of the organization that has hired you. Organizational culture refers to the way an organization operates, the attitudes the employees have, and the overall tone and approach to any given business (Wahl & Simmons, 2018). Taking time to learn the organizational culture is essential to your success as a communicator and a necessary part of the KEYS approach. Learning an organization's culture provides you with information necessary to evaluate the audience and context. Furthermore, you can't effectively step back and reflect on your communication without taking into account the organizational culture in which it occurred.

Learning a new culture is stressful. In fact, for many new employees, the excitement felt prior to starting a new position plummets as they undergo the assimilation process—the adjustment period and "settling in" that's common for anyone starting a new job. During this time, you will learn the organization's culture. If you successfully assimilate into the organizational culture, your job satisfaction should increase, and you can begin to excel. If you don't effectively assimilate into the organizational culture, chances are you will remain at a low level of job satisfaction and will once again begin job seeking. To help you better negotiate this assimilation process, as well as help you establish yourself as someone with professional excellence, let's walk through the assimilation process and discuss the keywords noted above in more detail.

Organizations begin to assimilate you into their culture before you are even hired. Websites are developed to attract not only customers but future employees. The recruitment process, from the way the job posting is written to the signing of the contract, contributes to your socialization into an organization. Most likely, this will be a positive experience; otherwise, you would not have taken the job. But remember, both you and your future employer are putting your best foot forward, which may result in unrealistic expectations for both parties.

Once hired, you step out of the fantasy world and into the reality of your new organizational culture. Every organization, large or small, has its own culture. According to Edgar Schein (1992),

> An organizational culture is a pattern of shared basic assumptions that have been invented, discovered, and/or developed by a group as it learns to cope with problems of external adaptation and internal integration in ways that have worked well and are considered valid, and, therefore, can be taught to new members of the group as the correct way to perceive, think, and feel in relation to a problem.

As a new member of an organizational culture, you will be formally and informally taught the acceptable ways to think and behave. According to Jablin (1987), "The newcomer learns the requirements of [their] role and what the organization and its members consider to be 'normal' patterns of behavior and thought." In many ways, it's like entering a foreign land.

As you get to know the diverse workplace, you should begin asking yourself reflective questions, including the following: What is the mission statement? Did you have an employee orientation? What was discussed in orientation? Where are the offices located (for workers, supervisors)? What do the offices look like (e.g., small, large, cubicles, open floor plans)? Does the company even have an office, or do people work entirely or partly from home? Are the furniture and computers old or new? What kinds of items are displayed (e.g., cartoons, degrees, awards, family photos)? How do people dress? What metaphors do employees use to discuss the organization (e.g., family, team)? What stories do employees tell about the organization, about leadership, about each other? What jargon is specific to this company and this department? What rituals are present (e.g., office birthday parties, having lunch together)? What behaviors are rewarded? How are employees rewarded?

FIGURE 5.1 ■ Workplace Culture at Zappos

One way an organization can promote a positive culture is in the language it uses. At Zappos, the company extends the use of the term into its list of organizational values, which is entitled "Zappos Family Core Values":

- Deliver WOW Through Service
- Embrace and Drive Change
- Create Fun and a Little Weirdness
- Be Adventurous, Creative, and Open-Minded
- Pursue Growth and Learning
- Build Open and Honest Relationships with Communication
- Build a Positive Team and Family Spirit
- Do More With Less
- Be Passionate and Determined
- Be Humble

iStockphoto.com/NoDerog

At Zappos, the workplace culture is all about being positive, spontaneous, and even a little strange, all of which strengthen the bonds the employees have as members of the Zappos family. Zappos also continues the "family" theme on its website, even devoting an entire page to all of the members of the Zappos family, and using fun, amusing language to describe each section of the company. To learn more about Zappos, visit the sections of the company website devoted to explaining workplace culture: http://www.zappos.com/c/meet-zappos-family and http://www.zappos.com/d/about-zappos-culture

Using fun language throughout its site allows Zappos to further promote its workplace culture not only as upbeat and positive, but also as one big happy family. What do you think of the Zappos workplace culture? Does the "family" approach work for a company like Zappos? Why or why not?

FIGURE 5.2 ■ Starbucks Coffee Mission Statements

Today, more companies and organizations are focusing aspects of their mission statements and workplace cultures on diversity and inclusion, with Starbucks being one of them. In a message on the company's website, Starbucks CEO Howard Schultz tells the audience the following:

> We deeply want to be respected and appreciated for our differences. There is a longing for human connection, for an emotional relationship . . . we've been able to create this environment that has great universal appeal and local relevancy. The secret sauce is the culture and values of our company.

To learn more about Starbucks, visit the sections of the company website devoted to explaining diversity and inclusion: http://www.starbucks.com/responsibility/community/supplier-diversity/message-from-howard and http://www.starbucks.com/responsibility/community/diversity-and-inclusion

iStockphoto.com/jfmdesign

As you can see, Starbucks is serious about its approach to diversity and inclusion, both within the company and with those that it serves. How important do you think diversity and inclusion should be to an organization's culture? What suggestions, if any, would you give to an organization like Starbucks regarding its approach to diversity and inclusion?

ASSIMILATING COLLEGE STUDENTS

To illustrate the assimilation process more concretely, let's examine an assimilation process you've experienced—entering a college or university as a new student. How do you learn information about the college or university you are currently attending? Most likely, you learned formally through things such as first-year orientation and welcome packets that included brochures and student handbooks. In addition, you learned informally by watching other students and observing how they did things.

How did you gain information about the organizational culture? According to Jablin (1987), there are six tactics a newcomer can use to learn about an organization. They are overt questioning, indirect questioning, third-party questioning, testing limits, disguising conversation, and surveillance. Although overt questioning is obviously the most direct way to gain information, there may be reasons to use the other tactics. For example, if the person you would like to question directly is not available, you may need to ask a third party. Or, depending on the question, you may feel that you can get a more accurate answer through observation or surveillance, rather than asking directly only to receive the politically correct response, not the truth.

You will also gain information about your organization's culture by evaluating artifacts, rituals, language and jargon, and narratives and stories. Let's look at some examples of each.

Recall from Chapter 2 that artifacts are temporary embellishments (e.g., jewelry, sunglasses, perfume) or objects characteristic of a particular culture or institution (e.g., furniture, buildings, technology, artwork, logos) that provide information about personalities, attitudes, group affiliation, and organizational membership (Ivy & Wahl, 2019; Varlander, 2012; Wahl & Simmons, 2018). According to Goodall (1991), artifacts found in parking lots can provide valuable insight into an organization's culture. The alma maters (Penn State and Nebraska) of the coauthors of this text have highly competitive football programs. The importance of football to these organizations' cultures is manifested in many ways, including in bumper stickers. At either university, it's rare to see a vehicle that does not have some sort of university-football-fan bumper sticker. Attending sporting events, particularly football games, and being a proud fan is a big part of the organizational culture at both campuses.

Historically Black colleges and universities (HBCUs) such as Howard University have a strong history involving civil rights and the education of Black Americans, and they continue to foster a culture of activism today (Sanders, 2020). How would you describe the organizational culture at your college or university?

iStock/Kelvin Sterling Scott

YOUR COMMUNICATION INTERACTION

Derek's Communication Choices

As you read the passage below, consider what would be a more effective communication strategy in this situation.

In his first semester of college, Derek took a public speaking class with Professor Harrison. On the first day of class, Professor Harrison emphasized the importance of audience analysis and diversity awareness in the presentation process. Derek already believed that he was an excellent speaker and chose to ignore Professor Harrison's advice about presenting to culturally diverse audiences. Unfortunately, Derek offended several students of color in the class by using insensitive language during his presentation.

After delivering his first speech, Derek was shocked when he saw that he was given a significantly lower grade than he had expected. Derek's frustrations only grew when he learned that all of his friends in the class had received higher scores than he had. Derek knew his speech was the best among his and his friends' and concluded that Professor Harrison was singling him out for no reason. Instead of contacting Professor Harrison and attempting to find out why he received a low grade on his speech, Derek was convinced that he had been treated unfairly and decided to take his frustrations to the department head in an attempt to get back at Professor Harrison. He did so by typing up an angry email to the department head, telling him how awful Professor Harrison was as an instructor and how unfairly he had been treated.

Questions to Consider

1. What could Derek have done differently when he received the low grade on his speech?
2. What could Derek have done differently when writing the email to the department head?
3. Which is the better option when a student wishes to discuss a grade with their instructor: email or face-to-face communication? Why?

While writing this book, both coauthors were employed by Texas A&M University–Corpus Christi. At TAMUCC, sports teams have been on campus for only a few years, and there is no football program. To date, sports have had little impact on the organizational culture. However, the university is located on an island, and that has been highly influential on the culture. At the "Island University," there are few university bumper stickers in the student parking lots, but the majority of student vehicles display beach permit stickers. Relaxing and socializing at the beach is an important part of this organization's culture. What do the artifacts on your campus tell you about the organizational culture? In online courses, what are some different types of artifacts you might see in the background of your professors' lectures that might indicate different aspects of the organization's culture?

As a new student, you learned cultural rituals—practices, behaviors, celebrations, and traditions common to people, organizations, and institutions (Wahl & Simmons, 2018). Rituals include activities such as professors passing out syllabi on the first day of class and rush for Greek organizations. Graduation is the most important ritual at a college or university and one you most certainly aspire to take part in someday. What are some other rituals on your campus? What do they tell you about the organizational culture?

As a new student, you also had to learn the jargon of higher education. For example, students seeking admittance into college learn acronyms such as SAT and ACT. Those graduating learn new acronyms such as GRE, MCAT, and LSAT. Every organization and profession has its own language or jargon (introduced in Chapter 3) that you must learn in order to communicate effectively in your chosen field. Part of your education will be learning that jargon so you can communicate with other professionals once you graduate. Can you think of any examples of miscommunication that occurred as you were learning the jargon? What is some of the jargon you have learned as part of your major? What jargon is used in your current workplace?

Communication scholar Walter Fisher (1984) argues that humans are all storytelling creatures. Through our narratives or stories, we come to understand the organizational culture and one another. Paying attention to an organization's stories is important to understanding the culture (Briody et al., 2012; Mitroff & Kilmann, 1975). Many of you probably used stories to determine which courses to take and from which professors. All of you have heard delightful tales and horror stories about various faculty members on your campus. In fact, today's high-tech world has taken organizational storytelling to a whole new level with programs such as RateMyProfessors.com allowing students to hear stories from students they have never met (Edwards et al., 2007; Zhu, 2012). Listening to what students use as criteria to deem a professor good or bad will tell you a lot about your campus's culture. What are the criteria on your campus? What stories helped you assimilate into the culture on your campus? How will what you learned while assimilating into the organizational culture in college help you in "the real world"?

DIVERSITY IN YOUR WORKPLACE: SOME IMPORTANT CONCEPTS

Part of the assimilation process involves getting to know the people who make up your organization. A common mistake among so-called professionals is neglecting to take an inventory of others in the working environment. In today's world, getting to know your diverse workplace is important for two reasons. First, for you to succeed in any professional environment, you must be aware of and sensitive to differences between yourself and others. Second, your ability to communicate effectively when encountering difference (e.g., ethnicity, race, language barriers, religion, spirituality, gender identity, marital status, sexual orientation, age, and others) is an essential component of professional excellence. Our point is this: The people you'll be working with may present you with differences you've never encountered before, and your communication choices will make or break the experience. Let's begin by exploring a few important concepts related to effective communication and workplace diversity.

Cultural Diversity Awareness and Worldview

As a professional beginning a new job, you must strive for cultural diversity awareness—being aware of diversity that's present in any working or social environment (Fine, 1996; Muir, 1996; Trenerry & Paradies, 2012; Wahl & Simmons, 2018). You may be thinking, *How do I prepare for the diverse workplace? What do I need to do to achieve cultural diversity awareness?* These questions are not easy to answer, because we all have varied worldviews.

According to Samovar et al. (2007), worldview refers to a culture's orientation to supernatural, human, and natural entities in the cosmological universe and other philosophical issues influencing how its members see the world. How can we understand what makes up our worldviews? Redfield (1953) devised a system that includes some of the following elements: self, other, gender differences, "us versus them," religious differences, various ways people manage time (e.g., fast paced, relaxed), and spirituality.

The preceding foundations of worldview give you a sense of how complicated it is to understand the variety of viewpoints in our world. Indeed, it's a challenge to prepare for and predict the diverse people you'll encounter at work. What are some ways to approach the diverse workplace to avoid misunderstanding? What's the connection between getting to know the diverse workplace and professional excellence?

Cultural Competence

As the economy has gone global and customers and clients have diversified, many organizations have increased their efforts to diversify their workforces. There are many advantages to diversity among employees, such as multiple perceptions in decision-making and increased understanding of the customer base. With professional excellence as your goal, you must engage in the diverse terrain of your workplace environment. One way to engage and get to know the diverse workplace is by striving to improve your cultural competence. The term cultural competence refers to the level of knowledge a person has about others who differ in some way in comparison with themselves (Wahl & Simmons, 2018). A culturally competent professional not only has the knowledge of difference but also is continually striving to learn more. People who are viewed as having cultural competence are usually masters of a practice called perception checking—asking others if their perceptions or sense of understanding is correct or incorrect. Even if your intention is one of respect for other people, the way you communicate messages regarding difference can make or break you as a professional and tarnish your journey toward excellence.

Mutual Respect

When getting to know the diverse workplace, it's important to foster relationships. We can develop positive personal and professional relationships with people who are different in terms of race, ethnicity, religion, age, gender identity, sexual orientation, disability, and other forms of diversity by coming to understand those differences. When individuals and groups communicate with the goal of mutual respect—also known as mutual understanding—cultural tensions, misunderstandings, and conflict can be avoided (Christian et al., 2006; Kals & Jiranek, 2012; Wahl & Simmons, 2018). Mutual respect is about people seeking understanding through the vehicle of open dialogue; attempting to understand others with an open mind leads them to respond with mutual respect and understanding. When cultural competence and mutual respect are absent, discrimination—the act of excluding people or denying them products, rights, and services based on their race, ethnicity, religion, age, gender identity, sexual orientation, or disability—can occur. As a result, organizations are implementing workforce training programs to increase cultural sensitivity, tolerance, and appreciation of diversity in the workplace (Burkard et al., 2002; Okoro & Washington, 2012). Professional excellence can't happen in a diverse workplace without cultural competence, perception checking, and mutual respect. (Review Table 5.1 Tools for Professional Excellence for specific ways to practice perception checking statements.)

ETHICAL CONNECTION

Caleb's Blunder

As you read this passage and answer the questions, consider how the way that you communicate has an ethical dimension.

Growing up and in college, Caleb was not exposed to Hispanic or Latino people. In fact, he had no idea what these terms meant. He had always been comfortable using the term

Mexican with his white friends and family in West Virginia. There was no negative intention in their use of the term, and Caleb never dreamed that another person would be offended by the word. During one of his first days on the job, Caleb had a lengthy email exchange with a trainer named Rosa. As Caleb and Rosa exchanged messages, Caleb wrote the following: "I've noticed that there are lots of Mexicans who work around here." He continued, "But you don't really look like a Mexican, Rosa. You have a very fair complexion." Rosa was offended. In response to Caleb's comment, Rosa took the time to message Caleb that some people who identify as Hispanic may be offended if labeled "Mexican." She went on to explain that in her case, her mother was of Irish descent and her father's family came from El Salvador, so she was not Mexican. She also added that Hispanics are a diverse group and do not all have one look. Caleb did not set out to offend anyone, but by failing to understand and evaluate his professional context, he offended Rosa just the same.

Questions to Consider

1. Do you consider Caleb's communication unethical? Why or why not?
2. How could Caleb have handled the situation with cultural competence?
3. What ethical issues could or should be considered in regard to not respecting workplace diversity?
4. How can Caleb use the KEYS process to develop more effective cultural competence?

Nasdaq, which is a major stock exchange marketplace, recently implemented a new policy that requires all of its listed companies to hire at least one woman on their board of directors along with one person who is of color or self-identifies as LGBTQ+ (Kelly, 2021). Diverse teams of professionals have many advantages over teams that lack diversity. Can you name some of those advantages?

iStockphoto/tobiasjo

TABLE 5.1 ■ Tools for Professional Excellence. Perception Checking Statements

A perception checking statement is a message a person creates to check their understanding of someone's words or behavior, especially when nonverbal communication is used. Perception checking statements can be beneficial because they help in decoding messages more accurately, as well as reducing defensiveness and the potential for conflict, both of which are essential in the workplace. To effectively recognize and use perception checking in the workplace, consider the following three parts of perception checking and corresponding examples:

Description: when a person describes the words they heard or behavior they noticed	1. I noticed you rolled your eyes during my presentation. 2. You slammed the door when you left our meeting.
Interpretation: when a person interprets the potential meaning(s) behind the words or behavior	1. I don't know if I said something that annoyed you, or if you were just having a bad day. 2. I'm not sure if you were angry about the meeting, or you shut the door harder than you intended.
Clarification: when a person asks others to clarify the words or behavior, as well as their interpretation(s)	1. Did I do something wrong? 2. Is there anything you want to talk about?

Source: Conflict Resolution Education, "Perception Checking Procedure." Retrieved from http://www.creducation.org/resources/perception_checking/perception_checking_procedure.html

EXAMPLES OF DIVERSITY IN PROFESSIONAL CONTEXTS

In the previous sections, we've established the importance of getting to know the diverse workplace. In this section, we survey a number of examples of diversity that you may encounter in professional contexts. Gender, sexual orientation, ethnicity and race, language differences, religion, disabilities, and age are just a few examples of the diversity you'll encounter in the workplace.

Gender

You may not think of men and women as being part of different cultures, but communication scholar Deborah Tannen (1990) argues that men and women are indeed part of very different cultures. Further, according to communication and gender scholar Julia Wood (2015), women have a different way of knowing and communicating than do their male counterparts. As a result, you should get in the habit of approaching gender diversity in the same fashion you would approach any other form of diversity—with cultural competence.

Let's look at some examples. Women are more likely to use communication to establish relationships, resulting in something known as rapport talk (Ford & Stickle, 2012; Tannen, 1990). If asked, "How was your weekend?" a woman is likely to give a detailed description of the events that occurred. Furthermore, women often add tag questions to their statements to invite conversation and help develop rapport. So a woman might say, "That is an excellent opportunity for the department, isn't it?" By adding the tag question, she has invited a response from the other party. Conversely, men are more likely to communicate in a style know as report talk (Stamou et al., 2012; Tannen, 1990). If asked, "How was your weekend?" a man might reply, "Great. We took the kids to a Giants game." He reports what occurred without much detail. Men are also more likely to talk in statements and commands, excluding tag questions: "That is an excellent opportunity for the department."

Understanding the cultural differences in the ways men and women communicate can help you avoid miscommunication and false stereotypes. For example, a woman who uses tag questions is not unsure of herself; she is simply developing rapport and inviting conversation. Similarly, a man may still consider rapport and relationships important even if he communicates using report talk.

Another critical aspect of gender to discuss is gender identity, and it is important to understand the difference between sex and gender. Sex is a label (i.e., female or male) a person is assigned at birth based on biological characteristics. Gender, on the other hand, is cultural and involves a person's internal concept of oneself as female, male, a blend of both, or neither. Some individuals also identify as gender nonbinary, meaning their gender identity does not fit within a traditional gender binary of male and female.

Our gender identity is a fundamental aspect of who we are, and many transgender individuals—or individuals whose gender identity differs from the sex they were assigned at birth—carry an additional emotional weight due to the actual or potential discrimination they may face at work. Compared to cisgender individuals—or individuals whose gender identity aligns with the sex they were assigned at birth—transgender employees are far more likely to experience discrimination at work due to their gender identity. While the Supreme Court ruled in 2020 that transgender employees are protected from discrimination under the Civil Rights Act of 1964 (Totenberg, 2020), it is still important for employers and employees to actively work to help make the workplace a trans-inclusive one.

Employers can do this by creating gender-neutral restrooms, or if they are unable to do so, they can encourage transgender employees to use restrooms that align with their gender identity. Employers should also institute gender neutral dress codes that allow every employee to select from a range of clothing options that destigmatize varying clothing expressions of gender. When making such accommodations, employers also have a responsibility to ensure transgender employees are not harassed for using their correct bathrooms and wearing the clothing of their choosing.

Employees can help make the workplace more trans-inclusive by using the correct names and pronouns of their coworkers. Many transgender employees identify on the traditional binary scale and use pronouns such as *he, him*, and *his* or *she, her*, and *hers*. However, genderqueer, gender-fluid, and gender nonbinary individuals may prefer gender neutral pronouns such as *they, them*, and *theirs* (Thoroughgood et al., 2020). If you are unsure of a person's pronouns, it is usually best to ask them instead of guessing or assuming.

Sexual Orientation

Similar to transgender employees, sexual orientation is another important concept to understand. Sexual orientation involves who a person is attracted to romantically, emotionally, and sexually. Employees who belong to a minority group with regard to sexual orientation—such as gay, lesbian, bisexual, pansexual, and others—recently gained workplace protections when the Supreme Court ruled in 2020 that sexual orientation is protected under the Civil Rights Act of 1964 (Totenburg, 2020). However, while it is now illegal to fire, harass, or otherwise mistreat an employee on the basis of their sexual orientation, discrimination in the workplace still exists for those belonging to a sexual minority group. Below is a list of a few important terms related to sexual orientation:

- *Ally*: People who embrace and advocate for LGBTQIA+ concerns.

- *Asexual*: Having little, if any, interest in sex.

- *Bisexual*: Physical and romantic attraction to people of all genders.

- *Gay*: Physical and romantic attraction to people of the same sex.

- *Heterosexual*: Physical and romantic attraction to people of different sexes.

- *Lesbian*: Physical and romantic attraction to people of the same sex (women).

- *Pansexual*: Physical and romantic attraction to anyone, including people who do not identify as a specific gender; pansexual individuals often describe themselves as being attracted to personality rather than gender.

- *Queer*: An umbrella term often used to describe LGBTQIA+ people in general; used by some as an activist term and by others to refer to an identity that does not conform to common labels and terms of sexual identity.

- *Questioning*: People who are exploring or questioning their sexual identity.

As a current or future employee who will likely work alongside people of various sexual orientations, it is important to keep a few things in mind. First, it is a best practice not to ask a person what their sexual orientation is; a person may choose not to discuss their sexual orientation in the workplace for privacy reasons or for fear of potential discrimination. It is also a good idea not to ask coworkers questions that could indirectly reveal their sexual orientation (e.g., "Are you seeing anyone?"). If a person does share their sexual orientation with you, it is a best practice not to discuss that information with other coworkers; a person has the right to discuss their sexual orientation with the people of their own choosing. Finally, if you hear coworkers using discriminatory remarks or jokes (e.g., "That's so gay."), you should intervene or else report their behavior to your supervisor if you do not feel comfortable intervening.

Ethnicity and Race

Differences in race or ethnicity often come to mind when we think of diversity in the workplace. Although the terms *race* and *ethnicity* are often linked to each other, it is important to know that they are different. Race is the categorization of people based on physical characteristics such as skin color, dimensions of the human face, and hair. Even though racial workplace discrimination has been outlawed in the United States since the 1960s, racism continues to oppress many people of color at work. For example, applicants with "White-sounding" names have been found to receive, on average, 50% more callbacks for job interviews compared to equally qualified applicants with "Black-sounding" names (Livingston, 2020). Systemic discrimination also impacts people of color who have landed a job; racial bias has been shown to impact starting pay negotiations, future wages, and upward mobility (Avery & Ruggs, 2020). Therefore, it is critical that employers address implicit bias in their hiring practices and day-to-day business interactions.

As an employee, there are many things you can do to help combat racism in your workplace. For example, you should report any racial discrimination you witness in your workplace, such as if you learn a hiring manager has passed over a candidate because they are of a certain race. You should also intervene if you overhear racist jokes and microaggressions, which are everyday, subtle interactions that communicate hostile or derogatory attitudes toward marginalized groups (e.g., "You don't sound Black"). While intervening when you hear such jokes and phrases may seem like it doesn't do a lot, it sends a message to others that such behaviors will not be tolerated at work.

Ethnicity refers to a social group that may be joined together by factors such as shared history, shared identity, shared geography, or shared culture. If you rely on nonverbal cues to detect someone's ethnic background, you do so without taking into account that what you see visually may not always be accurate. In other words, a person's physical qualities may lead you to perceive them as being a part of one particular ethnic group, when in fact they identify with a different ethnic group. Thus, as you get to know the diverse workplace related to ethnicity, remember that what you see visually through nonverbal dimensions of physical appearance does not always shape accurate perceptions of another person's ethnicity.

To understand the impact of ethnicity on communication, you must understand stereotypes. Although this term tends to have a negative connotation, stereotypes merely describe the way humans categorize or understand. This may cause one to perceive others as belonging to a particular ethnic or social group. These perceptions can be positive, neutral, or negative. When developing professional excellence as it relates to cultural competence, it is important to begin by *knowing yourself*. What are your experiences with this ethnicity? What stereotypes (positive or negative) do you hold? What questions or concerns do you have about communicating with someone from this ethnicity? The next step is to *evaluate the professional context*. You can do this by researching a culture to increase your understanding of difference. You can also ask questions of the person with whom you are communicating in the professional context. Open and respectful communication is a must when getting to know people of diverse ethnic backgrounds in the workplace.

How have you handled language barriers in your own life?

iStockphoto/stocknroll

For example, when James traveled to India on business, he researched ethnic differences. He learned that the custom in India is to get to know the other party prior to doing business. In New York City, he had always made it a point to do business first and, once an agreement was reached, then go for dinner or a drink. Understanding this difference increased his cultural competence. When

Suzette traveled from France to Iowa for a business meeting, she greeted her coworker, Sam, with a hug and a kiss on each cheek. She noticed that Sam seemed a bit uncomfortable. Instead of ignoring her perception, she asked, "What is the customary greeting in the United States?" Sam explained the simple handshake, and Suzette increased her cultural competence with perception checking.

Language Differences

According to intercultural communication scholars McDaniel et al. (2009), the impact of globalization is "a seemingly unstoppable process that brings each of us into greater contact with the rest of the world and gives our daily lives an increasingly international orientation." Have you thought at all about globalization and how it will influence your career? Keeping your own professional goals in mind, how do diversity and globalization impact the industry or profession in which you're interested?

One way globalization will affect your communication is through differences in accents, dialects, and languages. The word accent refers to a person's pronunciation of various words in a language. An accent can give us a clue as to where a person is from, for example, "She speaks with a French accent." Dialect differences include variations in the pronunciation of words, as well as in vocabulary and syntax. You may encounter a coworker or customer who does not speak the same language as you. Nevertheless, you will still need to communicate with each other. Clearly, accent, dialect, and lack of a shared language impact communication effectiveness in professional settings with coworkers and customers. Language differences will compound other cultural differences that surely exist.

When you experience language barriers, be prepared to ask and answer many questions to ensure a clear understanding. Try to avoid the common mistakes of losing patience and giving up or speaking to the person as if they can't hear you. Speaking louder or, even worse, yelling at another person when a language barrier is present can often lead to frustration and further misunderstanding.

Many industries regularly deal with language barriers. Workplaces involved in the service industries, such as health care facilities, airports, and hotels, have implemented translation services—interpretation systems available to assist with language barriers and other communication-related concerns. If your organization offers translation services, be certain to use them.

In addition to language differences, language preferences can create language barriers. For example, all employees in one department can speak English, but three of them prefer to speak Japanese. When they are speaking to one another, they use Japanese. The rest of the department is unable to understand what is being said and often feels left out. If the manager tells the Japanese-speaking employees to stop using their language, is the manager discriminating against them or violating their rights? Bergman et al. (2008) considered the use of foreign language in a professional setting—specifically, the way individuals perceive those who speak a foreign language in the workplace. Although a group of coworkers speaking a foreign language together may signal camaraderie, it may also cause them to be labeled as outsiders by those who do not speak the language. The choice to speak a foreign language is based on personal and professional factors, but the results of this study indicate that language use has important implications for how individuals are treated in the workplace.

As a leader or manager, what would you do to manage a conflict resulting from a language barrier? Consider the following example:

Terry was a new shift leader at a manufacturing plant. Half the unit he was in charge of spoke English as a second language, preferred to speak Spanish, and identified as Hispanic. The other half of the unit spoke English as their first language and identified as White or Black. Terry was warned by some of the other shift leaders that he really needed to pay attention to the cultural tensions before they got completely out of hand. The guy he replaced, Cecil, had never taken the time to do anything about the tensions and conflict taking place in the unit. Miguel, one of Terry's best employees, stopped by to report that there had been several verbal and physical confrontations that needed to be addressed. Miguel explained that the employees who spoke English as a first language had a problem with the Hispanic employees speaking Spanish at work. Miguel was one of the employees who liked to speak Spanish. He expressed that the native English speakers felt as though they were being talked about in a negative way. Terry decided to take action. He wrote up an "English Only Please" policy for his unit and gave it to Miguel. Terry never communicated with his unit in person about the situation. The conflicts continued to worsen. After several more complaints, Terry decided to put up a sign in the break room asking everyone in his unit to speak "English Only Please." Soon after, Terry started to see production problems as tensions increased. Terry couldn't figure out what he was doing wrong. After all, he had communicated the new policy in writing twice. Why wouldn't the guys in his unit simply follow his new rule? How could the KEYS approach help Terry with this problem?

Religion and Spirituality

Religion and spirituality are other areas of diversity among coworkers (Deshpande, 2012; Driscoll & Wiebe, 2007). How can religion or spirituality come into play with people you're working with or serving professionally? Let's turn to an example of a new employee, Jonathan, who is still getting to know the diverse terrain at his new job. One person on the team whom Jonathan really related to was Alex. Jonathan had observed that several members of the team would get together for happy hour on Fridays, and he thought it would be fun if he and Alex joined the group. Jonathan invited Alex out for happy hour several times, but Alex always declined. After the third rejection, Alex took the time to explain to Jonathan that she and her family were members of the LDS Church (also known as the Church of Jesus Christ of Latter-Day Saints). Alex further explained that she did not drink alcohol. What can we learn from Jonathan's experience? Clearly, people with various religious perspectives make up your diverse work environment (Bhunia & Das, 2012; Lewis & Geroy, 2000). Another common example of religion and spirituality coming into play in the workplace is when someone plans a workplace party to celebrate holidays that are associated with a particular religion. Can you think of other ways religion and spirituality impact professional contexts? Take a look at the Step Back and Reflect feature, which features Abby's experience with the company holiday party.

STEP BACK AND REFLECT

Abby Decorates for the Company Holiday Party

As you read this passage and answer the questions, step back and reflect on what went wrong in this professional situation.

Abby was in charge of decorating for the annual company holiday party. She had been working in financial planning for five years, but this was the first time she'd been able to help with the decorations. The prior year, Abby had helped decorate for the annual Christmas play at her church. Since she had paid for the Christmas play decorations with her own money, she felt comfortable reusing them at her work party. This would allow her to save money on decorations and purchase more door prizes. One of her favorite decorations was a nativity scene. It fit perfectly on the head table; Abby just knew that the scene would be a big hit with everyone! She also had a beautiful tree to display in the entryway. As Abby started to decorate for the party, the lead partner called her to the side and asked her to rethink the decorations. One of his concerns was that the decorations were culturally insensitive to some of the people at the office. Abby was asked to remove the nativity scene from the head table, and the tree had to come down. Abby was devastated.

Step Back and Reflect

1. What went wrong?
2. What had Abby failed to consider about the professional context in a diverse workplace?
3. How could Abby use the KEYS approach to improve her communication interaction?

People With Disabilities

Your diverse workplace may also include people with disabilities. We recognize that some of you are limited in your experience with people with disabilities, while other readers live with a disability or have friends, family, or significant others with a disability. Regardless, we can all develop cultural competence in this area and support fair treatment and respectful communication.

Your communication with people with disabilities is important in your personal and professional life. We usually know that a person is living with a disability based on their physical appearance, but remember that some forms of disability are invisible (Braithwaite & Thompson, 2000; Houtenville & Kalargyrou, 2012; Ivy & Wahl, 2019). The physical appearance of a person with a disability can lead you to communicate or act differently (Braithwaite, 1990, 1996; Braithwaite & Braithwaite, 2009; Braithwaite & Thompson, 2000; Ivy & Wahl, 2019; Konrad et al., 2012). In an interview situation, how would you react to a potential employee who arrives in a wheelchair or with a guide dog? Have you considered ways in which a video interview over Zoom might be more accessible and less accessible for people with various types of disabilities? Can you think of other situations or experiences to increase knowledge and awareness of this topic related to business and professional contexts? People with disabilities have a major presence in professional settings today, and it's critical that you as a professional strive for respectful communication with people with disabilities and promote a supportive and considerate attitude in the professional environment where you work (and that you may in some cases be responsible for maintaining). State and federal laws promote equal and fair treatment of people with disabilities in professional contexts, but we encourage you to go beyond minimal, legal compliance by educating yourself and striving to communicate with and respect people with disabilities in any personal or professional setting.

Listed below are various best practices for interacting with people who have disabilities:

- Don't touch someone's wheelchair, cane, or other assistive devices unless you have permission, even if you think you are helping them. Also, avoid touching the person without permission; many people with disabilities are treated as though they do not have normal bodily autonomy.

- Don't pet, feed, or distract service animals.

- If arranging an event, check the accessibility of the location.

- Don't ask invasive questions about someone's disability.

- Don't refer to them as "inspirational" or say things like "I could never live with [their disability]." This is felt by many people with disabilities to be condescending and insulting.

- Avoid euphemistic language like "differently abled," "special needs" or "handicapped/handicapable." It is a best practice to use people-first language that puts the individual before the disability (e.g., "people with disabilities.").

Generational Differences

Age can also influence the level of communication among group members, especially given that we live in a world where members of different generations are increasingly working with one another. It is important, then, to understand how generational differences may affect communication among group members. Older group members, for example, may take on a heavier workload because they do not trust younger group members to do the work correctly or efficiently. In turn, younger group members may feel that older group members are standing in their way of succeeding in the group by not allowing them to display the skills they have developed. Generational differences are also important to consider because they affect our lives from the beginning. Many of our earliest experiences with those around us—family, friends, and peers—heavily influence how we view the world later on in life, as well as how we communicate with others, such as those in groups. Therefore, much of our communication style is based on influences from people of different generations. Generational differences can also help group members bond with one another: Understanding the emotions and experiences of an older or younger group member can help you establish some sort of common ground and improve your overall communication.

People with disabilities work in a variety of business and professional contexts, but people with disabilities remain underrepresented in the workforce, particularly within the federal workforce. A few years ago, the government set a benchmark calling for every agency to commit to having at least 12% of its workforce made up of people with disabilities, but many argued that benchmark fell short since 26% of American adults have a disability (Shivaram, 2021).

iStockphoto/kali9

Often, the time period in which we are born affects how we view and interact with the world as we get older. Our own personal worldview forms from an early age and can be influenced by major, often historical, events. A person who was navigating adolescence during the Vietnam War likely has a significantly different worldview than a person who was navigating adolescence during the Great Depression, or the September 11, 2001, terrorist attacks. Adams and Galanes (2009) explain that "our early influences from family, friends, and institutions such as the media affect the way we perceive the world around us and the way we communicate, which in turn affects our behavior in small groups." As Generation Z continues to enter the workforce, what are some other major historical and cultural events—on top of those listed in Table 5.2—may have helped shape how they communicate and perceive the world?

TABLE 5.2 ■ Generational Differences					
	Builders	**Boomers**	**Generation X**	**Millennials**	**Generation Z**
Born	**Before 1946**	**1946–1964**	**1965–1976**	**1977–1997**	**1998–2012**
Formative events	Great Depression World War II	Post–World War II affluence Sexual revolution Vietnam War Civil rights	Struggling economy Divorce/single-parent households MTV	Internet Technology AIDS	Smartphones and social media COVID-19 Gig economy
Values	Financial security Sacrifice Trust government Extended families Teamwork Delayed gratification Careful with resources Plan ahead Disciplined **Source:** Adapted from Hicks & Hicks (1999)	Disillusionment with institutions Civil rights Individualism Material wealth Personal fulfillment Work as fulfilling Education Challenge old ways **Source:** Adapted from Hicks & Hicks (1999)	Skepticism of big organizations Divided loyalties Cautious Distrust institutions Endure education Sensitive/tolerant Computer literate Pessimistic/negative **Source:** Adapted from Hicks & Hicks (1999)	Access to information Family/parents Consumerism Networking Tolerance Innovation Collaboration **Source:** Adapted from Hicks & Hicks (1999)	Adaptability Flexible schedules Self-direction Security Universalism **Sources:** Evans-Reber, 2021; Sakdiyakorn et al., 2021

The most significant conflict caused by generational differences deals with the different sets of values that members of each generation possess. Hicks and Hicks (1999) explore these values in depth, along with the specific events that contributed to different generations' set of values (see Table 5.2). In a group setting, members from different generations—with different sets of values—often clash over misunderstandings caused by their respective values, especially when applied to making group decisions. Consider the following example: You are a recent college graduate and just began your dream job writing for a local publication. At your first staff meeting, the editor-in-chief says that the lead story for the next issue is an exclusive interview with the chief of police about recent violent incidents involving officers that made national headlines. You immediately express interest in conducting the interview, because the chief is a close family friend and you could potentially get him to answer some hard-hitting questions that no one else could. The editor-in-chief ignores you and instead gives the interview to one of the experienced staff writers. After the meeting, the experienced writer pulls you aside and tells you that you are too new to be trusted with such an important story, and that at future meetings you should keep quiet and do what you are told. Although you were eager to hit the ground running by showing your willingness to work, you did not account for the hierarchical structure of the publication, one based on generational differences.

As this example illustrates, the values of different generations can influence how they approach the decision-making process, as well as how they interact with group members of different generations. The older group members value experience and tradition, while the younger members value innovation and proving themselves. In this example, as with any group dealing with generational differences, it is important that both the older and the younger members acknowledge one another's values, and try and understand the motivating factors behind those values. In doing so, both older and younger group members are likely to find something they have in common, which can enable them to make better decisions for the group and equip them to better address future generational conflict.

Dealing with differences can seem like an overwhelming task when, in reality, it is a simple process. You can come to understand your coworkers and customers, even if they have views and practices different from your own, if you practice cultural competence, perception checking, and mutual respect.

Strategies for Adapting to Diversity in the Workplace

There are various strategies you can employ to help you and your workplace adapt to diversity. One such strategy involves listening. It is important to acknowledge diverse employees by treating them with respect and listening to them with empathy and enthusiasm. One way in which to apply listening would be to keep an "open door" policy that allows coworkers to be candid about how they perceive their work environment.

A second strategy for adapting to diversity involves training; challenge employees to release preconceived notions of certain groups and individuals. For example, create a team-building event designed to make employees work outside their typical work groups.

A final strategy for adapting to diversity is to be understanding. Set up company gatherings that celebrate similarities and differences between employees of varying backgrounds. For example, create a lunch or social gathering that highlights different types of ethnic foods or artwork.

KEYS TO EXCELLENCE IN GETTING TO KNOW YOUR DIVERSE WORKPLACE

Remember the chapter opener that featured Microsoft, Centene, Target, Gap, and Biogen as being among the top companies to work for in terms of diversity? In relation to the first key, *know yourself*, those companies should have practiced cultural competence, and part of that entails improving communication with people from different cultural backgrounds and worldviews. Other companies' inability to create a representative makeup of cultural diversity has led to poor public perceptions pertaining to those companies' hiring practices. Those companies might make the effort to ask how their hiring policies affect people from different backgrounds. The goal should be to check perception more and focus on open and honest conversations with people about areas with which those companies are not familiar. In all, those companies simply need to get to know their employees better in relation to cultural diversity.

The next key, *evaluate the professional context*, is essential for those companies because they should strive to become more audience centered and aware of the potential for cultural differences in both professional and personal contexts. Those companies' managers should become more mindful of differences in their surroundings and use the skill of perception checking to avoid making assumptions about different cultural groups.

The third key, *your communication interaction*, can make those companies more successful communicators. Company officials should frame their questions during hiring interviews to accommodate potential employees with diverse cultural backgrounds. As the communication interaction occurs, managers should work more at planning their messages and asking for clarification to avoid misunderstanding.

Once supervisors for those companies finish implementing good communication practices with their employees, it becomes necessary to *step back and reflect*. Those companies should become more open to reflecting on communication with others. Managers should ask themselves some of the following questions as they step back and think about the communication that has occurred: Was I respectful to the employee in our conversation? Did I ask questions that revealed a genuine interest and human decency toward others different from me? Was I a good listener? Was I open to the other person's point of view? If something seems off or the manager or employee is uncomfortable, it is important to revisit the conversation or check in with the other person to make sure the situation was handled well. This key can help people be more thoughtful about both verbal and nonverbal communication.

EVALUATE THE PROFESSIONAL CONTEXT

Madison's First Day

As you evaluate the passage below, consider whether this behavior is appropriate for this professional context.

Madison arrived at work early on the first day, dressed in professional attire and ready to take on her first day. She was greeted by her direct supervisor, Dan, and given a quick lay of the land. The supervisors were housed on the second floor in offices with doors. Madison noticed that the supervisors' doors, which were shut and remained shut most of the day, displayed only a nameplate and title. The midlevel employees, such as Madison, had cubicles on the first floor. The administrative staff shared one large open desk area. All the employee spaces on the first floor were decorated with family photos and cartoons. The cartoons poked fun at the dysfunction of corporate America and bureaucracies. The administrative staff had similar cartoons, as well as a large sign that read, "I have one nerve left, and you are on it."

Madison was introduced to a coworker, Ann, who was responsible for training her. Once the supervisor walked away, Ann told Madison that the department was understaffed and she had a lot of work piled up on her own desk, so she hoped Madison learned quickly. Ann ran Madison through her duties using a lot of acronyms and jargon Madison did not understand. By lunch, her head was swimming.

About that time, the rest of Madison's coworkers assembled at her cubicle. They were all dressed casually and seemed friendly. They invited her to a local pizza buffet for lunch. During lunch, they told her stories about "their team." Madison was pleased to hear some of her coworkers' comments, such as "We are a really tight-knit group" and "Welcome to our team." However, some of the comments about the supervisors caused her some concern. Supervisors were continually referred to as "them" and "those people," never part of "we." Many of the stories included advice on how to manage the administrative staff.

For example, David told a story about the last new hire, who quit after three weeks. "He was rude to the administrative staff. He demanded things, and they did not like it. So all of his stuff was 'accidentally' processed inaccurately. He got so frustrated that he quit."

When Madison returned from lunch, almost 45 minutes late, she was told to work on some of the things Ann had taught her. As she began, she discovered she had no computer access. When she asked the administrative assistants for help, they started laughing, saying, "You don't have a computer account or password yet." Madison just smiled and said thank you. Madison left work that day worried that she had made the wrong decision by accepting this job.

Questions to Consider

1. Put yourself in Madison's place for a moment. What have you learned so far about the organizational culture?
2. How should Madison use information about the context and organizational culture to guide her communication interactions at work on the second day?
3. How can the KEYS approach help Madison communicate effectively in this situation?

Do you think it is or will be difficult to communicate in a diverse workforce? Do you have any concerns? How can the KEYS approach help you succeed at understanding the organizational culture and communicating with coworkers and customers from other cultures?

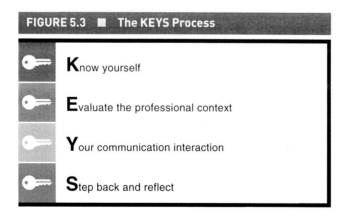

FIGURE 5.3 ■ The KEYS Process

Know yourself

Evaluate the professional context

Your communication interaction

Step back and reflect

EXECUTIVE SUMMARY

Now that you have finished reading this chapter, you should be able to

Assess the culture in your organization:

- From the day you were born, your parents, siblings, relatives, friends, teachers, and even strangers have been working to socialize you into the culture(s) that make up their experiences.

- Learning an organization's culture provides you with information necessary to evaluate the audience and context. Furthermore, you can't effectively step back and reflect on your communication without taking into account the organizational culture in which it occurred.

Describe each phase of the assimilation process:

- The assimilation process is the adjustment period and "settling in" that's common for anyone starting a new job.

- Organizations begin to assimilate you into their culture before you are even hired. The recruitment process, from the way the job posting is written to the signing of the contract, contributes to your socialization into an organization.

- Once hired, you step out of the fantasy world and into the reality of your new organizational culture. Every organization, large or small, has its own culture.

- As a new member of an organizational culture, you will be formally and informally taught the acceptable ways to think and behave.

Define key concepts related to diversity in the workplace and the important role they play:

- Cultural diversity awareness involves being aware of diversity that's present in any work or social environment.

- Worldview is a culture's orientation to supernatural, human, and natural entities in the cosmological universe and other philosophical issues influencing how its members see the world.

- Cultural competence refers to the level of knowledge a person has about others who differ in some way in comparison with themselves. A culturally competent professional not only has the knowledge of difference but is always striving to learn more.

- Perception checking involves asking others if one's perceptions or sense of understanding is correct or incorrect. Even if your intention is one of respect for other people, the way you communicate messages regarding difference can make or break you as a professional and tarnish your journey toward excellence.

- Mutual respect is about people seeking understanding through the vehicle of open dialogue; attempting to understand others with an open mind leads them to respond with mutual respect and understanding.

Discuss examples of different kinds of diversity that you may encounter as you enter the workplace:

- Diversity in groups can relate to differences in gender, sexual orientation, ethnicity and race, language, religion and spirituality, disabilities, and generational differences.

- Employees can be trans-inclusive by using correct names and pronouns.

- Avoid asking coworkers questions that could indirectly reveal their sexual orientation.

- Report any racial discrimination you witness, and intervene if you overhear racist jokes or microaggressions.

- Many organizations have implemented translation services to help with language barriers.

- Be mindful of how a coworker's religion might influence what they will and will not be able to participate in during workplace events.

- Be mindful of best practices when interacting with people with disabilities (don't touch someone's wheelchair, avoid feeding service animals, etc.).

Apply the KEYS approach to conduct yourself with professional excellence as you get to know your diverse workplace:

- Know yourself—You should want to achieve professional excellence, and part of that entails improving your communication with people from different cultural backgrounds and worldviews.

- Evaluate the professional context—It is essential for you to become more audience centered and aware of the potential for cultural differences in both professional and personal contexts.

- Your communication interaction—This key can make you a more successful communicator. Start to think before making statements or assumptive comments to coworkers with diverse cultural backgrounds.

- Step back and reflect—Try to become more open to reflecting on your communication with others.

EXPLORE

1. Locate a website and take a cultural sensitivity test. After completing the test, analyze your score. Does your score reflect your personal opinions concerning the importance of workplace diversity? How can this information help you in future career interactions?

2. Visit your local or state government website and research employment demographics as they relate to racial and cultural diversity. Compare the posted findings with census information about the population makeup of your city or state. Are the different cultural and ethnic groups represented fairly in the workforce? Write a short response giving your opinion as to why this is the case.

3. Locate a website for a nationally recognized company and examine its statements and positions about workplace diversity within the organization. Does the company's position accurately reflect its population of employees, or is there a large discrepancy in the employee makeup of the company? Write a summary that either endorses or criticizes the company's hiring practices.

REVIEW

1. What do assimilation and socialization refer to?

2. Define *organizational culture*.

3. _____ are practices, behaviors, celebrations, and traditions common to people, organizations, and institutions.

4. Being aware of diversity that is present in any working or social environment is known as _____.

5. _____ refers to a culture's orientation to supernatural, human, and natural entities in the cosmological universe and other philosophical issues influencing how its members see the world.

6. List the different types of questioning used to gather information about an organizational culture.

7. People who are viewed as having cultural competence are usually masters of a practice known as _____, which asks others if their sense of understanding is correct or incorrect.

8. _____ refers to the categories of people based on physical characteristics such as skin color, dimensions of the face, and hair.

DISCUSSION QUESTIONS

1. Discuss the attitude or mindset you have about work and finding a job. What are the primary factors (e.g., family, prior work history) that have influenced your attitude? Do you think these factors will positively or negatively influence you as you assimilate into your new organization?

2. How would you describe the organizational culture at your college or university? How were you assimilated into the culture?

3. What artifacts, rituals, language and jargon, and narratives and stories have you observed in your workplace?

4. Can cultural diversity be fostered in the workplace through employee education and training? What experiences have you had, if any, concerning diversity training or education?

5. Related to organizational culture, what are your impressions of companies such as Starbucks and Zappos? What, if anything, stands out to you about their organizational cultures that makes them different in comparison with others? What other companies stand out to you as having a unique culture?

Know Yourself

The Organizational Assimilation Index

As you read the index below and answer the questions, think about how this knowledge can help you be a better communicator.

This questionnaire contains statements about your assimilation into your workplace. Please indicate the extent to which each statement applies to you by marking whether you *strongly disagree* = 1; *disagree* = 2; *neither agree nor disagree* = 3; *agree* = 4; or *strongly agree* = 5.

_____ 1.   I feel like I know my supervisor pretty well.

_____ 2.   My supervisor sometimes discusses problems with me.

_____ **3.** My supervisor and I talk together often.

_____ **4.** I consider my coworkers friends.

_____ **5.** I feel comfortable talking to my coworkers.

_____ **6.** I feel like I know my coworkers pretty well.

_____ **7.** I understand the standards of my organization.

_____ **8.** I think I have a good idea about how this organization operates.

_____ **9.** I know the values of my organization.

_____ **10.** I do not mind being asked to perform my work according to the organization's standards.

_____ **11.** My supervisor recognizes when I do a good job.

_____ **12.** My supervisor listens to my ideas.

_____ **13.** I think my supervisor values my opinions.

_____ **14.** I think my supervisor recognizes my value to the organization.

_____ **15.** I talk to my coworkers about how much I like it here.

_____ **16.** I volunteer for duties that benefit the organization.

_____ **17.** I talk about how much I enjoy my work.

_____ **18.** I often show others how to perform our work.

_____ **19.** I think I'm an expert at what I do.

_____ **20.** I have figured out efficient ways to do my work.

_____ **21.** I can do others' jobs, if I am needed.

_____ **22.** I have changed some aspects of my position.

_____ **23.** I do this job a bit differently than my predecessor did.

_____ **24.** I have helped to change the duties of my position.

Scoring

1. Add your scores for items 1, 2, and 3. This is your familiarity with supervisors score.
2. Add your scores for items 4, 5, and 6. This is your familiarity with coworkers score.
3. Add your scores for items 7, 8, 9, and 10. This is your acculturation score.
4. Add your scores for items 11, 12, 13, and 14. This is your recognition score.
5. Add your scores for items 15, 16, and 17. This is your involvement score.
6. Add your scores for items 18, 19, 20, and 21. This is your job competency score.
7. Add your scores for items 22, 23, and 24. This is your role negotiation score.
8. Add your scores for all 24 items. This is your overall organizational assimilation score.

How did you score? What surprised you about your score? Does your score ring true with your personality or feelings about having to adjust to a new job?

Source: Originally published in Myers, K. K., & Oetzel, J. G. (2003). Exploring the dimensions of organizational assimilation: Creating and validating a measure. _Communication Quarterly, 51_, 438–457. Adapted in Galliard, B. M., Myers, K. K., & Seibold, D. R. (2010). Organizational assimilation: A multidimensional reconceptualization and measure. _Management Communication Quarterly, 24_, 552–578.

TERMS TO REMEMBER

accent (p. 118)

assimilation process (p. 107)

cisgender (p. 115)

cultural competence (p. 112)

cultural diversity awareness (p. 111)

cultural rituals (p. 110)

culture (p. 107)

dialect (p. 118)

discrimination (p. 112)

disguising conversation (p. 109)

ethnicity (p. 117)

gender (p. 115)

gender nonbinary (p. 115)

globalization (p. 118)

indirect questioning (p. 109)

language barriers (p. 118)

mutual respect (p. 112)

narratives (p. 111)

organizational culture (p. 107)

overt questioning (p. 109)

perception checking (p. 112)

race (p. 116)

sex (p. 115)

sexual orientation (p. 115)

socialization (p. 106)

stereotypes (p. 117)

surveillance (p. 109)

testing limits (p. 109)

third-party questioning (p. 109)

transgender (p. 115)

translation services (p. 118)

worldview (p. 111)

DEVELOPING IN THE WORKPLACE

6 INTERPERSONAL COMMUNICATION AT WORK

CHAPTER OBJECTIVES

After studying this chapter, you should be able to

6.1   Define the three types of workplace relationships and communication strategies used for each

6.2   Explain the difference between professional and personal communication

6.3   Discuss professional etiquette in the workplace

6.4   Apply the KEYS approach to conduct yourself with professional excellence in interpersonal communication in the workplace

Fortune magazine lists the 100 best companies to work for in 2021. The top five companies are Cisco Systems, SalesForce, Hilton Worldwide Holdings, Wegmans Food Markets, and Rocket Companies (*Fortune*, 2021). The similarity of the top-rated companies is that their employees are all satisfied with their company's great interpersonal communication. A company would not be a corporate giant without having effective interaction with its employees and consumers.

As you read this chapter, try to relate interpersonal communication with success in the marketplace. You will find that many successful companies remain so because they listen to their customers, their employees, and the general public as a whole. After reading this chapter, you should be able to see the myriad ways that interpersonal communication is critical to professional excellence.

Interpersonal communication at work occurs among supervisors, subordinates, coworkers, and customers. Beyond policies about appropriate relationships in the workplace, employees sometimes have problems communicating with clients as well as coworkers. This chapter reviews the essentials to connecting with other people professionally on an interpersonal level. Much, if not all, of the information we cover on interpersonal communication can help people achieve professional excellence. Interpersonal communication, also referred to as people skills or soft skills, is an area you will need to develop and foster throughout your career if you wish to achieve professional excellence (Conrad & Newberry, 2011; McKnight, 1995; O'Connor, 1993).

As we established in Chapter 5, once you begin a new position, getting to know the organizational culture and diverse workforce is essential. Part of that process will no doubt include the formation of relationships in the workplace. These relationships are developed through interpersonal communication. Interpersonal communication, the cocreation of meaning as people interact, is a powerful skill that will help you *develop* in the workplace. Interpersonal communication is dyadic, meaning it occurs in dyads (two people). Through these dyads, you'll make connections with others and come to establish a network of professional relationships. As you strive for professional excellence, your interpersonal communication with coworkers, leaders, and clients is critical.

You might be thinking, "I'm a people person. Friendships and interacting with others come naturally to me, so why do I need to study this stuff?" If you've had a positive experience with interpersonal communication in other jobs or as you've made progress in college, it's natural to think that you do not need to work on your people skills. However, interpersonal communication is a process that we need to understand *at* work and *as* work. That is, even if you've had positive experiences in the past, part of striving for professional excellence is to hone your skills and be as effective as possible in your connections with other people in any given professional environment. We describe interpersonal communication as work because it's something you must always be aware of and always seek to improve. There's always a need to connect and relate with others, whether they're our coworkers, leaders, or clients. Further, interpersonal communication skills are not just about developing relationships or getting along with others. You will also encounter difficult people and conflict (a topic covered in Chapter 10); the way you respond in these not-so-comfortable situations or with not-so-nice people will be informed by our focus on interpersonal communication in this chapter.

Interpersonal communication is important for the following reasons: (1) Your ability to relate with other people is central to achieving professional excellence; (2) interpersonal communication helps you form professional connections with other coworkers, leaders, and clients; and (3) your interpersonal relationships at work provide a supportive social system that will increase your job satisfaction (Karl & Peluchette, 2006; Simon et al., 2010). Remember the huge impact effective communication played when you were *entering the workplace?* Well, effective people skills and interpersonal communication will play an equally important role in your success as you *develop in the workplace.* Let's begin this chapter with a look at the important role of interpersonal communication at work.

EXPLORING RELATIONSHIP TYPES AT WORK

Interpersonal communication at work can be classified into three dyadic interactions or relationships: superior–subordinate relationships, coworker relationships, and customer–client relationships.

Superior–Subordinate Relationships

In the language of the workplace, the superior (supervisor/employer) is typically the higher status person and the subordinate (employee) the lower status person.

Communicating Information

The interpersonal communication between supervisors and subordinates is not limited to the relational layer (see Chapter 2), nor does it focus exclusively on conveying status. After all, some content has to be communicated if any work is ever to get done. Unfortunately, the status differences between supervisors and subordinates contribute to the creation of less-than-ideal communication conditions.

One such condition is known as *semantic information distance*—a term that describes how employees and supervisors do not share the same view of some fundamental areas such as organizational issues or basic job duties (Jablin, 1979). Furthermore, employees and supervisors do not have the same view of employees' participation in decision-making (Harrison, 1985; Zhou et al., 2011). For example, Tom believes his employees are highly involved in decision-making. Tom's employees, by contrast, believe they have little input in decision-making because even when Tom asks for their opinions and insights, they are rarely implemented. The good news is, even though supervisors and employees may suffer from semantic information distance, chances are good that neither party realizes it. In fact, most organizations continue functional operations—despite the lack of response to employee feedback.

As you study relationship types in the workplace, consider how the relationships between characters like Steve Carell as Michael Scott and Jenna Fischer as Pam in classic shows like *The Office* help us to understand or define our own relationships in the workplace.

LaylaBird/Getty Images

- In addition to the communication problems resulting from semantic information distance, communication between supervisors and subordinates often is affected by a communication phenomenon known as upward distortion (Foste & Botero, 2012; Fulk & Mani, 1986). Upward distortion occurs when the messages sent up the chain of command, from subordinates to supervisors, are altered (see Tools for Professional Excellence 6.1).

According to Fulk and Mani (1986), messages are altered in one of four ways: gatekeeping, summarization, withholding, or general distortion. Gatekeeping occurs when some, but not all, of the information is passed on to the supervisor. Summarization occurs when the employee summarizes the message in such a way that emphasis is placed on certain aspects of the message. Withholding occurs when information is not passed on to the supervisor. And general distortion, a close cousin to out-and-out lying, occurs when the message is changed to serve the subordinate's purposes. As a supervisor, you must take steps to limit message alteration by doing some, if not all, of the following: (1) Limit the number of people a message must travel through before it gets to you, (2) go to the source of the message for clarification, (3) keep communication channels open with subordinates and customers, and (4) never "shoot the messenger."

Communicating With Your Supervisor

In Chapter 10, we will spend some time discussing how you should communicate with subordinates when you become a leader or supervisor. In this chapter, we are going to focus our discussion on strategies you can use as a subordinate for communicating effectively with your supervisor(s).

Wouldn't it be great if you had some sort of cue to let you know about a distorted message? Be aware of ethical problems such as lying in the workplace—set boundaries and try to stay away from toxic people. Can you think of an example from a television show when a character's lie in the workplace snowballed and caused more problems than simply telling the truth would have caused?

iStockphoto/fizkes

No doubt, you are familiar with terms such as *teacher's pet* and *brown-noser*. These terms are often reserved for individuals who ingratiate themselves with or "suck up" to the person in authority, and the terms have a negative connotation. Still, ingratiation, which occurs when an employee acts warm and friendly toward the supervisor, can be an effective strategy for communicating with the boss. However, if the ingratiation is insincere or not your style, or if your boss doesn't like the attention, your resulting communication will come across as less than professional. For those seeking professional excellence, advocacy is the strategy of choice when communicating with supervisors. Advocacy utilizes a simple persuasive technique. Specifically, you evaluate your boss's needs and preferences and then develop messages, arguments, and proposals that line up with those needs and preferences (Foste & Botero, 2012; Riley & Eisenberg, 1992). Advocacy falls in line with the KEYS process, as it requires you to know yourself and evaluate the professional context (see Table 6.1).

TABLE 6.1 ■ **Tools for Professional Excellence.** Self-Monitoring for Message Alteration
To monitor your own message alteration habits, consider these questions:

- Can you remember a time when you altered a message?
- In what way did you alter it?
- Why did you alter it?
- Could your supervisor have done something differently to cause you not to alter the message?
- If so, what could they have done?

There is no single effective strategy that works every time when communicating with supervisors. To communicate effectively with your supervisor, you must evaluate them in the same way you evaluate everyone else. As you strive for professional excellence as a superior or a subordinate, remember the power of communication; appropriate verbal and nonverbal behaviors often make or break your chances of being viewed positively on the job. In terms of interpersonal communication in the workplace, it is important to consider the way a supervisor communicates with a subordinate.

Coworker Relationships

Although communication with your boss is important, effective interpersonal communication with your coworkers is equally important. Across industries, employees need to work together to complete common tasks. In fact, the *co-* in *coworker* is a prefix meaning "together or jointly." Common tasks are what bring you together and form that working relationship—some professionals form personal relationships initiated from the time spent completing workplace tasks and assignments.

Coworker relationships may also be based on needs or, more accurately, the fulfillment of needs. These needs may be task related. For example, if your computer is not working properly, you may need the expertise of the computer specialist, resulting in an interpersonal communication interaction between the two of you. Coworkers can also fulfill the need for support on the job. Having coworkers who can help you complete tasks, provide professional advice, and laugh with you is a real plus to your professional development and stress level on the job.

Physical and spatial closeness also has an impact on which coworkers you will develop relationships with. Coworkers who work in adjacent desks, cubicles, or offices are more likely to develop close relationships than people who work for the same organization but on different floors or opposite ends of a building (Ivy & Wahl, 2019). Professionals today stay connected with technology, such as email or instant-message exchanges, text messaging, social networking sites, and virtual work teams (Diaz et al., 2012; Riggio, 2005).

Another common factor that serves as the basis for coworker relationships is shared communication networks. A *communication network* is defined as "a group of individuals who regularly share a line of communication" (Eisenberg et al., 2007, p. 256). In some cases, these lines of communication are predetermined by the organization. For example, the organizational chart at Company U indicates that Ethan, Virginia, and Diana report to their supervisor, Don. If they have information that needs to be shared with the district manager, Margot, they must first report it to Don, who will then pass the information on to Margot. This type of communication network is known as a formal communication network because it is formally prescribed by the organization. But, as we all know, this is not the way all communication flows in the workplace. The majority of communication occurs in what is known as the white space, the part of the organizational chart that has not been prescribed.

The communication networks that develop in this white space are collectively known as the informal communication network, also commonly referred to as the grapevine. As someone with professional excellence, you should avoid the grapevine, right? Wrong. According to a study by Hellweg (1987), the information found on the grapevine is more efficient and more accurate than the information shared through formal communication channels. Communicating via the informal communication network allows employees to speak directly and not change the message being altered as it moves its way through several people in the formal communication network. Just remember, when using the informal communication network, continue to communicate with professional excellence. For example, be certain that you are not disrespecting

Remember that your workplace environment has a major impact on interpersonal communication. How might this outdoor workspace at Google's headquarters impact impersonal communication when compared to a typical indoor working environment?

iStockphoto/Purplexsu

anyone by going "over their head" without permission. If you need to discuss an issue with a coworker in a different department, be certain to get your superior's okay first. Furthermore, make certain that the information you give and receive is professional in nature (see Table 6.2). The grapevine is often associated with gossiping. You will encounter difficult people in the workplace, but gossiping about them or their behavior with other coworkers only makes you a difficult employee as well. If you have an issue with a coworker, you must discuss it with that person face to face, over a video call, or with the appropriate supervisor. Don't turn it into a hot piece of grapevine gossip or office drama. And remember, listening to gossip is just as bad as spreading it.

In the 21st century, the channels for communicating with coworkers seem to expand daily. Should you send the message via a phone conversation, a video call, a voice message, a text, an email, or an in-person meeting? Although each channel has strengths and weaknesses, when it comes to developing interpersonal relationships, good old-fashioned face-to-face communication—whether it be in person or over a video call—is still the best way (Rhoads, 2010; Waldeck et al., 2005).

People or entities that your organization serves or provides products to are known as customers. For our purposes, we are going to refer to them as external customers, because they are external to the company. An internal customer, then, is an employee—an internal part of the organization—who needs services or products from other parts of the organization to complete their work. If you take a holistic view of any organization and see serving the external customer as the ultimate mission, then the vast majority of employees are directly or indirectly one another's internal customers.

Do you think of your coworkers as internal customers? Do you give your coworkers the same respect and professional courtesy that you give your external customers? How do you treat your external customers? In the next section, we discuss how to achieve professional excellence

Unfortunately, gossip and rumors can serve as roadblocks to business and professional excellence. How would you manage gossip in your own professional life?

iStockphoto/katleho Seisa

TABLE 6.2 ■ **Action Items.** Skills for Interpersonal Communication		
Skill	**Strategy**	**Application**
Leadership	Delegate important tasks fairly and effectively.	In a group project, make sure different tasks are allotted to the most effective people (and ensure they understand their responsibilities).
Networking	Identify and open communication with people who can benefit your education or career.	Use cocurricular functions (e.g., fraternities, sororities, clubs) to begin to develop professional relationships after graduation.
Teamwork	Collaborate with classmates or coworkers to ensure your job is done in a timely and effective manner.	Use group project meetings to ensure everyone is informed and up to date with the different parts of the project, and identify potential problems or barriers to success.

with customers. This information is applicable to your communication with your coworkers, as they should be treated as your internal customers. Achieving professional excellence with your coworkers is accomplished most easily by following the KEYS process and thinking of your coworkers as internal customers.

Customer–Client Relationships

Maintaining positive customer relations centers on effective communication and is essential in today's business world. Customer relations, or customer service, is the interaction between employees or representatives of an organization or business and the people the organization serves or sells to (Ivy & Wahl, 2019). All organizations have customers or clients, and anyone claiming to have professional excellence must excel at communicating with these individuals. Samsung Home Applications, for example, was ranked number one in reliability and customer service by the American Customer Satisfaction Index Survey in 2021. What did Samsung do to excel? It trained employees in services and products, and they established a professional environment that made its customer service agents feel, and ultimately sound, upbeat and friendly when talking to customers.

Communication can be extremely challenging when dealing with angry customers or coworkers.
iStockphoto/georgeclerk

Excellent customer service is ingrained in the organizational culture of successful organizations; therefore, you should seek out organizations that value and foster customer service when you are job searching. Such organizations see customer service as the central focus and avoid defining the customer as a nuisance (Albrecht, 1992; Teece, 2010). According to Tom Peters (1987), organizational cultures that foster excellent customer service provide quality as defined by the customer, respond quickly, and are obsessed with listening.

THE LINE BETWEEN PROFESSIONAL AND PERSONAL

Given the vast amount of time you will spend in the workplace, chances are some of your interpersonal relationships at work will include intimacy. Intimacy is characterized by feelings of closeness and trust that you share with other people. What comes to mind when you hear the word *intimacy*? Most people typically think of physical intimacy, but it's important to understand that there are other types of intimacy as well. Intimacy is not just about romantic or sexual activity. In situations where you share physical closeness with others (e.g., coworkers, clients, close friends), you have intimacy. As communication scholars Andersen et al. (2006) explain, intimacy is defined as "an experience consisting of felt emotions and perceptions of understanding, or as a relationship that is characterized by affection and trust" (p. 260). And as you develop a feeling of trust and affection toward coworkers, even toward clients and bosses, you will find yourself maintaining interpersonal relationships with coworkers *at* as well as *away* from work.

However, in order to develop professional excellence in the workplace, you must have a clear understanding of the line between personal and professional relationships, as well as what constitutes professional versus personal communication.

Romance in the Workplace

In some ways, developing personal relationships, affection, and trust with coworkers, clients, and supervisors is not only a positive experience for you but also good for your employer. After all, having a sense of social belonging is a core motivational factor on the job (Kirkhaug, 2010; Maslow, 1965). But what happens when feelings between cohesive colleagues turn into something more? Be forewarned that many organizations have norms and in some cases written policies that discourage or forbid romantic relationships in the workplace.

Why do such policies exist? One reason workplace romance is discouraged or forbidden is because it's a distraction. Flirting, courting, and breaking up can all distract from the work that needs to be done. In fact, the plots of many television shows center on the distraction and drama created by romance in the workplace. What would *Grey's Anatomy* be without romance? Another reason romance is discouraged in the workplace is favoritism. The fear is that romantic relationships and sexual favors, as opposed to hard work and merit, can be used to advance one's career.

Sexual Harassment

What is sexual harassment? The Equal Employment Opportunity Commission (2004) defines sexual harassment as follows:

Unwelcome sexual advances, requests for sexual favors, and other verbal or physical harassment of a sexual nature. Sexual harassment is tied to communication excellence because it is a result of communicative behaviors and sense making (Bingham, 1991; Dougherty, 2001; Scarduzio & Geist-Martin, 2010; Taylor & Conrad, 1992). As clearly stated by the Equal Employment Opportunity Commission, sexual harassment is not only quid pro quo (i.e., something for something) but also the creation of a hostile work environment. Saying to an employee, "Have sex with me or you are fired," is clearly sexual harassment. But eyeing an employee up and down, referring to someone's spouse as hot, displaying provocative calendars, or making someone uncomfortable by pursuing them romantically are also forms of sexual harassment.

As you strive for professional excellence, continually monitor your own communication for comments or behaviors that might be inappropriate. If you're doing anything that might be questionable, stop it immediately. Furthermore, if a colleague demonstrates a behavior, makes comments, or creates an environment that could be construed as sexual harassment, don't ignore it. If you sit by and allow someone else to be sexually harassed, you are contributing to the problem even if you are not the perpetrator.

What should you do if you are sexually harassed? Tamaki (1991) provides the following steps for dealing with a harasser. If you feel comfortable doing so, confront the harasser. You may not feel comfortable confronting the harasser directly, or you may confront the harasser but still the behavior continues. You might also find it helpful to indirectly intervene if you notice potential harassment occurring (e.g., "Hey, Sam, do you have a minute to help me with something?"). In any case, you should report the behavior to a supervisor or your Human Resources Department.

Creating a hostile work environment is a form of sexual harassment.

iStockphoto/fizkes

In addition, you should keep a written record of the behaviors and comments that you feel constitute harassment. It may also help to have a support system. Talking to supportive individuals, whether they are from your personal or professional life, is recommended.

Communication Privacy Management at Work

Because most employees do develop friendships with people they meet in the workplace, non-work-related conversations are fairly commonplace. What topics are deemed acceptable or professional? What constitutes friendly office chitchat? What topics are too personal for the workplace or invade coworkers' privacy? According to Sandra Petronio (2000, 2002, 2007), who developed Communication Privacy Management theory, privacy is regulated by rules. We each develop our own set of rules that helps us determine what information we share, or self-disclose, and what information we keep private. For instance, many people in leadership positions believe that sharing private information with their employees is inappropriate and can confuse the relationship between leader and employee.

To understand the relationship between privacy management, interpersonal communication, and professional excellence, let's look at an example you are likely to encounter in the workplace. You're on a job interview, and your future boss asks you about your marital or relational status. Does this question display professional excellence? In fact, as noted in Chapter 4, this question is illegal.

Now, let's say that you have the job and you are getting to know your coworker. The two of you are making small talk. Since you are both already employed by the company, it's perfectly fine to ask a coworker about their marital or relational status, right? Although you may be asking this question to show interest in your new coworker, they may have been raised believing that this sort of questioning is intrusive and "none of your business." Some people feel that details about their love lives are not to be shared with many people, especially with someone at work.

In recent years, many people in powerful positions have faced investigations for sexual harassment allegations. New York Governor Andrew Cuomo resigned as Governor in 2021 after a state attorney general report concluded he sexually harassed multiple women (Ferré-Sadurní & Bromwich, 2021).

Because family and loved ones are a fairly common discussion topic, it may seem natural when getting to know someone to ask if the person is married, dating, or single. Are you comfortable with people at work knowing about your marital or relational status? If you are married, are in a traditional heterosexual relationship, and have children, you likely don't have much trouble at all talking about your family and spouse: "Yeah, my wife and I are settling into the community. Julie loves her new job at the art museum. The kids are both playing soccer for Hamlin Middle School. We really like it here." The person on the receiving end of this message, if they also have a family, would likely reciprocate with their spouse's name and number of kids. Topics such as family and kids are safe, professional topics of conversation, right? Review Tools for Professional Excellence 6.2 to explore the dark side of personal communication at work, especially when social media and other forms of technology come into play.

As you learned in Chapter 5, gender identity and sexual orientation are important factors to consider with regard to workplace diversity. Lesbian, gay, bisexual, transgender, questioning, intersex, and ally (LGBTQIA+) people will no doubt make up part of the diverse population in any professional setting (Bell et al., 2011; Fleming, 2007; McDermott, 2006; Wahl & Simmons, 2018).

For the LGBTQIA+ readers of this text, we also want to recognize the choice you'll have to make regarding being open or private about your identity at work. Being "out" at work is easier for some LGBTQIA+ people than for others. Regardless of your own identity, it's critical to recognize that LGBTQIA+ communication and culture is present in both professional and social contexts (Wahl & Simmons, 2018).

Single, married, gay, queer, or straight, it's unprofessional to ask about the relationship statuses of others at work. As you're adjusting to new coworkers or taking a new role as a leader, be sensitive to the varied degree of acceptance when it comes to talking about marital or relational status in the workplace. You'll find that there are varying levels of acceptance regarding discussion of marital or relational status, from personal preferences to organizational policy (see Table 6.3).

TABLE 6.3 ■ Tools for Professional Excellence. The Dark Side of Personal Communication at Work

More and more, employees are using their own personal devices to communicate while on the job, whether for work purposes or not. Employees using their own cell phones, for example, has become commonplace, which can pose risks to their employers. If anything negative occurs because an employee was using their personal communication device while on the job, the employer could be found liable for any repercussions. Here are four examples of risks that an employer can face when employees use their own communication devices while working:

Communication Risk	Description
Sexual harassment/"sexting"	● Instances of sexting (sending sexually explicit text messages) are on the rise, especially among adults in their 20s. ● Sexting while at work is no different than an employee telling a dirty joke at the water cooler. ● Unlike verbal sexual harassment (which may result in a game of "he said, she said"), sexting results in concrete evidence that can be used in legal action against the company.
Distracted driving	● Many states have laws that prohibit using personal communication devices while driving. ● Despite these laws, nearly 70% of adults admit to using a cell phone while behind the wheel. ● If an employee gets caught using their cell phone while driving on company time (i.e., if they cause an accident), then the employer can be found liable for any damages.
Social media content	● Personal cell phones allow employees to access social media, even if the company has a strict ban on social media in the workplace. ● Offensive content that is posted on social media while an employee is on the job can be used as evidence against the company in any legal action.
Lost devices with unsecured data	● Whether company owned or personal, lost devices can negatively affect a company if they fall into the wrong hands (i.e., sensitive information may be leaked to the public). ● Any sensitive or private information that goes public opens up the potential for legal action against the company from any party negatively affected by the leak.

Based on this information, what can a company do to protect itself from the risks of employees using personal communication devices? The best thing a company can do is to have a clear, enforceable policy regarding personal communication in the workplace. The policy should explicitly state any consequences for violating the terms of the policy, information that enlightens employees about the potential risks (for both them and the company) of using personal communication devices while on the job, and security measures that can help the company avoid any situation in which it could be found liable. Taking these steps can help a company make sure its employees use personal communication devices safely and ethically, as well as help the company stay afloat should a crisis occur because of an employee's personal communication in the workplace.

Source: Haun, B. (2013, April 29). "4 Risks When Employees Bring Their Own Devices to Work." *Inc.* Retrieved and adapted from www.inc.com/bzur-haun/legal-backlash-of-bring-your-own-device-policies.html

Marital or relational status is just one example of a topic that might be deemed private. Other topics, such as religion, political affiliation, and even hobbies, may be private issues for your coworkers, clients, or supervisors. To maintain professional excellence as it relates to privacy management is to avoid asking questions that may be deemed private, unless the other party initiates the topic. Do not feel pressured to reveal information about yourself that you deem private. And if you do develop a personal relationship with another professional, keep your personal conversations private. As we discussed in the last section, sharing personal information about others through the company grapevine is completely and totally unprofessional.

PROFESSIONAL ETIQUETTE

It doesn't take a rocket scientist to understand that you can't have professional excellence if you don't display professional etiquette. Professional etiquette means practicing the behaviors of social etiquette or good manners in a professional setting. You have been taught good manners. You know not to talk with your mouth full and to cover your nose when you sneeze. So do we really need to talk about professional etiquette? You bet we do, because the workforce is increasingly full of people who lack professional etiquette; therefore, your ability to display it not only will help you achieve professional excellence but also will set you apart from the pack.

Let's begin with the basics: politeness. Greet people when you see them. Do not interrupt others when they are speaking or when they are having a conversation with another party. Make requests in a manner that is polite as opposed to demanding. Respect your supervisors', coworkers', and customers' time. Say "please" and "thank you." Turn off your cell phone in a meeting. Be punctual. Don't eavesdrop on conversations. And, as noted earlier, don't spread gossip.

You may be thinking, "Don't patronize me. I know all this." Of course you do, but do you practice it? We have been in meetings and witnessed all of the following (more than once, we might add): so-called professionals showing up late, wasting everyone else's time, and then asking, "What did I miss?"; high-level employees not only getting cell calls but answering them during meetings; a complete lack of manners displayed by employees on all levels; customers being ignored; employees being reprimanded in front of others; gossip and office drama getting so out of hand that work literally stops. Even though many people in professional positions display poor manners, it is still not professional and certainly is unacceptable behavior for someone striving for professional excellence.

KEYS TO EXCELLENCE IN INTERPERSONAL COMMUNICATION

Refer back to the companies mentioned at the beginning of the chapter—Cisco Systems, SalesForce, Hilton Worldwide Holdings, Wegmans Food Markets, and Rocket Companies—as excellent places to work. Those companies have such an outstanding reputation because of their emphasis on effective interpersonal communication. Think about how you should strive for excellence during interpersonal communication. When studying the KEYS approach to professional excellence as you develop in the workplace, try to make some changes and improve your people skills and interpersonal communication.

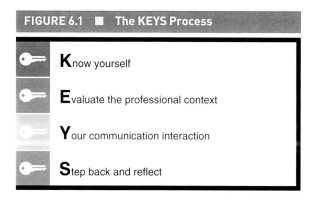

FIGURE 6.1 ■ The KEYS Process

Know yourself

Evaluate the professional context

Your communication interaction

Step back and reflect

Know Yourself

Understanding Professional Etiquette

As you read the index below and answer the questions, think about how this knowledge can help you be a better communicator.

A great place to begin practicing your professional etiquette is in the classroom. Take the following quiz and see how many times you have displayed less-than-professional etiquette during your college career. Place a check beside every violation you have committed.

1. Came to class without completing the homework
2. Came to class without completing the required readings
3. Made the following statement or one like it: "I missed class last week. Did we do anything important?"
4. Asked your professor, "Will this be on the test?"
5. Forgot to silence your cell phone before class
6. Left class to answer your cell phone
7. Answered your cell phone during class
8. Sent a text or instant message during class
9. Browsed the internet during class
10. Sent an email with punctuation and/or spelling errors
11. Called your professor by the wrong title—for example, "Mrs." instead of "Dr."
12. Requested a reference letter via email
13. Requested a reference letter less than two weeks before it was due
14. Gossiped about a professor or classmate

How did you do? For true professional excellence, you should not have a single check. Take some time to explore why each of the above behaviors is considered an example of poor professional etiquette. If you did earn some checks above, what can you do to eliminate those behaviors in the future? Are there other behaviors that you believe should be listed above? What are those behaviors, and why do you consider them violations of professional etiquette?

When examining the first key, *know yourself*, decide if you want to achieve professional excellence, and know that part of that entails improving your interpersonal communication with both your coworkers and your clients. Realize that getting to know yourself better involves adjusting your communication style in professional settings. Remember that using your cell phone and texting in front of your coworkers and customers can be rude or insensitive. Examine your strengths and weaknesses as they relate to interpersonal communication. Set a goal to improve your impression management and be more mindful of your communication decisions at work. For example, avoid making comments in front of coworkers about things going on in your personal life. In addition, review your company's performance standards and try to improve both verbal communication and body language in service encounters. Smiling and tone of voice can be improved—these are both factors that can positively impact the way other people view you.

The next key, *evaluate the professional context*, is essential because you want to become more audience centered and aware of how you come across to coworkers and clients. Become more mindful of the topics you bring up at work, and give more attention to how loudly you talk about particular topics when customers are present. The evaluation of your audience and workplace context can lead to improved interpersonal communication with your coworkers and clients.

The third key, *your communication interaction*, can make you more genuine during interpersonal encounters with coworkers and clients. Start to practice good eye contact as well as active listening strategies, and realize that these skills are valuable to your development as a professional. As you walk away from interpersonal conversations and service encounters, think about what you communicated both verbally and nonverbally. As your communication interaction occurs, work more at making appropriate decisions regarding your people skills and interpersonal communication.

As you strive to improve your people skills, engage in the fourth key, *step back and reflect*. Become more open to reflecting on your interpersonal communication with others. Ask yourself some of the following questions as you step back and think about the message you sent:

Was I communicating a positive attitude to the customer? Was I engaged in active rather than passive listening? Did I sound sarcastic when I responded to the customer's complaint? Did I talk about personal issues that other people may have viewed as offensive or unprofessional? Revisit the conversation or check in with the other person, whether coworker or customer, to make sure you handled it well.

STEP BACK AND REFLECT

Jessica and Vinnie

As you read this passage and answer the questions, step back and reflect on what went wrong in this professional situation.

Jessica had recently been promoted into a new position with Company K when she was instructed to work with Vinnie on a project. When their meeting ran late, Vinnie suggested that they continue talking over some food. He commented that his wife and kids were out of town, so he did not have to hurry home that evening. Jessica saw nothing unprofessional about the invitation. She was starving, and they were in the middle of an excellent brainstorming session, so she agreed. At dinner, Jessica began to feel uncomfortable. Twice, Vinnie brushed his hand against hers. It did not seem professional, but she excused it as an accident. Then he began making personal comments, such as "I just can't believe a gorgeous woman like you is single. You are too attractive to be spending your evenings alone." Jessica responded by mentioning the photos of his wife and kids displayed in his office. "I am sure one day I will be lucky enough to have a beautiful family like yours. Now about the project timeline . . ." When the meal ended, Jessica declined the offer for a nightcap and headed for the parking lot. Vinnie followed her to her car, at which point he physically stood in front of her car door, blocking her access to the vehicle. He then stated, "Well, if you will not have a nightcap with me, at least give me a hug." Jessica replied, "I'm not much of a hugger," and she extended her hand. Vinnie grabbed her hand with both of his and began to caress it. Luckily, at that moment her phone rang; she pulled her hand free and answered it. She stayed on the phone, saying, "I have to take this." Vinnie backed up a bit, and Jessica threw her car door open, jumped in her car, and sped off.

Jessica did not know what to think. Was she overreacting? Could she have misunderstood? The next day, she approached a female supervisor, Michelle, described what had happened, and asked for her thoughts on the situation. Michelle listened to the events of the evening and then replied, "If someone as good-looking as Vinnie hit on me, I would be thrilled. Anyways, if you were not interested in him, you should not have gone to dinner with him. I think you should be flattered, not whining." Jessica did not mention the situation again, but she did start searching for a new job that afternoon.

Step Back and Reflect

1. What went wrong?

2. Was Vinnie's behavior appropriate? Was it professional? Was it sexual harassment?

3. Was Michelle's reaction appropriate? Was it professional?

4. What advice would you give Jessica?

5. How could Jessica or Michelle have used the KEYS approach to improve her communication interaction?

Do you need to improve your interpersonal communication in the workplace? What have you learned in this chapter that could help you improve?

EXECUTIVE SUMMARY

Now that you have finished reading this chapter, you should be able to

Describe different kinds of workplace relationships:

- In the language of the workplace, the superior (supervisor/employer) is typically the higher status person and the subordinate (employee) the lower status person.

- People or entities that your organization serves or provides products to are known as external customers.

- An internal customer is an employee—an internal part of the organization—who needs services or products from other parts of the organization to complete his or her work.

- Maintaining positive customer relations centers on effective communication and is essential in today's business world. Customer relations, or customer service, is the interaction between employees or representatives of an organization or business and the people the organization sells to or serves.

Explain the difference between professional and personal communication:

- As you develop a feeling of trust and affection toward coworkers, and even clients and bosses, you will find yourself maintaining interpersonal relationships with coworkers at as well as away from work.

- To maintain professional excellence as it relates to privacy management is to avoid asking questions that may be deemed private, unless the other party initiates the topic.

Discuss professional etiquette in the workplace:

● Professional etiquette means practicing the behaviors of social etiquette or good manners in a professional setting.

● Greet people when you see them. Do not interrupt others when they are speaking or when they are having a conversation with another party.

● Even though many people in professional positions display poor manners, it is still not professional and certainly is unacceptable behavior for someone striving for professional excellence.

Apply the KEYS approach to conduct yourself with professional excellence in interpersonal communication in the workplace:

● Know yourself. Know how you want to achieve professional excellence, and know that part of that entails improving your interpersonal communication with both coworkers and clients.

● Evaluate the professional context. This is essential for you because you will become more audience centered and aware of how you come across to coworkers and clients.

● Your communication interaction. Work more at making appropriate decisions regarding your people skills and interpersonal communication. This makes you more genuine during interpersonal encounters with coworkers and clients.

● Step back and reflect. Become more open to reflecting on your interpersonal communication with others.

EXPLORE

1. Use the internet search engine of your choice (Google, Bing, etc.) to search for "the top 10 best companies to work for." After looking over the rankings and explanations for each company, do you notice any recurring themes among these companies? How can interpersonal communication be attributed to the best practices of these companies?

2. Examine how interpersonal communication occurs within your college or university. How easy is it to get into contact with other students, professors, or administrators? Write a statement discussing how open you believe communication is within your school, as well as if you find it effective and balanced.

3. Pick a social media platform and evaluate the communication interactions that occur there. Does the interpersonal communication on the platform foster open discussion, or are many people maligned for their opinions? Discuss the pros and cons of engaging in interpersonal communication in an online environment.

REVIEW

1. Define *interpersonal communication*.

2. _____ describes how employees and supervisors do not share the same view of some fundamental areas such as organizational issues or basic job duties.

3. _____ occurs when some, but not all, of the information is passed on to the supervisor.

4. _____ occurs when an employee acts warm and friendly toward the supervisor.

5. Explain the difference between an internal customer and an external customer.

6. Explain the foundations of Communication Privacy Management theory.

7. _____ means practicing the behaviors of social etiquette or good manners in a professional setting.

8. _____ in the workplace refers to feelings of closeness, trust, and affection in professional and interpersonal relationships with coworkers, clients, or bosses.

DISCUSSION QUESTIONS

1. What are your strengths when it comes to interpersonal communication? What areas do you plan to develop?

2. Make a list of several positive customer service experiences you've had. Did interpersonal communication impact your service experience? If so, what makes the difference in these experiences compared with others?

3. As a manager or leader, what steps would you take, if any, to educate your employees about interpersonal communication?

4. Do you believe companies should have policies that forbid dating among employees? Why or why not? Should companies have policies forbidding supervisors and subordinates to have nonromantic relationships outside work? Why or why not? Should companies have policies that forbid coworkers to develop nonromantic relationships outside work? Why or why not?

5. Make a list of private topics that you believe should not be discussed in professional settings, and then think of a time when your privacy was violated by someone. Was it an invasion of your private space or of your private information? How did the invasion make you feel, and how did you react?

YOUR COMMUNICATION INTERACTION

Riley's Angry Email

As you read the passage below, consider what would be a more effective communication strategy in this situation.

After a hectic morning at work, Riley is ready to unwind during her lunch break. She heads to the break room, already salivating at the thought of the leftover chicken casserole she brought from home. When she opens the refrigerator, however, Riley is stunned to see that her lunch is gone. She immediately suspects a coworker, Penny, of stealing her lunch, as the two of them have never gotten along. Back at her desk, Riley types up a nasty email to send to her group of close friends, in which she heavily insults Penny. Only after she sends the email does Riley realize that she accidentally sent it in a thread to the entire company, instead of to her friends. Mortified, Riley quickly leaves work, and tries to concoct a story that will help her save face. A few minutes later, Riley receives a call from another coworker asking about the email. Riley plays dumb and claims that her email account must have been hacked.

Questions to Consider

1. What could Riley have done differently when she realized her lunch was missing?
2. Was using her work email the best way for Riley to vent her anger? Why or why not?
3. Was denial the best way for Riley to save face, or should she have owned up to her mistake? Why?
4. If you were Penny, how would you respond to Riley's email?

ETHICAL CONNECTION

Emma's Marital Status

As you read this passage and answer the questions, consider how the way you communicate has an ethical dimension.

Emma is a single professional. When her coworkers, Stephanie and Derek, ask about her relationship status, she feels as if her privacy is being violated, but she answers, "I'm single," and tries to change the topic. Her less-than-professional coworkers, Stephanie and Derek, then go on to ask questions such as the following: "Are you dating anyone? So, you don't have a boyfriend yet? Would you like for me to set you up on a blind date with our friend Darren?" Although some professionals are open about their marital or relational status and enjoy sharing information about their family life at work, not everyone feels the same way about the disclosure of marital or relational information. In Emma's case, she wishes to maintain privacy around her relational status and her sexual identity in the workplace.

Questions to Consider

1. What are the ethical issues involved in asking coworkers personal questions at work?
2. How could you offer social opportunities to Emma without violating her privacy?
3. What methods of communication could you use to build trust with Emma and get to know her more personally outside of the professional context?
4. How could Stephanie and Derek use the KEYS approach to strengthen their interpersonal sensitivity skills?

EVALUATE THE PROFESSIONAL CONTEXT

Katie and Joey's Misunderstanding

As you evaluate the passage below, consider whether this behavior is appropriate for this professional context.

When Katie learned a good-looking guy had been hired in the marketing department, she quickly found an excuse to head that way and check him out. Joey *was* cute and did not have on a wedding ring, so Katie wasted no time making her move by asking him for his phone number. Joey had heard through the grapevine that Katie often planned company events and happy hours, so when she extended an invitation to him, he thought nothing of it and accepted. Katie had also sent him several text messages that didn't suggest anything beyond friendship. Joey had relocated for this job, and he had not yet made any friends in the community. He was excited about the opportunity to hang out with coworkers. It seemed as though things were going well at work, and now he was even establishing what seemed to be a new social network.

Friday afternoon arrived, and Katie met Joey at the local club. After grabbing a table, Katie said the following to Joey: "Wow, I have not been on a date with a nice-looking guy like you in several months. I really picked up on your sense of humor in our texts."

Joey was shocked and didn't know what to say. He was just looking for another coworker to hang out with. He had just come through a painful divorce, and he did not want to discuss it.

Questions to Consider

1. How should Joey respond to Katie?

2. Do you believe Katie and Joey displayed professional excellence? Why or why not?

3. How could the KEYS process help Katie and Joey in this situation?

TERMS TO REMEMBER

advocacy (p. 137)

communication network (p. 138)

Communication Privacy Management (p. 143)

customer relations (p. 140)

dyads (p. 134)

external customers (p. 139)

formal communication network (p. 138)

gatekeeping (p. 136)

general distortion (p. 136)

grapevine (p. 138)

informal communication network (p. 138)

ingratiation (p. 137)

internal customer (p. 139)

interpersonal communication (p. 134)

intimacy (p. 141)

organizational chart (p. 138)

professional etiquette (p. 146)

self-disclose (p. 143)

semantic information distance (p. 135)

subordinate (p. 135)

summarization (p. 136)

superior (p. 135)

upward distortion (p. 136)

white space (p. 138)

withholding (p. 136)

Executive and coach Gregg Popovich of the San Antonio Spurs

Jim McIsaac/Getty Images Sport/Getty Images

7 STRENGTHENING TEAMS AND CONDUCTING MEETINGS

CHAPTER OBJECTIVES

After studying this chapter, you should be able to

7.1   Distinguish between a group and a team

7.2   Explain the impact of the environment, the topic(s), and the participants on communication when conducting meetings

7.3   Describe the concept of shared leadership and how it relates to the roles and norms displayed by a group or team

7.4   Discuss the concepts involved in effective problem solving

7.5   Describe ways to foster innovative thinking in a team context

7.6   Discuss the need for conflict and the strategies for productive conflict

7.7   Apply the KEYS process to professional excellence as you develop your groups into teams

Gregg Charles Popovich is an American basketball executive and coach of the San Antonio Spurs of the National Basketball Association (NBA). Popovich is considered one of the greatest coaches in NBA history. One of his famous quotes on coaching and teamwork is "It is not about any one person. You have got to get over yourself and realize that it takes a group to get this thing done" ("23 Best Gregg Popovich Quotes," 2017). Popovich's coaching philosophy is focused on teamwork, and the proficient communication teamwork helped his team win over 1,000 NBA games.

As you study this chapter, try to use Popovich's teamwork strategy as a yardstick for your own educational and professional life. Do you receive enough collaboration and feedback from your peers and professors in school? How about work? After reading this chapter, you should be able to identify what teamwork practices make for an effective organization.

Many college students make the mistake of picking a career under the assumption that it will not require them to interact with other people on a regular basis. In the communication age, however, you will almost certainly be expected to work well with others in a team environment. This chapter identifies the needs and functions of communication in a team setting and shows what benefits can be gained by working well in a group with your coworkers.

Have you had unpleasant group experiences? Are there times you'd prefer just to do the project yourself because it would be easier? Well, if you don't like working in groups, we have some bad news for you—working with others is part of every job, regardless of the field. If you want to excel in your field of interest, you need to learn how to work with others. The good news is that by using the KEYS process, you can turn your groups into innovative, functional teams. In this chapter, you'll be introduced to a variety of communication strategies that will help you lead this transformation.

Team communication is important for the following reasons: (1) Your ability to relate with other people in teams is central to achieving professional excellence, (2) team communication helps you form professional connections with coworkers and accomplish professional projects, and (3) your ability to work effectively in teams is a critical skill that will play an important role in your success as you *develop in the workplace.* Let's begin with a look at the important role of team communication at work.

HOW DO GROUPS DIFFER FROM TEAMS?

Is there a difference between groups and teams? Although executives and managers often use these terms interchangeably, their definitions do differ (Katzenbach & Smith, 1993; Kinlaw, 1991; West, 2012). For those seeking professional excellence, understanding this difference is essential. The small-group theorist Marvin Shaw (1981) states that a group is "two or more persons who are interacting with one another in such a manner that each person influences and is influenced by each other person" (p. 8). Central to this definition are the concepts of relationship, interaction, and influence.

If you go to see a blockbuster movie on opening night, you'll be part of an audience that you might refer to as a "group" of people. You may call the audience a group, but it would not fit our definition of a group since the moviegoers have no relationship, interaction, or influence on one another. For our purposes, a *group* is defined as three or more individuals who are working toward a common goal or share a common purpose. As a result of their common goal or purpose, they have relationships, interactions, and influence with one another.

Similar to groups, teams have common goals and purposes. Further, like group members, team members have relationships, interactions, and influence with one another. The difference between groups and teams resides in the nature of those relationships and interactions (Levi, 2011; Myers & Anderson, 2008). A *team* is defined as a group in which members share leadership responsibility for creating a team identity, achieving mutually defined goals, and fostering innovative thinking (Lumsden & Lumsden, 1997; Moe et al., 2010). This definition highlights four key differences between groups and teams. First, unlike group members, team members share leadership responsibilities. There may be one team member who has a leadership title such as manager, vice president, or coach, but all team members demonstrate leadership when it comes to defining goals, making decisions, and implementing ideas. Second, team members share an identity. They refer to their team as "us" and "we," as opposed to "the group" or "them." Third, group members work toward common goals, while team members not only work toward common goals but also help define what those goals will be. Finally, teams strive for innovation. According to Katzenbach and Smith (1993), "A working group relies primarily on the individual contributions of its members for group performance, whereas a team strives for a magnified impact that is incremental to what its members could achieve in their individual roles" (p. 88).

What would be some advantages of firefighters who operate as a team rather than firefighters who operate as a group?

iStockphoto/xavierarnau

Understanding Group Behavior

As you read the index below and answer the questions, think about how this knowledge can help you be a better communicator.

Most students have many opportunities to develop their communication skills during class projects that require group work. The first step in developing your group into a team is to know yourself. Think about the last group project you completed for school. Take the following quiz and see how many times you displayed behaviors that did not reflect a team attitude or professional excellence while working with that group. Place a check beside every violation you have committed.

_____ **1.** Came to meeting without completing your assigned task

_____ **2.** Made the following statement: "No one told me what I had to do" or "I was not sure what to do, so I didn't want to do it wrong."

_____ **3.** Missed a meeting without giving your group members advance warning

_____ **4.** Missed a group meeting and did not proactively find out what you needed to do for the next meeting

_____ **5.** Participated in a meeting without an agenda

_____ **6.** Gossiped about a fellow group member

_____ **7.** Pushed your ideas forward without allowing others to express their ideas

_____ **8.** Did not share a concern because you did not want to start a conflict or cause the meeting to last longer

_____ **9.** Discussed a problem with the professor before discussing it with your group member(s)

_____ **10.** Wasted others' time by coming to a meeting late and/or discussing issues that were not relevant to the project

_____ **11.** Accepted the first "okay" solution, as opposed to working toward an innovative idea

How did you do? For true professional excellence, you should not have a single check. Throughout this chapter, we will discuss why each of these areas is important for excellence in team communication. If you did earn some checks, what can you do to eliminate those behaviors in the future? Are there other behaviors that you believe should be listed here? What are those behaviors, and why do you consider them violations of excellence as a team member?

CONDUCTING MEETINGS

According to an old adage, groups outperform individuals, and teams outperform groups. If you wish to achieve professional excellence in the workplace, you must learn to transform your groups into teams. Effective communication is essential for this transformation.

Meetings are the central form of team communication (Boerner et al., 2012; Myers & Anderson, 2008). During meetings, leadership can be shared, goals and purposes can be defined, a team identity can be developed, and innovation can be fostered. The ability to effectively participate in and lead meetings is an important component of professional excellence and a key to transforming groups into teams. On the flip side, poorly run meetings are a major roadblock

Meetings can be stressful, especially when you have too many projects to keep up with. In our consulting practices, we have met numerous professionals frustrated with their time spent in meetings just thinking about the stacks of information waiting for them afterward. To make matters more challenging, the rise of virtual meetings has made it easier for people to multitask and do other work while in a meeting, which makes it difficult for them to give the meeting their full attention.

iStockphoto/Su Arslanoglu

stopping many groups from ever becoming teams and many group members from achieving professional excellence.

For meetings to run effectively, a few basics must always be considered. These basics include the meeting environment, the meeting topics, and the meeting participants.

Meeting Environment

Creating the proper meeting environment is a vital but often overlooked component of effective communication. What is a meeting environment? It includes both the time a meeting is held and its location. The meeting environment is as much a part of the communication that occurs as the words that are said. Unfortunately, despite the importance of the meeting environment, most people spend little time thinking about it when they plan their meetings.

Currently, there are hundreds of shows and entire television networks dedicated to designing the perfect room or creating the perfect space. Why? The physical environment, from the color on the walls to the furniture to the lighting, has a major impact on us (Ivy & Wahl, 2019; Kupritz & Hillsman, 2011). Look around the room you are in right now. Why did you select this room for studying? How does this room make you feel? How does the room positively impact your studying? How does it negatively impact your studying? Now think about various places where you have attended meetings. How did those environments impact communication? We hope you are beginning to see the importance of meeting environment (see Tools for Professional Excellence 7.1).

If you wish to create an effective meeting environment, what factors should be considered? First, you must consider the time. Time of day, time of week, and time of year can all influence communication. For example, holding a meeting at 8:00 on a Monday morning, 4:30 on a Friday afternoon, or right after lunch may not be the best choice if you want your team members to be fully engaged and alert. Trying to implement a large-scale change is probably a bad idea during the busy holiday season in November and December, but it may be the perfect thing to do in January to kick off the New Year. When selecting meeting times, be aware of differences in team members' schedules. If team members work different shifts with different days off, meeting times should be varied. For example, if half the team works from 7:00 a.m. to 3:00 p.m. and the other half from 3:00 p.m. to 11:00 p.m., holding every meeting at 9:00 a.m. would repeatedly inconvenience the same half of the team. When team members work varied schedules, there is no ideal time to meet. Yet alternating the meetings between shifts shows that all team members are valued and respected, which positively impacts communication interactions.

Location is also an important component in creating a positive meeting environment. In fact, you should consider the convenience, aesthetics, and comfort of the location. As far as convenience, Maelia learned the impact it can have on communication in a meeting. When Maelia began her job as the district supervisor, she held all the district meetings at 8:00 on Monday mornings in her office. Her intention was to start each week fresh by clearly communicating goals and priorities. Unfortunately, this was not the message Maelia sent; both the time and the location were inconvenient for the rest of the group. Most of the managers found themselves commuting to and from Maelia's office during rush-hour traffic. Furthermore, the managers felt they were needed in their stores first thing on Monday mornings, not at a meeting across town. The location and time of the district meetings indirectly sent the message that Maelia considered herself the most important person in the group and that she didn't care about her managers' schedules or duties. This message didn't support the notion of shared goals and shared leadership necessary for transforming groups into teams. In fact, it created a negative environment that hindered communication during the meetings. Fortunately, Maelia realized her mistake. When she moved the district meetings to Mondays at 2:00 p.m., she allowed her managers to have the time they needed in their stores on Monday mornings. She also varied the location from week to week,

A meeting or seminar room may seem like an ideal place to hold a meeting, but be aware of environmental factors such as lighting, temperature, and overall comfort. What would be some pros and cons of the hybrid meeting environment pictured above?

iStockphoto/AndreyPopov

holding meetings at different stores throughout her district. By considering the time and location, she was able to improve the meeting environment and begin transforming her group into a team.

When selecting a meeting location, you should also consider aesthetics and comfort. Many leaders get in the habit of holding all their meetings in the same room. For example, there is only one conference room in our building, so a lot of meetings are held there. The problem is that the conference room has an extremely long and narrow table. When sitting at the table, team members can't see one another, making it very difficult to hold discussions or brainstorming sessions. Further, the room is very dull and uninspired, with no windows and poor lighting. Fortunately, there is another room two floors down that has movable tables, excellent lighting, and a great view outside the window. Using this room does require proactive scheduling, a short elevator ride, and some furniture rearranging, but the aesthetics create an atmosphere that is more conducive to effective communication.

The length of the meeting should factor into your assessment of comfort. Pay close attention to the furniture. Make certain that the chairs are comfortable and that team members have enough elbow room. If you cram your team members into a small space with uncomfortable furniture for any length of time, it will be difficult for them to remain productive.

Keep in mind that comfort extends beyond furniture. For longer meetings, you should consider taking short breaks, allowing people to stretch, visit the restrooms, and refresh their perspective. If your budget allows for it, consider providing food and beverages in meetings.

If you are preparing to conduct a virtual meeting, the virtual environment you choose is an important part of your planning. With so many video conferencing tools available (Microsoft Teams, Webex, Zoom, etc.), it can be tricky to pick one. Generally speaking, it is often best to choose the program your meeting participants use most regularly for their virtual meetings so they aren't late from having to download, install, and learn a new piece of software. That being said, you may discover that a different video conferencing tool has a feature you would really like to use during your meeting; if you choose to use a different tool from what your participants usually use, it is a good idea to let them know beforehand that they may need to install the program. You will learn more about conducting virtual meetings later in this chapter.

TABLE 7.1 ■ Tools for Professional Excellence. The Meeting Environment

To set up an effective meeting environment, consider these questions:

- Is the time convenient to those who will be attending?
- Has enough time been allotted to discuss all the topics?
- Are there too many topics?
- How long is the meeting? Will we need breaks?
- How long is the meeting? Will we need beverages or food?
- Are there audiovisual needs? Is the location equipped to meet those needs?
- Does the furniture support conversations? Can everyone see one another easily?
- Is the furniture comfortable? Is there enough elbow room?
- Is the location convenient to those who will be attending?
- Does the location send any unintended messages? Is the location considered anyone's turf?
- Is the location aesthetically pleasing?
- Is this the best time and location available?

In the end, you may not always have the ability to change the time or location of your meetings. Regardless, considering both time and location for every meeting is part of professional excellence.

STEP BACK AND REFLECT

A Day at the Museum*As you read this passage and answer the questions, step back and reflect on what went wrong in this professional situation.*

I (Kelly Quintanilla, one of your coauthors) have taught many successful workshops to business professionals over the years, workshops in beautiful locations with enthusiastic participants. I also taught one workshop that appeared to be doomed to fail before it even began. The topic of this six-hour workshop was conflict management. The group was a department whose members were currently engaged in a battle with one another. Literally, half the department was not speaking to the other half. Some of the best department members had put in for transfers. Productivity and customer service were suffering.

Knowing all this in advance, I had carefully selected a large room with comfortable chairs, round tables, and good lighting. I had planned for several breaks with food and drinks in an attempt to foster informal communication. The meeting environment was ideal. Unfortunately, an emergency power outage caused the workshop to be moved to a room in one of the local museums. The meeting was scheduled to begin at 8:00 a.m., but many people arrived late due to the last-minute change in location. Those who arrived on time became increasingly agitated as they waited. Part of their agitation stemmed from the fact that there was no coffee, no food, nothing. Despite several calls, the food order never made it to the new location. The only place to get a drink or snack was a small, extremely overpriced gift shop that did not open until 10:00 a.m. To make matters worse, the room had about 40 mounted animal heads hanging from the walls. The animal heads, most of which were in a growling pose, were very dusty, causing anyone with allergies to begin sneezing and sniffling. The final problem was the furniture. The chairs were the small, metal, folding kind. The tables were also small, and there were not enough of them, so the participants were crammed together. I could not imagine a worse meeting environment for any group, let alone a group already engaged in conflict. I needed to do something quickly.

Step Back and Reflect

1. What went wrong?
2. What would you do if you were in my position?
3. Could you overcome the meeting environment?
4. Could the situation be used to your advantage somehow?
5. Should the workshop be called off and rescheduled?
6. How could I use the KEYS approach to improve this communication interaction?

Meeting Topics (Agenda)

One essential component of any well-run meeting is an agenda. An agenda is a guide or an overview of the topics that will be covered during the meeting. An agenda can be simple or complex. Either way, an agenda is a useful channel for informing team members about meeting topics and, if used properly, can serve as a communication tool for facilitating meetings (see Figure 7.1).

Agendas should be distributed several days in advance of the meeting. This will allow team members to comment on the agenda items and give the leader time to revise the agenda if necessary. It will also give team members time to think about issues in advance of the meeting. If you'd like the participants to brainstorm ideas or share information, the agenda is a valuable preparation tool for team members.

Noting the allotted time for each topic also helps the leader determine which topics and how many can be covered in any given meeting. Leaders with professional excellence prioritize agenda items. Items should be prioritized based on importance and urgency. Items that require extensive discussion time should be handled at a separate meeting or series of meetings dedicated solely to that topic. If a leader is truly seeking the input of team members, then they should not try to force too many items into one meeting.

Meeting Participants

When it comes to planning meetings, you should ask yourself two important questions. First, who should be at this meeting? Determining the participants in a meeting should not be based on office politics. Leaders with professional excellence avoid the trap of inviting a representative of each department in order to be politically correct. Invite people who can contribute to the purpose of the meeting. Take time to assess the meeting's purpose, and then determine who can best serve that purpose. Second, can all key members attend this meeting at this time? If key team members can't be present, the meeting should be rescheduled. For example, you should not hold a meeting about budgetary issues if the CFO (chief financial officer) can't attend. You'll waste the time of everyone who does attend, and the team will still need to meet again with the CFO.

Sometimes meetings go extremely well. Sometimes meetings are a nightmare. It's really all about the people who make up your meeting or project group. Nearly everyone can relate to what it's like to attend a meeting, so meetings are often used to set up funny scenes in comedy shows like *The Office* and *Schitt's Creek*. As you study conducting meetings in this chapter, what is your general mindset about attending meetings? What expectations do you have for a meeting to be successful? What qualities of a meeting tend to be a turnoff or deal breaker to you?

iStockphoto/AzmanL

FIGURE 7.1   ■   Agenda Format

Heading: Should include date, time, and location. May include a list of participants.

I. Welcome/opening
The leader should always orient the team and focus the meeting during the opening.

II. Approve minutes from the previous meeting
Minutes are a written record of the meeting.

III. Specific points to be discussed
The majority of the agenda will be a list of the specific items that will be covered during the meeting. Beside each item, state who will lead the discussion and/or report on this item. It is also wise to include the estimated time it should take to cover each item.

IV. Old business
Allow time for the team to discuss items from previous meetings that may still be unresolved.

V. New business
Allow time for the team to discuss any new items that may have come up after the agenda was finalized or during the meeting itself.

VI. Arrangement of the next meeting.
Summarize any assignments that must be completed by the next meeting. Also make certain to discuss the time and location of the next meeting.

VII. Closing
Always provide some sort of closing statement.

Failing to consider meeting environment, meeting topics, and meeting participants hinders the chances for a successful meeting, but covering the basics does not, in and of itself, guarantee success. For meetings that will transform groups into teams, all members must share leadership, develop positive problem-solving strategies, strive for innovation, and participate in productive conflict. Let's take a moment to explore each of these important elements.

SHARED LEADERSHIP

As you learned earlier in this chapter, teams require members to share leadership. How do team members share leadership? What is the role of the designated leader if all members are sharing duties?

There are many designated leadership titles (e.g., director, manager, supervisor, vice president, president, queen). Regardless of your title, if you're the designated leader, think of yourself as a coach. A coach has a very distinct role in meetings. Remember, a coach does not play the game. The coach must remain on the sidelines. The coach doesn't have to be an expert on everything, have all the answers, or do all the talking. However, the coach does need to call the meetings, set the agenda, and then facilitate the discussion. A coach facilitates the discussion by supporting positive team roles and norms while eliminating self-centered roles and unproductive norms.

Team Roles

Within every team, members can play a host of possible roles. Some of these roles are functional roles that help the team achieve goals or maintain positive relationships among members (see Table 7.2). These roles are known as task roles and relationship roles, respectively.

Unfortunately, there are also many dysfunctional roles that can interfere with the positive functioning of the team. These roles are known as self-centered roles. For a group to become a team, all team members must actively engage in the functional roles while working to limit the dysfunctional roles.

As a coach utilizing the KEYS approach, you should *know* the skills and strengths you bring to the team and *evaluate* the skills and strengths of your team members. After *your communication interaction* occurs, coaches must *step back and reflect* to determine if all the functional roles are being covered. If not, redesign the agenda or add team members who will cover the gaps. For example, if no one is giving their opinion, the coach might add an agenda item that calls for everyone to provide input on a topic. If the group lacks a harmonizer, the coach may add a new member to the team who is skilled at handling conflict. You should never hesitate to talk about the way the team is interacting. It's a sign of professional excellence to address weaknesses head on. So if you're the coach, make certain your team is aware of the various tasks and relationship roles. Make it a habit to discuss the team's strengths and weaknesses. Make it a habit to step back and reflect on the communication as individuals and as a team. And when the team notes dysfunctional roles, be prepared to address those behaviors directly. (We discuss dealing with difficult people in more detail in Chapter 10.)

Team Norms

When you attend class, you probably sit in the same seat every time. Why? You don't own the seat; it's not yours. Still, if someone else sat in the seat, it would bother you, right? You might even ask that person to move. There's no written rule, no seating chart stating that this is your seat—it's simply a norm.

TABLE 7.2 ■ Team Roles

Task roles: Roles that help the team carry out tasks and get the work done

Role	Characteristics
Initiator	Proposes solutions; suggests ideas; introduces new approaches to problem-solving
Information giver	Offers facts or generalizations; relates one's own experience to the problems to illustrate points
Information seeker	Asks for clarification of suggestions; requests additional information or facts
Opinion giver	States an opinion or belief concerning a problem and suggests solutions to that problem
Opinion seeker	Looks for an expression of feelings from group members; seeks clarification of values, suggestions, or ideas
Coordinator	Shows relationships among various ideas or suggestions; tries to pull together ideas and suggestions
Procedural developer	Takes notes; records ideas; distributes materials; guides group through the agenda
Summarizer/ evaluator	Restates ideas and describes relationships; details agreements and differences

(Continued)

TABLE 7.2 ■ Team Roles *(Continued)*

Relationship roles: Roles that strengthen or maintain team relationships

Role	Characteristics
Supporter	Expresses togetherness; encourages others; gives praise; suggests solidarity
Harmonizer	Mediates and reconciles differences; suggests areas of agreement between disagreeing members; suggests positive ways to explore difference
Gatekeeper	Asks opinions of members who are not participating; prevents dominance by others; facilitates overall interaction

Self-centered roles: Roles that interfere with the team's ability to complete tasks

Role	Characteristics
Blocker	Gives negative responses to most ideas; is negative about any positive solutions; raises continuous objections
Dominator	Controls through interruptions, superiority of tone, and length of conversation control
Attacker	Aggressive to achieve personal status; expresses disapproval; critical of status of others
Clown	Disrupts with jokes and other diverting behavior; brings up tangents; refuses to take ideas seriously

Source: Adapted from Benne, K., & Sheats, P. (1948). Functional roles of group members. *Journal of Social Issues, 4,* 41–49.

What's a norm? A norm is an unwritten rule of behavior. Although norms are unwritten, they are as powerful as (if not more powerful than) the written rules. Think about the organizations for which you have worked. Do they have an employee handbook or a policy book? Ever taken the time to read a handbook? Many employees fail to take the time to learn the written rules. Instead, they follow the unwritten rules or norms they see other people enacting in the workplace.

Our point is this—if you want to function with professional excellence, you should read your employee handbook! You should know the written rules and expectations. (We also recommend you spend some time familiarizing yourself with your student handbooks.) Knowing both the written and unwritten rules is important for communicating with professional excellence. At times, these written and unwritten rules will complement each other and lend themselves to norms that are productive for your team. At other times, the written and unwritten rules will contradict each other, resulting in negative consequences for both you and the team.

Let's look at Lina for an example. In Lina's office, the written rule related to cell phones was very clear: "No use of personal cell phones during company time." Yet the norm was for employees to take personal calls all day long. Further, employees would leave meetings to answer their cell phones or send text messages during the middle of group discussions. This was clearly a negative norm.

All groups have both positive and negative norms. The important thing is to step back and reflect on the norms and assess how various norms are affecting your group. Your objective is to turn your group into a team by eliminating the negative norms and building on the positive norms.

But how do you eliminate negative norms? You have to address them. You can't ignore them and just expect them to fix themselves. To achieve professional excellence, you must be willing to say, "Here is something that is going wrong; let's find a way to correct the problem as a team." It's equally important to recognize the positive norms. When a norm is contributing to the success of the team, it should be acknowledged and actively supported by the team.

Smartphones, cell phones, and other electronic devices can serve as major distractions during meetings. In one study published in the journal, *Mobile Media and Communication*, the researchers found that those who use their phones during a meeting were evaluated lower in terms of both perceived competence and meeting effectiveness (Piercy & Underhill, 2020). What is your view of the use of technology in the classroom or other professional settings?

iStockphoto/PeopleImages

PROBLEM SOLVING

In the opening section of this chapter, we introduced you to the definition of a team. If you recall, a team is defined as a group in which members share leadership responsibility for creating a team identity, achieving mutually defined goals, and fostering innovative thinking.

To achieve mutually defined goals, teams engage in problem solving. *Problem-solving* and *decision-making* are not interchangeable terms. Decision-making is actually a step in the problem-solving process. According to Dennis Gouran (1982/1990), a leading scholar in group communication, decision-making is "the act of choosing among a set of alternatives under conditions that necessitate choice" (p. 3). Problem-solving involves not only making a choice but also coming up with quality alternatives from which to select and then working to implement the choice your team selects.

How can you ensure that your team generates innovative alternatives or successfully implements its choice? Begin by understanding all the steps in the problem-solving process. At some point in your academic career, you probably learned John Dewey's Reflective Thinking Process or some other problem-solving model based on his process. According to Dewey (1910), five steps make up problem solving:

1. Describing and analyzing the problem

2. Generating possible solutions

3. Evaluating all solutions

4. Deciding on the solution

5. Planning how to implement the solution

Within each step, you have the opportunity to excel or struggle. Let's examine each of the steps to see how effective communication can help team members achieve professional excellence.

Describing and Analyzing the Problem

It seems only logical that the first step in problem-solving is to describe and analyze the problem. After all, how can you solve a problem if you do not know what the problem is? Alas, this vital step is often shortchanged or skipped altogether. The reason for this mistake is simple. There is an assumption that "we already know what the problem is." The leader has defined the problem in their own mind, so they may feel that the group's time would be better spent discussing solutions. Group members are comfortable with skipping this step because they, too, have defined the problem in their minds. Unfortunately, the group leader and various group members, in all likelihood, do not share the same definition. Based on their individual experiences and perceptions, they probably have a different take on the nature of the problem or unsatisfactory state. By failing to understand the problem from all sides, a group limits its chances of generating a solution that will truly correct all facets of the problem.

Teams take time to discuss the problem. Team members share their own insights and experiences. In addition, they actively seek and share feedback from other employees and relevant parties who are not part of the team. When determining meeting participants, careful consideration is given to the makeup of the team in an attempt to include diverse perceptions of a problem. When analyzing a problem, group members must look at the current conditions realistically to determine the nature, extent, and probable cause(s) of the problem (Choy & Oo, 2012; Gouran & Hirokawa, 1996; Kauffeld & Lehmann-Willenbrock, 2011). Further, failure to recognize potential threats or to clearly understand the situation can result in poor decisions.

Generating Possible Solutions

Once a problem is clearly understood, team members can begin generating possible solutions. Avoid tossing around a few ideas; find one that is satisfactory, and then move on to the next step. Do not stop with an "okay" solution. Teams seek innovative solutions that address all facets of a problem.

For better or for worse, your formal education has trained you to look for the "right answer" (Von Oech, 1983). One consequence of taking thousands of multiple-choice exams in your lifetime is that you have become skilled at marking the right answer and then moving to the next question. This skill is useful when demonstrating your knowledge of a given subject area, but it's not very useful when trying to think critically and develop innovative solutions. There's an old proverb that states, "There are seven right answers to every question." Teams subscribe to the wisdom of this proverb.

Fortunately, there are many tools that can aid your team in generating possible solutions. Those tools include brainstorming, nominal group technique, idea writing, and role-playing.

TABLE 7.3 ■ **Tools for Professional Excellence.** Tools for Innovation	
To generate innovative ideas or solutions, consider these practical tools:	
Tool	**Description**
Brainstorming	A technique for generating many ideas quickly. The goal is quantity, not quality, so all ideas should be expressed and written down. No ideas should be criticized or praised. Members are not permitted to speak for longer than 10 seconds at a time—no long explanations. Ideas will be evaluated and elaborated on at a later point in the problem-solving process.
Nominal group technique	A type of brainstorming designed to incorporate all team members. Rather than having team members yell out their ideas, nominal group technique has members brainstorm independently, writing down their ideas on a piece of paper. After a set amount of time has passed, members stop writing and read what they have written. All the ideas are then recorded on a chalkboard or somewhere the entire group can view them.
Idea writing	This technique combines brainstorming and the nominal group technique. With this technique, team members begin brainstorming and write their first idea down on the top of a piece of paper. Each member then passes their paper to the right, reads the idea on the paper, and then adds another idea. This process continues until the paper is full. All the ideas are then read aloud and displayed for the group to see.
Role-playing	A technique used to increase team members' understanding of various points of view. A team member will put themselves in the place of someone else. It may be another group member or someone not present at the meeting, such as the customer. The team member will then try to answer questions about the problem from the point of view of the person they are playing.

See Tools for Professional Excellence 7.3 for a detailed description of each tool. (We will continue our discussion of innovative thinking later in this chapter.)

Evaluating All Solutions

Once possible solutions have been generated, the team must begin the process of evaluating the merit of each solution based on criteria. Criteria are the standards used to make a decision. For example, if your company was developing a new advertising campaign, the criteria might include that it must reflect the company's current image, be easy to remember, have a positive feel, reach the target audience, be in place within six months, and not cost more than $10,000 to implement. Your criteria should always include budgetary considerations and deadlines. Your team may come up with a highly innovative solution, but if you can't afford to implement it or if it can't be implemented by a preset deadline, then that solution is not the right choice.

How do you evaluate solutions? Teams develop a systematic process for evaluation. Just as there are tools to help generate possible solutions, there are tools to help teams evaluate solutions. These tools include keep/scratch, value rating, *T*-chart, and decision matrix. See Tools for Professional Excellence 7.4 for a detailed description of each.

If the leader is actively facilitating discussion and if the team members are actively engaged, a thorough evaluation of solutions will be a natural function of the team. All teams should routinely test and question the quality of information used as the basis for both problem analysis and possible solutions. In addition, teams should routinely question their assumptions and biases.

TABLE 7.4 ■ **Tools for Professional Excellence.** Tools for Evaluation	
To evaluate ideas and possible solutions, try these practical tools:	
Tool	**Description**
Keep/scratch	A technique for limiting the number of alternatives the team will discuss in detail. Display all the alternatives so that all team members can see them. Have the leader read each alternative. If a member of the team wishes an alternative to be considered further, they will yell, "Keep." If no one yells, "Keep," the leader will cross out or scratch the alternative. No one should ever yell, "Scratch."
Value rating	A technique for reducing the number of alternatives the team will discuss in detail. Team members are given a set number of points (or stickers). Each member distributes their points to the alternatives they would most like to discuss. If each team member has 10 points, they may give 5 points to Alternative A, 3 points to Alternative C, and 2 points to Alternative F. The alternatives that receive few or no points will be cut before the discussion begins.
T-chart	A visual representation of the pros and cons of each alternative. Team members draw a T, large enough for everyone to view easily. One side of the T is labeled "Pros," and the other side is labeled "Cons." The team then brainstorms the pros and cons of the alternative in question, recording their comments on the chart. The pros and cons are rated in accordance with the criteria.
Decision matrix	A decision matrix is similar to a T-chart. It is a visual representation of the merits of various plans. It allows team members to compare alternatives easily. The merits are rated in accordance with the criteria.

- If this type of critical evaluation is not occurring naturally, one or more team members should be assigned to the role of devil's advocate. The devil's advocate has the task of making sure dissenting points of view are discussed. The questions provided in Tools for Professional Excellence 7.4 can help guide the team through this evaluation process.

Deciding on the Solution

Once the merit of all the solutions has been thoroughly evaluated and discussed, it's time to make a decision. This decision will become the goal or desired state that the team will then work toward. Four approaches to decision making are available to the team. These approaches include decision by the leader, voting, compromise, and consensus.

Decision by the Leader

When the decision by the leader approach is used, members are not truly functioning as a team. The role of the members is to recommend or advise the leader. The leader then makes the ultimate decision. As a result, the goal is not mutually defined. In some instances, this approach may be the best way to make a decision. For example, if an emergency room team needs to make a quick decision about an unfamiliar medical situation, the physician in charge may ask the advice of colleagues and/or medical staff. Yet, due to the need for a quick decision, the physician will ultimately determine the course of action. Although this approach has benefits in pressure situations, it's not the preferred approach for building teams.

Team communication is the foundation of negotiation and problem solving seen across industries.

iStockphoto/Rawpixel

Voting

The concept of voting is another way to reach a decision. With this approach, team members cast a vote for the solution they find most meritorious. The solution that receives the most votes is implemented. There are some obvious advantages to voting. First, all team members have equal input in the decision. Next, it is an easy process that often requires little more than raised hands or slips of paper for casting votes. Finally, it requires little time in comparison with the compromise or consensus approaches. However, voting as a decision-making approach also comes with some disadvantages. Because it is quick and easy, voting is often used to speed up the decision-making process and avoid any lengthy discussions or conflict. Conflict, as we discuss later in this chapter, is a valuable, needed resource in innovative problem solving and team building. Limiting this process can result in quick decisions that lack innovation and cause division. Voting is a win–lose approach to decision making. Unfortunately, not everyone makes a good loser—or a good winner, for that matter—so voting can divide the group and stop it from becoming a team.

Compromise

Team members approaching decision-making with a "let's compromise" attitude is a positive thing, right? After all, compromise is a win–win approach, isn't it? Actually, compromise is a lose–lose approach to decision making. Although it is a commonly held belief that compromise is a good thing, compromise can limit innovation. With compromise, all parties are willing to give up something in order to gain something they want; so the goal becomes narrowing options, not developing innovative ideas. Jake and Marilyn used the compromise approach on their last date. Jake wanted to eat ribs and see an action movie. Marilyn wanted sushi and a romantic comedy. So they compromised and spent their evening eating ribs, which made Marilyn miserable, and watching a movie that Jake hated. Both parties were unhappy for half the evening; it was a lose–lose situation. If they had searched for some additional options, they would have discovered that pizza and bowling would have made them both happy for the entire evening.

TABLE 7.5 ■ Tools for Professional Excellence. Questions to Guide the Evaluation
To help guide a team through the evaluation process, consider these questions:
● Do we have enough information?
● Do we understand the information we have?
● Are we missing any information? Are any areas not covered by the information we have?
● Are our sources reliable, credible, and appropriate?
● Are the criteria appropriate given our objectives and constraints?
● Did we generate a variety of innovative alternatives?
● Did we limit our alternatives?
● Did we apply the criteria to each alternative fairly and appropriately?
● Did the team agree on the mode of decision making?

Source: Gouran (1982/1990).

Consensus

The final approach to decision making is consensus. Consensus occurs when a solution or agreement that all team members can support is reached. This does not mean that the final solution is one that all team members prefer; rather, it means that the solution has the support of all team members. In an ideal world, team members might be able to come up with an idea that everyone loves and thinks is the best way to go, but most times, that doesn't occur. Thus, finding a solution that everyone supports has many positive benefits. This support results in a stronger commitment to implementing the solution and strengthens the relationship between team members. Further, working through the consensus process lends itself to innovative decision-making.

So why aren't all decisions made using consensus? Because consensus is time consuming. Many leaders or groups do not see the value in spending time working through the consensus process. Although consensus is more time consuming as a decision-making approach, decisions reached using consensus can often be implemented quickly because they have the support of all members. As a result, consensus may be less time consuming than voting or compromise, especially when the process is looked at from beginning to end (see Table 7.6). It certainly is the most likely to result in mutually defined goals.

TABLE 7.6 ■ Tools for Professional Excellence. Implementing Your Solution
To create a clear plan for implementation, take note of the following points:
● State the objective clearly and concisely.
● List the major steps that must be completed in order to accomplish the objective.

- Prioritize the steps. What are the most critical elements? Which are less critical? What can you do now? What will you need additional resources for?

- Under each major step, list all the tasks (substeps) that must be completed in order to accomplish the step in question.

- Place all the steps and tasks on a timeline. Focus on the sequence in which steps and tasks must be completed. Adjust the timeline accordingly.

- Estimate the cost of each step and begin to develop a budget. Revisit the budget often.

- Assign a lead for each step. Multiple leads may be needed for some steps—different leads for different tasks.

- Anticipate obstacles. What obstacles stand in the way of success? How will your team deal with these obstacles?

Planning How to Implement the Solution

Once the solution is reached, it must be implemented. Walking away from the table with a great solution is not a success if that solution never comes to fruition. Teams make certain their solutions are implemented by developing a thorough, detailed plan. When implementing a solution, all facets of the implementation must be accounted for in both a timeline and a budget. In addition, a   —the person who's accountable for a given task—must be designated. Designating leads is an excellent opportunity to share leadership. The team member with the leadership title should not be the lead in all facets of the implementation plan. Rather, leads should be selected based on their areas of expertise and their passion for various parts of the plan. To ensure a thorough plan, your team should address all of the suggestions found in Tools for Professional Excellence 7.5.

CULTIVATING INNOVATIVE THINKING

Whereas groups conduct problem-solving meetings with little thought of innovative solutions, teams structure their meetings and facilitate the problem-solving process in such a way that innovation is stimulated. After all, teams, by their very definition, must foster innovative thinking.

One way to foster innovation in team problem solving is to incorporate Von Oech's (1986) explorer, artist, judge, and warrior into the process. Incorporating Von Oech's cast of characters doesn't require team members to dress up in costumes and run around acting like explorers or warriors. Rather, the skills and tools displayed by explorers, artists, judges, and warriors are meant to highlight or reinforce the skills and tools essential to creative problem solving. Let's examine each character to better understand its role in cultivating innovative thinking.

Explorer

When analyzing a problem and preparing to generate solutions, team members should act as explorers. Explorers seek out new information in uncharted lands. As explorers, team members follow their curiosity, create a map, leave their own turf, and look for a lot of ideas and information (Von Oech, 1986). Research is the central skill used during this phase of the creative process. A team in the explorer mode might ask, "What's the problem?" or "Why aren't we the leader in sales?" or "How can we do it better?" Then, team members are given the task and the time to seek new information that addresses the question(s). This task turns into a map of sorts, as it provides team members with a general guideline to follow when searching. The interesting thing is, once this map is in your mind, you will begin to see relevant information everywhere. If you have your doubts, think about the last time you purchased a car—did you suddenly start seeing similar cars (color and type) everywhere you went? Were they there before? Of course they were, but they were not on your map, so they blended into the background scenery.

As long as you have your map, leaving your turf can become a rewarding adventure. For example, the famous football coach Knute Rockne discovered his "four horsemen defense" while watching a chorus-line dance, and Picasso's art was the inspiration for World War I military camouflage (Von Oech, 1986). Looking both inside and outside your field and your type of business or industry for information and insight is what will make your team innovative. In fact, one distinct advantage of team members with diverse backgrounds is that they bring different perspectives into the team. Put simply, send the team members out to explore and make certain they come back with lots of information that can be molded into innovative solutions during the artist phase.

Artist

As the team begins to generate solutions, members move from the role of explorer to the role of artist. The   puts ideas together in new ways. When you hear the word *artist*, what images come to mind? Do you see a painter, a sculptor, or someone who's handy with a hot-glue gun? That's certainly one way to look at an artist, but in reality an artist includes those images and so many more. Someone who puts ideas together in a new way is an artist. You may not be able to paint or sing, but if you can develop a chart or a schedule, you, too, are an artist. Earlier in this chapter, we discussed some tools useful to the artist (see Tools for Professional Excellence 7.2). Three additional tools your team can utilize to enhance the artist are asking "what if" questions, connecting concepts, and incubating (Von Oech, 1986).

Two small words—*what if*—are essential to finding innovative solutions. For example, a team of hospital administrators was determined to improve patient satisfaction scores. During the explorer phase, they examined successful hospitals and medical arenas for information. In addition, they left their turf and explored other places where people stay overnight, such as hotels. In the artist phase, they asked themselves "what if" questions, such as "What if we were a five-star hotel?" By connecting hotels and hospitals, they gained a new perspective on the problem. They began to offer free valet parking at the emergency room, and they added a staff position—patient and family liaison—that functioned much like a concierge in a hotel. Not surprisingly, patient satisfaction scores increased.

Just as explorers need time to explore, artists need time to incubate. When do you have your most inspired ideas? Is it during a meeting within moments after a problem has been thrown on the table? Or does your inspiration come to you in the shower or after a good night's sleep? Maybe your creative ideas come when you're on the treadmill, sweating away your stress or streaming music on your phone. Truth be told, we have yet to meet a single person who can achieve creative inspiration on command. We certainly can't. If you want innovative solutions, your team needs time to explore resources and discover information. Then team members need time to allow that information to germinate in their minds and grow into something that is more than just okay or so-so.

Judge

Once a team has developed lots of innovative ideas, it moves into the judge mode as team members evaluate the possible solutions and then select one solution for implementation. Judges begin with the question, "Are we meeting our objective?" Then, they systematically examine the positives and negatives of each solution and render their decision (Von Oech, 1986).

Warrior

Innovative problem solving does not end with the judge mode. Warriors are needed to make certain that the plan is implemented successfully. The role of the warrior is to develop and carry out the plan. We have already discussed how to develop a thorough plan and the importance of leads who will act as warriors overseeing or carrying out various parts of the plan. Yet warriors must do more than that. Ask yourself, "Why did Von Oech select a warrior to represent the skills needed in this phase of innovative problem solving?" First, all plans will hit obstacles and roadblocks. As a result, team members must be strong and ready to overcome inevitable difficulties. Furthermore, innovative ideas are more likely to be criticized and attacked because they are different. When your team moves forward with a plan that is outside the box, others may want to stuff it back in the box. Therefore, team members must act like warriors, carrying out the plan with persistence (see Figure 7.2).

FIGURE 7.2 ■ Quotations for Warriors

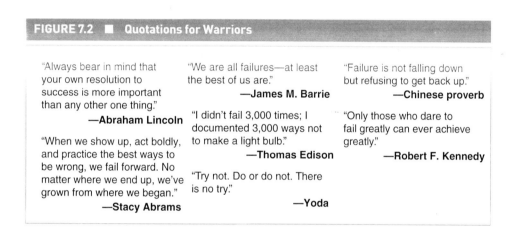

"Always bear in mind that your own resolution to success is more important than any other one thing."
—**Abraham Lincoln**

"When we show up, act boldly, and practice the best ways to be wrong, we fail forward. No matter where we end up, we've grown from where we began."
—**Stacy Abrams**

"We are all failures—at least the best of us are."
—**James M. Barrie**

"I didn't fail 3,000 times; I documented 3,000 ways not to make a light bulb."
—**Thomas Edison**

"Try not. Do or do not. There is no try."
—**Yoda**

"Failure is not falling down but refusing to get back up."
—**Chinese proverb**

"Only those who dare to fail greatly can ever achieve greatly."
—**Robert F. Kennedy**

Supporting Each Role

As you reviewed the skills and qualities of each role, you may have noticed that you are stronger in some roles than in others (this is normal). Some of us are natural artists, while others are outstanding warriors. The benefit of working in a team is that you don't have to be strong in every area to ensure innovative solutions. To ensure innovation, teams must have at least one member who is strong in each area and share leadership to maximize those strengths. In addition, meetings should be structured to support each phase of the innovative problem-solving process. For example, begin exploring the problem at your first meeting. Then send every member of the team out to explore the problem further and collect information that might aid in finding solutions. Dedicate at least one meeting, more if time allows, to the artist. Allow team members time to brainstorm, ask "what if" questions, and so on. Develop criteria and a clear process for assessing solutions during the judge phase. And finally, as a warrior, develop a clear plan and work as a team to overcome roadblocks, obstacles, and setbacks. Being innovative is not easy, but it's a central component to functioning as a team and achieving professional excellence. In the 21st century, innovation is no longer an option; it's a necessity.

TABLE 7.7 ■ Action Items. Skills for Teamwork		
Skill	**Strategy**	**Application**
Listening	Ensure that all team members have a fair say in the decision-making process.	Offer every team member a five-minute opportunity to list their ideas, expectations, and concerns at the end of every meeting.
Helping	If team members are having difficulties with their responsibilities, make sure the team is equipped to help them.	Set aside at least one team meeting during which the only goal is to help other team members in areas where they are struggling.
Participating	Be an active listener and doer in all phases of the team exercise or project.	Create benchmarks for yourself to reach before each team meeting.

CONFLICT IN TEAM MEETINGS

When was the last time you thought to yourself, "I have a meeting today. I hope it's full of conflict"? Chances are you've never had those thoughts. In fact, you may have thought the exact opposite on occasion: "I hope my meeting today has no conflict." Believe it or not, lack of conflict isn't a good thing. Lack of conflict is a strong sign that your group has some serious problems, will not develop innovative ideas, and will never reach "team" status. The whole purpose for having meetings is to get different people together to share a variety of ideas and develop innovative solutions to problems. If this is to occur, then conflict must occur, too.

The problem for most of us is that the word *conflict* has a negative connotation. So let's use a different word. If you replace the word *conflict* with something such as *discussion* or *sharing of ideas*, then the phrase sounds more appealing: "I hope my meeting today is full of discussion and sharing of ideas." To better understand the need for conflict in meetings and strategies for facilitating productive conflict, let's explore each area in more detail.

Some people are difficult to work with and play the role of the shouter—especially when they have emotional outbursts and bully other people in meetings.

iStockphoto/skynesher

Need for Conflict

As groups develop into teams, some naïve leaders think that a positive by-product of this transformation will be a lack of conflict. Nothing could be further from the truth. If you're part of a group that is not experiencing conflict, chances are you're part of either a groupthink or a meetingthink situation.

Groupthink

Groupthink is the tendency of highly cohesive groups to suspend critical thinking and make faulty decisions (Janis, 1982, 1989; Shirey, 2012). You may recall from history class that in 1961, President John F. Kennedy supported a group of Cuban exiles who returned to Cuba in an attempt to overthrow the communist government headed by Fidel Castro. Instead of claiming a quick and easy victory as Kennedy and his advisers had planned, the mission failed. The scholar Irving Janis studied the incident, known as the Bay of Pigs, and concluded that the defeat was a result of groupthink.

Causes of Groupthink.   For groupthink to occur, several conditions must exist. First, the group must be highly cohesive. Not all highly cohesive groups suffer from groupthink; however, if highly cohesive groups are combined with other elements, the chances of groupthink increase. For example, groupthink is more likely to occur if the group functions in isolation, is very homogeneous, lacks norms for critically analyzing information, or is dealing with high-stress threats. In addition, these groups are often headed by a charismatic, directive leader. Because of the strong desire to maintain the cohesiveness with leader and group, group members begin to self-censor. No one in the group wants to be the voice of dissent, so members remain silent even though they have doubts or concerns. If a group member does voice disagreement, "mind guards" jump in and silence the dissent until the dissenting member begins self-censoring. (Just as bodyguards protect the group from physical harm, mind guards protect the group from conflict and dissention.) Since these groups often function in isolation, they do not receive feedback from the outside. In the end, it appears as if everyone agrees, assumptions go unchallenged, and faulty decisions are made.

Avoiding Groupthink.   The way to avoid groupthink is to introduce conflict systematically. Norms should be developed for seeking additional information, testing assumptions, and incorporating the role of devil's advocate. Having the larger group divide into subgroups when brainstorming or having the leader withhold thoughts are additional strategies used to reduce groupthink.

Meetingthink

As consultants, we have seen the by-product of groupthink occur in many different organizations—not groupthink itself but the *by-product* of groupthink, which is the suspension of critical thinking that results in faulty decisions. The groups we have observed are not highly cohesive, don't have charismatic leaders, and don't function in isolation. Yet their members still make faulty decisions due to a lack of critical thinking. We refer to this phenomenon as meetingthink. Meetingthink has the same outcome as groupthink, but it doesn't require the same inputs. It's the suspension of critical thinking due to more common variables, such as false empowerment, overload, or poorly run meetings.

False Empowerment.   False empowerment occurs when a leader acts as if they plan to involve the group in the decision-making process when, in reality, the leader is going to make the decision regardless of the input received from the group. At first, group members believe they are empowered to make a decision, but in the end this proves to be false. Over time, group members learn that their opinions, ideas, and thoughts are not valued, so they remain silent during meetings. As a result, critical thinking is suspended.

Overload.   Overload occurs when group members have so much on their plates that they cannot truly concentrate on and engage in the meeting at hand. While the meeting is occurring, group members are thinking about the 10 other items they have to do that day at work, as well as the list of things they must take care of when they leave work. Being overloaded may also cause members to come to meetings without preparing. For example, if members fail to read a report in advance of a meeting, they may be unable to take part in the discussion. Overloaded group members also withhold valuable input because they fear it will somehow lead to more work. They are afraid the boss will say, for instance, "Great idea, Susan. I'd like you to head up a committee examining that issue and report back in two weeks."

Poorly Run Meetings.   Poorly run meetings are a third contributor to the meetingthink problem. The next time you are at a meeting, look around the room. How many people appear to be engaged and listening? How many people's eyes are glazed over, or how many are sleeping with their eyes open, doodling, or looking out the window? If the majority of the group is not engaged, chances are the meeting is being poorly run. Poorly run meetings can be the result of some or all of the factors we discussed earlier. The meeting may be disorganized due to a lack of an agenda. It may be too long or include too many topics. The meeting may include the wrong participants. Overtalkers may be dominating the meeting. The leader may be doing all the talking and failing to do any facilitating. Regardless of the reason, poorly run meetings result in group members disengaging, which results in poor decision-making.

Avoiding Meetingthink.   What can you do about it? How can you avoid this in your own groups? First, make it a practice to follow the suggestions discussed earlier in this chapter. Consider the meeting environment. Always evaluate the meeting topics and use an agenda. When planning the meeting, ask yourself the following questions: Is this topic relevant to the participants? (If you are not positive, ask them.) Am I being respectful of my team's time? If you have a meeting scheduled but some of the key participants can't make it, cancel the meeting. Similarly, if you have a standing meeting scheduled but there are no agenda items, cancel it. Your team members will be more engaged in the meetings they do attend if you respect their time. Finally, if you have the leadership title, facilitate the discussion. Make certain all the functional roles are present. If they're not, bring it to the attention of the team.

What if you're not the leader of the meeting in question? What can you do to avoid meetingthink? On a personal level, challenge yourself to be fully prepared and engaged in every meeting you attend. Avoid becoming overloaded by actively managing the number of meetings you attend. If you are invited to participate in a meeting, ask the leader why you were selected to participate. What role do they want you to play? If you will play a valuable role, attend the meeting. If you were invited out of courtesy, decline to attend. Similarly, ask if you are the person who needs to attend or if a representative from your team is needed. If a representative is needed, look within your team for support. There may be equally qualified members of your team who could go in your place. What may have been a burden to you might well be an exciting opportunity for another member of your team.

Whether group members are suffering from groupthink or meetingthink, the results are the same—critical thinking is suspended, and faulty decisions occur. By design, groups and teams should have conflict. The trick is to make sure the conflict is positive and productive.

People have many competing priorities that may distract them from fully paying attention during a meeting, especially if they are working from home. Lack of engagement can lead to meetingthink, so remember to stay engaged and to do your best to avoid distractions.

iStockphoto/Chaay_Tee

Productive Conflict

By now, you may be convinced that conflict is a necessary part of teams, but you still may not be excited about the idea of engaging in conflict, especially if you've experienced negative, counter-productive conflict in the past. Achieving professional excellence in teams involves the utilization of positive, productive conflict as a valuable resource.

Stages of Team Development

Conflict is present in three of the five stages that make up team development (Posthuma, 2012; Tuckman & Jensen, 1977). The five stages of team development include forming, storming, norming, performing, and adjourning. During the *forming stage*, group members tend to be polite and impersonal as they test the waters. Conflict appears in the second stage, known as storming. During the *storming stage*, members engage in infighting and often clash with the leader. In the *norming stage*, the group develops procedures for organizing, giving feedback, and confronting issues. In the *performing stage*, the members carry out the duties of the group. In the final stage, *adjourning*, the group completes its work, resolves issues, and comes to a close. This is not a linear process. Group members don't march neatly from stage to stage. It's normal for groups to revisit stages and circle through the process repeatedly. The point here is that groups encounter conflict in the storming, norming, and performing stages of development. If a group is going to become a team, it will encounter conflict in the storming stage, develop productive ways to handle conflict in the norming stage, and utilize the kind of innovative thinking in the performing stage that can come only through productive discussion or conflict.

Handling Conflict

To achieve professional excellence, you must determine the best way to handle conflict so that it's both positive and productive. Every time you are faced with a conflict, you must select one of three modes of conflict resolution: flight, fight, or unite. Let's take a look at each.

Flight occurs when you choose not to engage or deal with a conflict. There are times when this is the appropriate strategy. Some issues are not worth the time or the energy. However, if there is a problem that must be solved or a behavior that must be changed, flight is not the appropriate response, and avoidance only makes the problem worse.

Fight is another alternative for handling conflict. Using the fight approach will require you to engage in some type of confrontation. This approach is also known as a win–lose approach to problem solving. Both parties face off as opponents, and one party will come out the winner, while the other party will come out the loser. Clearly, this approach can have some negative consequences. In fact, the losing party often holds a grudge, which can damage relationships in the long run. However, there are times when an issue is important enough to warrant the fight approach. If handled properly, even conflicts that are solved using the fight approach can be positive.

The Unite Approach

The third mode for conflict resolution is the   approach, which requires team members to move away from stating positions to exploring interests (R. Fisher et al., 1991; Hackman, 2012). The unite approach defines team members as joint problem solvers rather than as adversaries. Instead of approaching the conflict as team member against team member, it becomes the team united against the problem. A position is a demand that includes each person's solution to the problem. Under the unite approach, team members look beneath the surface of each position to see all the interests. Interests are the needs and concerns underlying each position.

An example of two competing positions might be "The wait staff should only wait tables and not do side jobs such as filling ketchup bottles or rolling silverware in napkins" and "The wait staff must wait on tables and do side jobs." There are only two positions, but under each position are many interests. For example, under the wait staff position are interests (needs and concerns) such as *I want to be a good employee. I like working here. I want to do a good job. I want to be a team player. I do need to have the ketchup filled and silverware rolled. I do not have time to do side jobs and properly serve my customers. I want to earn the most tips possible. Not all the wait staff take turns with the side jobs. Hostesses and busboys do not do side jobs. I am paid only $2 an hour, while hostesses and busboys are paid $6 per hour.* Under the manager position are some similar needs and concerns: *My wait staff are excellent servers. I want to retain this wait staff. I want my wait staff to get the most tips possible. I want the customers to have an excellent dining experience. The side jobs must be done. Traditionally, wait staff do the side jobs. I want the entire staff to function as a team.*

When the team members look beyond the positions and focus on the interests, they are able to identify interests they share and establish common ground for joint problem solving. Instead of arguing positions, the team can look for solutions that support the interests or common ground members share.

Raise the Issue

For this approach to work, it's critical for the opening communication to reflect the unite attitude. According to R. Fisher et al. (1991), you should begin by preparing to raise the issue. Preparation includes many of the elements we have already discussed, such as considering the meeting environment, meeting participants, and meeting topic. Because this process can take some time, be certain to schedule the meeting at a time when participants are not rushed (X. Chen et al., 2012).

Begin the meeting by stating the issue concisely and in a neutral tone. Focus on behaviors and facts, not opinions. For example, you would not want to begin by saying, "Clearly, the wait staff think they're too good to take care of the side jobs, and it's causing us to lose business. Do I have to fire someone in order to get this problem resolved, or do you have a better idea?" Rather, begin with something such as "Recently, there has been a shortage of rolled silverware and filled condiments during peak serving times." The latter statement is concise with a neutral tone.

When stating the problem, be as brief as possible. As illustrated in the example above, you should keep it to a sentence or two. Leaders have a tendency to state the problem and the solution without allowing others to talk—this will shut down the entire communication process.

Invite Cooperation

Once the problem is stated, invite cooperation (R. Fisher et al., 1991; Kress & Schar, 2012). For example, you might say, "How can we solve this problem together?" By listening, you and the other team members will gain a better understanding of everyone's perceptions of the issue.

If your team is not familiar with this approach, you may need to guide team members through the process. Prior to addressing any issues, talk to the team about the benefits of using the unite approach. Have the team members imagine themselves on one side of the table, united against whatever issue or problem arises. Emphasize that the unite approach requires effective listening and participation from all team members. To develop listening and participating as a norm, incorporate the round robin technique. After you've raised the issue and invited cooperation, go around the circle and allow everyone to share their perceptions of the issue. The round robin technique requires members to listen and not interrupt while other team members are speaking. Team members may ask one another clarification questions to improve understanding, but they can't argue for or against positions. As the team members discuss their perceptions of the issue, the underlying interests will become clearer. Only then can the team begin generating options and select the best solution(s). (As you think about the best communication choices related to meetings, review Tools for Professional Excellence 7.6 for a list of tips focused on preparing for virtual meetings.)

TABLE 7.8 ■ **Tools for Professional Excellence.** Conducting Effective Virtual Meetings

To prepare for a virtual meeting, follow these practical tips:	
Key Points	**Practical Tips**
Prepare for the meeting.	● Be upfront when preparing for the meeting: Send out the agenda ahead of time, along with any visual or supporting material, to make sure everyone is on the same page.
	● Decide on what technologies and software are most appropriate for the setting of the meeting, as well as for those involved.
	● Make sure all technologies, software, and other electronic materials for the meeting are functioning, and have backup plans in place in case of any issues or malfunctions.

(Continued)

TABLE 7.9 ■ Tools for Professional Excellence (*Continued*)	
To prepare for a virtual meeting, follow these practical tips:	
Key Points	**Practical Tips**
Plan for technology tools and requirements.	● When it comes to technology, think small: Use only the tools that are needed, so as to avoid any potential problems or embarrassment. ● Be knowledgeable of all tools that are being used, so that you know how to troubleshoot any issues that arise.
Stay focused.	● Encourage attendees to check into the meeting from a quiet, distraction-free environment. ● If outside noise becomes an issue, ask attendees to make sure their microphones are muted if they are not speaking. Chat boxes or other text-based tools can also be used to help conduct the meeting. ● Don't try and squeeze everything into one meeting: Spread points across multiple smaller meetings to keep attendees comfortable and able to focus. ● Whether directing or attending the meeting, avoid wearing clothing or accessories that can be visually distracting on camera, such as bright colors or shiny jewelry.
Use good meeting etiquette.	● Be courteous and respectful of other meeting attendees, just like you would in any face-to-face meeting. ● Speak clearly and concisely, and avoid shouting. ● Keep body movements to a minimum, to prevent the video quality from deteriorating. ● Avoid interacting with people or objects on the side, as this may distract other attendees.
Engage participants.	● Break the ice by asking each attendee to introduce and share something interesting about themselves. ● Always ask for audience input when posing a question or proposing an idea, which helps to stimulate group discussion. ● Do anything you can think of to simulate face-to-face meetings and keep attendees attentive and engaged.

Source: Thomas, F. (2010, December 20). 5 Tips for Conducting a Virtual Meeting. *Inc.* Retrieved and adapted from www.inc.com/guides/2010/12/5-tips-for-conducting- a-virtual-meeting.html

KEYS TO EXCELLENCE IN TEAM COMMUNICATION

Refer back to the discussion of Gregg Popovich's approach to teamwork, at the beginning of this chapter. When thinking about how you interact with others in a team setting, be aware of the KEYS process to improve your communication. During the first step, *know yourself,* do a self-inventory of how you have interacted with others in the past and how your team members reacted to your communication. Did they react positively or negatively to the way you communicated with them? Understanding different workplace cultures is critical to avoid offending the people you work with.

The second step, *evaluate the professional context,* requires you to identify what is considered professional communication and what is not. What types of jokes are tolerated in your working environment? Is cursing frowned upon or ignored? What behavior is considered acceptable when venting your frustrations to your coworkers? Try to make sure that your team communication fits the culture of your workplace.

The third step, *your communication interaction*, requires you to be critical of your communication while talking with your team members. Be sensitive to others' nonverbal cues, and try to notice when somebody feels threatened or offended by your communication. Take what you have learned from evaluating your professional context to craft a message that can be well received by your coworkers.

The final strategy, *step back and reflect*, involves taking a reflexive inventory of your communication with other team members. Both verbally and nonverbally, how did your coworkers react to what you said? Was your body language offensive or threatening, or did you choose a more amiable approach in your communication? Continually be aware of how others react to your communication, and make the proper changes to your approach when necessary.

EVALUATE THE PROFESSIONAL CONTEXT

Winter Carnival in Snowy Mountain

As you evaluate the passage below, consider whether this behavior is appropriate for this professional context.

The Snowy Mountain Tourist Department was tasked with developing new promotional events to attract skiers during the upcoming season. Over the years, this resort community had been steadily losing business to other ski destinations. Sasha Adams, the department manager, was willing to admit that her ideas were just not competitive, so she turned the task over to her department.

Sasha was thrilled to learn that her department generated three creative ideas. The problem was that supporters of each idea felt very strongly that their idea was the best, and they could not narrow it down to one event. Sasha honored her commitment to allow the group to make the decision, so she had department members vote. Three votes went to a winter comedy festival, three votes went to a winter sports event, and four votes went to a winter carnival.

Sasha had high hopes that the winter carnival would increase tourism, but it decreased department morale instead. The four members who had voted for the carnival were very involved, but more than four people were needed to run the event. In the end, it was not a success. The other six members felt that their events would have achieved much better results. Were they right?

Questions to Consider

1. What went wrong?
2. Was voting the best way to make this decision? Why or why not?
3. How would you have handled the decision-making process?
4. Could the KEYS approach have helped Sasha? If so, in what way?

Think of a group or team to which you belong. How does that group or team make decisions and handle conflict? Are your decisions innovative? Are your conflicts productive? Based on what you have learned, could you improve the communication in your group or team?

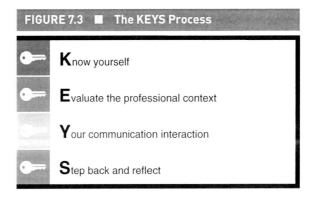

FIGURE 7.3 ■ The KEYS Process

Know yourself

Evaluate the professional context

Your communication interaction

Step back and reflect

EXECUTIVE SUMMARY

Now that you have finished reading this chapter, you should be able to

Distinguish between a group and a team:

- A group is defined as three or more individuals who are working toward a common goal or share a common purpose.

- A team is defined as a group in which members share leadership responsibility for creating a team identity, achieving mutually defined goals, and fostering innovative thinking.

Explain the impact of the environment, the topic(s), and the participants on communication when conducting meetings:

- Location is an important component in creating a positive meeting environment. In fact, you should consider the convenience, aesthetics, and comfort of the location.

- An agenda is a useful channel for informing team members about meeting topics; if used properly, an agenda can serve as a communication tool for facilitating meetings.

- Leaders with professional excellence avoid the trap of inviting a representative of each department just to be politically correct. Invite people who can contribute to the purpose of the meeting. Take time to assess the meeting's purpose, and then determine who can best serve that purpose.

Describe the concept of shared leadership and how it relates to the roles and norms displayed by a group or team:

- Designated leaders should think of themselves as coaches.

- Within every team, members can play a host of possible roles. Some of these roles are functional roles that help the team achieve goals or maintain positive relationships among members. These roles are known as task roles and relationship roles.

- A norm is an unwritten rule of behavior. All groups have both positive and negative norms. The important thing is to step back and reflect on the norms and assess how various norms are affecting your group.

Discuss the concepts involved in effective problem solving:

- Problem solving involves not only making a choice but also coming up with quality alternatives from which to select and then working to implement the choice your team selects.

- Remember John Dewey's Reflective Thinking Process. According to Dewey (1910), five steps make up problem-solving. These steps include describing and analyzing the problem, generating possible solutions, evaluating all solutions, deciding on the solution, and planning how to implement the solution.

Describe ways to foster innovative thinking in a team context:

- One way to foster innovation in team problem-solving is to incorporate Von Oech's (1986) explorer, artist, judge, and warrior into the process.

Discuss the need for conflict and the strategies for productive conflict:

- Lack of conflict is a strong sign that your group has some serious problems, will not develop innovative ideas, and will never reach "team" status. The whole purpose for having meetings is to get different people together to share a variety of ideas and develop innovative solutions to problems. If this is to occur, then conflict must also occur.

- To achieve professional excellence, you must determine the best way to handle conflict so that it's both positive and productive. Every time you are faced with a conflict, you must select one of three modes of conflict resolution: flight, fight, or unite.

- To develop listening and participating as a norm, incorporate the round robin technique. After you've raised the issue and invited cooperation, go around the circle and allow everyone to share their perceptions of the issue.

Apply the KEYS process to professional excellence as you develop your groups into teams:

- Know yourself. Be aware of the strengths and weaknesses you bring to the group or team.

- Evaluate the professional context. Know your workplace culture and the personalities of other people in your group or team. This will enable you to foster a positive group interaction.

- Your communication interaction. Develop an agenda and send it to the group a week before the meeting, giving everyone time to acquaint themselves with it.

- Step back and reflect. Listen to the input from your peers to better understand what is important to the group and the company as a whole.

EXPLORE

1. Find an example of a team-building exercise from your previous school or work experience. Did you find the exercise beneficial or effective? Write a brief response weighing positive and negative consequences from your experience.

2. Watch a video detailing some type of team-building function (e.g., military boot camp, exercise classes, athletics). Attempt to identify the purpose of the team-building exercise, as well as why it is important in the given context. Offer another example of how the same exercise could be used in a different setting.

3. Form several small teams within your classroom with the goal of reaching a shared objective (e.g., solving a math problem, puzzle, logic riddle, or anything else applicable). Have the teams try to complete the project while keeping track of who finished the fastest while also solving the problem. Have the team members offer reasons as to why their team-building exercise was successful.

REVIEW

1. Define a *team*.

2. A(n) _____ is a guide or an overview of the topics that will be covered during the meeting.

3. A(n) _____ is an unwritten rule of behavior.

4. Explain the difference between task roles and relationship roles.

5. _____ is the act of choosing among a set of alternatives under conditions that necessitate choice.

6. Identify the steps in John Dewey's Reflective Thinking Process.

7. _____ are the standards used to make a decision.

8. _____ is the tendency among members of highly cohesive groups to self-censor, suspend critical thinking, and make faulty decisions.

DISCUSSION QUESTIONS

1. Think about the last project you worked on with others. Would you define that as a group or a team experience? Why would you use that label?

2. Step back and reflect on some meetings in which you have participated. How did the environment, topics, and participants contribute to the communication in those meetings?

3. During meetings, do you share in the leadership? What roles do you play? When you have a designated leadership title, do you act as a coach? What norms do you use to help facilitate effective communication and shared leadership?

4. When it comes to innovative problem solving, in which role (explorer, artist, judge, or warrior) do you excel, and which role must you work to develop?

5. How do you handle conflict? Have you ever tried a unite approach? Why or why not?

ETHICAL CONNECTION

Overtalking vs. Undertalking

As you read this passage and answer the questions, consider how the way you communicate has an ethical dimension.

Team leaders can also use an agenda as a tool for facilitating communication during meetings. Let's say one member of your team, Anna, tends to dominate conversations, occasionally leading the discussion on irrelevant tangents. Anna is an overtalker. Another member of your team, Zach, tends to sit silently during meetings, failing to participate or give input. Zach is an undertalker. The few times Zach has tried to communicate during meetings, he is cut off by Anna, who often moves the conversation in a different direction. During several of your one-on-one sessions with Zach, you have noticed that he is very insightful and has many great ideas to help out the company. Although Anna is motivated and eager to participate in meetings, you notice she has a hard time focusing on one topic at a time. To keep your meetings moving effectively and professionally, you must find a way to curtail Anna's speeches while not cutting her off entirely. Also, you need to encourage Zach to interact more and to have the confidence to state his ideas to the entire staff.

Questions to Consider

1. What are the ethical issues with allowing one person to dominate or one person not to participate in a team or staff meeting?

2. How could you limit Anna's speaking without making her feel as though she is being cut off?

3. What methods or communication could you use to encourage Zach to be more active in team meetings?

4. Using the KEYS approach, how could both Anna and Zach strengthen their team communication skills?

YOUR COMMUNICATION INTERACTION

The Fundraiser

As you read the passage below, consider what would be a more effective communication strategy in this situation.

Henry is the chair of his organization's fundraising committee, and the organization's big annual fundraiser is quickly approaching. There are only a couple of meetings left before the fundraiser, and Henry and the rest of the committee are feeling the pressure to pull off another successful event. Tensions are high among the committee members, which leads to an argument between two members, Tim and Angela. During the meeting, every time Angela brings up which band to hire for the fundraiser, Tim interrupts her to talk about picking up more sponsors. After the third time, Angela snaps at Tim, demanding to know why he keeps interrupting her. Tim says that they are running out of time and that there are more important topics to discuss than what band to hire. Angela looks to Henry for support, but he stays silent. Feeling embarrassed, Angela storms out of the meeting, leaving awkward silence behind her. Henry decides to call the meeting then and there, and stays behind to get more work done. Later that night, after having a few drinks, Henry calls Angela and leaves her a voicemail saying how much he values her as a committee member and as a person.

Questions to Consider

1. As the committee chair, what responsibility (if any) does Henry have when committee members begin to argue?
2. Do you think Henry reacted appropriately to Tim and Angela's argument? Why or why not?
3. Was Henry's response to Angela appropriate? Why or why not?
4. If you were Angela, how would you respond to Henry's voicemail?

TERMS TO REMEMBER

agenda (p. 162)

artist (p. 174)

coach (p. 164)

compromise (p. 171)

conflict (p. 176)

consensus (p. 172)

criteria (p. 169)

decision by the leader (p. 170)

decision making (p. 167)

devil's advocate (p. 170)

explorer (p. 173)

false empowerment (p. 177)

fight (p. 180)

flight (p. 180)

group (p. 157)

groupthink (p. 177)

interests (p. 180)

judge (p. 174)

lead (p. 173)

meeting environment (p. 159)

meetingthink (p. 177)

norm (p. 166)

overload (p. 178)

overtalker (p. 187)

position (p. 180)

problem-solving (p. 167)

Reflective Thinking Process (p. 167)

relationship roles (p. 164)

round robin technique (p. 181)

self-centered roles (p. 165)

stages of team development (p. 179)

task roles (p. 164)

team (p. 157)

undertalker (p. 187)

unite (p. 180)

voting (p. 171)

warrior (p. 175)

EXCELLING IN THE WORKPLACE

iStockphoto/Sundry Photography

8 TECHNOLOGY IN THE WORKPLACE

CHAPTER OBJECTIVES

After studying this chapter, you should be able to

8.1   Discuss the impact technology has on business and professional communication

8.2   Discuss how the drawbacks of technology can prevent you from excelling as a professional

8.3   Discuss key challenges related to technology and social media in the communication age

8.4   Explain how to use professional etiquette with technology

8.5   Apply the KEYS approach to achieve professional excellence regarding communication and technology

---

Adobe, a computer software company, was named the best large company to work for in 2021 according to an annual report by the company review website, Comparably. This report, which looked at over 70,000 companies, identified various key factors that contributed to Adobe's high employee satisfaction. Some of these factors included monthly companywide days off, 20 new paid days off per year, flexible work schedules, and an increase of its wellness reimbursement to $600 per year. According to Gloria Chen, Adobe's Chief People Officer, the company also prioritized building community and staying connected while working apart during the COVID-19 pandemic (Liu, 2021). With the help of technology at the workplace, communication is becoming more and more convenient. However, with the added convenience of instant communication and feedback, there are drawbacks as well. Nonverbal communication becomes even more difficult to analyze with the lack of nonverbal cues in computer-mediated communication (Ivy & Wahl, 2019; Wahl & Simmons, 2018). Although face-to-face computer technologies such as Zoom and Microsoft Teams are now widely used, the cues in these online communication interactions are still lacking in richness.

In this chapter, you will learn how people have attempted to compensate for the difficulties associated with emotional communication when using technology, as well as the potential drawbacks of using technology to communicate as a professional. After reading this chapter, you should have the tools needed to adapt in the ever-changing technological landscape.

Communicating excellence through technology is a necessary skill in today's workforce. Learning to communicate effectively while using technology is important for the following reasons: (1) The way you communicate when using technology influences the impressions other people have of you, which is central to achieving professional excellence; (2) communication and technology help you establish contact and maintain professional networks and relationships with coworkers, leaders, and clients; and (3) communication and technology can lead to a number of obstacles that can hinder professional excellence. Recall the important role that professional excellence played when you were *entering and developing in the workplace*. Put simply, the KEYS process will help bridge professional excellence with communication and technology and help you *excel in the workplace*.

Adobe is one of the largest software companies in the world, and professionals from all types of industries use its products (Photoshop, InDesign, Illustrator, Captivate, etc.).

Video conferencing technology enables greater participation in common professional tasks such as interviewing, planning, and negotiating.

iStockphoto/SDI Productions

COMMUNICATION AND TECHNOLOGY: TOOLS FOR PROFESSIONALS

When you communicate by using any form of technology, you are taking part in computer-mediated communication (CMC) (Diaz et al., 2012; Li, Jackson, & Trees, 2008; Walther et al., 2005). Your methods of communicating with clients, colleagues, and managers with technology must be thought out carefully.

Communication and technology have helped people to conduct business virtually instead of needing to communicate face to face (Couch & Liamputtong, 2008; Langan, 2012). No doubt, many of you are or will be members of a virtual work team—a group of coworkers who use CMC to accomplish tasks and professional projects traditionally completed face to face, in order to save on time and travel (Schiller & Mandviwalla, 2007; Staples & Webster, 2007; Watson-Manheim et al., 2012). When team members are located all around the country or the world, technology is an excellent tool to enhance communication. But if you use technology to avoid face-to-face communication with people in your office, technology can become a barrier to effective communication.

If you decide to use technology, how do you determine which communication channel works best for a given situation? Is email the best way to get a message out? Is an instant message over Slack the best way to make an urgent request? Is your smartphone the best device to use when participating in a phone or video conference or interview? Table 8.1 features the pros and cons of many common devices designed to help us stay connected and manage information as professionals. Review the table and think about your technology preferences.

Maintaining Professional Excellence Online

Social networking can be a wonderful tool for sharing information and maintaining professional connections. However, you should be especially mindful of the kinds of information about you that others can retrieve from the internet.

TABLE 8.1 ■ Selecting the Channel: Pros and Cons		
Channel	Pros	Cons
Desktop/network email	• Robust software provides a full range of features and functions • Provides lots of storage for your email messages • Provides offline access to your email; you don't have to be connected to an email provider to compose new messages or read replies • Provides timestamped and uneditable documentation of your communication	• Limited mobility: must use desktop/laptop computer or be signed in to network to access software
Web email	• Freedom of movement: don't have to be logged on to own computer to send and receive email • Provides timestamped and uneditable documentation of your communication	• Limited features and functions compared with desktop email software • No offline access to email • Access to attachments is limited to the computer or network you are using at the time
Instant messaging/ texting	• Instant give-and-take associated with phone chat: unlike standard email, which involves composing and sending messages and then waiting for replies, instant messaging takes place in real time	• Incompatibility issues between competing instant-messaging software providers • Lack of basic email features and functions available on most desktop or web email programs • Messages can be edited and/or deleted, depending on the software
Smartphones/ tablets	• Portability: slip it into your pocket or briefcase, and off you go • Offline access to email received and messages being composed • Ability to sync smartphones/tablets to desktop computer so that email can be transferred between hardware devices	• Inconsistent coverage: if you are out of cell phone range, you are probably out of range to transmit and receive email messages • It can be more time consuming to type out a long email using a touch screen when compared to using a physical keyboard

Source: Flynn (2009) and Flynn and Flynn (2003, pp. 95–99).

Important to your study of business and professional communication is learning to assess and improve your effectiveness when utilizing technology in your communication (Hewett & Robidoux, 2010; Shipley & Schwalbe, 2008). Since much of our communication occurs through technology, you must make sure to present yourself as a professional both online and in person (Ivy & Wahl, 2019; Jovin, 2007; Locher, 2010; Walther et al., 2005; Wright, 2004).

The way people present themselves online does matter in professional life. Remember, even "private" electronic communication can easily become public. Genova (2009) argues that employers have legitimate business interests in monitoring workplace internet use: to minimize legal exposure, to increase productivity, and to avoid proprietary information loss. Since employees arguably have no expectation of privacy in their work on employers' computers, there are few grounds for complaint if they are disciplined for straying from corporate policy on such use. It is a good practice to read and become familiar with your workplace's technology use policies and to avoid using company technology for personal or private matters.

Images such as this are what some employers are looking for as a red flag in hiring applicants. Do you have any pictures posted online that could potentially lead to a negative impression?

istockphoto/PeopleImages

In this heavily scrutinized work environment, it is no small wonder that employees crave a place to unwind after hours. In unprecedented numbers, America's workers are using social media to post tidbits that their employers might not consider job appropriate. Here, many observers postulate that they do have an expectation of and, indeed, a right to privacy, especially in arenas that are used to express personal freedoms and exercise individualism and have no bearing on the workplace. Whether employers agree with this stance or not, an increasing majority are using employees' presence online to support discipline, termination, or simply not hiring of an individual. But is this fair if those actions are based on off-the-clock internet use? What do your social media profile(s), text messages, and email address say about you? What impression will others have of you based on what you post on social media such as Twitter, Instagram, and TikTok? Are these social media accounts private, and if not, would you allow workplace colleagues to follow you? Is your image online different from the image you present in person? If they are different, how are they different? What does each say about you as a professional? Understanding the impact of technology on your communication is critical to achieving professional excellence.

Electronic Communication

Have you thought about how communication has changed as a result of technology such as email, instant messaging, social media, and texting? With each change in technology, there are changes to our communication as professionals (Barley et al., 2011; Hermes, 2008; Ivy & Wahl, 2019; Yee, Bailenson et al., 2008). And, as noted earlier, some of the changes that result from technology positively influence our communication, while others have a negative influence.

As we move into the sections that follow, there are a number of things to keep in mind about technology, especially when writing and sending email professionally. Before composing and sending an email, consider the information provided in Table 8.2 Tools for Professional Excellence. These rules also apply to text messages, blogs, and other electronic messages.

Using an email system, as well as many other forms of technology, allows a sender to avoid some of the unpleasant parts of face-to-face confrontation. For example, if you had to fire an employee, you would not have to see anyone cry if you delivered the bad news via email, nor would you have to worry about the physical side of an angry outburst over the telephone (Li et al., 2008; Locher, 2010). Getting fired over email is just one example of a change resulting from increased accessibility to and affordability of technology. How we communicate with one another in professional settings continues to evolve. Some people welcome the constant evolution and emergence of new communication technology, whereas others find it difficult to adjust to these changes and feel pressured to keep up. Clearly, advantages and disadvantages emerge when it comes to the use of technology in managing our professional relationships. You've likely heard great stories about making professional connections online, then face to face, and then negotiating a big contract. You've probably also heard stories about employees shopping online or viewing porn on the company computer when they should be working.

While we often focus on *employee* appropriateness when using technology professionally, it is also important for an *employer* to use technology appropriately. Vishal Garg, who is the CEO of an online mortgage company called Better, learned this lesson the hard way after he fired 900 employees over Zoom. An employee recorded Garg's Zoom meeting, and the recording quickly went viral on various social media platforms and made headlines on national news. As a result, Garg took a leave of absence, and Better's top marketing, public relations, and communications executives resigned (Duffy & Nicoll, 2021).

People working in businesses and professional organizations constantly rely on their email systems to communicate with colleagues and accomplish their work (Ivy & Wahl, 2019; Kibby,

Better's CEO, Vishal Garg, received intense backlash after he fired 900 employees over Zoom. Why do you think Garg's use of Zoom made people so angry, and what could he have done differently?

iStockphoto/LeoPatrizi

2005; Lawson & Leck, 2006; Shipley & Schwalbe, 2008; Thompson, 2008; S. Young et al., 2011). Considering how prevalent email usage is in business and professional communication, let's examine how this form of technology impacts professional image.

As we suggested in Chapter 4, you should review and perhaps change your email address when applying for jobs. Think about the impression a job recruiter would have when receiving an email message from pimpinout@university.edu versus gabe.martinez@university.edu (Ivy & Wahl, 2019). Which address implies more professionalism? Which address communicates a better first impression? You need to think about the perception of you that others may form based on your email (Byron & Baldridge, 2007; Ivy & Wahl, 2019; Welch, 2012).

TABLE 8.2 ■ Tools for Professional Excellence. Being Aware of Email
To use email effectively in the workplace, remember these critical points:

- Email is never secure.
- Email can lead to misunderstanding.
- Inappropriate email can lead to workplace lawsuits.
- Your email may be monitored by your employer.
- Spending too much time on email can hinder your productivity and focus.
- Email abuse can lead to employee termination.
- Sending inappropriate emails can harm your reputation as a professional.

Source: Flynn (2009).

TABLE 8.3 ■ Tools for Professional Excellence. Checklist for Appropriate Email Content
To compose and send professional emails, make sure your messages:

- Are spell-checked to clean up mechanical and grammatical errors
- Are free of jokes
- Do not contain harassing, negative, or aggressive language
- Illustrate professional excellence
- Are free of racist, sexist, or discriminatory language
- Are free of sexual language, violence, and pornographic images

Source: Flynn (2009).

Know Yourself

CMC Competence

As you read the index below and answer the questions, think about how this knowledge can help you be a better communicator.

Directions: The following statements, modified from Spitzberg's (2006) CMC Competence Scale, describe the ways some people use and feel about new CMC. Please indicate in the space to the left of each item the degree to which you believe the statement applies to you. Use the following 5-point scale: *not at all true of me* = 1; *mostly not true of me* = 2; *neither true nor untrue of me; undecided* = 3; *mostly true of me* = 4; or *very true of me* = 5.

1. I enjoy communicating using computer media.
2. I always seem to know how to say things the way I mean them using CMC.
3. I don't feel very competent in learning and using communication media technology.
4. Communicating through a computer makes me anxious.
5. I know I can learn to use new CMC technologies when they come out.
6. I manage the give-and-take of CMC interactions skillfully.
7. I can show compassion and empathy through the way I write emails.
8. I take time to make sure my emails to others are uniquely adapted to the particular receivers to whom I'm sending them.
9. I try to use a lot of humor in my CMC messages.
10. I use a lot of the expressive symbols [e.g., for "smile"] in my CMC messages.
11. I have no trouble expressing my opinions forcefully on CMC.
12. I avoid saying things through email that might offend someone.
13. My interactions are effective in accomplishing what I set out to accomplish.
14. My comments are consistently accurate and clear.
15. I am generally pleased with my interactions.
16. I come across in conversation as someone people would like to get to know.
17. My CMC interactions are more productive than my face-to-face interactions.
18. CMC technologies are tremendous time-savers for my work.
19. I rely heavily on my CMCs for getting me through each day.
20. I can rarely go a week without any CMC interactions.

How did you score? What surprised you about your score? You can also try the assessment on others. Simply fill out the measure with another person's behaviors in mind. For instance, you might find it interesting to fill out the survey for one of your friends to determine whether their use of CMC might play some role in the degree to which you interact with them online. Do you notice differences in that person's use of CMC and face-to-face interactions? Be aware of how you assess communication between CMC and face-to-face interactions among your friends, family, coworkers, and acquaintances.

Source: Modified scale from Spitzberg, B. H. (2006). Preliminary development of a model and measure of computer-mediated communication (CMC) competence. *Journal of Computer-Mediated Communication, 11*(2), 629–666.

But communicating effectively through email involves much more than just having a professional email address. The checklist in Tools for Professional Excellence 8.2 also applies to other forms of electronic communication, such as text messages and blogs. Unfortunately, many people fail to put the same level of professionalism into their email messages. This can lead to the start of conflicts or the escalation of existing conflicts. According to Wollman (2008), electronic conflicts are common. Can you think of a time when you sent an email message that was less than professional? How could you have changed the message to present yourself with professional excellence?

Professional excellence requires you to know yourself as a communicator. Using the KEYS approach, you must know what kind of email style you have, in both sending and receiving, to see what impression you communicate through your emailing behavior. You also need to expand that self-analysis to all forms of CMC. For example, do you have a habit of using smiley faces and "lol" with friends? Have you carried those habits into your professional texts? Do you carefully proofread your professional emails but send text and instant messages full of typos and errors? Do you forward things you think are funny or inspirational to colleagues or other professional contacts? Now ask yourself, "Would I pass that same information on in hard copy? Would I repeat that joke in person?" As you analyze yourself online, remember that you want to portray the same image and the same level of communication professionalism electronically that you would portray in person or in written, hard-copy correspondence, because the need for professionalism is the same. This is a different channel, but the same rules apply. Similarly, remember that you must evaluate the audience or the receiver of the message. For example, some people love to text, and others love virtual meetings, but some people and some topics require face-to-face communication. If you apply the KEYS approach and carefully select the communication channel you use, you will be one step closer to communication excellence with technology.

DRAWBACKS OF TECHNOLOGY

We recognize that communication and technology will help you to be more productive, to network, and *to excel* as a professional. However, part of professional excellence is also being able to recognize the drawbacks of technology and avoid violating professional etiquette (explained further in Chapter 4). Those of you who excel into leadership positions should be aware of the drawbacks of technology, as the need for more workplace policies is emerging to help manage risks associated with technology (e.g., security breaches, privacy violations, decreased production, employee conflict, viewing of pornography, miscommunication; Diffle & Landau, 2007; Kelleher & Hall, 2005; Roberts & Wasieleski, 2012).

Employee Surveillance

How privacy is managed in the workplace is certainly part of the organizational culture that you need to get to know (Cozzetto & Pedeliski, 1996; Langan, 2012; Rule, 2007). Be aware of the private information you communicate to other people (e.g., relationship problems, health, money troubles), as well as the private information or activities you might manage at work (e.g., personal email, virtual communities, online banking; Cho & Hung, 2011; Solove, 2008). In fact, companies and organizations are using workplace surveillance systems in an effort to monitor and track employee behavior in terms of the information they access or communicate while at work.

The goal of workplace surveillance is to alleviate productivity concerns and discourage employees from doing things such as looking up personal banking information or viewing pornography at work (Sheriff & Ravishankar, 2012; Watkins-Allen et al., 2007). In addition to blocking employee access to particular sites or tracking web-browsing behaviors, companies are now asking employees to waive their privacy rights when it comes to using work-related email. That is, personal or private affairs are not to be included in any company email. Remember, the intensity of workplace surveillance depends on the industry, but holding a conversation on your personal smartphone as you walk down the hallway or sit in a meeting is unprofessional, regardless of the topic of the conversation. Let's explore in more detail the concerns or problems that emerge with communication and technology in business and professional situations.

Time Management

Chronemics is the study of time as communication or as a communication function. Drawing from research on the nonverbal dimensions of time in CMC, Ivy and Wahl (2019) explain that some messages are posted at one time (referred to as asynchronous), while others are more interactive, often fostered by social media (referred to as synchronous). As a result, email systems and other forms of communication technology make employees more efficient while simultaneously increasing their workloads (Ballard, 2008; Biggiero et al., 2012; Bruneau, 2012; Ivy & Wahl, 2019). Do you think technology helps or harms your own time management? How, if at all, do you use technology to help manage your time? What expectations do you have related to response time for text messages, email, instant messages, and the like?

In virtual meetings and with the use of messaging features such as instant messaging, texting, and email, professionals can communicate with little delay between messages (Ivy & Wahl, 2019; Z. Wang et al., 2012). Indeed, technology helps professionals be more productive and stay connected with clients; respond quickly; and accomplish tasks despite geographic distance, travel time, and the like. But what are the drawbacks when we consider how much of the time we are wired? A good friend of ours gets so stressed out with email responses and phone calls at work during the week that he advocates for times of being *unplugged*—a term referring to the avoidance of checking email, sending text messages, watching television, or answering the phone (see Tools for Professional Excellence 8.3). No doubt, some of you might think of watching television, talking to your friends on the phone, sending text messages, or listening to your Spotify playlist as ways to recharge—the use of technology may very well make your downtime possible. We must also consider the demands of many jobs, which would never allow several days without communication.

Information Overload

Spending a lot of time on tasks that seem to take away from your productivity instead of helping you accomplish your work can make you feel off balance and stressed, leading to burnout (covered at length in Chapter 14). You might be experiencing information overload. This happens when information, requests for feedback, new projects, responses to questions, phone calls, and required online trainings for work—on top of taking care of loved ones, children, pets, and other family matters—leave you feeling as though things are spinning out of control (Chen et al., 2012; Savolainen, 2007).

Contributing to information overload are several unprofessional distractions or threats to privacy. Here are a few examples:

- Email forwards consist of virus alerts, chain letters, stories disguised as warnings, petitions or calls for help, jokes, pictures, and the like (Kibby, 2005).

- Spam is the use of a user's email address for a purpose to which the user didn't agree. It is junk email sent by "spammers" who obtain email addresses by buying company customer lists or using programs to produce email addresses randomly.

- Phishing involves sending authentic-looking but fraudulent emails designed to steal sensitive personal information.

Addressing information overload means more than just deleting emails; it can also include dealing with threats to your privacy and to the overall security of your computer (Flynn, 2009).

Computer viruses and security breaches can tarnish professional activities and productivity, and falling for a phishing or malware scam on your workplace's device could lead to negative professional consequences for you. Remember to always verify the email addresses of those who send you emails, and be wary of any strange or unexpected links or attachments.

iStockphoto/Ridofranz

TABLE 8.4 ■ Tools for Professional Excellence. Managing Your Email Inbox	
To manage your inbox effectively, follow these practical tips:	
Key Points	**Practical Tips**
Set aside time to read and respond to email.	● Don't leave your email program open all day long. Alerts and beeps from incoming messages can interrupt your work flow and leave you unfocused. ● Schedule specific blocks of time throughout the day for checking your email. ● Turn off your cell phone and shut your office door to prevent interruptions by family members (if you work from home) or employees. ● The amount of time required for reviewing email and replying will depend on how frequently you check messages and how many you typically receive, so find the right balance for your situation.
Take action immediately.	● Making quick decisions and pursuing immediate action will help keep your email inbox under control. ● When you check your messages, browse the inbox for emails that can be deleted immediately such as spam or promotional emails. Then select messages that don't require a response and delete or archive them. Once you've pared down the number of messages in your inbox, you'll be able to better evaluate which ones are the most critical. ● Don't let important emails sit in your inbox for days. Reply to the sender as soon as you've read the message. ● If you're unable to respond immediately, communicate to the sender that you received the message and will be in touch as soon as you can.

(Continued)

TABLE 8.4 ■ Tools for Professional Excellence (*Continued*)

To manage your inbox effectively, follow these practical tips:

Key Points	Practical Tips
Organize an inbox with labels, folders, and categories.	● Although a majority of emails can be deleted, you'll most likely want to retain messages related to key aspects of your business, such as correspondence between clients, colleagues, and employees.
	● Prioritize, group, sort, and file messages to keep your inbox organized.
	● Before you file a message, ensure the subject line is search friendly. If it doesn't accurately describe the content of the email, edit the subject line before it's categorized and archived.
Unsubscribe from unwanted promotional emails.	● Clean out the clutter: Newsletters and advertisements can overwhelm your inbox and bury important messages.
	● Unsubscribe from specific email lists if you no longer want to receive the senders' messages or don't have the time to read them.

Source: Whitmore, J. (2015, January 15). 4 Tips to Better Manage Your Email Inbox. *Entrepreneur.* Retrieved from http://www.entrepreneur.com/article/241423

Information overload is certainly a drawback to technology, and overcoming it serves as more of a maintenance function for professionals globally (Flynn, 2006b; Marulanda-Carter & Jackson, 2012), but let's return to the drawbacks of communication and technology for professional excellence. We consider Barb and Alex—two professionals who happen to work at the same company and maintain an intimate relationship. As you'll see in this "Step Back and Reflect" feature, technology can be used to attack other people when romance in the workplace goes south.

STEP BACK AND REFLECT

Barb's Email Response

As you read this passage and answer the questions, step back and reflect on what went wrong in this professional situation.

Barb was having a bad day. One of her coworkers, Alex, whom she had been dating for several years, broke up with her using a text message! Needless to say, Barb was angry—she couldn't believe that Alex was impersonal and cold enough to break up with her in that way. Both women worked in an accounting office at a large oil refinery. Alex and Barb socialized with a group of coworkers on Friday nights—a social network clearly existed outside of work. To get back at Alex, Barb wanted to make a statement. She decided *not* to use a text message to respond to Alex and didn't want to confront her face to face at work. Instead, she used the workplace email list (the same list used to organize the Friday night gatherings for everyone in the accounting office). Barb sent a "Reply All" email in response to one of Alex's old email messages and told the entire story about the text-message breakup. The next day, Barb received a formal reprimand from her boss and almost lost her job. As you can see, this is an example of someone using email to attack another person.

Step Back and Reflect

1. What went wrong?

2. Was Barb out of bounds in sending this message to coworkers, since this group socialized outside of work?

3. Have you ever used text messages or emails to break up with someone or to display your anger about a breakup?

4. How would you respond, if at all, if you were in Alex's situation?

5. How could Barb use the KEYS approach to improve her communication interaction?

The circumstances surrounding Alex and Barb's breakup may sound rare, but it should encourage you to think about how communicating with technology requires the same level of consideration as face-to-face communication. Sometimes you may get mad at another coworker inside or outside of work, but that doesn't mean the confrontation needs to be distributed to everyone in the company. Do you know someone who has the bad habit of using the "Reply All" function in email?

Electronic Aggression

Electronic communication allows people like Barb in any workplace situation to sit behind their computer screens or other digital devices and fire off responses in many forms (see Tools for Professional Excellence 8.5). Professionals in a variety of industries take topics in need of discussion, or controversial topics, and place them in electronic formats, often termed —exchanges of messages about a particular topic using email, professional blog space, and other electronic tools to encourage participation that will ideally lead to new ideas, strategic planning, and sound decision making.

Managing all the information sent electronically can be especially distracting when you're trying to meet a deadline.

iStockphoto/artiemedvedev

Email dialogues can be fruitful, and we don't want to advocate avoidance of this type of exchange; however, email dialogues have a drawback that many of you have already experienced. The dark side of these electronic exchanges is electronic aggression—a form of aggressive communication filled with emotionality that is used by people who are interacting on professional topics. Topics that begin with a professional spirit can get unprofessional when people don't agree with the direction of the discussion or if particular language is used to disagree about a program or idea others support. One way to fuel the aggression is to send an email flame—"a hostile message that is blunt, rude, insensitive, or obscene" (Flynn & Flynn, 2003, p. 54; Nitin et al., 2012).

Electronic aggression and email flames, similar to the one discussed in the "Step Back and Reflect" feature, can occur when someone posts a highly charged message to a corporate blog, a web log used to improve internal communication at work or for external marketing and public relations (Flynn, 2006a; Jang & Stefanone, 2011); a listserv, a computer service that facilitates discussions by connecting people who share common interests; or an electronic bulletin board, an online service that anyone, not just a subscriber, can access to read postings (Doyle, 1998; Hult & Huckin, 1999; Ivy & Wahl, 2019).

TABLE 8.5 ■ Tools for Professional Excellence. Tips for Avoiding Electronic Aggression

- Would you say the same thing to someone in person?
- Would this message be seen as unprofessional by anyone?
- Is your read of the electronic aggression correct? Give people the benefit of the doubt and request a face-to-face conversation.
- Avoid the temptation to use the "Reply All" option.
- Avoid using obscene or threatening language.
- Control your emotions. Revisit the issue when you've had time to calm down.

Source: Flynn (2009).

SOCIAL MEDIA AND TECHNOLOGY: KEY CHALLENGES IN THE COMMUNICATION AGE

Although new technologies such as smartphones, social media, and video conferencing can make communication a more convenient task, these relatively new channels of communication create their own sets of problems if not used effectively (Edwards et al., 2019). Simply because you have the ability to communicate with different people and cultures across the globe does not mean you are ready to work with these people if you lack training and cultural sensitivity. Also, when relying almost exclusively on computer-mediated communication for business and professional interactions, you run the risk of letting your face-to-face communication skills suffer. Another issue is that constant availability and connection with your work life can lead to stress, burnout, and information overload if you do not "unplug" from work from time to time. Here are some common challenges to business communication in the information age.

- **Knowing when to use** computer-mediated communication **or face-to-face communication can be challenging.** A common problem now is that we have almost too many choices available to us for communicating with others. Email, texting, and instant messaging have become the de facto choice of communication for many people, but what about those who are not as connected to their smartphones or computers? There are still many "traditional" communicators who prefer the intimacy of face-to-face interactions and find email or text interactions to be dismissive or insulting, especially if the conversation is a serious or important one.

- By this same reasoning, new media are inhibited in their ability to transmit nonverbal cues of intimacy and familiarity. How many times have you read a text message and not been able to decipher if the text is a joke, sarcastic, or completely serious? These types of miscommunications happen continually, and they have the potential to unintentionally ruin business relationships.

- So when is it appropriate to use face-to-face or computer-mediated communication? Current literature suggests that new media are appropriate for sending routine and simple information, but face-to-face communication is better for complex, urgent, or controversial messages. Keep in mind there is no "one size fits all" approach to choosing the appropriate communication channel. Your continued study and application of business and communication are what will ultimately allow you to make the right decisions about what communication channels to use.

- **Practicing cultural sensitivity can be difficult.** As business and commerce increasingly take place on a global scale, the ability to communicate with cultural sensitivity cannot be overstated. Many businesses rely on global exposure for success, and part of that success involves communicating with individuals who can be quite different from you. For intercultural communication competence, you must be an active learner of values, language systems, and cultural communication norms.

- *Intercultural communication* involves the communication between and among individuals and groups across national and ethnic boundaries (Wahl & Simmons, 2018). Understanding and effectively engaging in this type of communication can put you head-over-heels above other professionals in your organization. For the most part, your personal cultural background determines the way you communicate—how personal beliefs influence what you say, what language you use, and even your nonverbal gestures. These in turn will alter how others respond to your communication. For example, a common job interview or negotiation strategy in the United States is to make consistent eye contact with your communication partner. However, in many Asian cultures, prolonged eye contact can be construed as a sign of disrespect, or even belligerence. This lack of cultural awareness could easily disrupt business negotiations across cultures.

- **Information overload can negatively affect your work and health.** The price we pay for convenience and immediacy with computer-mediated communication is the difficulty of disconnecting from it. Constant connectivity can sometimes be abused by making yourselves or others constantly available. Have you ever had a day off from work ruined because your boss emailed new work after business hours? All the digital media you use for convenience, work, and enjoyment (smartphone, social media, email) can result in *information overload*, which exposes you to more messages than you can process. Research has shown that a growing number of employees are feeling overwhelmed by the seemingly endless flow of email and text messages, and feeling pressured to respond to messages as soon as they receive them (Edwards et al., 2019;

Ivy & Wahl, 2019; Wahl & Simmons, 2018). Remember that although being connected is important and sometimes essential to business communication, it is also equally important to give yourself an avenue to step away from constant digital interaction.

YOUR COMMUNICATION INTERACTION

Making Social Media Choices

As you read the passage below, consider what would be a more effective communication strategy in this situation.

Anne is interviewing applicants for a vacant position at her company. A new component of the interview process is examining applicants' social media accounts, so as to get a better idea of who they really are when not on the job. Based on the process thus far, Anne has narrowed down the candidates to three applicants: Jen, Brian, and Jack. After some searching, Anne manages to find the Facebook pages for all three applicants and begins her examination. Because of privacy settings, Anne can only see each page's profile picture and a limited number of photos and posts. On Jen's page, Anne notices that her profile picture features her posing with her dog, while the first post that appears shows Jen and a group of friends partying and chugging bottles of beer. On Brian's page, Anne sees that his profile picture features him posing with a small child whom he identifies as his nephew, while further down the page is a series of pictures from a weekend he spent with his fraternity brothers in Las Vegas, some of which feature heavy drinking and gambling. On Jack's page, Anne finds that he is wearing a T-shirt with an expletive written on it in his profile picture, while in another post he mentions how much fun he had volunteering at the local animal shelter. Anne spends a bit more time looking over each page, and then logs off.

Questions to Consider

1. Do you think Anne has enough information to decide whom to hire? Why or why not?
2. Based on each candidate's profile, whom would you hire? Why?
3. What suggestions would you give to the candidates regarding what they post on their profiles?
4. How important do you think social media profiles are in the hiring process?

PROFESSIONAL ETIQUETTE WITH TECHNOLOGY

The previous sections of this chapter explored the advantages and disadvantages of communication and technology in professional contexts. Remember to think about professional etiquette when communicating with technology (see Tools for Professional Excellence 8.6). Again, a great place to begin practicing your professional etiquette with technology is in the classroom. Students and teachers alike are using technology in the classroom. Laptop computers, smartphones, smart watches, and tablets are the beginning of a long list of electronic devices that help us manage our everyday lives (Arlat et al., 2012; Flynn, 2009). What concerns, if any, do you have regarding technology use during class? Have you ever been distracted by other students' use of technology? Similarly, think about how the use of technology (e.g., talking, texting, tweeting, gaming) can disrupt the workplace experience. Where's the professional etiquette when employees are texting their friends instead of taking care of work-related tasks? Has professional etiquette changed with the growth of technology? What do you think?

Are policies that establish a sense of respect and courtesy related to technology use a good idea? Weigh the pros and cons and then determine why you think they would or wouldn't be a good idea.

iStockphoto/AzmanL

TABLE 8.6 ■ Action Items. Skills for Navigating Technology		
Skill	Strategy	Application
Digital etiquette	Learn what online behaviors are appropriate and which are not.	Visit any accredited etiquette website and familiarize yourself with its online section.
Digital safety	Learn what skills are needed to keep both you and your hardware safe from hackers and malware.	Review general online interaction tips from any major computer security company's website (e.g., Norton, McAfee).
Safety in e-commerce	Familiarize yourself with safe online purchasing practices.	Call your bank or credit union representative for tips and warnings about what to watch out for when shopping online.

KEYS TO EXCELLENCE WITH COMMUNICATION AND TECHNOLOGY

In the story at the beginning of the chapter, Adobe was rated as one of the best companies to work for in 2021, according to its employees' reviews. As you continue as a communication professional in your life, you must make a conscious effort to stay informed about ever-changing and growing technologies. If you want to excel and get promoted to a higher position in leadership, you need to improve your communication—especially when using technology to communicate and collaborate. When studying the KEYS approach to professional excellence as you try to *excel in the workplace*, make some adjustments and improve your email style. When examining the first key, *know yourself*, know that achieving professional excellence entails improving your communication. Thus, both your electronic and face-to-face communication have to improve if you want to advance professionally. Examine your strengths and weaknesses related to all aspects of your communication (verbal, nonverbal, and electronic). Set a goal to be more respectful of the employees who work on your team when communicating one on one, during meetings, or through email. In all, you need to get to know yourself better in all aspects of your communication, with the use of technology being just one of them.

TABLE 8.7 ■ Tools for Professional Excellence. Professional Etiquette with Technology	
To use technology with professional etiquette, follow these best practices:	
Technology	**Professional Best Practices**
Voicemail—your personal greeting	Record your own greeting.
	Indicate if you will be out of the office.
	Refer the caller to another person for help.
	Check messages daily.
Voicemail— leaving messages	Speak clearly and slowly.
	Leave your name and number.
	Keep messages short and to the point.
	Leave the date and time you called.
Ringtones	Use the silent or vibrate setting when a ringtone might be disruptive.
	Many ringtones are unprofessional—use the standard tones offered by your provider.
Text messaging	Don't replace all communication with texts.
	Use texts that leave little room for misunderstanding.
	Don't deliver bad or good news in a text.
	Don't use text messages to have a conversation.
	Don't send texts during meetings.
	Don't type in all caps.
Cell phone usage	Don't answer your phone during a meeting.
	Don't take personal calls at work.
Social Media	Watch what you post—before you post anything, consider what your family, friends, coworkers, or boss might think.
	Don't post all of the time—go for quality over quantity.
	Don't be selfish—use your posts to support others around you.
	Don't post while under the influence of alcohol or drugs.
	Don't go overboard with symbols or emojis, and avoid using emojis that might have inappropriate double meanings.

Source: Cowan (2011) and Flynn (2009).

The next key, *evaluate the professional context*, is essential for you to become more aware of your professional context as well as how you come across to other people when sending information via email. Become more mindful of how your communication could be hurtful, even if you are just trying to make a point.

The third key, *your communication interaction*, can make you a more professional communicator. Start to think before making certain statements to members of your team, and be much more mindful of your tone and word choice in emails. If you send out information electronically, think about how your email can be received. Follow up with people in person after sending information electronically. Follow up or ask questions, such as "Did you get my email?" and "I hope my description of the new product was clear. Let me know if you need my assistance with anything that might come up." As your communication interaction occurs, work more on planning your message and don't simply rely on sending messages electronically. Realize the value of follow-up, respect, and courtesy in all aspects of your communication.

When you meet a new hire or send out information to your team, engage in the fourth key, *step back and reflect*. Become a more reflective communicator. Ask yourself some of the following questions as you step back and think about the communication that has occurred, especially electronically: Was my email response appropriate? Did my questions in the email sound sarcastic? Did my team think it was rude when I answered my cell phone during the meeting? Should I use all caps in my text message? Was sending a response to everyone inappropriate? Did my coworker view my email as negative and critical? What will my staff think if I don't respond at all? This fourth key can make you more thoughtful about all aspects of communication, not just when you use technology.

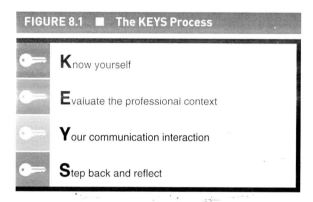

FIGURE 8.1 ■ The KEYS Process

Know yourself

Evaluate the professional context

Your communication interaction

Step back and reflect

EXECUTIVE SUMMARY

Now that you have finished reading this chapter, you should be able to

Discuss the impact technology has on business and professional communication:

- Communication and technology are important for the following reasons: (1) The way you communicate when using technology influences the impressions other people have of you, which is central to achieving professional excellence; (2) communication and technology help you establish contact and maintain professional networks and relationships with coworkers, leaders, and clients; and (3) communication and technology can lead to a number of obstacles that can hinder professional excellence.

Discuss how the drawbacks of technology can prevent you from excelling as a professional:

- Companies and organizations are using workplace surveillance systems in an effort to monitor and track employee behavior in terms of the information they access or communicate while at work.

- Electronic messages can occur in asynchronous time—messages are posted at one time, then read at another time—but CMC also offers more interactive features, such as communication in synchronous time. As a result, email systems and other forms of communication technology make employees more efficient while simultaneously increasing their workload.

- Information overload occurs when information, requests for feedback, new projects, responses to questions, phone calls, and required online classes for work—on top of taking care of loved ones, children, pets, and other family matters—leave you feeling as though things are spinning out of control.

- The dark side of electronic exchanges is electronic aggression—a form of aggressive communication filled with emotionality that is used by people interacting about professional topics.

Discuss key challenges related to technology and social media in the communication age

- There are many challenges to business communication in the information/communication age: knowing when to use computer-mediated communication or face-to-face communication, practicing cultural sensitivity, and information overload can negatively affect your work and health.

Explain how to use professional etiquette with technology:

- Thinking about professional etiquette in the use of technology means examining your use of voicemail (personal greetings and messages), ringtones, text messaging, smartphones, and social media in the workplace.

- Inappropriate use of technology can disrupt the workplace experience.

Apply the KEYS approach to achieve professional excellence regarding communication and technology:

- Know yourself. Determine if you want to achieve professional excellence, and know that part of that entails improving your communication.

- Evaluate the professional context. This is essential because you become more aware of your professional context, as well as how you come across to other people when sending information via email.

- Your communication interaction. This will help you become a more professional communicator. Start to think before making certain statements to members of your team, and be much more mindful of your tone and word choice in emails.

- Step back and reflect. Become a more reflective communicator. This fourth key will make you more thoughtful about all aspects of your communication, not just when you use technology.

EXPLORE

1. Go to a major technology company's website and look over some of its latest consumer products. How much more developed are they than what you currently use? Write a short response that compares and contrasts how old your personal technologies are (e.g., computer, smartphone, smart watch, tablet) compared with what's on the market right now. What does this tell you about the changing communication landscape?

2. Have a "mock" face-to-face discussion with a friend, coworker, or family member about a descriptive subject of your choice. Afterward, try to replicate the same conversation via text or email. What nonverbal cues are lost during the computer-mediated

communication? What tools (acronyms, emojis, or symbols) did you use to substitute for nonverbal cues, and how effective were they?

3. On any social networking site, conduct a self-inventory of your knowledge about the jargon and acronyms used. How often do you use these shortcuts in your online interactions: lol, imo, ftfy, tldr, and the like? Write a brief response in favor of or in opposition to using abbreviated communication in online environments.

REVIEW

1. Define a *virtual work team*.

2. Explain the goal of workplace surveillance systems.

3. _____ is the study of time as communication or as a communication function.

4. _____ refers to the avoidance of checking email, sending text messages, watching television, or answering the phone.

5. _____ occurs when information, requests for feedback, new projects, responses to questions, phone calls, and required online classes for work—on top of taking care of loved ones, children, pets, and other family matters—leave you feeling as though things are spinning out of control.

6. _____ refers to sending authentic-looking but fraudulent emails designed to steal sensitive personal information.

7. A(n) _____ is a hostile electronic message that is blunt, rude, insensitive, or obscene.

8. _____ are exchanges of messages about a topic using email and other professional electronic tools to encourage participation that will ideally lead to new ideas, strategic planning, and sound decision-making.

DISCUSSION QUESTIONS

1. Discuss an example of a time when you misunderstood another person in a text message, an email, or an instant message. How did you respond to the misunderstanding? Did you and the other person clear things up in person, or was it done electronically?

2. Do you have an Instagram, LinkedIn, Twitter, TikTok, or related account? Are there any posts or information associated with your profile that you think could potentially harm your credibility as a professional?

3. How do you express emotion when communicating with various forms of technology covered in this chapter?

4. Can the drawbacks and risks associated with communication and technology be alleviated with employee education and training? What experiences have you had, if any, concerning training or education related to security, privacy, and professional etiquette?

5. Have you ever experienced information overload? If so, what are some strategies you implement to help you with time management, filtering spam and email forwards, excessive text messages, and other distractions?

TERMS TO REMEMBER

Review key terms with eFlashcards: https://edge.sagepub.com/quintanilla5e.

chronemics (p. 200)

computer-mediated communication (CMC)
  (p. 193)

corporate blog (p. 204)

electronic aggression (p. 203)

electronic bulletin board (p. 204)

email dialogues (p. 203)

email flame (p. 204)

email forwards (p. 200)

information overload (p. 200)

listserv (p. 204)

phishing (p. 200)

spam (p. 200)

unplugged (p. 200)

virtual work team (p. 193)

workplace surveillance systems (p. 199)

Written communication across a range of print and digital platforms is an essential professional communication and PR skill.

iStockphoto/PeopleImages

9   BUSINESS AND PROFESSIONAL WRITING

CHAPTER OBJECTIVES

After studying this chapter, you should be able to

9.1   Discuss the importance of written communication

9.2   Apply strategies for developing written communication

9.3   Discuss the different types of written communication

9.4   Apply the KEYS approach to achieve professional excellence regarding written communication

Effective writing is a critical aspect of all effective communication, but perhaps nowhere is it more important than in public relations. Press releases are one of the primary tools in a public relations professional's toolbox, and they have evolved. Just like your marketing plans have changed in the last 10 years, your PR strategy and distribution methods need to change as well. Keys (2017) offers several strategies to help a story stand out:

- **Research your audience.** Know whom you are writing for and the topics that will pique their interest.

- **Be relevant.** Your audience goes beyond journalists to include bloggers, your industry, your partners, and the general public.

- **Understand what drives search traffic.** Research the words and phrases that are trending today. Select the ones most relevant to your release, but also use words that give you a chance at winning in the rankings.

- **Place your words strategically within your release.** The first 250 words matter. Use your headlines and subheads as opportunities to fluidly place a keyword. Be creative, but be natural.

- **Multimedia releases win.** A press release with text, photo, video, and links is 77% more likely to be engaged with than one with text only.

- **Measure the results.** Review the report from your distribution service; monitor your website analytics for page visits and traffic quality, add in social monitoring and listen to the chatter, and look at your sales data.

Above all, make sure that the product or service you are presenting to the public is very clear and easy to understand, whether the reader works in the industry or is a random person off the street.

In this chapter, we explore the importance of *written communication* as it connects to professional excellence. All the chapters in this book have focused on human communication. We have spent a great deal of time emphasizing the importance of culture in the workplace, interpersonal relationships, team communication, leadership, and communication and technology. These topics are essential to your study of business and professional communication. Further, human relationships are essential as you enter, excel in, and survive in your career. Yet our study of business and professional communication is not complete without attention to written communication. In Chapter 4, we reviewed a number of written communication essentials, such as cover letters and résumés, in the process of *getting the job*. Now we turn our attention to some basic principles for excellence in all types of written communication. In addition, we cover some specific types of written communication that you are likely to encounter on the job. What types of written communication skills do you think you may use *on the job?* What can you do on the job regarding your written communication that will ensure professional excellence?

THE IMPORTANCE OF WRITTEN COMMUNICATION

What would you do if you were hired for a new position that required you to communicate in a variety of styles and formats? Written communication can challenge professionals entering a variety of positions, regardless of industry. We point this out because many readers of this text may have some of the same concerns as Yolanda (discussed later in this chapter): How do I select the correct format to get the message out? Is it appropriate for me to send this document via email? What tone should I strive for in this message? How much detail about the new company initiative should I include in the press release? How should the memo be organized? Indeed, these questions about written communication that are emerging as you take this course may continue to present a challenge as you transition into your career or excel as a professional.

Written communication is important for the following reasons: (1) Official documents, memos, emails, and other forms of written communication reveal something about you as a professional; (2) important policies, requests, and organizational procedures are conveyed through written communication; (3) proposals, employee terminations, media relations, and the like are achieved with written communication; and (4) written communication must be present in order to achieve professional excellence. To address these important topics, let's take a look at ways to strive for written communication excellence.

STRATEGIES FOR WRITTEN COMMUNICATION EXCELLENCE

So how do you develop excellence in written communication? In this section, we review some strategies that will help your development: message structure, message clarity, and message presentation.

Message Structure

Excellent written communication begins with a clear general purpose, a clear specific purpose or thesis, and clear organization. Begin by asking yourself, "What is the purpose of this written communication? Am I presenting new information? Am I clarifying? Am I requesting? Am I persuading?" Once you have identified your general purpose, ask yourself, "What is the key message I want my audience to take away from this email, report, or memo?" By answering this question, you will have identified your specific purpose or thesis statement. From there, you can begin to organize your message. We strongly recommend that you develop an outline before you begin writing. This outline will help you determine the organizational structure of your message. Remember this: Poor organization will lead to ineffective communication. Simply put, if the reader cannot follow your message, the reader cannot understand your message.

Written communication and organizational skills are critical in managing large amounts of information in today's business and professional world, and these skills are vital in both large and small organizations.

iStockphoto/_ultraforma_

Message Clarity

Developing clear organization is the first step to message clarity. However, clear organization alone does not guarantee that your message will be clear. To maximize message clarity, you must evaluate your audience and avoid generalities.

As with all forms of communication, excellence in written communication requires you to evaluate your audience. Ask yourself, "Who will read this written document?" In many cases, you will have both a primary audience—the person or persons the message is addressed to—and a secondary audience—other readers who may need or use this information. Keep all readers in mind as you draft your message. Consider details such as the reader's place in the organization (supervisor, employee, customer), their level of understanding (both educational level and experience in your industry), and the amount of interest in and involvement with the topic at hand. This evaluation will help you determine if jargon can be used and if background information is needed.

Message clarity is also achieved by using specific language as opposed to general language (Bly, 1999; Travers, 2012). General language is usually characterized as vague statements that can easily be misunderstood, whereas specific language makes precise references. For example, Dr. Jones could write the general statement that she has excellent patient satisfaction scores, or she could make the specific, clearer claim that 97% of her patients reported the highest level of satisfaction. During a reprimand, the manager could write, "You need to return from lunch in a timely fashion." But his message would be much clearer if he wrote specifically, "You must return from lunch by 1:00 p.m."

Message Presentation

In addition to considering message structure and message clarity, you must consider message presentation. Unlike spoken communication, there is a lasting visual element to your written communication. Message presentation refers to that visual component. Carelessly written communication will send the message that you are a careless employee or leader. With spelling and grammar check, as well as good old-fashioned proofreading, you can correct typos (mistakes in typing), misspellings (mistakes in spelling), and grammar errors (sentence fragments, inappropriate use of punctuation, and the like). Just as a typo on your résumé can lose you a job, a typo on a report can cause you to lose credibility. Misspellings, typos, and sending something to the wrong department are all roadblocks to professional excellence. As the KEYS approach has taught you, know yourself. For some of you, knowing yourself will mean realizing that you are not very good at editing your own work. Many of us who are good at editing others' work struggle to edit our own work. If that is the case, get a colleague to proofread your document before you send it out.

To achieve professional excellence, your documents and emails should be printed in black and should be legible. In addition, your typeface must be dark enough to read, and it should be set against a lighter background (e.g., white paper) for contrast. Documents with poor toner quality look unprofessional and are ineffective.

In addition to the preceding tips for written communication, we recommend using a writing startup sheet—a list of questions that encourage the writer to think about audience, purpose, key issues, and delivery (see the "Know Yourself" feature).

Know Yourself

Writing Startup Sheet

As you review and answer the questions below, think about how this knowledge can help you be a better communicator.

Audience

1. Who is my primary reader or audience? Who else will be reading this?

2. Did I provide the necessary information?

3. How does the information relate to the reader or audience?

4. How does my reader or audience feel about this information or subject?

Purpose

5. The purpose of this written communication is to _____ so that my audience will _____.

Delivery

6. What's the best channel for this message? Hard copy? Email? Phone? In person?

7. When should I send this message?

Would you find the writing startup sheet useful in a professional setting? What types of written communication are you the most concerned about?

Source: Adapted from Lindsell-Roberts (2004, p. 24).

TYPES OF WRITTEN COMMUNICATION

What types of written communication will you encounter as a professional? Although the various types of business letters, memos, emails, and the like depend on the industry you work in, it's important for you to be prepared and begin to fill a toolbox that you can use as a professional. In the sections that follow, we cover the following types of written communication: business letters, employee reviews, recommendation letters, thank-you letters, memos, proposals and reports, planning documents, press releases, proactive media writing, and email.

Business Letters

The business letter is used to address formal matters in professional communication including cover letters, information sent to customers, announcements about business events, and the like. As you strive for professional excellence, remember that business letters, when not composed appropriately, can be ineffective and lead to miscommunication. Have you ever received a letter that did not keep your attention? What reaction do you have when your name is misspelled in a document? See the basic business letter template provided in Writing Sample 9.1.

In addition to providing price quotes for services with business letters, you will communicate with other departments and businesses. Downsizing letters are used to inform other businesses about skilled employees available for employment due to company downsizing (e.g., layoffs, fired employees).

Employee Reviews

Written communication is central to providing feedback to employees regarding job performance. Employee reviews serve as a form of written communication used in business and professional settings to provide feedback to employees about how they are performing on the job (see Writing Sample 9.2). These reviews are typically filed with personnel documents. Written communication related to employee reviews must be accurate and reflect actual employee performance. Remember, this type of document should be used carefully to document positive performance and areas for the employee to improve. If an employee is a candidate for mandatory leave, an improvement plan, or termination, these review documents must be used to document a pattern of employee performance. Further, employee review documents serve as a method of informing employees how to improve on the job.

Recommendation Letters

Another type of letter that is commonplace across industries and academic disciplines is the recommendation letter—a form of written communication used to provide a documented reference for students and professionals. A letter of recommendation is needed when a college or university or employer requests one, and it's something that many, if not all, of the readers of this text will need throughout their careers. Your professors are asked to write

TABLE 9.1 ■ Action Items. Skills for Professional Writing		
Skill	**Strategy**	**Application**
Drafting	Write your ideas in sentences and paragraphs, giving your work a basic structure.	Create an initial draft of a research paper, before fine-tuning.
Revising	Edit your writing (an outside editor is useful here). Make changes that will improve your writing.	Take an initial draft to your college or university's writing lab for guidance.
Proofreading	Finish your editing. Check for errors in grammar, spelling, capitalization, and punctuation.	Ask a friend, family member, or work professional to review your document.
Publishing	Choose a way to present your work to your target audience.	Place what you have written into a presentational form (e.g., PowerPoint, Prezi).

many recommendation letters for current and past students. Your careful preparation will help your professor write the best letter possible. You as a student must take responsibility and initiative in the letter-writing process. Although professors will vary in their preferences, Table 9.1 Tools for Professional Excellence and Tables 9.2 and 9.3 offers some tips. See Writing Sample 9.3 for an example of a recommendation written by a professor for a student applying for a professional position.

Thank-You Letters

In our consulting practice, we encourage professionals at all levels across industries to set a goal for using thank-you letters—written communication used to express appreciation to coworkers and clients. With the intensity of email, text messages, and all the information professionals manage, it's easy to forget a simple thank you. Thank-you letters can be sent via email (which is great for delivery speed), but think about how impressive it is to actually receive a handwritten note. We encourage you to keep professional thank-you cards in your work area to write letters or notes of appreciation. In addition to helping you achieve professional excellence on the job, thank-you letters can be used as networking notes—a form of thank-you letter used to remind employers of your interview and to emphasize that you're the right person for the job. In fact, employers often say that a sincere thank-you letter can give a job candidate the edge over another competing candidate. Review Writing Sample 9.4 and set a goal to use thank-you letters both on the job and to network for new jobs or promotions.

Memos

Memos (the word *memo* is short for *memorandum*) are another type of written communication used in professional settings. They are typically short notes or updates distributed in business. Memos should be reserved for communicating information that's critically important. The memo format we recommend is provided in Writing Sample 9.5.

As you can see, the four major elements of the basic memo are "date," "to," "from," and "re" (regarding what topic). Be careful with memos in terms of frequency and topic. Frequent memos will come to be expected, leaving important information ignored. Employees may also respond negatively to the topics addressed and the tone of a memo. To illustrate our point regarding topic and tone in business memos, review the case study of Yolanda's use of memos (in the "Step Back and Reflect" feature) to see what can go wrong with memos if used inappropriately.

Memos can also be used to communicate process directives—descriptions of new policies and procedures and changes to those already in place. Process directives are distributed to the employees or departments that the directive impacts and are filed as official documents of organizational policy. Yolanda has the task of writing a process directive for Company ABC. Her process directive is to be placed inside a memo and distributed as an internal communication announcement to let everyone know about a new company newsletter. The executive team wants to make sure that everyone in the organization is informed about the newsletter. The goal is for employees to feel a sense of community in the workplace by being informed about Company ABC activities. In addition to the employees knowing about the newsletter, Yolanda includes specific information in the process directive regarding to whom information for the newsletter should be sent, as well as deadlines for submitting information (see Writing Sample 9.5).

WRITING SAMPLE 9.1

Business Letter With Price Quote

WRITING SAMPLE 9.1

Business Letter With Price Quote

XYZ Corporation
650 Wayward Avenue
Houston, TX 73850
(Letterhead)

January 10, 2022 **(Date)**
ABC Global Services (Address of the recipient)
PO Box 32555
Tyrone, PA 16801
Dear Mr. Stobbs, **(Opening/greeting)**

XYZ proposes to furnish all necessary labor, supervision, materials, tools, and equipment for the installation of the electrical work for the above referenced project, as detailed herein, in accordance with our interpretations of the intent of the design for the Lump Sum price of **Fourteen Thousand Six Hundred Forty Nine Dollars and No Cents . . . . $14,649.00.**

Breakdown:

1. Labor: $1,068.00
2. Material: $13,581.00

Scope of work:

1. Furnish and install:
   a. Battery Monitoring System
   b. (1) Duplex Receptacle in computer room
   c. (1) Cat 5E cable from UPS to computer room

Clarifications:

1. All work to be based on straight time first shift.
2. Due to rising cost of materials and/or labor, we reserve the right to adjust this proposal if not accepted within thirty (30) days of the above date.

Scope of work:

Respectfully yours, **(Closing)**

Cheryl Banks

Project Manager

YOUR COMMUNICATION INTERACTION

The Terminator

As you read the passage below, consider what would be a more effective communication strategy in this situation.

Tyler recently received a promotion at his workplace and now oversees a small group of new employees. While spending time with the new employees, Tyler has begun to bond with one in particular, Joey, who reminds him a lot of his younger brother. Tyler takes it upon himself to take Joey under his wing and make sure he succeeds within the company. One day, Tyler's boss notifies him that they have to make some cuts in the company, and that includes some of Tyler's employees. The terminations are based on evaluation scores, and Tyler is devastated to see that Joey is in the terminated group. Later that day, Tyler sends a short email to his employees informing them of the cuts, and sends Joey a separate email inviting him to get together after work for drinks, so that he can tell him about the termination face-to-face. Tyler and Joey meet up after work, but Tyler doesn't have the courage to terminate Joey. By the end of the night, Joey still believes that he is employed, and Tyler feels even worse for not telling him.

Questions to Consider

1. Was Tyler correct in terminating his employees through email? Why or why not?
2. Was Tyler correct in choosing to inform Joey of his termination face-to-face, instead of via email? Why or why not?
3. What should Tyler's next step be?
4. What is the best way for an employer to inform an employee of termination: written communication (such as email), face-to-face, or another way? Why?

TABLE 9.2 ■ 10 Reasons Letters Fail	
Reason	**Description**
Poor message	The message is poorly written.
Insensitive salutation	The salutation is too impersonal. For example, avoid "Hey" or just jumping right in to the message.
Too much on one page	People often try to fit too much on one page.
Lack of signature	Many people forget to sign their names on letters or to include their names in email messages.
Spelling errors	Spelling errors harm your credibility.
Grammatical errors	Grammatical mistakes harm your credibility.
Self-absorbed sender	The letter is focused on the sender, leading the reader to lose interest. Try to focus on "we" instead of "me."
Poor font choice	The reader should not be exposed to numerous font styles and colors.
Tone	The tone is not conversational.
Long paragraphs	The paragraphs are too long, leading the reader to lose focus.

Source: Lindsell-Roberts (2004, p. 4).

WRITING SAMPLE 9.2

Annual Performance Evaluation

WRITING SAMPLE 9.2

Annual Performance Evaluation

Annual Performance Evaluation   January 10, 2022
Ms. Alexis Hernandez
To: Personnel Annual Review File
From: Samantha Wilson, District Manager
                                              Terry White, Store Manager

This review is for the 2022 calendar year. As per the company policy, Ms. Alexis Hernandez may choose to include additions or corrections to this review.

*SALES

Ms. Alexis Hernandez meets weekly and monthly sales quotas in a timely manner. She surpassed her December sales quota by almost 40%, exceeding that of the other sales consultants in our division. Additionally, Ms. Hernandez surpassed her February sales quota by 30%, exceeding that of the other sales consultants in our district.

*COMMUNICATION

In attempting to create and maintain an all-around safe and secure environment for all employees, our company values feedback from its employees. Ms. Alexis Hernandez offers managers and supervisors innovative methods for maintaining the sales floor. Additionally, Ms. Hernandez has initiated constructive feedback to other sales consultants in order to boost sales for our division.

*TIMELINESS

Ms. Hernandez always arrives on time to begin her shift. However, when Ms. Hernandez breaks for lunch, she has returned late 60% of the time. On average, her lunch breaks are exceeded by 45 minutes. Although she makes up the time and exceeds her sales quotas, her tardiness impacts the other members of the sales staff. It is vital for all of our sales consultants to be reliable. As work schedules are constructed in efforts to suit peak sales hours, sales consultants should always maintain that schedule. In making timeliness a priority, sales consultants are able to maintain their weekly and monthly sales quotas. In all, timeliness is a key aspect to success in our company and in individual locations throughout our organization.

*CUSTOMER SERVICE

Being in the retail industry, we strive to provide the best customer service to our consumers. Being honest, reliable, and responsible is beneficial to gain repeat consumers. Ms. Alexis Hernandez properly illustrates the ways to interact with consumers on a day-to-day basis and provides clients with excellent support. In our regional division, Ms. Hernandez has received the most unsolicited positive feedback. She rated a 5 out of 5 in all areas with our consumers. One consumer stated, "Alexis does what she says she will do." Another states, "She is always helpful. I can tell she is truly invested in my satisfaction." With these statements it is clear to see that Ms. Hernandez has the necessary customer service skills.

*SUMMARY

Ms. Alexis Hernandez's performance is excellent. Her sales, communication, and customer service skills are above average. She exceeds the necessary elements in being a sales consultant for our organization.

   Although having excellent marks elsewhere, Ms. Hernandez will have to initiate change in her timeliness . Ms. Hernandez has agreed to limit her breaks to the allotted time of one hour. Additionally, Ms. Hernandez is now aware that this behavior impacts not only her, but also her team members and their sales.

Print on company stationery. Generally, employees are evaluated every 6 months to a year.

Always be certain to keep a file of annual evaluations and performance reviews for each individual employee.

Headings should outline the different aspects of job duties and requirements.

Always provide specific feedback when discussing weaknesses. Honesty shows the employee that you are serious about job performance expectations.

It is important to include information on how the employee's behavior impacts the organization as a whole, as well as the specific expectations for improvement.

"You may want to give more information about the type of performance you expect from your employees" (Guerin & DelPo, 2015, p. 202).

TABLE 9.3   ■   Tools for Professional Excellence. Obtaining a Recommendation Letter

When requesting a recommendation letter, consider these professional tips:

Plan ahead.	● Ask for letters well ahead of the deadline. Never assume your professor will have the time to write a strong letter if the deadline is only days away.
	● Give your professor plenty of advance warning (at least several weeks).
Ask nicely.	● When contacting your professor, it is preferable to do so in person. If that is not possible, then a telephone call or email will suffice.
	● Explain to your professor what you are applying for (and why), and ask whether they may be willing to write you a letter.
Ask what type of letter you may receive.	● You need to know whether the letter you will receive will be a strong letter, or one that is perhaps less in depth.
	● If the professor you ask has only taught you in one class, for example, then they may not have enough information to write an in-depth letter.
	● Knowing what type of letter to expect from the beginning can help you reevaluate your decision, and seek a letter from a different professor if necessary.
Write well.	● In all correspondence with the person who is writing a letter for you, ensure there are no grammatical or spelling errors.
	● Be professional, respect credentials (i.e., referring to a professor with a PhD as Dr.), and make sure what you write is readable.
	● Avoid common writing mistakes. Sloppy writing, poor grammar, and spelling mistakes can make the professor think less of you, and may affect the strength of their letter.
Include all relevant details.	When contacting the person, include all of the following (when applicable):
	● Detailed description of what you are applying for
	● A reminder of who you are (i.e., what classes you took under the professor)
	● Any helpful technical information, such as GPA or CV
	● Any and all deadlines for the letter
	● Links to any online forms or pages your professor will have to fill out
Make it easy.	● Always make the process of writing a letter of recommendation as easy as possible. In many cases, PDF fillable forms have parts that are to be filled out by the candidate ahead of time. Do this.
	● For hard copies, make sure to fill in parts that you are supposed to, and always include a stamped envelope with the address written out.
	● If you are required to pick up the letter and send it in as part of an entire application package, provide two envelopes, one for the confidential letter and another that the writer can slip the official envelope into, and arrange a system by which you can pick up the letter.
Send a reminder.	● A few days before the deadline, send a reminder email to politely remind the professor that the deadline is approaching.
Say thank you.	● It is always professional to say thanks to whomever writes letters of recommendation for you.
	● If your application ends up being successful, or you get that scholarship, you can even send a postcard or a short thank-you letter that leaves a positive and lasting impression.
	● As a minimum, send a short thank-you email.

Source: Adapted from Buddle, C. (2013, March 20). Ten tips when asking for a letter of recommendation. *Arthropod Ecology.* http://arthropodecology.com/2013/03/20/ten-tips-when-asking-for-a-letter-of-recommendation/

WRITING SAMPLE 9.3

Recommendation Letter

Recommendation Letter

WRITING SAMPLE 9.3

KELLY JONES

7609 Tanzanite Drive • Houston, Texas 78044 • 361.518.4900

---------------------------- kelly.jones@gmail.com ----------------------------

January 10, 2022

Natalie Contreras

HDS Life, Inc.

2727 Allen Parkway

Houston, Texas 77019

RE: Recommendation of Heather Gutierrez for Assistant Director of Communications

Dear Ms. Contreras,

It is my pleasure to recommend Ms. Heather Gutierrez, B.A., for the Assistant Director of Communications position with your organization. I worked with Ms. Gutierrez in the student-professor capacity during her time at the University of Houston. Additionally, I supervised her work as a student worker for the College of Liberal Arts, Associate Dean's Office.

Ms. Gutierrez has received her B.A. from the Communication Department of the University of Houston. During the time she was receiving her B.A., she demonstrated willingness to work hard in her studies, as well as in the office. In her studies, she prepared and delivered professional presentations, worked in teams, and led group meetings in order to produce the best quality work. Ms. Gutierrez served as the lead on a team-based project, ABC Read With Me. Under her leadership, this project exceeded its fundraising goal by 150%.

Not only did Ms. Gutierrez maintain a 4.0 GPA in her communication studies, but she also held a part-time position as an office assistant for the College of Liberal Arts. During her time at work, she routinely exceeded expectations. She organized events, maintained personnel files, and also created correspondence for my office. Based on Ms. Gutierrez's advanced skill set, she was responsible for special projects and duties not typically assigned to an office assistant.

Ms. Gutierrez has been an outstanding student and office assistant within the College of Liberal Arts. Overall, Ms. Gutierrez has demonstrated competencies that should serve her well in helping to lead the communications department of your organization as Assistant Director of Communications.

In closing, I would like to reiterate that based on my experiences with Heather Gutierrez, I would give her the highest recommendation. If you have any questions or need additional information, you may contact me at your convenience.

Sincerely,

Kelly S. Jones, PhD

Associate Dean, College of Liberal Arts

Include contact information.

Include the position you are recommending for.

Provide the employer with information regarding the candidate's qualities and skills that speak directly to the job posting.

Providing specific data on performance is very valuable.

As a reference, always highlight performances that are exceptional. As a student, always seek opportunities to utilize and advance your skill set.

Reiterate your recommendation of the candidate.

ETHICAL CONNECTION

Andrea's Trouble With Plagiarism

As you read this passage and answer the questions, consider how the way you communicate has an ethical dimension.

Andrea was a graduate assistant in her final semester at the university. She had never been an excellent writer, and her job required her to make significant contributions to an academic paper being published by the university. When Andrea found her contributions to be entirely too short, she took large sections from another article, which was already published, to meet the page requirements. Although she did not simply copy and paste entire sections into her paper, she made only trivial changes to the wording and did not give proper credit to the original article's author. Andrea was incredibly surprised when she was informed the university was letting her go as a graduate assistant. When she talked with the head of her department, Dr. Jones, he said that he was familiar with the paper she got her information from and considered it plagiarism since there were no citations. Dr. Jones also informed Andrea that it would be hard for her to find employment at another university with a plagiarism charge on her record.

Questions to Consider

1. What ethical boundaries did Andrea cross by taking research from another paper?

2. Why would a charge of plagiarism hurt Andrea's chances of finding another job at a university?

3. How could Andrea have avoided this outcome through the decisions she made about her writing?

4. Use the KEYS process to explain what steps Andrea could have taken to become a more effective writer.

Clearly, Yolanda's memo includes specific information about the goals and processes of the Company ABC Newsletter. With so many changes and new initiatives flying around in an organization, effective written communication is a must. What if Company ABC started a newsletter without informing the frontline employees and those in management about what to expect?

Proposals and Reports

Proposals are used in many business and professional settings to propose products and services to potential clients. Writing Sample 9.6 is a short proposal that describes the major components of a workforce communication assessment—an inventory or evaluation of the communication practices of an organization (also known as a communication audit). The proposal describes what the client can expect from the communication assessment. Notice how the proposal includes an objective and description of each component of the assessment (e.g., survey, focus groups, recommendations, project completion, project hours).

Now that you have a basic understanding of what a short business proposal looks like, let's review reports—written communication used to summarize research or assessment findings to inform managers about important issues related to business (e.g., customer service, employee satisfaction, employee morale). Reports are used to summarize both quantitative data (characterized

WRITING SAMPLE 9.4

Thank-You Letter: On The Job

WRITING SAMPLE 9.4

Thank-You Letter: on The Job

HEATHER GUTIERREZ

3606 Bon Soir Drive • Houston, Texas 78044 • 361.815.4949
----------------------------------- heather.gutierrez@gmail.com --------------------
-----

January 10, 2022

HDS Life, Inc.

2727 Allen Parkway

Houston, Texas 77019

Attention: Ms. Natalie Contreras

Re: Assistant Director of Communications

Dear Ms. Contreras:

I greatly appreciated the opportunity to meet with you to discuss the Assistant Director of Communications position, as well as the values and history of HDS Life, Inc.

After our conversation, I am confident my skills, education, and experience are an ideal match for this position and organization. As we discussed, I have a proven record of success with all position requirements. My ability to prepare and deliver professional presentations is ideal for the Assistant Director of Communications position. Additionally, my leadership and communication skills would greatly enhance the company's productivity and the quality of work being produced.

In all, I am eager about the prospect of joining HDS Life, Inc. Thank you again for your time and consideration. I hope to hear from you in the near future.

Sincerely,

Heather Gutierrez

This should be written in formal language.

Include the position for which you interviewed.

◀ *Remind the interviewer why you are the best candidate.*

◀ *Thank the interviewer again.*

---

by numbers, percentages, statistics, and surveys) and qualitative data (characterized by actual words, phrases, responses to open-ended questions, and interviews). The report provided in Writing Sample 9.7 is an example of what could be presented at the completion of a workforce communication assessment. As you see, this sample focuses on reporting focus-group data.

This focus-group report with recommendations, as well as other forms of research about businesses and organizations, can lead to changes in business strategies. Once an executive leadership team has had time to review recommendations made by a particular department or outside consulting firm, it's not uncommon to begin planning for the future of the organization. The next section explores the role of planning documents as forms of written communication.

Planning Documents

Once the organization knows its strengths and weaknesses, business leaders often engage in strategic planning—the development of a plan that emphasizes goals, initiatives, strategies, and targets utilized to help employees strive for a shared vision and commitment to the organization's core values. What do planning documents look like? Virginia has asked Yolanda to put together an internal communication plan (a plan that focuses on communication taking place inside the daily operations of any given business) and an external communication plan (a plan that focuses on communicating information about the organization or business to citizens or employees' families outside any given business). Planning documents are forms of written communication usually presented with maps and other visual designs to lay out a broader vision of where the company is going and what specific strategies will be used in the near future. Since Yolanda was struggling with her written communication on the job, she asked Virginia to help her come up with some basic planning documents for the internal and external communication plans at Company ABC. The two samples provided (Writing Samples 9.8 and 9.9) are good starting points to help employees understand components in the two communication plans at Company ABC.

Press Releases

When an organization or business wants to make an announcement to the community, it uses press —forms of written communication used to send messages and make announcements to a variety of media organizations, including newspapers, radio, television news, and internet reporters. Read the press release in Writing Sample 9.10 and grade Yolanda's effort. What changes or edits, if any, could improve the press release? What words did you identify that are vague?

Proactive Media Writing

Press releases cover topics beyond workforce layoffs, bankruptcies, and corporate scandals. There are a number of positive things that organizations announce in press releases (e.g., scholarship programs, donations, community events). Industries that affect the environment and community safety (e.g., petrochemical facilities, oil refineries) are often held to standards set by the federal government. If you work for an organization that has the potential to harm people or the environment, it's critical to be ready to respond to news that can put your company in a negative light.

In addition to writing the press release about the Company ABC literacy initiative, Yolanda needed to focus on proactive media writing—a form of written communication similar to a press release that emphasizes an organization's commitment to safety and compliance. There are certainly other components to a proactive media strategy. For example, oil refineries may choose to post billboards with images of their employees helping kids in the community. Put simply, if citizens in the community maintain a positive image of an organization, they will not immediately think of the potential harms brought on by the industry. Therefore, using written communication as a proactive media strategy helps the organization prepare for negative news that could tarnish the organization's reputation at the local, state, national, and perhaps even global levels. Read the proactive media release in Writing Sample 9.11 and grade Yolanda's effort. Do you think she does a good job of damage control? Remember, written communication can make or break a company's image and overall success, regardless of the industry.

Email

People working in businesses and professional organizations rely on their email systems to communicate with colleagues and accomplish their work (Khan & Khan, 2012; Kibby, 2005; Shipley & Schwalbe, 2008; Thompson, 2008). Given how prevalent email usage is and will continue to be in business and professional communication, we can't emphasize enough how important it is to strive for written communication and professional excellence when using email.

Indeed, written communication is just as important when composing email messages as it is with the other forms reviewed in this chapter (see discussion of concerns related to email in Chapter 8). Tools for Professional Excellence 9.3 offers tips for writing email with professional excellence.

Indeed, written communication is just as important when composing email messages as it is with the other forms reviewed in this chapter (see discussion of concerns related to email in Chapter 8). As you work to develop your written communication skills, give special attention to Tools for Professional Excellence 9.2 and 9.3. While 9.2 provides practical tips for creating documents and collaborating using Google Docs, 9.3 offers tips for writing email with professional excellence.

WRITING SAMPLE 9.5

Process Directive Memo

WRITING SAMPLE 9.5

Process Directive Memo

[COMPANY LOGO]
PROCESS DIRECTIVE 126

DATE: January 10, 2022
TO: All Company ABC Employees
FROM: Yolanda Smith
RE: Company ABC Quarterly Newsletter, Process Directive 126

Objective: To communicate important information from the Executive Team to the employees of Company ABC, as well as to the community. The primary goals of the Company ABC Quarterly Newsletter are to

- provide a newsletter to distribute information, both internally and externally, about plant operations and employee news in a QUARTERLY format;
- recognize employee social activities, retirements, and accomplishments;
- communicate information from the lead team, gain sharing, safety, employee social activities, etc.;
- share the Company ABC Values with employee families and community leaders;
- establish a positive impression of the business in the community and enhance the workplace culture.

Frequency: The Company ABC Newsletter has been designed and approved to be distributed electronically, mailed to the employees' homes, and mailed to community leaders in a QUARTERLY format.

Process: The Lead Team and Business Unit Managers will contribute information to Virginia Wolf to prepare for distribution quarterly.

Newsletter Contact: Virginia Wolf will collect information for each section of the newsletter. Members of the Executive Team should

- send information to Virginia Wolf to prepare for distribution each quarter;
- pay attention to activities, such as social clubs and activities, to be included;
- support internal and external distribution of the newsletter;
- respond to calls for information to be included in the newsletter.

Directive: Company ABC provides access to the newsletter in both electronic and printed formats. Members of the Executive Team and all Company ABC employees should support the distribution of the newsletter to institutionalize effective communication, enhance workplace culture, and build positive impressions of the business in the community.

WRITING SAMPLE 9.6

Proposal for Services

WRITING SAMPLE 9.6

Proposal for Services

WORKFORCE COMMUNICATION ASSESSMENT
COMPANY ABC
Prepared By
[INSERT NAME]

WORKFORCE COMMUNICATION ASSESSMENT
PART I: SURVEY
OBJECTIVE: Evaluate communication preferences of Company ABC workforce

DESCRIPTION:

1. Survey Planning with Company ABC Leadership Team
2. Workforce Communication Survey will be designed
3. Company ABC survey will

- focus on communication effectiveness (best way to get the message out);
- identify what is ineffective (communication channels that don't work);
- include areas in which the Leadership Team is interested;
- evaluate important factors related to employees' on-the-job experience (satisfaction, morale, managerial support, communication expectations); and
- be reviewed and approved by Leadership Team.

4. Workforce will be surveyed
5. Information from survey will be prepared and presented to Leadership Team

PART II: FOCUS GROUPS
OBJECTIVE: Collect specific preferences about how to communicate effective messages at Company ABC

DESCRIPTION:

1. Focus-Group Planning with Company ABC Leadership Team
2. Workforce Focus Groups will be designed
3. Company ABC Focus Groups will

- collect specific information about employee communication needs;
- identify specific ways to communicate effective messages at Company ABC;
- include questions in which the Leadership Team is interested; and
- explore specific factors related to employees' on-the-job experience (satisfaction, morale, managerial support, communication expectations).

4. Focus Groups will be conducted
5. Information from Focus Groups will be prepared and presented to Leadership Team

PART III: RECOMMENDATION
Based on the information collected from the surveys and focus groups, recommendations will be made to the Company ABC Leadership Team. Information will be provided about how Company ABC can communicate effectively during reorganization and as it moves forward.

PROJECT COMPLETION: Early January 2022
PROJECT HOURS: Not to exceed contract

WRITING SAMPLE 9.7

Focus-Group Report and Recommendations

Focus-Group Report and Recommendations

(REMINDER: Reports like the one in this sample usually include an appropriate title page, table of contents, and bibliography.)

Private and Confidential
Prepared for Company ABC by Strategic
Company ABC: Focus-Group Report and
Recommendations
Yolanda Smith,
Director of Communications

DATA COLLECTION INFORMATION
- Number of Focus-Groups: 10
- Number of Focus-Group Participants: 99
- Length of Focus-Group Interviews: 62–87 minutes

OVERVIEW
The report that follows includes major themes and specific responses to the current communication, morale, safety, and benefits at Company ABC. Hourly, salaried, and executive leadership employees participated in focus-group forums in which they discussed major topics connected to communication at Company ABC (communication about change, workforce preferences on how to communicate/get the message out, morale, safety, and benefits). In order to articulate a clear sense of the focus-group responses, the report is organized as follows: (1) overall reaction and tone, (2) communication, (3) safety, and (4) benefits/rewards and recognition. In addition, the report includes recommendations regarding communication methods and strategies to support the future of Company ABC.

Thematic Analysis of Data
Overall Reaction and Tone

The overall reaction and tone in the focus-group discussions were extremely negative. Focus-group participants all expressed dissatisfaction, low morale, and uncertainty about their jobs at Company ABC. The participants specified that they feel "in the dark" and that all they hear are rumors about people getting fired, big layoffs, and contract negotiations. Lack of communication, job uncertainty, and poor working conditions were central themes in all 10 groups. The participants noted that this is the worst they have ever seen Company ABC in terms of morale. Themes of job uncertainty, low morale, and poor communication were consistent across all groups. The themes are summarized with the following comments:

- "We are completely in the dark about what is going on around here."

- [Insert other responses or comments.]

Communication

All 10 focus groups provided insight into specifics and/or priorities for improving communication. In doing so, they addressed what is not currently working and what they would like to see in terms of improvement.

Communication About Change. All 10 groups were clearly confused about the direction of Company ABC, as well as organizational changes.

- "They tell us that change is coming, but we don't know what that is. They intentionally keep us in the dark."
- [Insert other comments.]

Methods of Communication. All 10 groups noted methods of communication available but not used, such as email, technical tools, electronic message boards, bulletin boards, and memos. This theme was summarized with the following comments:

- "People do not use email. There are over 1,100 employees here; only about 450 use email."
- [Insert other comments.]

Overall, there was an agreement in all 10 groups that there are communication methods (mechanisms) available at the plant that work but are simply not being used. Information is not current.

Safety

All 10 focus groups expressed major concerns about safety procedures and poor working conditions. *Safety Procedures and Workplace Conditions.* In all 10 groups, discussions about safety focused on poor workplace conditions at Company ABC as demonstrated by the following comments:

- "This place gives lip service to safety. They do not care about safety. The only thing they are interested in is production."
- [Insert other comments.]

Benefits/Rewards and Recognition

Throughout the discussions, all 10 focus groups expressed major dissatisfaction with benefits and a lack of reward/recognition at Company ABC. All 10 groups discussed a need for increased wages and more reward/recognition. Of the 10 groups, 8 specifically discussed the need for more clarity when it comes to gain-sharing goals.

(Cotiued)

(Continued)

Benefits and Pay. All the focus groups made comments about their dissatisfaction with the benefits and pay at Company ABC.

- "We used to make a good living around here. Our health insurance has gone up, our copays are higher, and the company has done nothing to offset our costs."
- [Insert other comments.]

Gain Sharing. All 10 focus groups expressed major dissatisfaction with gain sharing.

- "They lie to us about gain sharing."
- [Insert other comments.]

Rewards and Recognition. Of the 10 focus groups, 9 expressed major concerns with the current reward and recognition of Company ABC employees. Interestingly, one focus group argued about reward and recognition. Several participants believed that a paycheck should be enough incentive. The individuals who disagreed with the majority contended that reward and recognition are never good enough for people and that someone will always complain. However, the majority of focus-group participants emphasized that reward and recognition need to be improved.

- "The newsletter used to let us know who retired and who was new to the plant. They don't inform us about accomplishments or what's going on. We are never recognized and are not appreciated."
- [Insert other comments.]

Recommendations

1. Bulletin Board Locations
   - All locked bulletin boards need to be cleaned up. All old announcements need to be removed. There needs to be a date and posting system in place. All messages approved for distribution should be monitored. After a designated period of time, messages/postings should be removed.
   - [Insert other recommendations.]
2. Terminate Wide Distribution of Company ABC Daily Report
3. Replace Company ABC Daily With Company ABC Monthly Newsletter
   - Company ABC must revive a monthly newsletter that is both distributed at work and mailed home so that employees and their families are exposed to the message. The newsletter should be made available at designated locations at the plant.
   - [Insert other recommendations.]
4. Revive Use of Electronic Message Boards

- Company ABC must revive use of Electronic Message Boards.
- [Insert other recommendations.]

5. Emphasize Traditional Face-to-Face Communication
   - There must be designated communication and team time.
   - [Insert other recommendations.]
6. Train Leaders as Information Facilitators
   - Team leaders, managers, or those designated as leaders at Company ABC must be trained in effective oral communication and meeting facilitation.
   - [Insert other recommendations.]
7. Town Hall Meetings Hosted by Executive Team
   - After the Journey to Excellence plan moves forward, host town hall meetings about Company ABC.
   - Insert other recommendations.]
8. Craft a Message and Disseminate to Community
   - Advertise positive message about Company ABC to external audience.
   - [Insert other recommendations.]
9. Utilize Professional Communication and Marketing Consultants
   - Administration should continue to seek outside professional communication/transition experts
   - (e.g., Strategic Communication Concepts, The Turnover Team) for technical assistance and advice.
   - [Insert other recommendations.]
10. Develop Employee Orientation Program
    - As Company ABC makes the transition, develop employee orientation program that can be first used with all current employees who are on board with the transition. The orientation should be required for everyone who is going to stay and, of course, all new employees.
    - [Insert other recommendations.]
11. Employee Development Series
    - As Company ABC makes the transition, develop employee education series on topics that support Company ABC Values.
    - [Insert other recommendations.]

Appendix A
Focus-Group Participants

	SALARIED	HOURLY	EXECUTIVE
Total	41	58	3

Total = 99 participants
Executive Leadership Representatives = 3 participants

KEYS TO EXCELLENCE IN WRITTEN COMMUNICATION

Remember that it is essential for you to use professional excellence in writing, not only through electronic communication but in traditional writing as well. When examining the first key, *know yourself*, determine if you want to achieve professional excellence, and know that part of that entails improving your written communication. Examine your strengths and weaknesses related to all aspects of your written communication (see Table 9.4 Tools for Professional Excellence). Set a goal to improve your written communication skills, and realize that you need members of your team to edit your writing.

Written communication entails paying special attention to confidential records and information privacy.

iStockphoto/nirat

TABLE 9.4 ■ **Tools for Professional Excellence.** Collaborating Using Google Docs	
To create documents and collaborate using Google Docs, follow these practical tips:	
Key Points	**Practical Tips**
Creating a document	● To create a document, first go to your Google Drive interface and log in with your Google account.
	● Click on "My Drive" and this drops you into a screen that lists all of your current documents (if you have already created any).
	● To create a new document, click on the "New" button.
	● You can add a new folder to store documents in, or you can just create a new document. You can also create a new spreadsheet (similar to Excel) or presentation (similar to PowerPoint).
	● Once you create a new document, you'll be presented with a blank page with a standard set of word processing tools at the top.
	● Additionally, your document is stored in the cloud, which means you don't have to worry about saving it to your computer or losing it. It's auto-saved every minute, so all you need to do to get back to it is open your web browser, go to your Google Drive, and click on it.

To create documents and collaborate using Google Docs, follow these practical tips:	
Key Points	**Practical Tips**
Collaboration	● Traditionally, if you are working on a document that requires feedback and input from others in your office, chances are that each person will make notes and changes in the document and email it back, leaving you with five different versions that you need to consolidate back into one.
	● Google Docs eliminates this headache. All you need to do is "share" the document with your coworkers and ask them to make their changes directly in the same document. You are now working on one document as opposed to five different ones.
	● To do this, click on the "Share" button in the upper right. This will open up a screen that allows you to share the document.
	● By default you are inviting people to edit the document. This means that the people you invite will be able to make changes. However, you can always undo their changes. Once you click "Done," an email with a link to the document will be sent to the people you invited. They will then be able to click the link and view the document, as well as edit it.
	● You can also add a personal message to the document (which is a good idea) so that the people you are inviting have some context.
	● Using Google Docs for collaborative editing is an efficient process. It means that everyone is editing only one document; everyone always sees the latest version; and all changes and comments are tracked and saved. Additionally, the document can be edited on a tablet or mobile devices, for even more flexibility.
	● If anyone wants to download a copy of the document in another format, like Word or PDF, go to the File menu and hover over "Download" to export it to another format.
Different uses	● Drafting a memo or policy in your office that needs group feedback
	● Taking notes for a meeting and sharing the document with meeting attendees
	● Sharing a Google Spreadsheet with your sales team and asking them to keep it up to date with stats
	● Working on a blog post or an article as a team
	● Collaborating on meeting agendas
	● Planning for group work when serving on boards and committees

The next key, *evaluate the professional context*, is essential for you to become more audience centered and aware of how you are coming across to other people in your writing. Become more mindful of whether your written communication sounds demanding or negative.

The third key, *your communication interaction*, makes you a more professional communicator in that you can make better choices when using written communication. Start to think before sending out memos and emails, and be much more aware that your passion to perform and motivate can affect your written communication. When there is a need for a company announcement via written communication, think about the best way to get the message out. If there is a need for written communication, engage in careful planning and editing of the written message. As the message is sent, also communicate with members of your staff face-to-face to make sure they understood the message.

Graphs, charts, and maps are integral to writing with communication excellence.

iStockphoto/HAKiNMHAN

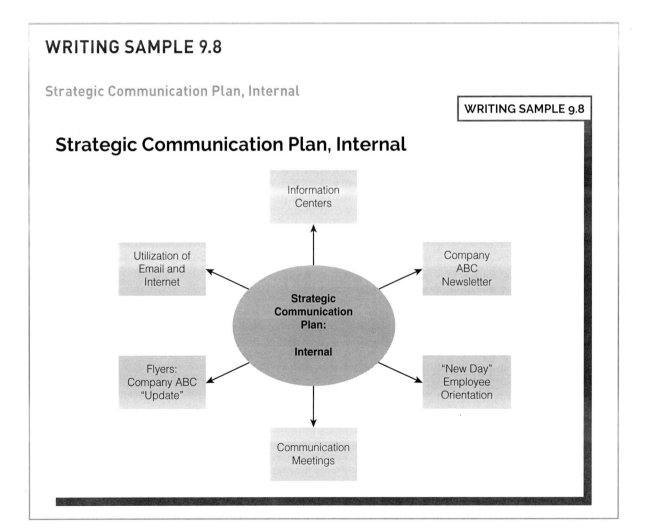

Working from home can be valuable during difficult times, but think about the advantages and disadvantages of checking email from your home computer or personal phone. Employees often experience increased anxiety, decreased sleep quality, and lower relationship satisfaction when they feel emails from work could arrive at any moment, regardless of the time of day or day of week (Thomas, 2021). Technology tends to blend our personal and professional lives in many ways, and it is important to set boundaries that help with your work–life balance.

iStockphoto/Charday Penn

WRITING SAMPLE 9.9

Strategic Communication Plan, External

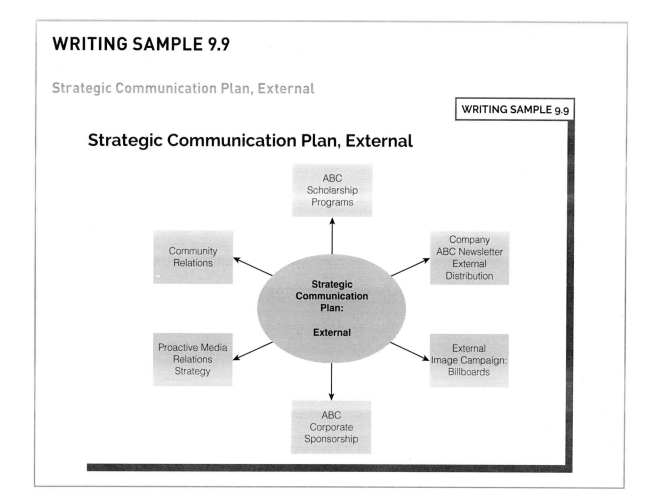

WRITING SAMPLE 9.10

Sample Press Release

WRITING SAMPLE 9.10

Sample Press Release

For Immediate Release:

ABC: *Read With Me* Triples Initial Fundraising Goal

CORPUS CHRISTI, TX January 10, 2022 - ABC: Read With Me spokesperson Jennifer Rodriguez announces the final count of books the non-profit organization was able to donate to a local elementary school library and its students as 1,228. In attempts to raise awareness of the low levels of literacy in the Coastal Bend, the members of the organization were excited to find they had more than tripled their original goal of purchasing 400 books for the low-income school.

The organization was founded by six university students attempting to "light up literacy" in the Coastal Bend. In an effort to raise awareness of the low literacy levels, the students began raising funds to purchase books for three grade levels at a local elementary school. After a week's worth of fundraising, the students found they had exceeded their initial goal. As a result, a total of 1,116 students, ranging from kindergarten to fourth grade, were gifted a book. Additionally, 112 books were donated to the school's library.

In an attempt to spread awareness for low literacy rates in the Coastal Bend, ABC: *Read With Me* raised funds to purchase books for a low-income elementary school. Furthermore, in continuing to aid their efforts, the members of this organization urge individuals to "light up literacy" in your home today!

Contact Information:

Jennifer Rodriguez

Spokesperson

ABC: Read With Me

361-815-0000

This is a usual introduction for most press releases.

Include city, state, and date.

The first paragraph is the most important. This should capture the editors' attention.

Be concise. Do not provide too many details.

Include contact information for the organization.

When you use written communication, engage in the fourth key, *step back and reflect*. Become more reflective of written communication and realize how it could be misunderstood and send the wrong signal.

Ask yourself some of the following questions as you step back and think about your written communication: Was my memo response appropriate? Did my questions in the letter sound negative? Did my team think it was rude when I passed out the process directives printed in red? Should I use all caps in my email message? Is sending a memo about attitude and productivity to everyone inappropriate? The fourth key also makes you more thoughtful about all aspects of your written communication, not just when you send out a memo or write a letter (see Table 9.5 Tools for Professional Excellence). Your evaluation and reflection can result in positive changes that other people will notice.

WRITING SAMPLE 9.11

Proactive Media Writing

WRITING SAMPLE 9.11

Proactive Media Writing

Company ABC in Compliance With Mercury Vapor Regulations

In recognition of a recent study released on the link between mercury exposure and cancer, Company ABC emphasizes its commitment to operations and community safety with assurance of state and federal environmental compliance. Company ABC understands the importance of medical and environmental research that helps support company operations that are safe for its workforce and community. While the recent study raises some important discussion points for future research, the study does not substantiate any links between environmental pollutants and autism. Further, the amounts of mercury vapors released from the plant are minimal, according to state and federal environmental regulations.

Realizing that some concern has been raised by one study, here is some information about the role of mercury in our operations at Company ABC. Mercury is a naturally occurring metallic element found throughout the crust of the earth in concentrations averaging about 0.5 ppm (1/2 of 1 part per million, equivalent to about 1/2 a teacup in a railroad tank car). Normally, it is found compounded with sulfur as the mineral cinnabar. In the pure or metallic form, it is a silver-colored liquid at ordinary temperatures and for centuries was called "quicksilver." It has long been used in making pharmaceuticals, in the mining industry, and to treat fur and hides. The most common exposure

most people have to mercury is in dental fillings, called amalgams, which are about 50% mercury.

Bauxite, like most soils, contains trace amounts of mercury in amounts ranging up to about 1/2 part per million. Each year, Company ABC processes about 3.8 million tons (about 7.7 billion pounds) of bauxite. Most of the mercury contained in the bauxite, typically 1,200 to 1,400 pounds per year, leaves the plant combined with the plant's main solid waste stream, bauxite residue, in the same solid mineral form in which it arrived. The residue is stored in large surface impoundments. The plant has permits that actually allow it to emit up to about 60 pounds per year into the air, but favorable plant chemistry stabilizes nearly all the material as a solid. Typically only 4 to 7 pounds per year are released into the atmosphere either as metallic mercury vapor or as an oxide.

Company ABC continues to modernize the plant to improve processing efficiency, energy efficiency, product quality, safety, and respect for the environment.

Our ultimate goal is to secure the long-term potential of this business and to become a serious competitor in the global market.

For more information, please contact:
Yolanda Smith
Media and Community Relations Coordinator
ABC Company
215-999-0000

TABLE 9.5 ■ **Tools for Professional Excellence.** Tips for Writing Email	
To write email with professional excellence, follow these practical tips:	
Key Points	**Practical Tips**
Slow down.	● Effective communication and good writing take time, so take the time to formulate your thoughts and figure out exactly what you want to say.
	● If you're struggling to find the time, block out time on your calendar to devote solely to email.

(Continued)

Key Points	Practical Tips

TABLE 9.5 ■ Tools for Professional Excellence (*Continued*)

To write email with professional excellence, follow these practical tips:

Key Points	Practical Tips
Always have a beginning, middle, and end.	● An email introduction should always start with a greeting, and then follow with the nature of the email (i.e., a friendly greeting, or a preface to why you're emailing the person). ● An email body should always include all the information that the recipient needs to accomplish whatever you are asking of them (i.e., contextual information, details, or data), and it should be presented in a logical, reasonable manner. ● An email conclusion should always include some sort of action plan (i.e., reminding the recipient of any deadlines), as well as a final greeting and full signature.
Proofread and fact-check.	● Once you've typed out your email, don't send it off right away. Always reread the email at least once. ● Besides checking for basic spelling and grammar mistakes, always make sure you correctly spelled any proper names and that any facts (such as dates) are accurate. ● Check the overall tone of your email: Does it sound too businesslike when you're trying to be friendly? Does it come across as too lighthearted when you meant to be professional? This is also a good time to decide whether using things such as exclamation points or emojis is appropriate for that particular email. ● It's never a bad idea to ask someone else to look over your email, especially if it's an important one.
Think about how you would feel if it went public.	● Imagine how you would feel or respond if your email was seen by anyone other than its recipient (i.e., your boss). ● Picturing these scenarios will help ensure that your email sounds respectful and professional and is an accurate representation of how you want the world to see you.

Source: Adapted from Muse, T. (2013, November 19). An editor's guide to writing ridiculously good emails. *Forbes.* www.forbes.com/sites/dailymuse/2013/11/19/an-editors-guide-to-writing-ridiculously-good-emails/

EVALUATE THE PROFESSIONAL CONTEXT

Austin Needs a Recommendation Letter

As you evaluate the passage below, consider whether this behavior is appropriate for this professional context.

Austin found out about a new scholarship, and he needed to fill out the application as soon as possible. The only problem was that he found out about it at the last minute, and a recommendation letter from a professor on campus was required. He had taken several courses taught by Dr. Chang, so he felt it was okay to ask for a recommendation letter. Austin had so many things going on and didn't have time to make an appointment or call, so he dropped by during Dr. Chang's office hours. The following interaction took place regarding the letter:

Austin: Hi, Dr. Chang! I'm really in a bind. I need you to write me a recommendation letter today. I figured that since your office hours were from 1:00 p.m. to 3:00 p.m., you would have time to get it done before your next class. I'm really in a hurry, and I figured I could count on you.

Dr. Chang: Austin, I actually have an appointment with another student about a project, and she's about to come in any minute.

Austin: Oh, that's okay. I'll just wait outside until you're done with the other student. If you can get it done by 2:45 p.m., that will work for me.

Dr. Chang: Unfortunately, I will not be able to get to the letter today. I really need more notice. I am more than happy to help but would need some specific information about the scholarship and where to send the letter.

Austin was not happy about Dr. Chang's response. What was he supposed to do? We all have busy schedules and encounter sudden deadlines that are out of our control, but requesting a recommendation letter has to be done with professional excellence at the core. Clearly, Austin was not successful in his approach to getting a letter from Dr. Chang.

Questions to Consider

1. Did Austin act appropriately, given the professional context?
2. Was Dr. Chang's behavior professional? Why or why not?
3. What can you learn from Austin's experience?
4. How could the KEYS process (see Figure 9.1) help Austin improve his communication skills?

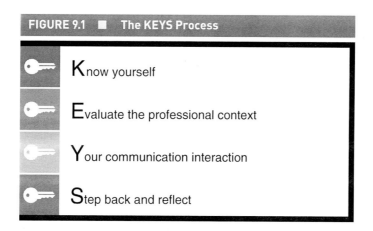

FIGURE 9.1 ■ The KEYS Process

Know yourself

Evaluate the professional context

Your communication interaction

Step back and reflect

EXECUTIVE SUMMARY

Now that you have finished reading this chapter, you should be able to

Discuss the importance of written communication:

- Official documents, memos, emails, and other forms of written communication reveal something about you as a professional.

- Important policies, requests, and organizational procedures are conveyed through written communication.

- Proposals, employee terminations, media relations, and the like are achieved with written communication.

- Written communication must be present to achieve professional excellence.

Apply strategies for developing written communication:

- With spelling and grammar check, as well as good old-fashioned proofreading, you can correct typos (mistakes in typing), misspellings (mistakes in spelling), and grammar errors (e.g., sentence fragments, inappropriate use of punctuation). Just as a typo on your résumé can lose you a job, a typo on a report can cause you to lose credibility. Misspellings, typos, and sending something to the wrong department are all roadblocks to professional excellence.

Discuss the different types of written communication:

- The business letter is used to address formal matters in professional communication including cover letters, information sent to customers, announcements about business events, and the like.

- Employee reviews provide feedback to employees about how they are performing on the job.

- The recommendation letter is a form of written communication used to provide a documented reference for students and professionals.

- Thank-you letters are written communication used to express appreciation to coworkers and clients.

- Proposals are used in many business and professional settings to propose products and services to potential clients.

- Reports are written communication used to summarize research or assessment findings to inform managers about important issues related to business.

- Press releases are forms of written communication used to send messages and make announcements to a variety of media organizations, including newspapers, radio, television news, and internet reporters.

Apply the KEYS approach to achieve professional excellence regarding written communication:

- Know yourself. Determine that you want to achieve professional excellence, and know that part of that entails improving your written communication. Examine your strengths and weaknesses related to all aspects of your written communication.

- Evaluate the professional context. This is essential for you to become more audience centered and aware of how you are coming across to other people in your writing. Become more mindful of whether your written communication is sounding demanding and negative.

- Your communication interaction. Make yourself a more professional communicator by making better choices when using written communication.

- Step back and reflect. Become more reflective of written communication and how it could be misunderstood and send the wrong signal.

EXPLORE

1.   Visit the website of public relations firm Affect (www.affect.com). In the blog section, pick a blog of your choosing and analyze the writing. As a professional communicator, do you find the writing to be clear and concise? How can public relations writing be applied to your personal career path?

2. Find a video example of a company currently in damage control over bad publicity. What (if any) steps has the company taken to improve its public relations? As a communication professional, what public relations strategy would you recommend to a company in that situation?

3. Find an example of how your workplace or school practices written communication with you personally (e.g., course syllabus, job orientation newsletter). Is the overall message easy to read and comprehend? What (if any) improvements could help make the message more effective?

REVIEW

1. Describe the difference between general language and specific language.

2. A(n) _____ is a list of questions that encourage the writer to think about audience, purpose, key issues, and delivery.

3. _____ serve as a form of written communication used in business and professional settings to provide feedback to employees about how they are performing on the job.

4. What type of documented letter would you need as part of a university admission or employment application?

5. _____ are descriptions of new policies or procedures and changes to those that are already in place.

6. A(n) _____ is an inventory or evaluation of the communication practices of an organization (also known as a communication audit).

7. Explain the difference between quantitative and qualitative data.

8. _____ refers to the development of a plan that emphasizes goals, initiatives, strategies, and targets utilized to help employees strive for a shared vision and commitment to the core values in an organization.

DISCUSSION QUESTIONS

1. Discuss an example of a time when you were offended by written communication. How did you respond? Did you use written communication for your response, or did you respond in person?

2. Do you have concerns about other forms of written communication not covered in this chapter? As a professional, what steps would you take if you were asked to use a form of written communication with which you were not familiar? Would you delegate the task to someone else? Would you be honest that you were not comfortable with the project?

3. What steps do you or will you take on the job that will help you strive for professional excellence with written communication? What strategies do you have, if any, that work for you?

4. Take a moment to reflect on your experiences with written communication. Have you ever been caught in an email or letter exchange that crossed the line from professional to uncivil? What can organizations do to prevent uncivil written communication?

5. Some scholars are concerned about the negative impact of text messaging and other forms of technology on written communication. Do you share this concern? Do you think technology encourages you to be less professional in your written communication? Why or why not?

STEP BACK AND REFLECT

The Attitude Memo

As you read this passage and answer the questions, step back and reflect on what went wrong in this professional situation.

Shannon: Did you see that memo from Yolanda?
Joel: No, what's going on?
Shannon: She sent another memo about team attitude. The team is getting really annoyed.
Joel: Has anyone responded?
Shannon: No, but I heard that several employees have been complaining.

Based on this brief conversation between Shannon and Joel, it seems that Yolanda has done some damage using written communication. Yolanda is the assistant director of communication at Company ABC. Attitude and having fun are really important to Yolanda, so she decided to communicate her standards of performance with the following memo:

DATE: January 10, 2022
TO: Communication Team
FROM: Yolanda Smith
RE: Team Attitude

I expect my team to showcase a positive attitude when working on projects. If you all have any questions about attitude, see me in my office.

Yolanda sent out memos like this once a week. Her goal was to have a highly cohesive team, and she wanted to be respected. However, things were not going very well. Her team seemed to get more and more negative and unmotivated as each week passed.

Step Back and Reflect

1. What went wrong with Yolanda's memo?

2. How would you respond if you received a memo like this at your job? How could Yolanda's memo be improved?

3. How could she benefit from the KEYS process related to her written communication?

TERMS TO REMEMBER

business letter (p. 218)
downsizing letter (p. 218)
employee reviews (p. 218)
external communication plan (p. 227)
general language (p. 216)

grammar (p. 217)
internal communication plan (p. 227)
memo (p. 219)
misspellings (p. 217)
networking notes (p. 219)

"No one person can know or do it all. And the more we can collaborate and work together as a team, the better product we will have." —Gary Kelly

iStockphoto/s-cphoto

10 LEADERSHIP AND CONFLICT MANAGEMENT

What constitutes a great leader is a subject that is debated continually. Depending on your field of study or career choice, there can be many different traits that are preferred when trying to establish ideal leadership.

Dan Price, the founder and CEO of credit card processing company Gravity Payments, made headlines when he announced he was cutting his own salary to raise his company's minimum salary to $70,000 for its 120 employees. Before this salary increase, the company's starting wages were roughly $35,000. This change resulted in a 10-times increase in the number of first-time homeowners for Price's employees every year since increasing the minimum salary, and Price's employees went from having between no and two babies born per year among the team to over 65 born within 6 years. The company's revenue also soared every year since increasing the minimum salary, with the exception of 2020 when COVID-19 started (Tayeb, 2021). Whether you're CEO of a megabrand or owner of a doggy day care startup, investing in your personal brand is always a sound investment in your company. When the individual at the helm has the right image and reputation, they impact everything from boosting the company brand to forging emotional connections with employees, investors, customers, and media (Cohen, 2017).

WHAT IS LEADERSHIP?

To develop professional excellence as a leader, you must have a firm grasp of what constitutes leadership. To understand what leadership is, we must first understand what leadership is not. Although leaders may possess some desirable personality traits, be charismatic, be born into a family of leaders, or have a job title such as manager or executive, true leadership is not defined by any of these things. Let's explore each of these more closely for a better understanding of why they don't equal leadership.

Leadership is something that takes work. Leadership excellence demands constant attention and self-evaluation. Leaders at many different companies, such as Amazon, Starbucks, Chick-fil-a, Target, and Wells Fargo—have started offering college tuition benefits as an incentive to attract talent. The number of companies offering this type of benefit increased as employee turnover rates soared in 2021 (Farrington, 2021).

iStockphoto/JohnFScott

Leadership is not a trait. A trait is a distinguishing characteristic or quality that's part of one's individual character; traits are often seen as inborn or genetically based. For example, some people have the personality trait of being extroverted or outgoing, while others are introverted, less outgoing, or shy. In the 1920s and 1930s, scholars focused on determining the traits that make up a leader, exploring which traits all great leaders share, as well as traits that differentiate *leaders* from *followers*. Scholars studying the leadership traits concluded that there are indeed traits that distinguish a leader from a follower (Barbuto & Gifford, 2012; Mann, 1959; Stogdill, 1948). The traits thought to make up a great leader were many (see Table 10.1). But if you begin to compare various leadership traits with various leaders, you will see quickly that great leaders are not all alike, and the traits they possess can vary greatly. In addition, both leaders and followers have many of these leadership traits. Furthermore, these leadership traits have been criticized for biasing traits that male leaders display while ignoring traits possessed predominantly by female leaders (Powell, 2012; Rosener, 1997).

Extending from the leadership-as-traits approach is the notion that charisma or birthright equals leadership. Definitions of *charisma* include characteristics such as magnetic charm, allure, and the supernatural or magical ability to appeal to followers. "Charisma is, literally, a gift of grace or of God" (Wright, 1996, p. 194). History is full of charismatic leaders who possessed confident, assertive styles that drew loyalty and support from followers. There is no doubt that charisma is a wonderful characteristic for a leader to possess. Yet charisma alone doesn't make a great leader, nor is the lack of charisma a mark of poor leadership. There are many great leaders who will never be labeled as charismatic. Conversely, there are many people who possess charisma but never ascend to leadership excellence.

TABLE 10.1 ■ Leadership Traits	
Trait	**Description**
Physical traits	Young to middle-age, energetic, tall, and handsome
Social background traits	Educated at the "right" schools and socially prominent or upwardly mobile
Social traits	Charismatic, charming, tactful, popular, cooperative, and diplomatic
Personality traits	Self-confident, adaptable, assertive, and emotionally stable
Task-related traits	Driven to excel, accepting of responsibility, having initiative, and being results-oriented

Source: G. Allen (2002).

Leadership has also often been seen as a birthright. The thinking here is that if there are certain inborn traits that make a great leader, then those traits will be passed on from parent to child. Monarchies are based on the notion of birthright. In some cultures, subjects believed that their kings, queens, czars, or chiefs were superior to the rest of the population. In extreme cases, they were elevated to godlike status. Similarly, many business empires are passed on from one generation of a family to the next with the belief that each new generation will bring with it the drive and skills of the business founder. Alas, this concept of leadership is also flawed. Within every monarchy, there are examples of leadership excellence and failed leadership all in the same family tree. In the Roman Empire, Claudius and Nero illustrate this point. Claudius, due to a disability, was viewed as a poor choice for emperor—but in the end, he proved to be an effective leader. Under his rule, many public works were built, and Rome expanded its territories into Britain. However, his grandnephew and successor, Nero, holds an infamous place in history for being a horrible leader. He is remembered for his extravagant lifestyle and cruelty and for "fiddling while Rome burned." The same holds true in the business world. Conrad Hilton may have built one of the most prestigious hotel chains in the world, but his great-granddaughter Paris likely has a different take on leadership than her great-grandpa did.

In the United States, the break from the English monarchy and the establishment of an elected government reinforced a link between leadership and job title. The person who's hired or voted into the leadership role gets the title. Those with the leadership job title lead, and the rest follow. In fact, during the Industrial Revolution, the idea that "management thinks and workers work" was developed, two-way communication was stifled, and managers literally told employees, "We don't pay you to think." Again, a little reflection on your own experiences should help you spot the weakness with the notion that job title equals leadership. Do you know people with leadership titles who are poor leaders? Do you know people without leadership titles who are excellent leaders? Leadership skills and leadership titles are not mutually exclusive. Remember, leadership is something that team members share regardless of title.

If leadership is not a trait, a matter of charisma, a birthright, or a job title, what is it? Leadership is "a dynamic relationship based on mutual influence and common purpose between leaders and collaborators in which both are moved to higher levels of motivation and moral development as they affect real, intended change" (Freiberg & Freiberg, 1996, p. 298). As you study this definition, the role of communication should be clear to you. According to this definition, *change* is dependent on a dynamic relationship, mutual influence, and a common purpose. As you've already learned, you can't have a *dynamic relationship* without effective communication. In addition, *mutual influence* and *common purpose* both rely on two-way communication. Furthermore, having leaders and *collaborators*, as opposed to leaders and followers, again implies the need for effective communication. By examining this and other definitions of leadership, you should see that the role of communication is clear—it's intrinsically woven into every facet of leadership excellence. Everyone has leadership potential, and by using the KEYS process for communication excellence, you can unlock your leadership potential.

In this chapter, we focus on specific communication skills that you'll need to achieve leadership excellence. The areas that can make or break you as a leader include utilizing power, improving communication with leadership theory, hiring the right team, following up and following through, communicating about your team, dealing with difficult people, giving feedback, and managing your public image.

UTILIZING POWER

Let's review for a moment our discussion of superior–subordinate relationships from Chapter 6. Status is a person's rank or position in an organization. Typically, the superior (supervisor/employer) is the higher status person, and the subordinate (employee) is the lower status person. Typically, people who hold a higher status have more years of experience, training, knowledge, and rank than do those with lower statuses (this may not always be the case). For example, a doctor has the leadership title and status over the nursing staff. This title and status hold true even if the doctor is right out of medical school and the nursing staff is full of veteran nurses with years of experience and hands-on training.

Job title is about status, but as we discussed in the preceding section, job title does not equal leadership. True leadership is about power. Both professional and personal relationships have a power dimension. To better understand the role of power in your relationships and the resulting communication, let's look at the six types of power as defined by John French and Bertram Raven (1968): legitimate power, coercive power, reward power, expert power, referent power, and connection power.

Legitimate power is based on a position of authority. The manager has legitimate power over the department budget and employee schedules. Although a position or job title may give someone legitimate power, it doesn't mean that person exercises that power.

Coercive power refers to the ability to control another person's behavior with negative reinforcement, whereas reward power describes control over another person's behavior with positive reinforcement. Clearly, a person with legitimate power has both coercive and reward power over subordinates. For example, a manager could reward an employee with a good schedule and a raise or punish the employee with an undesirable schedule and no raise. But people with legitimate power are not the only ones who have coercive and reward power. Anyone who can offer positive or negative reinforcements has power. So the staff member who can process your paperwork quickly versus slowly and the administrative assistant who can choose to squeeze you in or make you wait for a meeting with the boss both have coercive and reward power.

Expert power is based on one's superior expertise in a specific field. In our fast-paced, increasingly specialized world, it is no wonder experts are given power. For example, Madison has an entry-level position at a large company, but she is the only person in her division who speaks fluent Spanish. In this situation, Madison holds expert power in all projects that contain Spanish components.

You give referent power to someone because you want that person to like you. You may feel a connection to that person, or you may wish to be like that person—either way, it gives them power over you. High school peer pressure is a form of referent power. Tiana has been a member of the accounting firm for years. She's organized, highly knowledgeable, and excellent with customers. Tiana has a positive attitude about life and has found a healthy balance between work life and home life. Although she has never taken a leadership title, many of the young accountants look to her as a role model. They follow her lead and seek her advice because they have granted her referent power.

Connection power is based on the old expression, "It's not what you know but who you know." Having a connection to people in positions of power or having a strong support system definitely acts as a source of power. If the CEO's son works in the mailroom, he will likely be treated differently from the other members of the mailroom staff.

Leaders face both positive and negative confrontations. Leadership excellence is about turning those negatives into positives.

istockphoto/fizkes

Examining types of power reveals a critical difference between managers and leaders. *Manager* is a title, which brings with it legitimate power. Managerial functions include important duties such as being in charge of and responsible for various goals and functions in an organization. It also involves supervising subordinates. Leaders may be managers, and they may have legitimate power, but neither is a requirement for leadership. Leadership functions include influencing and guiding followers as opposed to subordinates, as well as being innovative and creating a vision for future direction. Leaders often have multiple types of power, with referent power likely in the mix.

Now that you understand the different types of power as well as the difference between status and power, it is important to apply this knowledge to the KEYS process. *Know yourself.* Begin by asking yourself, "What kind of power do I possess? How does my power affect my communication interactions? How do I react when communicating with coworkers or supervisors who possess each of the types of power noted above?" When *evaluating the professional context*, ask yourself, "What kind of power do various members of my workplace exhibit? How effective are the legitimate leaders and people with status? What are their strengths? How could they improve?" Make it a habit when *your communication interaction* occurs to *step back and reflect*. Ask yourself, "How does power affect communication in my workplace?"

Ineffective leaders rely solely on their legitimate power to motivate others and fail to take into account the power of other members in the workplace. As you achieve professional excellence, you will reflect on the role that power plays in all your communication interactions.

STEP BACK AND REFLECT

Rosa's Review

As you read this passage and answer the questions, step back and reflect on what went wrong in this professional situation.

A regional manager could not make sense out of the dramatically different ratings that were given to Rosa, the administrative assistant for the western office. Some members of the team had given her extremely high ratings, while others had given her extremely low ratings. The written comments ranged from "She is the glue that holds us together" to "She plays favorites, deliberately delays projects, and should be fired." How could they be talking about the same person?

During her annual review, Rosa explained the office dynamic as follows:

I have worked here for 15 years, and I know how everything is run. I know the procedures like the back of my hand. The problem is, some people don't care about the procedures. They don't listen to me when I tell them they are doing it wrong, and then they want me to fix their messes. That's not my job. Another problem is timelines. I am busy, and I will get to things when I get to them. But poor planning on their part does not equal a crisis on my part. Plus, when I have bailed them out or dropped everything to help them, they are never grateful. They have no respect for me or my job.

Now I will bend over backward for the people who follow the rules and respect my time. And you know what? Those people are always grateful. They give me thank-you cards, take me to lunch, and remember my birthday. They see me as part of the team, not "the secretary."

Step Back and Reflect

1. What went wrong?

2. What types of power are coming into play in this office?

3. Does Rosa have power in her position?

4. Is Rosa's behavior professional?

5. How could the regional manager use the KEYS process to improve communication in the western office?

IMPROVING COMMUNICATION WITH LEADERSHIP THEORIES

Just as understanding theories on power can improve your communication as a leader, so too can studying leadership theories. Over the past century, scholars have studied leadership-developing theories and models designed to help us understand what effective leadership is and to train us to be better leaders. Implementing the knowledge and insight contained in various leadership theories is a must if you ever plan to excel as a leader.

Imagine yourself at a fork in the road. Each path before you represents a different choice you could make as a leader. If you select the wrong path, you may never find your way. If you select the right path, you will still have a journey ahead of you, but your chances for success will improve dramatically. Each leadership theory discussed in this section will help you select the right path for communicating as a leader given your team, your task, your situation, and your vision. Let's begin by reviewing various leadership theories developed through the years.

Behavioral Theories

As we noted earlier, the traits approach to leadership was among the first formal attempts to study leadership. But when it became clear to scholars that leadership was more than merely a list of traits, they began to turn their attention to the behaviors of leaders.

In elementary school, you were probably taught three leadership styles: authoritative, laissez-faire, and democratic. Under the authoritative style, the leader makes all the decisions with little input from the team. With the laissez-faire style, the team makes the decisions with little input from the leader. (*Laissez-faire* is a French expression meaning "allow to do.") In the democratic style, the leader follows the will of the people, or at least the majority of the people, with decisions often being made through voting. Although these terms create a classification for leaders based on behaviors, they were designed as broad categories for explaining systems of government, not as a formal study of leadership behavior.

Fortunately, behavioral theorists such as Douglas McGregor did develop categories for leaders that were based on research into leader/manager behavior. McGregor (1960) observed two very different leadership styles that he labeled   and   . The differences between Theory X managers and Theory Y managers are derived from their opposing views of employees. Theory X managers believe that

- The average employee dislikes work

- Because most employees dislike work, they must be controlled, directed, and threatened so they will perform their job duties

- Employees prefer to be told what to do, avoid responsibility, have little ambition, and value job security above all

By contrast, Theory Y managers believe that

- The need and desire to work is as natural as the need and desire to play or rest

- Controlling, directing, or threatening are not the only means for getting employees to perform their job duties

- The average employee is motivated by achieving goals

- The average employee not only accepts responsibility but many times seeks it

- The average employee's full intellectual and creative potential is not utilized in most organizations

What can you learn from studying McGregor's work that will make you a better leader? Managerial attitudes about employees have a direct effect on communication style. It should come as no surprise that Theory X managers have a very different communication style from that of Theory Y managers. Theory X managers support a top-down communication. The vast majority of information flows down the organizational chart from managers to employees in the form of commands. Since employees are seen as disliking work, rewards and punishments are used to keep them motivated. The idea that managers think and workers work stems from Theory X's roots in classical management theories.

Those subscribing to a Theory Y style of management support two-way communication. The Theory Y manager acts more as a facilitator or a coach working to empower employees. They seek employee feedback and insight. Employees are encouraged to take part in decision-making.

So which communication style is more effective: (1) the top-down style of Theory X or (2) the two-way communication of Theory Y (see Tools for Professional Excellence 10.1)? It depends on the situation. There are times when the authoritative communication styles associated with Theory X are a must for effective leadership. Think about an emergency situation: A building is on fire; a platoon is under attack; a patient has been wheeled into the ER with life-threatening injuries. Having the senior-most person take charge and begin barking orders as the rest of the team members perform their duties with speed is, without question, not only appropriate but also necessary in these examples. This realization led researchers to the next wave of leadership theories, known as the situational leadership approach.

TABLE 10.2 ■ Tools for Professional Excellence. What Is Your Attitude About Work?

- ● Do you subscribe to the Theory X or Theory Y style of management? Why?

- ● Do you believe people inherently dislike work, or do you believe work is as natural as play?

- ● Have you ever worked for a Theory X manager? Was this style effective or ineffective?

- ● Have you ever worked for a Theory Y manager? Was this style effective or ineffective?

Situational Leadership Theories

According to Sadler (1997), one of the major limitations of the traits approach was its failure to take into account the importance of the situation. This same limitation holds true for the work of McGregor. However, researchers such as Blake and Mouton, Fiedler, and Hersey and Blanchard studied the impact of situation on assessing leadership effectiveness.

The Managerial Grid, developed by Robert Blake and Jane Mouton (1964, 1978), includes five managerial styles: impoverished, country club, authoritative, middle-of-the road, and team. Unlike researchers before them, Blake and Mouton incorporated into their model two dimensions: concern for people and concern for task (see Figure 10.1). The impoverished manager has a low concern for both people and task. The country club manager has a high concern for people and a low concern for task. The authoritative manager has a high concern for task and a low concern for people. The middle-of-the-road manager has a moderate level of concern for both people and task, while the team manager has a high concern for both people and task.

What can you learn from studying Blake and Mouton's Managerial Grid? When selecting an effective leadership style, you have to consider multiple factors. Be careful not to make the mistake of glancing at the grid and thinking that team manager is the best way to lead. There may be times when the task at hand is small or less than urgent, so an effective leader might use the country club style to increase the cohesion of the group. At another time, the task might be urgent, opening the door for an authoritative style—it depends on the situation.

This idea was reiterated and expanded on by other researchers, such as Fiedler. According to Fiedler's Contingency Theory, there's no best way for managers to lead. Excellent leaders assess the situation and then select the leadership style and accompanying communication style that best fits the situation. When assessing the situation, Fiedler reports the need to look at three factors: the leader–follower relationship, the task structure, and the position power (Fiedler, 1997; Fiedler & Garcia, 1987; Wisse & Rus, 2012). Let's say that Christy and Michael are trying to determine how best to lead their respective teams. Christy has a positive relationship with her team, and they share a history of mutual respect. The structure of the task is clearly defined, and she has strong position power because the executive team has given her the funds and the order to get the job done. Michael has just started his position, so there is little history or trust between him and the team. The task at hand is somewhat ambiguous. Furthermore, this initiative is Michael's idea. It has not been mandated by the executive team, so he has little position power. How should Christy communicate with her team? Should Michael use the same style as Christy since she has the kind of relationship with her team that he wants with his team?

Before you give any advice to Christy or Michael, you should first review Hersey and Blanchard's (1977) Situational Leadership Theory (see Table 10.3). According to this theory, to select the most effective communication style, leaders should take into account task behavior, relationship behavior, and level of maturity/readiness of the followers.

Based on Hersey and Blanchard's work, which leadership style should Christy use with her team? Which style would work best for Michael, given his task, his relationship, and his team's readiness? As you can see, the research of situational leadership scholars will allow you to better *evaluate the professional context* as you work your way through the KEYS process to professional excellence as a leader.

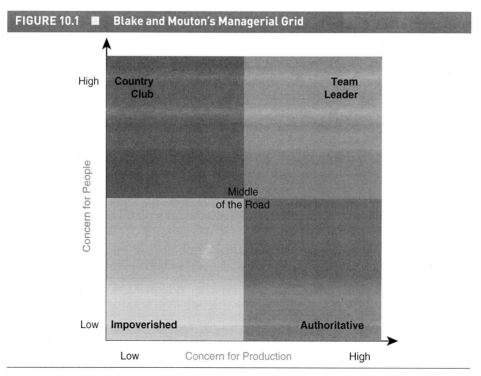

FIGURE 10.1 ■ Blake and Mouton's Managerial Grid

Source: Grid International. "The Fifth Achievement" by Robert Blake and Jane Srgley Mouton, *Journal of Applied Behavioral Science: A Publication of the NTL Institute 6*, no. 4. Published by SAGE Publications on behalf of the NTL Institute for Applied Behavioral Science.

Leadership is about bringing people together.

iStockphoto/Edwin Tan

TABLE 10.3 ■ Hersey and Blanchard's Situational Leadership Styles	
Leadership Style	Description
Telling (high task/low relationship behavior/low level of readiness)	Leader provides detailed instructions; a useful style with new employees, when things must be completed quickly, or when employees lack motivation.
Selling (high task/high relationship behavior/moderate level of readiness)	Leader works to persuade the team to support the task; involves two-way communication, but the leader is still in the position of authority.
Participating (high relationship/low task behavior/moderate to high levels of readiness)	Leader facilitates the discussion, and the decision-making is shared between leaders and followers; the main role of the leader is to facilitate.
Delegating (low relationship/low task behavior/high level of readiness)	Leader assigns the task or identifies the problem, but the team is empowered to develop and carry out the plan of action.

Source: Hersey and Blanchard (1977).

Transformational Leadership

One final area that must be addressed is that of transformational leadership. Transformational leaders are defined as leaders who articulate a goal or vision to an organization and then inspire followers to make that vision a reality, requiring them to transcend their own personal interests for the good of the organization (Bolman & Deal, 1997; Wright et al., 2012). Transformational leaders are often known for being charismatic. In addition, their leadership style can be characterized as empowering, which helps develop innovative thinking and initiative among followers. Be warned—the effectiveness of transformational leaders is difficult to measure (Den Hartog & Belschak, 2012; Wright, 1996).

What you learn from this research into transformational leadership is that truly outstanding leaders in the 21st century have a vision of where their teams or organizations are heading and communicate that vision to their teams. They also empower their teams, allowing them to become a part of that vision.

HIRING THE RIGHT TEAM

Leadership should be something that you share with the other members of your team. You will be acting as a coach, so you should be engaged in the recruitment process. It's highly unlikely that you'll be placed in a leadership position that allows you to select your entire team or department; it just doesn't work like that. You will most likely accept a leadership position and begin working as the titled leader with a preexisting group. Developing this group into a team may be challenging. Our point is this: You must begin by developing the players you have been given. Over time, some of those players will leave or your organization will grow, and you'll have the opportunity to hire new team members. Leaders with professional excellence know that hiring is a process that begins long before the first candidate arrives for an interview and lasts long after orientation and training. Let's review each step in this process from a leader's perspective.

Developing the New Employee Profile

When hiring opportunities occur, it's incredibly important that you, as the leader, participate in every stage of the hiring process. It's also important to get the rest of the team involved. So begin by framing the problem as a challenge facing the team—there's a vacant position that must be filled. If someone has left an existing position, there's a tendency among status quo groups simply to place an advertisement for that identical position. In contrast, innovative teams use the vacancy as an opportunity to evaluate team duties and needs as they currently exist, not as they were written years ago. As companies grow and change, so do the duties of their employees. In addition, according to McGregor's Theory Y, each new team member brings with them a host of skills not being utilized.

As the leader with professional excellence, you should facilitate a discussion about the opportunities this new position creates and what the team really needs. This may be the time when some current team members shift their duties, allowing them to put some of their underutilized skills to work. It also might be the time to add new skills to the team.

Leadership excellence focuses on hiring the right people.

iStockphoto/Cecilie_Arcurs

As the team evaluates which skills will be needed, make certain that people skills and attitude are part of the conversation. As a professional, you should not only pay attention to your own people skills and attitude—you should also pay attention to the people skills and attitudes of those hired into your team. If you make a hiring decision based solely on technical training, you'll be making a terrible leadership error. Successful organizations focus on how people skills and attitude contribute to a positive organizational culture with enhanced employee and customer satisfaction (Gilbert et al., 2012; Krapels, 2000). When hiring new employees, you must be certain the employees have all the following: the competencies needed for the position, an openness and excitement about training and developing new skills, a positive attitude, career goals that will fit into your organizational culture, and, most important, professional excellence.

During the Interview

Once the position has been advertised, the interview questions must be drafted. You may or may not be responsible for drafting the questions, but as the leader, you should always review the questions, giving your input and ultimately your approval. When drafting or reviewing questions, keep your purpose in mind. What are we looking for in a candidate? Then ask, how do these questions inform us about those skills or qualifications? Let's say you need an employee who can work under the pressure of a short deadline. You could ask, "Do you work well with deadlines?" Any smart interviewee will answer, "Yes, I do." So a better question might be, "Tell me about your experience working under deadlines." As the interviewee provides examples, you can probe each situation to determine how successfully they really functioned. This would also be a good question to ask professional references to verify the information the interviewee gave you.

EVALUATE THE PROFESSIONAL CONTEXT

I Hire Only Nice People

As you evaluate the passage below, consider whether this behavior is appropriate for this professional context.

Paul was the branch manager of a car rental chain. Although the chain had thousands of branches all over the globe, the employees at Paul's branch stood out. Their customer satisfaction scores were exceptionally high. Their turnover was very low. They had promoted a record number of entry-level employees into managerial positions throughout the corporation. When problems arose, such as low sales or budget cuts, the team members worked together to address issues, as opposed to bickering and backbiting. To what did Paul attribute the success of his team? He attributed it to the "nice" factor.

When Paul interviewed potential employees, he made sure they met all the qualifications listed in the job posting, and then he asked the deal-breaking question: "How would you describe your personality? What kind of person are you?" If they gave an answer that included the word *nice* or a self-description that translated into "nice," they were still in the running. He would also check references, always asking, "Would you describe so-and-so as a nice person? Why would you describe them this way?" He would then ask various members of the staff who had interacted with this potential employee to describe their interactions. Of course, he was looking for interactions that would indicate a "nice" quality. Once he hired a new employee, he would provide them with an orientation and training process that included frequent reminders that "we hire only nice people around here."

> **Questions to Consider**
>
> 1. What do you think of Paul's hiring strategy?
> 2. What qualities will you look for when you hire new employees?
> 3. How will you know if a candidate has these qualities?
> 4. Should "nice" be a goal when developing a professional context?

During the interviewing process, professionals set the tone. As the leader, you may not be the one conducting the initial interviews. Yet you should meet with all potential team member(s) *before* they are hired and engage in open dialogue with others who will be participating in the interviewing process about the importance of hiring people with professional excellence.

When conducting an interview, remember that everyone gets nervous—you should take the first few minutes to help put the interviewee at ease. Make some small talk and allow the interviewee to get comfortable with you and the setting. This will create an environment in which you can see beyond this prospective team member's nerves to see their true potential.

As you learned in Chapter 4, interviewees are also assessing the organization to determine if they even want this position. As the leader, you must be sure you and your team treat all interviewees with professional excellence.

After the Interview

A leader with professional excellence makes certain that new team members feel like part of the team from Day 1. You should make it a point to greet all new employees on the day they arrive. In addition, you must make certain they will be properly oriented and trained. Training and orientation may or may not be part of your job duties. Regardless, you must make sure new employees are given the tools they need to succeed. Assign training duties—don't just think training will occur magically—and follow up to make sure the new employee is getting what they need to succeed.

FOLLOWING UP AND FOLLOWING THROUGH

Excellent leaders know the meeting does not end when they say "adjourned." As we discussed in Chapter 7, teams must allow for innovation and shared leadership. To achieve these goals, team members should leave most meetings with homework—send them out to explore information. Allow them time to incubate ideas so that they can brainstorm more effectively. Give them tasks to complete as the team accomplishes its goals. Remember, excellent leaders don't do all the work alone. Excellent leaders involve the team members so that they, too, can share in the leadership, which will make your job more manageable.

To achieve this, you must follow up after each meeting. A poor leader makes one of two mistakes. First, some poor leaders assign homework but then fail to ask about the results at the next meeting. If this occurs once or twice, team members will stop participating and will not bother to do the things you have assigned. The second mistake is "taking care" of team members who don't perform their duties. If tasks are assigned but the team members fail to perform those assigned tasks, they must be held accountable. Poor leaders see that an assignment has not been done and just do it themselves. This teaches team members that they are not accountable or responsible, and the leader will end up doing most, if not all, of the work.

As the leader, you must create a "follow up and follow through" norm within your team. To begin enacting this norm, send out an email thanking the team members for their participation in a recent meeting, state the homework to which each team member has agreed, and remind everyone of the next meeting time. By doing this, you have reaffirmed in people's minds what they have to do for the next meeting. Let's say this team meets once a month. Two weeks before the next meeting, send out a reminder to each team member saying, "You are on the agenda for our next meeting." Then, ask if there are any additional items team members would like included on the agenda or if they need any supplemental materials. One week prior to the meeting, send out the agenda, and be sure to list the name of each team member who will be reporting during the meeting. Also note areas in which the entire group should be prepared, and be ready to discuss. During the meeting, call on each person even if they aren't prepared. Make the individual responsible for saying, "I did not do my assigned task." Do not remove that person from the agenda. Make them accountable. This will set up a norm in which you follow up so that team members follow through. As a result, your meeting will be more productive and everyone can share in the leadership.

COMMUNICATING ABOUT YOUR TEAM

As we discussed in Chapter 6, no matter how many times you say, "This is confidential," "What happens in this room stays in this room," or "This is just between us," information still leaks out. Somehow, some way, gossip almost always finds its way to the informal communication network (aka the grapevine). You can rest assured that the way you communicate about your team will get back to your team. And your message, positive or negative, will have a major impact on the way you and your team interact. Furthermore, the way you communicate about your team will have a major impact on the way others view you as a leader. When it comes to communicating about your team, follow two simple rules: When there are problems, the buck stops with you; and when there are successes, you never take the credit. Let's explore each rule in more detail.

If your team makes a mistake, if your department has a shortcoming, if something goes wrong in your department, or if there is an error, the buck stops with you. You're the leader of that team; therefore, in a public forum, you assume responsibility for whatever the problem may be. Excellent leaders don't make excuses. They take responsibility when their teams do not perform at the expected level. In doing so, you'll earn the respect of your coworkers, supervisors, customers, and team. Your professionalism and integrity will be remembered. Watch an episode or two of a reality show like *Survivor* if you want to see how unprofessional a leader appears when they start blaming team members and pointing fingers because the team failed to meet expectations of group efforts. Leaders with professional excellence acknowledge the problem, apologize if necessary, and correct the problem. Privately, some team members' behavior may need to be addressed, but publicly, the professional leader stands up and takes responsibility.

On the flip side, when your team has met expectations, exceeded expectations, or had an outstanding performance, you don't take the credit. In fact, you should publicly give credit to your team. You may be thinking, "Wait a minute. I have to take responsibility for the mistakes, but I don't get credit for the successes. That seems unfair." Fair or unfair, it's a characteristic that all leaders with professional excellence must demonstrate. Don't worry, others know that you led the team, and they understand that great teams are a product of great leaders. If it's a team effort, the whole team should share in the praise, and you should be the first one cheering for them. Even if they are not there to hear your praise, it will get back to them. The results will lead to strong morale and loyalty from your team members.

YOUR COMMUNICATION INTERACTION

Questions About Leadership

As you read the passage below, consider what would be a more effective communication strategy in this situation.

Kelly recently began her career at a large advertising agency. After her first 2 weeks, Kelly realized she was receiving ambiguous directions from her supervisor. Her fellow team members never seemed to be on the same page, and oftentimes they were assigned to the same piece of work while other duties were never assigned at all. After their weekly meeting, Kelly's team decided it was time to confront their boss about their conflicting responsibilities. Since their boss was out of the office constantly, Kelly decided against trying to set up a face-to-face meeting because it would be nearly impossible for everyone to have a shared meeting time set aside. A phone meeting or group email exchange appeared to be the best options, but members of Kelly's team had different opinions about which medium would be more useful in clearing up the redundancies and the confused communication with their boss. Kelly realized time was of the essence, as her team needed clear communication from their supervisor before the quarterly performance review the following week.

Questions to Consider

1. What communication channel do you believe would be the most effective for Kelly's team?
2. What are the pros and cons of the members of Kelly's team meeting with their boss face to face, over the phone, or via email?
3. Which communication tactic do you use most often, and why?
4. What other communication technologies might be useful to Kelly's team in this situation?

DEALING WITH DIFFICULT PEOPLE

As consultants and corporate trainers, we often ask employees, "What is it like working in your department or organization?" The vast majority of them reply, "We are like a family." The idea that employees and supervisors function as a family or a team is promoted heavily in corporate America. Since we already have explored the team metaphor, let's use the family metaphor to examine an extremely important duty of every leader who aspires to professional excellence: namely, dealing with difficult people.

Meeting Your Organizational Family

The family metaphor can have both positive and negative ramifications. To many supervisors, the thought of employees running around saying, "We are all one big, happy family here at Company X," is wonderful. But let's remember that families can be dysfunctional, too. In fact, even the most functional families have problems from time to time. So let's begin our discussion by meeting some of the difficult people you might encounter in your organizational family.

Brother Steven is a bully (Bernstein, 2001). As is the case with most schoolyard bullies, Steven has a bad temper. He uses aggression and anger to get his way. Other family members allow him to have what he wants to avoid a blowup. Steven's behavior also gets him out of a lot of responsibilities, because no one wants to work with him or hold him accountable.

Sister Angela is a sniper. During meetings or discussions, she pops in with nasty comments meant to wound her targets. She's full of sarcastic remarks and masks inappropriate comments

It takes a leader with integrity to hold difficult people accountable for their actions.

iStockphoto/PeopleImages

with humor. Some of Angela's comments include "Who came up with that lame idea?" "That's a great suggestion coming from a blonde!" and "That never worked before, but I am *sure* it will work now."

Aunt Madison loves drama. She loves to create drama in the workplace by starting arguments, gossiping, holding grudges, and the like. She will blow small things out of proportion for attention. Her communication includes angry outbursts, tearful breakdowns, and the silent treatment.

Uncle Jason is a slacker. He finds any excuse not to work. His excuses include "I don't know how," "No one trained me," "That's not my job," and "You didn't tell me to do that."

Cousin Kathy is a different type of slacker, known as a vampire. She is more appealing than your run-of-the-mill slacker. When Kathy is around, there always seems to be laughter and fun, but in the end, others always do her work. Like a vampire, she draws you in and then drains you dry (Bernstein, 2001).

Cousin Paul is the office grump. A dark cloud follows him wherever he goes. He often rolls his eyes, breathes hard, and presents a bad attitude. He makes comments such as "I can't believe we have to do this," "This is stupid," and "Why do I always have to do all the work?"

Grandpa Bill is the roadblock to change. He doesn't like change. In fact, he often refuses to carry out changes in his duties. Grandpa Bill can be heard saying, "Back in my day . . ." or "Things used to be different (or better) around here."

Grandma Millie can be a distracter. She may mean well, but she often leads the team on tangents. Her examples, comments, and questions are long-winded and stray from the purpose of the meeting.

Nephew Robert is a patient, turning his coworkers and sometimes even his bosses into his counselors. He brings personal problems to work and discusses them on company time. His personal life often affects his attendance and performance on the job.

Finally, there are the nieces. Niece Elaine is the team player. Niece Marie is the star. Both nieces are hardworking and dependable. For Elaine, the goal is to complete her tasks, get along with her coworkers, and serve her customers. As for Marie, she shares Elaine's goals, but in addition, she wants to take on extra duties, learn more, and advance in her career. Unfortunately, in many organizations, both nieces are rewarded for a job well done with extra work and little praise.

It's quite likely that your workplace will have a different mix of "family members." For example, none of these labels is gender specific. You can have female grumps and bullies as well as males who are stars but enjoy drama. You may not have all these family members in your workplace, and you may have some others we didn't mention. Even worse, you may have one person who embodies several (or all) of these dysfunctional roles.

So take a moment to reflect on your workplace. One important step in achieving professional excellence, even with difficult people, is *knowing yourself.* As our 86-year-old neighbor often says, "A skunk never smells its own tail." In other words, everyone around the skunk knows he stinks, but the skunk doesn't have a clue. You don't want to be that skunk, so take a long, hard look at yourself and determine which family member best represents you. You may come to realize that while most of the time you are a star, on occasion you can be a bully, slacker, or dramatic. None of us is perfect, so we all have qualities that can at times make us difficult to work with. That's okay as long as you know your own weaknesses and actively seek to control and improve them.

Once you've identified your role(s) in the organizational family, reflect on the rest of your group. Who makes up your organizational family tree? How do the different family members positively or negatively impact your work environment? How effectively or ineffectively do you communicate with each type of family member? As a leader, what have you done or what will you do to foster professional excellence within all members of your organizational family? Remember, communication is a process, and even if the other person is behaving in a way that's less than professional, you must still work to maintain professional excellence. Furthermore, as the leader, you must work to develop professional excellence for all your team members, both functional and dysfunctional. For tips on improving employees' attitudes in the workplace, see Tools for Professional Excellence 10.2.

TABLE 10.4 ■	**Tools for Professional Excellence.** Improving an Employee's Work Attitude
To help improve an employee's work attitude, consider these practical tips:	
Key Points	**Practical Tips**
Know the facts.	● If you are a supervisor or another employee tasked with addressing someone's attitude problem, know exactly what you should be addressing.
	● Talk with anyone who has experienced the employee's attitude problem and get their account of the issue.
Ensure privacy.	● Helping someone improve their attitude can be a touchy subject, especially at work. Only include those people who are directly affected by the employee's attitude.
	● When addressing any kind of issue regarding an employee's attitude, always do so in a private, one-on-one setting to help those involved avoid any additional embarrassment.
Lay down the law.	● When addressing an employee's attitude problem, make sure the employee is clear on any workplace codes of conduct they have violated.
	● Be clear on any consequences for the employee's behavior tied to their attitude, especially for future reference.

To help improve an employee's work attitude, consider these practical tips:

Key Points	Practical Tips
Develop a plan of action.	● Once the problem has been addressed and the employee is aware of the behavior, set up steps that the employee can take to improve their attitude.
	● Be specific about what actions the employee should take. For example, if they are prone to angry outbursts, consider anger management classes. Make sure the plan of action is tailored to the needs of the specific employee.
End on a positive note.	● Addressing an employee's attitude problem can be stressful enough; ending the meeting on a positive note lets the employee know that you have faith in them and that the problem will be resolved.
	● Find something about the employee to praise: Let them know that even though the behavior needs to change, the employee is still a value to the company. This will keep the employee motivated and help them to resolve the attitude problem.

Source: McFarlin, K. (2015). How to tell an employee about attitude complaints. *Chron.* Adapted from https://smallbusiness.chron.com/tell-employee-attitude-complaints-10541.html

Leader as Parent

If the department or organization is like a family, then, metaphorically speaking, the leader is a parent. Again, this can have both positive and negative ramifications. On the positive side, good parents are understanding, focus on developing their children, and serve as role models. The same holds true for good leaders. A good leader understands employees' duties, workloads, constraints, and goals because they are open to giving and receiving feedback. Good leaders also develop their employees. If you have a quality employee in your organization, a star or even a team player, you should work to retain that employee. Clearly, they will not stay in the same job forever, so you should coach that employee, helping them advance within your organization. A big part of developing employees is giving them proper training and then empowering them to take on assignments and responsibilities. Finally, good leaders serve as role models. Telling employees that customer service is important and then failing to display it yourself is the mark of an unprofessional leader. "Do what I say, not what I do" is ineffective with children and adults. A leader with professional excellence makes certain that their behavior reflects the values and attitudes they want everyone on the team to emulate.

The "leader as parent" metaphor also has some negative ramifications. First, leaders may begin treating employees like children. This can result in the leader's making excuses when employees don't perform their duties. Second, the leader as parent may make all the decisions for the group and fail to share leadership. *Father Knows Best* was a clever title for a 1950s sitcom, but it is no way to develop a team in the 21st century. Leadership must be shared. The third negative ramification of leader as parent comes when leaders begin to feel as though they cannot fire their employees, since you cannot fire your children. As we discuss in the next section, learning to reprimand or fire employees is something a leader must do.

GIVING FEEDBACK

Can this family/parenting metaphor help in your quest for professional excellence as a leader? The answer is a resounding yes. We can learn many valuable leadership lessons from parenting skills and strategies because it often takes a good leader to manage unruly kids. Effective parenting often involves laying out the expectations, providing feedback, and following through with consequences. Good behavior is rewarded, and bad behavior has consequences. Although putting a time-out chair in your workplace will not work, the underlying principles will. Leaders with professional excellence set expectations; provide feedback for praise, accountability, and motivation; and enact consequences. A leader with professional excellence understands how to use feedback to mentor stars as well as to turn difficult family members into team players.

The good news is, laying out expectations, providing feedback, and following through with consequences works for all types of difficult employees, as well as star employees. You don't need to become a psychologist who analyzes each type of difficult employee and then develops a plan that fits their psychological profile. Instead, you must make sure everyone understands what's expected of them in terms of both job performance and professional behavior. You must provide constant feedback, praising those employees who meet expectations and reprimanding those who fail to meet them. You must follow through, which can mean a bonus, a reprimand, or termination. For tips on delivering constructive criticism, see Tools for Professional Excellence 10.3. Let's take a closer look at feedback as it relates to each of the principles noted above.

Setting Expectations

Parenting metaphor or no parenting metaphor, the first thing any leader must do is set clear expectations for performance and professionalism. In today's diverse workplace, you cannot assume that others share your vision of excellence in performance or professionalism. Furthermore, trying to impose a standard on others is almost certain to fail. When you assume a leadership position, hold a meeting in which you discuss performance and professionalism with your team. What rules and regulations are laid out by the organization? How has the team worked in the past? What should stay? What can be improved? How do team members see excellence in performance and professionalism? How do you visualize excellence in performance and professionalism? Through this discussion (or series of discussions), you and your team will collectively develop a vision of excellence in performance and professionalism that meets your expectations as a leader and simultaneously earns the team's support.

TABLE 10.5 ■ Tools for Professional Excellence. Delivering Constructive Criticism	
To deliver constructive criticism, take note of the following tips:	
Key Points	**Constructive Tips**
Admit your part in any mistake.	● If you never own up to your own mistakes, then your employees or team members are less likely to own up to theirs.
	● Taking responsibility for a mistake can encourage those around you to admit their own mistakes, which only empowers the group.
	● As a leader, taking responsibility for your mistakes will make it easier to deliver criticism in the future, as well as make it easier for your employees to take the criticism.
Begin in a positive way.	● No matter the circumstances, you can always find something positive to say about those receiving the criticism.
	● When giving constructive criticism, always use honest and sincere language to help those receiving the criticism feel valued.
	● Establishing a positive tone will help those receiving the criticism do so in a more relaxed, productive manner.

To deliver constructive criticism, take note of the following tips:	
Key Points	**Constructive Tips**
Use encouragement and make the fault seem easy to correct.	● Telling people that they made a lot of errors or have a lot of work left to do only overwhelms them, instead of motivating them to change.
	● Let those receiving the criticism know that you believe in their ability to get work done, and that you are always available to provide assistance should they need it.
	● Using encouragement helps those receiving the criticism feel confident about their ability to correct their mistake, and more likely to do so.
Praise the slightest improvement.	● No matter how big or small an improvement may be, always take the opportunity to praise people when they do something right, which encourages them to keep up the good work.
	● Be specific when delivering praise, so that the person knows exactly what they did correctly for future reference.

Source: Roberts. (2014, February 7). 4 ways to give constructive criticism in a positive way. *Dale Carnegie Training.* For more information about ways to give constructive criticism, see Forbes Coaches Council. (2017, June 19). 15 ways to offer truly constructive feedback. *Forbes.* https://www.forbes.com/sites/forbescoachescoun cil/2017/06/19/15-ways-to-offer-truly-constructive-feedback/#6ef07d446e9b

What if you're already in a leadership position? Is it too late to set clear expectations for performance and professionalism? No, of course it isn't. Select a time that marks a new phase for your team, such as after the completion of a big project or at the beginning of the new fiscal year. Then hold a retreat in which you celebrate the team's past successes and begin setting new goals for the future. As part of this discussion, address the previously noted questions on professionalism and performance. In the end, you can't expect success from your team members if they don't know what success looks like. Excellence in professionalism and performance must be clearly defined.

The best leaders provide honest feedback that helps employees improve and develop professionally.

iStockphoto/Lyndon Stratford

Providing Feedback Regularly

Once the expectations for performance and excellence have been clearly defined, you must discuss them on a regular basis. These discussions should become a part of your team meetings. In addition, you must give feedback on performance and professionalism to individuals both publicly and privately.

Poor leaders often fall into the annual feedback trap. Because many leaders are extremely busy or because they are conflict avoidant, they save all their feedback for the official performance appraisal. It is common for organizations to require some type of formal, written evaluation for employees once a year. This performance appraisal usually involves an interview and a written summary of the employee's strengths and weaknesses on the job. Annual performance appraisals are a useful communication tool. They give leaders an opportunity to learn about employees' long-term goals, which can be used for mentoring purposes. In addition, it's an opportunity to praise strengths formally, as well as a time to lay out action plans for improving weaknesses. But the annual performance appraisal is only one of many communication tools used by excellent leaders. Feedback exchanges should be held often between you, as the leader, and your team members. No one should have to wait an entire year to be praised. In addition, no behavior that warrants improvement should go an entire year without being addressed.

Praising Team Members

In terms of praise, a leader with professional excellence should give praise daily. Make it a habit to let employees know they are valued. Your team members should be complimented on a job well done every time the job is done well. Major successes or accomplishments should be marked with a celebration of some type. In fact, celebrating successes should be a part of the organizational culture under your leadership. In addition to publicly praising and acknowledging success, take time to privately acknowledge outstanding performance and professionalism. For example, Margie keeps a pack of thank-you cards in her desk. When an employee or coworker goes the extra mile, she then can immediately send that employee a handwritten note thanking them for those efforts or congratulating them on the recent success. It doesn't take her a lot of time to do this, but the gesture is meaningful and makes Margie stand out as a leader.

Holding Team Members Accountable

In an ideal workplace, once the expectations are laid out, all you ever need to do is praise employees for meeting and surpassing those expectations. Unfortunately, we have never met anyone who is in an ideal workplace. This means that just as you must learn to praise success on a regular basis, you must also learn to hold others accountable when they fail to meet expectations in performance or professionalism.

Unlike praising, which should be done both publicly and privately, holding someone accountable should be done only privately. There are two reasons why privacy is so important. First, discussing someone's shortcomings or weaknesses privately shows respect for the other person. Rather than embarrassing the other person in front of their coworkers—or worse yet, customers—you can create a comfortable environment in which you can talk honestly and work toward a solution. It is really a matter of saving face. Face-saving behavior is both verbal and nonverbal communication that honors and maintains the other person's sense of self-respect in a given situation (Clare & Danilovic, 2012; Ting-Toomey, 1990). When you show the other person respect, they save face. This makes that person more open to engaging in improvement. If you disrespect the other person, they lose face. As a result, the other person may feel the need to disrespect you or ignore your comments in an attempt to reclaim face, becoming less likely to engage in improvement.

Second, discussing shortcomings or weaknesses one on one in a private setting increases the chances that the message is heard. For example, Jane makes a habit of taking long lunches. Her boss, Steve, has noticed this behavior as well as the frustration it is causing among her coworkers. At the next team meeting, Steve states, "I have noticed that our punctuality is becoming a problem and some of you are beginning to make tardiness a habit. Let's all try to make sure we are on time for the start of shifts and after our lunches and breaks." Following the meeting, Steve's star employee, Dana, comes up to Steve and apologizes: "I know I was late for work one day last week when my battery died in my car. I am so sorry." Steve assures her that the comment was not directed at her, but she still seems upset. As for Jane, Steve's comments rolled off her back. In fact,

TABLE 10.6 ■ Tools for Professional Excellence. Developing Performance Plan Discussions

To develop clear performance improvement plans, consider these practical tips:

Key Points	Practical Tips
Prepare for the discussion.	● Review documents that provide information on your role or plans that relate to your wider workplace.
	● Reflect on what you need and want to discuss, such as what you find most rewarding or challenging about the job, or you career goals.
	● Arrange a time and a place that suit both people, where interruptions are unlikely and confidentiality can be maintained.
	● Allow adequate time for the discussion, which may depend on how long you have been doing the job, how long you have worked with your supervisor or manager, the level of change that has happened since the last discussion, and the nature of the issues to be discussed.
Know what to do during the discussion.	● You can positively influence the discussion by
	○ Keeping honest communication going
	○ Being respectful
	○ Taking a positive approach and focusing on the future
	○ Having realistic and reasonable expectations of each other
	○ Seeking and confirming that you both understand what the other is saying by summarizing key points and agreements
	● Confirm what has been agreed upon, including any actions, such as who will do what and by when.
	● Decide what will be recorded during the discussion, and how it will be recorded.
Know what to do after the discussion.	● Prepare the performance plan by recording the main points and what was agreed upon.
	● Implement what has been agreed upon, including any follow-up actions.
	● Continue to have performance discussions on a regular basis, such as at quarterly meetings.

Source: ACT Government. (n.d.). *ACTPS performance framework.* http://www.cmd.act.gov.au/__data/assets/pdf_file/0005/463730/dev_a_perf_plan.pdf

she did not even realize they were directed at her. Had Steve met with Jane one on one, she would have realized he was talking to her, and Dana would not have become upset unnecessarily.

As you begin to increase the amount of feedback flowing throughout the team, the question "How do I (or we) improve?" will inevitably come up. Telling someone they have done something wrong or needs to improve, without discussing how, is the mark of a poor leader. Take your typical toddler as an example. We daresay all toddlers at some point in time throw a temper tantrum. Why? They throw tantrums because they are angry and they do not know any other way to express that anger. An experienced parent knows that to stop the tantrums you must teach the toddler not only that this behavior is unacceptable but also how to handle anger in a more productive way. Seasoned parents can often be heard saying, "Use your words when you are upset." The same strategy holds true with adults. You must let them know if a behavior is unacceptable, and then you discuss how to improve. For example, if you tell an employee, "You need to take more initiative," the results will most likely be disappointing. The employee needs specific instructions about what your expectations are and what they should be doing. You may be thinking, "That's silly. They just need to take more initiative. It is self-explanatory." Actually, it is not self-explanatory. Let's look at Charles's case.

TABLE 10.7 ■ Action Items. Leadership Development Skills

Self-development	Be critical of your management style and how it impacts your team.	Use the KEYS process daily to reflexively assess the actions and directions you set forth for your team.
Transactional development	Sustain your leadership roles by consistently interacting with your employees.	Set aside weekly one-on-one meetings and team meetings to encourage discussion.
Interpersonal development	Continually develop your team and engage in relationship-building exercises.	Have weekly team-building exercises that are informal and recreational (e.g., golfing, intramural leagues).

Charles had been "written up" in his last evaluation for not taking initiative. Charles walked out of the performance appraisal completely confused. In the beginning, he tried to take initiative, but every time he tried to do something on his own, he was told it was the wrong thing. After a while, he quit trying and just waited until someone told him what to do; then he did what he was told and did it well. He had no idea what his supervisor wanted or how to improve. Fortunately, Charles's supervisor, Stephanie, realized her mistake and developed a means for improving that was specific and clear. All performance improvement plans should be specific and clear (see Tools for Professional Excellence 10.4). So in Charles's case, he was told that, as soon as he completed one task, he should approach Stephanie for his next task. She did not want him to begin a new task unless she okayed it, nor did she want him to stand around waiting until she noticed he was not busy. For the next few weeks, Charles tried this approach. Stephanie noted a lot of improvement in his performance, and she praised his success. She also held a follow-up meeting to discuss his progress and listen to his feedback. During this discussion, Stephanie learned that Charles felt uncomfortable, as though he was interrupting her, every time he asked for a new task. He also was concerned that when she was busy, he was left without anything to do. Stephanie listened to Charles's feedback and used the information to change her communication with all her employees. Instead of giving each person one task at a time, she began assigning multiple tasks at once, trusting the employees to complete the tasks on their lists and then come to her for more assignments when they were done.

Discussing improvement plans with employees is much more effective than simply telling employees what to do. This two-way communication flow will allow for improvements in your leadership and for individual differences among your team members. No two people are alike, so there is no cookie-cutter, one-size-fits-all strategy for improving or motivating others.

Motivating Through Feedback

Leaders with professional excellence develop individualized means for motivating. Individualizing motivation is part of the KEYS process, which requires you to evaluate your audience. What motivates employees to continue to give outstanding performances and reach high levels of professionalism? What motivates employees to improve their areas of weakness? It depends on the individual person in question. The only way to determine what will motivate the individual is to ask them.

Although there are many theories on employee motivation, we have found (Locke & Latham, 1984) to be the most effective. According to this theory, goals are not merely assigned; rather, the leader and the team member develop the goal(s) together. Goals must be clear and specific, allowing both parties to have shared expectations. Goals should also be challenging yet attainable, increasing the likelihood for both growth and success. Finally, feedback must be frequent as team members work to achieve their goals.

Discussing an area that needs improvement or defining a goal should mark the beginning, not the end, of the communication on that subject. Leaders with professional excellence immediately schedule a follow-up meeting in which the employee can discuss their progress, questions can be answered, and additional support can be provided. The number of follow-up meetings must be determined on a case-by-case basis, but additional meetings should be called immediately if any signs of poor performance return.

Enacting Consequences

Part of the feedback process includes discussing consequences for both positive and negative behaviors and then making sure those consequences are enacted. For example, Sally was named "Employee of the Month" for April. For this honor, she was supposed to receive a prime parking spot for a month and $500. She did get her parking spot, but it was now August and she had yet to receive the money, which she had planned to use for a vacation. Her boss's failure to follow through made Sally feel demotivated instead of valued and honored.

Failure to follow through is the major reason why there are so many difficult people in the workplace. Despite repeatedly demonstrating unprofessional behavior, many leaders fail to hold these people accountable. As a result, they continue to act in ways that violate clearly defined standards of professionalism and performance, without consequences. Providing feedback, holding people accountable, and following through with consequences are critical leadership responsibilities, yet many leaders fail in these areas.

Giving someone negative feedback and holding them accountable is uncomfortable for most of us, but excellent leaders realize it is a necessity (Kuntz & Gomes, 2012; Patterson et al., 2005). Without honest feedback, employees cannot improve. If your team members are to grow and develop, they must come to understand the areas that are holding them back. By providing them with honest feedback, you are providing them with a service. Failure to provide honest feedback is a disservice. Furthermore, if the behavior in question has negatively affected other team members, the work environment, or customers, then it must be stopped, because it is making everyone uncomfortable. If you ignore it, you will be fostering a negative work environment, and you run the risk of losing your star employees.

One tool that can help you give negative feedback and hold others accountable is scripting. Scripting is the process of mentally rehearsing what you will say during the discussion. As part of scripting, you will anticipate the responses of the other party and think through what you will say to those responses.

When you are giving negative feedback and holding someone accountable, you should be direct. Don't beat around the bush or make irrelevant chitchat. You also should focus on facts and observations while avoiding judgments. For example, you should say, "You cut Ross off mid-sentence," as opposed to saying, "You're rude," or you should say, "You spoke so quietly, it was hard to hear," as opposed to saying, "You're afraid."

Remember, the ultimate goal is to create improvement in the other person's behavior. Therefore, whenever possible, use the unite strategies discussed in Chapter 7. You and your employee are trying to solve the problem together. State the problem as you see it, and then listen. Together, come up with solutions that meet the expectations of professionalism and performance your team has developed.

Firing Employees

Unfortunately, even if you lay out the expectations, provide honest feedback, and give support, some people will not meet the expectations of professionalism and performance needed to continue working for your team. If that is the case, then you are responsible for firing that person. For some of you, firing another person will be very difficult, but as a leader, it is your responsibility. There is no reason to feel guilty if you followed all the steps noted earlier. In the end, it is the other person's choice not to live up to the clearly defined expectations and their choice to face the consequences.

Unprofessional employees with negative attitudes can be especially challenging for employees and customers.

istockphoto/AndreyPopov

Harvard psychologist Martha Stout (2005) claims that 1 in every 25 people is a sociopath. This means that they have no conscience or feelings of guilt, shame, or remorse. If you have someone like this on your team, there's nothing you can do to develop them into a productive employee. Don't worry; not every difficult employee on your team is a sociopath. They may just be in the wrong job. Nevertheless, as the leader, you must look out for the good of the rest of the team, and sometimes firing that bad apple is what is best for the bunch.

When you step into a leadership role, familiarize yourself with your organization's termination policy. For most organizations, you must have documentation in order to fire an employee. In other words, you must document expectations, your feedback, and the employee's performance. As a leader with professional excellence, you will already have those things in place if and when someone needs to have their future freed up for new opportunities.

Putting It Together

We have spent much of this chapter discussing types of difficult people, as well as strategies for leading all types of employees—whether difficult or outstanding. Still, you may be questioning how defining expectations, providing feedback, and enacting consequences can lead to communication excellence for a diverse workforce. Don't you need a variety of different communication strategies to deal with a variety of personalities? No, not if you apply the KEYS approach to each phase of this process.

Let's say you have a department with many hardworking employees and a few stars, as well as two slackers, one who loves drama, and a bully/sniper. Begin by *knowing yourself*. Maybe you are conflict avoidant. As a result, you tend to ignore the problems among coworkers that result in work not getting done due to unprofessional drama and slacking in the workplace. In fact, you may even blame the employees who bring the problems to your attention. During meetings, you avoid topics that will "set off" the bully/sniper, and when their negativity overruns a meeting, you say nothing. On the rare occasions when you have tried to provide feedback and constructive criticism, the one who loves drama declares, "Everyone picks on me," which causes the discussion to go off course and never reach a solution. As for the slackers, they say they will improve, but that improvement is never clearly defined, you never follow up, and the negative behavior continues. You will never reach communication excellence if you allow this pattern to continue.

Even if you are not conflict avoidant, you must still *know yourself*. If there are problems with your team, then you must take charge and address them. But this requires you to take some time to assess how your communication style has been adding to the problems with your team. Are you too busy to follow through? Have you failed to define expectations clearly? Are you indeed providing feedback? Are you better at communicating with one type of difficult person than with another? For example, do the tears of someone who enjoys drama have no effect on you, or do you excuse behavior when the tears come? Does a bully intimidate you, or can you hold your ground? Do you tend to hold slackers accountable, or do you push their work on your stars? You must know your own strengths and weaknesses as a communicator so that you can factor those in when dealing with your teammates.

ETHICAL CONNECTION

Nora's Leadership Dilemma

As you read this passage and answer the questions, consider how the way you communicate has an ethical dimension.

Nora is a project manager for a large advertising firm. Although her team has always performed at a high level, two of her group members are making progress difficult and alienating other coworkers. Nora has tried all the coaching techniques available to her, but her problem employees still show no signs of improvement. Although firing employees has always been a last-ditch effort for Nora, she sees no other option but to let one or both employ-ees go. However, one of the problem employees has been with the company for years and is approaching retirement; if the employee is fired now, she will lose her chance for a company pension and could have financial issues into her old age. Nora needs to find a solution soon, because one of her largest clients is rolling out a massive advertising campaign, and the members of Nora's team need to be working at their finest.

Questions to Consider

1. What is the ethical dilemma facing Nora as a leader right now?

2. What other communication skills might Nora employ when dealing with her problem employees?

3. What action would you consider to be the most fair to the rest of the advertising team?

4. Outside of termination, what other options could Nora consider?

Next, you must *evaluate the professional context*. Think about the types of problems and excuses that occur due to the various personalities in your workplace. As the group is defining professional expectations, be certain that all these situations are discussed. Whatever the issue—gossiping, interrupting, negative attitudes, poor performance—discuss it as a group. Because this process is not focused on any one person, it will be easier to get a lot of issues out in the open. Once you have clearly defined, mutually defined expectations, you can quickly redirect any employee when you get to the providing feedback stage. As noted earlier, practice scripting prior to *your communication interaction*. Regardless of whether the bully/sniper tries to intimi-date you, the slackers make excuses, or the one who loves drama cries, you must remain focused on clearly defining the problem, developing a solution, and presenting the consequences. State the behaviors in question. Invite cooperation for solutions by asking, "How can we fix this situa-tion?" And do not end the meeting until a clearly defined plan is in place. At times, this will not be easy. You may have to make statements such as the following: "As a team, we defined respect as an expectation. I find it disrespectful when you call your coworkers derogatory names. This behavior is unacceptable. How can we fix this situation so that our work environment meets this expectation of respect?"

To help ensure success during the feedback sessions, review the steps for conflict resolution discussed in Chapter 7. When giving feedback, your ability to stay focused and not become defensive or lead everyone on a tangent is critical. Stay focused on behavior, and redirect all con-versation to that behavior. For instance, you can open a feedback session by saying, "Refusing to speak to a coworker about work is not acceptable. I can see that you two have issues outside work, but at work this lack of communication is unacceptable. Communicating with respect and professionalism is one of our expectations, regardless of personal issues. This cannot continue, so how can we—you and I—solve this problem? And I want our discussion to stay focused on your behavior, not your coworker's." Also, remember to use agendas in meetings, as discussed in Chapter 7. Agendas will help focus your meetings and control overtalkers and undertalkers.

Next, you should *step back and reflect* on all the communication that has occurred. You may find it necessary to discuss past communication interactions as part of the process, as in this example: "I have noticed that this behavior has continued. In the past, when we have discussed it, I do all the talking and you say nothing. Today, I would like to change that. I would like you to lead the discussion. How can we solve this problem?" This will help you more effectively *know yourself* and *evaluate the professional context* as you move into the follow-up. But remember, you must follow up to either enact the consequence or praise the improvement.

Leading difficult people isn't that difficult. In fact, the formula is simple. You must define expectations, provide feedback, and follow up. If you as the leader are consistent in these three functions, you will be on your way to leadership excellence, regardless of the types of difficult people you encounter.

MANAGING YOUR PUBLIC IMAGE

Take a moment and visualize a leader in your mind. What do they look like? What do they sound like? To excel as a leader with professional excellence, you must take time to reflect on your public image. Public image is the impression you give or present to others both verbally and nonverbally. Obviously, the public image you want to present is that of a leader with professional excellence. The way to ensure that this is the image you are presenting is through impression management— directing the formation of an impression, a perception, or a view that others have of you (Ali & Gulzar, 2012; Goffman, 1971; Harris & Sachau, 2005).

A word of warning is needed here. Impression management is not and should not be about creating a false or deceptive public image. If you want to be viewed as a leader, you must act as a leader and display professional excellence on all levels. Impression management is simply a self-monitoring technique meant to help you put the KEYS process into action.

When it comes to impression management, we often think of clothing. In fact, we would be willing to bet that you have been told at least once in your life to "dress for success." Why are *dress* and *success* linked together (besides their making a cute rhyme)? Clothing can convey your status within an organization (Key, 2012; Peluchette et al., 2006). As noted in Chapter 4, for superiors, conservative, solid-colored, well-fitting, and well-made clothing often communicates power and success.

An old adage states that you should dress for the job you want, not the job you have. This is good advice. Let's say your goal is to become a manager. If shorts are permitted on the job, but the management team always dresses in business-casual wear, you should put away your shorts and get out your slacks. Dressing for the job you want may not be possible in some organizations. For example, your position may require you to wear a uniform that designates your position. If that is the case, then you should make certain you look like a professional in your designated attire. In fact, regardless of your position or career aspiration, you should always look like a professional. If your position requires a uniform or scrubs, make certain that everything is clean and neatly ironed. If your position requires more casual attire, you should still look professional and follow the dress code. Hair, makeup, jewelry, and shoes should also be selected with professionalism in mind. You do not have to spend a lot of money to look like a professional—after all, even an Armani suit looks unprofessional if it is dirty or wrinkled. Bottom line: Attire is a part of your public image; therefore, dress in a manner that says "professional."

Although it can enhance or detract from your public image, clothing in and of itself does not make a leader. It is just one small part of your nonverbal communication that must be considered. Throughout this book, we have talked about verbal and nonverbal communication that conveys professional excellence; all those behaviors contribute to your public image. In a workshop, we once asked a group of leaders to evaluate the impression they were giving their teams. With just a little reflection, several leaders were shocked at the conclusions they reached.

For example, Nancy had noticed that her staff always began their conversations with her with statements like "I'm sorry to bother you," "I know you are busy," "I'll just be a minute," and "I know you have more important things to attend to." She realized she had unintentionally given the impression that communicating with her staff was not a priority. She also realized the potential problems that could stem from this impression, and she began to rethink her impression management.

Similarly, Rob recalled asking his team to join him for lunch. He was surprised when they all assumed they had done something wrong and that he was going to reprimand them. Clearly, he was not communicating enough praise, and the impression he was giving was that of dissatisfaction.

Finally, Stephanie noted a very different problem. All day long, her staff would pop in to chitchat about non-work-related issues. Her office was like a break room. As a result, she had to come to work early, stay late, and work weekends to get her tasks completed. She needed to maintain openness about work-related issues but change the impression that she had nothing to do or was there as a friend, not a leader.

By stepping back and reflecting, these leaders were able to more effectively manage the impressions they were giving. Again, impression management is not about creating a false impression, but rather it's about monitoring your communication so that you can present a truthful and professional image.

Know Yourself

Reflections on Leadership Excellence

As you answer the questions below, think about how this knowledge can help you be a better communicator.

- Whom do you consider an excellent leader?
- How would you describe their public image?
- What does an excellent leader look like? Sound like?
- How does an excellent leader behave?
- When you walk into a room, do your associates think you look like a leader?
- What are your positive leadership qualities?
- What leadership qualities do you need to develop?

KEYS TO EXCELLENCE IN LEADERSHIP

Think back to the leadership values identified at the beginning of the chapter. Gravity Payments CEO Dan Price changed workers' lives, and he has a high reputation among the employees. The first step, *know yourself*, requires you to understand how you act as a leader and to assess if you would like working for a boss like yourself. Place yourself in your employees' shoes, and learn what is important and motivating to them.

The second step, *evaluate the professional context*, involves learning more about the environment of your company. Price compared his wages and lifestyle with the lifestyle and wages of his employees and saw a large discrepancy.

The third step, *your communication interaction*, tasks leaders not to be afraid of engaging in open communication with their subordinates. As the first leadership strategy stated, leaders must be willing to confront ambiguity in communication and learn how to turn it to their advantage. Instead of looking inward for problem solving, leaders must be willing to use all the tools available to them, with teams and individuals being a crucial resource. When placed in a leadership position, you must keep an open line of communication with your employees.

The final step asks you to *step back and reflect* and assess the communication interaction before reaching a decision. Always make sure that you have the most complete and unbiased information possible before you make decisions that can affect both your and your employees' professional careers. Go over every segment of the interaction, and give considerable thought to how your decision can reflect on your position as a leader in your professional environment.

Do you consider yourself an effective leader? What are your expectations for professional excellence at work? Have you discussed it as a team? Are you comfortable giving feedback? Are you more likely to praise or criticize? *Step back and reflect* on your leadership. What would you most like to improve?

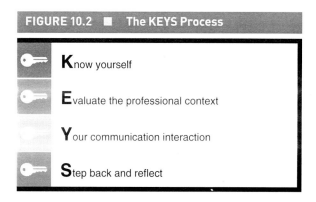

FIGURE 10.2 ■ The KEYS Process

Know yourself

Evaluate the professional context

Your communication interaction

Step back and reflect

EXECUTIVE SUMMARY

Now that you have finished reading this chapter, you should be able to

Define leadership:
- Leadership is a "dynamic relationship based on mutual influence and common purpose between leaders and collaborators, in which both are moved to higher levels of motivation and moral development as they affect real, intended change."

Discuss what constitutes power:
- Legitimate power is based on a position of authority. The manager has legitimate power over the department budget and employee schedules. Although a position or job title may give someone legitimate power, it doesn't mean that person exercises that power.

- Coercive power refers to the ability to control another person's behavior with negative reinforcement, whereas reward power describes control over another person's behavior with positive reinforcement.

- Expert power is based on one's superior expertise in a specific field.

- You give referent power to someone because you want that person to like you.

- Connection power is based on the old expression "It's not what you know, but who you know." Having a connection to people in positions of power or having a strong support system definitely acts as a source of power.

Explain the relationship between leadership theory and communication:

- Just as understanding theories on power can improve your communication as a leader, so, too, can studying leadership theories. Over the past century, scholars have studied leadership-developing theories and models designed to help us understand what effective leadership is and to train us to be better leaders. Implementing the knowledge and insight contained in various leadership theories is a must if you ever plan to excel as a leader.

Discuss communication strategies for hiring quality employees:

- Leaders with professional excellence know that hiring is a process that begins long before the first candidate arrives for an interview and lasts long after orientation and training.

- When hiring opportunities occur, it's incredibly important that you, as the leader, participate in every stage of the hiring process. It's also important to get the rest of the team involved.

- Once the position has been advertised, the interview questions must be drafted. You may or may not be responsible for drafting the questions, but as the leader, you should always review the questions, giving your input and ultimately your approval.

Understand the importance of following up and following through with employees:

- Leaders should create a "follow up and follow through" norm within their teams.

- Reaffirm in people's minds what they have to do for the next meeting.

- Ask if there are any additional items team members would like included on the agenda or if they need any supplemental materials.

Discuss the ways in which leaders should communicate about their teams:

- A leader with professional excellence makes certain that new team members feel like part of the team, starting on Day 1. You should make it a point to greet all new employees on the day they arrive.

- Excellent leaders involve the team so that they, too, can share in the leadership, which will make your job more manageable.

Identify strategies for dealing with difficult people:

- In addition to the team player and the star, the negative members of your organizational family may include the following: the bully, the sniper, the one who loves drama, the slacker, the vampire, the grump, the roadblock to change, the distracter, and the patient.

- Taking steps to improve an employee's work attitude and learning to deliver constructive criticism may help you to deal with some of the difficult people you may encounter in the workplace.

Provide feedback as a means to motivate team members:

- A good leader understands employees' duties, workloads, constraints, and goals, because they are open to giving and receiving feedback.

- A leader with professional excellence understands how to use feedback to mentor stars as well as to turn difficult family members into team players.

- You must provide constant feedback, praising those employees who meet expectations and reprimanding those who fail to meet them. You must follow through, which can mean a bonus, a reprimand, or termination.

Discuss ways to manage your public image:

- To excel as a leader with professional excellence, you must take time to reflect on your public image.

- Impression management is a self-monitoring technique meant to help you put the KEYS process into action.

- Verbal and nonverbal communication that conveys professional excellence also contributes to your public image.

Apply the KEYS process to develop professional excellence as a leader:

- Know yourself. Before assessing your team, realize first what you bring to the table.

- Evaluate the professional context. A participating approach is more likely to succeed. Instead of making the meeting about your goals and your vision, stress the importance of shared leadership and teamwork, asking the team to collectively develop goals and a vision for the department.

- Your communication interaction. Offer feedback to your team members, and give them the opportunity to give you feedback as well.

- Step back and reflect. Avoid future conflicts. See what is working for you, and hold people accountable for their performance.

EXPLORE

1. Read the Society for Human Resource Management's (SHRM) article on developing and sustaining high-performance work teams (https://www.shrm.org/resourcesandtools/tools-and-samples/toolkits/pages/developingandsustaininghigh-performanceworkteams.aspx). Review the characteristics of high-performance work teams, and apply those prerequisites with what you have learned in this chapter.

2. Attend a leadership or management training session at your college or community center. What key attributes do the facilitators teach all leaders to have? What similarities or running themes have you pinpointed through your study of this chapter so far?

3. Pick a community leader, politician, or professional executive to report on. What makes that person an effective leader in your particular community? Apply the context of your environment to the leadership attributes that are important in your community.

REVIEW

1. Define *leadership*.

2. Explain the difference in status between a superior and a subordinate.

3. _____ refers to the ability to control another person's behavior with negative reinforcement.

4. _____ include(s) influencing and guiding followers as opposed to subordinates, as well as being innovative and creating a vision for future direction.

5. Explain the position of Contingency Theory.

6. List the requirements set forth in Goal Setting Theory.

7. _____ is the process of mentally rehearsing what you will say during a discussion.

8. _____ involves directing the formation of an impression, a perception, or a view that others share of you.

DISCUSSION QUESTIONS

1. What type(s) of power do you have as a student? How does that source of power influence communication with other students, professors, and administrators?

2. How can you use the information you have learned about leadership theories to develop your leadership skills?

3. Think about the last job interview in which you participated. How effective was the interviewer? What could they have done differently to improve the interview process?

4. What goals have you developed for yourself in your career or in your workplace? What motivates you to reach these goals? In what ways does your motivation differ from that of other people you know?

5. Have you ever worked with a difficult person? If so, how did you communicate with this person? Was your communication effective or ineffective? Based on what you have learned in this chapter, how would you change your communication in this situation?

TERMS TO REMEMBER

annual feedback trap (p. 266)
authoritative (p. 252)
birthright (p. 248)
bully (p. 260)
charisma (p. 247)
coercive power (p. 249)
connection power (p. 250)
Contingency Theory (p. 254)
democratic (p. 252)
distracter (p. 261)
expert power (p. 249)
face-saving behavior (p. 266)
Goal Setting Theory (p. 269)
grump (p. 261)
impression management (p. 273)
job title (p. 248)
laissez-faire (p. 252)
leadership (p. 248)
leadership functions (p. 250)
legitimate power: (p. 249)
managerial functions (p. 250)
Managerial Grid (p. 253)

patient (p. 261)
performance appraisal (p. 266)
performance improvement plan (p. 268)
public image (p. 273)
referent power (p. 249)
reward power (p. 249)
roadblock to change (p. 261)
role models (p. 263)
scripting (p. 270)
Situational Leadership Theory (p. 254)
slacker (p. 261)
sniper (p. 260)
sociopath (p. 270)
star (p. 261)
status (p. 249)
team player (p. 261)
Theory X (p. 252)
Theory Y (p. 252)
trait (p. 247)
transformational leaders (p. 255)
vampire (p. 261)

PRESENTING IN THE WORKPLACE

The ability to connect and resonate with the audience is key to becoming an effective professional speaker.

iStockphoto/cipella

11 INFORMING AND PERSUADING

After studying this chapter, you should be able to

11.1   Discuss the importance of professional excellence in public speaking

11.2   Identify presenting opportunities and purposes

11.3   Design an informative speech

11.4   Design a persuasive speech

11.5   Apply the KEYS process to develop professional excellence as an informer and a persuader

Actor Jane Fonda received the Cecil B. DeMille Award—which is a prestigious lifetime achievement award—at the 2021 Golden Globes. During her acceptance speech, Fonda began by describing storytelling as an art form and praised the directors and actors in the room. She concluded her speech with a call to action for better leadership in the Hollywood film industry to make sure everyone's stories are told: "Stories—they really can change people. But there's a story we've been afraid to see and hear about ourselves in this industry—a story about which voices we respect and elevate, and which we tune out." She went on to say, "So let's all of us—including all the groups that decide who gets hired and what gets made and who wins awards—let's all of us make an effort to expand that tent. So that everyone rises and everyone's story has a chance to be seen and heard" (Shoichet, 2021). In some cases, the requirement of public speaking stops great employees from ever advancing in their career. However, when delivering a speech, it will increase your visibility to people. As you progress in your career, being articulate becomes more and more important, and becoming a competent and confident public speaker is critical for leadership roles. Here are often-overlooked pointers from people who are paid to stand out and engage their audiences on the speaking circuit (Arruda, 2017):

- Dan Pink, *New York Times* best-selling author: "Saying something important is better than saying important things. Your goal isn't to show how much you know or how many thoughts you've had, but to leave the audience with one idea to ponder or one action to take."

- Marcus Buckingham, motivational speaker and business consultant: "The best speaking advice I'd give is the best speaking advice I've heard—from Martin Luther King, Jr: When you're speaking, the most important thing is your takeoff and landing. You've got to know how you are going to launch the audience into your dream, and then land it by bringing the dream back down to them. But in between takeoff and landing, you can fly like crazy."

- Brene Brown, research professor: "You either walk inside your story and own it or you stand outside your story and hustle for your worthiness."

Do you fear giving presentations? For some of you, presenting is indeed a fear. For others of you, it may even be your greatest fear. It's doubtful, however, that any of you would rather die than give a presentation. Even if you don't consider presenting a fear, chances are that presenting isn't on your list of favorite activities; of course, there are a few of you who really do enjoy presenting opportunities. The good news is that whether you view presenting as a fear, an annoyance, or a joy, developing presentational skills will help you excel in your career. Our study of business and professional communication is not complete without attention to this type of oral communication. How will you use presentation skills *on the job?* How can presentational excellence enhance your professional excellence? The study and practice of oral communication discussed in this chapter and in Chapters 12 and 13 will help you overcome your fears and develop presentations with professional excellence.

Many of us think of audiences as mean and hostile. As this photo suggests, your audience can turn out to be supportive, interested, and friendly.

iStockphoto/SDI Productions

You will learn the basics, which have been around for more than 2,000 years. These speaking essentials are often connected with Aristotle—Greek philosopher, author of *The Art of Rhetoric,* student of Plato, and teacher of Alexander the Great. Clearly, after 2,000 years, these guidelines have passed the test of time. Yet many people either have failed to learn these basics or fail to implement them. As executive coaches, we have worked with dozens of top leaders in a variety of industries and often find ourselves telling them the same things you'll learn in these chapters. Use this knowledge and presentation opportunities offered in this course to develop the confidence and abilities needed for professional excellence.

THE IMPORTANCE OF PRESENTING WITH PROFESSIONAL EXCELLENCE

Just as effective communication skills are essential to your professional success, effective oral communication skills are essential if you want to excel in leadership. Presentational excellence is important for the following reasons: (1) Product presentations, team huddles, meeting leadership, press conferences, special events, and other forms of oral communication reveal something about you as a professional; (2) presentations serve as a tool to motivate employees and to communicate effectively about business goals; and (3) presentational excellence is required to achieve professional excellence. To address these important topics, let's take a look at ways to communicate excellence in presentations.

IDENTIFYING PRESENTATION OPPORTUNITIES AND PURPOSES

The first step in the presentation process is identifying opportunities. Once you have identified the presentation opportunities, you can identify the purpose within them.

Presentation Opportunities

Claire: "I get so tired of the huddle every morning."

Juan: "Why do Bill's morning huddles bother you so much?"

Claire: "When Jameela was doing the huddles, they really got me fired up and ready for the day. I get so bored listening to Bill's morning speech. I can't keep track of what he's saying with all those charts and numbers."

Juan: "Poor Bill. Maybe we just need to have an extra cup of coffee so we don't fall asleep."

This brief conversation illustrates that Bill has missed an opportunity to motivate his employees. Instead, he's boring them to death with charts and numbers. Let's explore presentation opportunities in more detail.

Television shows like *Shark Tank* that feature games and competitions emphasize the importance of presenting with professional excellence.

Maximum Film/Alamy Stock Photo

Two types of presentation opportunities are available to leaders. One is a formal presentation, which occurs in a traditional presentation setting. Presenting a sales pitch to clients and giving a progress report at the district meeting are examples of formal presentations. We have labeled the second type as the opportunity presentation. The opportunity presentation is identical in preparation and presentation to the formal presentation, but it occurs in a less traditional setting. For instance, many organizations have huddles, during which employees are pulled together to talk. This is not a traditional presentation setting, but it is still an opportunity. Meetings provide another possible setting for opportunity presentations. As a team leader, it will be your job to facilitate meetings. You may not be required to present at a meeting, but the opportunity remains. Giving a small opening address to kick off a meeting is an example of an opportunity presentation.

As a leader, you must begin to identify presentation opportunities and present yourself with professional excellence at each opportunity. You may consider preparing for presentations, especially opportunity presentations, a waste of time. If you've done okay in the past by giving an impromptu presentation—winging it or speaking off the cuff—you may be tempted not to prepare. Remember, professional excellence is not about being "okay." Think back to a presentation you delivered without preparation. How much better would your message have been if you had prepared? Let us reiterate that both formal and opportunity presentations require preparation and practice.

General Purpose

Once you've identified your presentation opportunity, the next step is to determine your purpose. Presentations can have one of two general purposes: to inform or to persuade. When speaking with an informative purpose, you present the facts. Informative speakers act as teachers relaying information. When speaking with a persuasive purpose, you are acting as an advocate or making an argument. Your role is to advocate for or against something. In some situations, you'll be trying to persuade the audience simply to agree or disagree with an idea—this is known as passive agreement. In other situations, you'll be trying to persuade the audience to take some sort of action—this is known as immediate action or a **call to action**.

Bill loves his flip chart and thinks of himself as a good presenter, but his employees have a different view.

iStockphoto/AndreyPopov

Determining your purpose may seem like a simple enough task, but speakers with professional excellence always think carefully when determining their purpose. For example, you may need to inform employees about a new policy in your organization. Ask yourself, "Am I merely informing them about the policy, or am I persuading them to follow the new policy?" In all likelihood, you will be persuading them. Although many presentation opportunities appear informative on the surface, a closer look reveals the need or opportunity to persuade. Let's look at another example. Say you're relaying some information on customer satisfaction scores. Are you simply presenting the information, or is there a secondary purpose? If the scores are low, the secondary purpose may be persuading your team that they need to do a better job the next time around. If the scores are high, it may be to celebrate as a team, acknowledge some outstanding performances, motivate team members to keep up the good work, or all of the above.

We will explore speaking to inform and speaking to persuade in more detail. But first, it is important to understand the difference between a general purpose and a specific purpose.

The audience and the presentation context can sometimes be difficult to predict or can present a challenge, such as presenting over a video conferencing tool like Microsoft Teams when you're more accustomed to using Zoom. Ensure you know which tool you will be using for your virtual presentation well ahead of time so you can install the most up-to-date version of it and practice using it.

iStockphoto/Eloi_Omella

Specific Purpose

Once you've identified the general purpose of your presentation, you'll begin to formulate a specific purpose. The specific purpose is to an oral presentation what a thesis statement is to an essay. A specific purpose is a declarative sentence telling the listeners what you want them to understand, know, or believe by the end of your presentation.

The following are some examples of specific purposes:

- I want my employees to understand and follow the new overtime rule.

- I want the executive team to believe our department deserves a 10% budget increase.

- I want Company X to select us as the health care provider for its employees.

- I want my team to feel recognized and appreciated for their hard work.

Designing a presentation is not a linear process in which you move from one step to the next. Instead, designing a presentation is a fluid process. Thus, you may develop a tentative specific purpose and then change it after you have done some analysis and research. In fact, identifying the general and specific purposes for any presentation opportunity will require you to analyze the audience and the context.

STEP BACK AND REFLECT

Trust Me: I've Been Here Awhile

As you read this passage and answer the questions, step back and reflect on what went wrong in this professional situation.

Kendall had been working in the same management position at an insurance company for several years. She was responsible for giving a presentation to all the area coordinators.

The report was important because the coordinators needed the updated information to help design marketing campaigns in areas where sales had decreased. For months, Kendall had been passing out a one-page sheet that was difficult for the coordinators to read. Rather than discussing specifics, Kendall would say, "I've been here awhile, and these sales decreases go away after a while." Instead of preparing a professional presentation, she would tell stories about what had happened at the company years ago. Kendall believed her experience and observation of sales patterns were enough informational support to assure the coordinators that things would turn around.

Step Back and Reflect

1. What went wrong?

2. What advice would you give Kendall about her presentation?

3. How can the KEYS process help Kendall in this situation?

SPEAKING TO INFORM

As noted earlier, when speaking with an informative purpose, your goal is to present the facts. Informative speakers act as teachers relaying information, striving to be   and not influenced or affected by emotions or their individual point of view.

According to Aristotle, a good persuasive speech includes three persuasive appeals: ethos, logos, and pathos. Although Aristotle discussed these appeals in relationship to persuasive presentations, we believe the first two appeals also are important for designing an effective informative presentation.

Ethos

Ethos refers to your credibility as a presenter as well as the credibility of the information delivered in your presentation. To present with professional excellence, you must demonstrate credibility and help your audience believe you and the information or argument you are presenting. Quintilian, a Roman philosopher and educator, viewed credibility as central to any effective rhetoric, which he defined as "a good man speaking well." The word *good* in Quintilian's quote refers to credibility.

How do you establish credibility? According to Aristotle, presenters must demonstrate ethos or positive character by demonstrating competence, trustworthiness, and goodwill. There are many ways to develop positive character within your presentation, but you must make sure the audience is aware of your expertise and knowledge on the subject matter. In addition, you must conduct research and then cite your sources.

Eileen is the vice president of security for a large resort chain. She's been invited to inform hotel managers about the effectiveness of their new security system at the annual retreat. When Eileen is introduced, both her title and her 15 years with the company are mentioned. This begins to develop her credibility. Within the body of her presentation, Eileen discusses a new security plan that was tested recently at one of the resorts in the chain. When discussing the success of the new plan, she cites improved security scores at that resort and emphasizes that the scores were gathered by an outside agency. By making certain that both she and her data are credible, she has succeeded in establishing ethos.

Logos

Logos is another type of appeal needed in effective presentations. *Logos* is a term that refers to the words of a presentation in the context of organizational structure and the supporting information. When developing an informative presentation, think of yourself as a teacher laying out information about a particular topic. After reviewing your research and analyzing the purpose, audience, and context, you will develop a clear organizational structure for your presentation (we discuss this in Chapter 12). However, that structure can't stand without support. The research that you've conducted will become that support. Together, the structure and the information will provide your audience with logical appeal.

What type of research should you include? Obviously, that will depend on the nature of your topic, your purpose, the audience, and the context. However, any or all of the following may have a place in your presentation: definitions, examples, statistics, and quotes. See Table 11.1 for a more detailed discussion of each.

Know Yourself

Credibility

As you read the index below and answer the questions, think about how this knowledge can help you be a better communicator.

Circle the number that best represents your feelings about the speaker.

1.	Intelligent	1 2 3 4 5 6 7	Unintelligent
2.	Ethical	1 2 3 4 5 6 7	Unethical
3.	Caring	1 2 3 4 5 6 7	Uncaring
4.	Trained	1 2 3 4 5 6 7	Untrained
5.	Honest	1 2 3 4 5 6 7	Dishonest
6.	Has my interests at heart	1 2 3 4 5 6 7	Doesn't have my interests at heart
7.	Expert	1 2 3 4 5 6 7	Not an expert
8.	Unselfish	1 2 3 4 5 6 7	Selfish
9.	Concerned	1 2 3 4 5 6 7	Unconcerned
10.	Informed	1 2 3 4 5 6 7	Uninformed
11.	Sympathetic	1 2 3 4 5 6 7	Unsympathetic
12.	Understanding	1 2 3 4 5 6 7	Not understanding
13.	Competent	1 2 3 4 5 6 7	Incompetent
14.	High character	1 2 3 4 5 6 7	Low character
15.	Responsive	1 2 3 4 5 6 7	Unresponsive
16.	Bright	1 2 3 4 5 6 7	Ignorant
17.	Trustworthy	1 2 3 4 5 6 7	Untrustworthy
18.	Understands how I think	1 2 3 4 5 6 7	Doesn't understand how I think

Now total your scores using the guidelines below.

The scores should range from 6 to 42 for each subscale.

Competence: Add items 1, 4, 7, 10, 13, and 16 for a total score of _____.

Character: Add items 2, 5, 8, 11, 14, and 17 for a total score of _____.

Caring: Add items 3, 6, 9, 12, 15, and 18 for a total score of _____.

Source: Modified from McCroskey, J. C., & Teven, J. J. (1999). Goodwill: A reexamination of the construct and its measurement. *Communication Monographs, 66,* 90–103.

TABLE 11.1 ■ Supporting Material	
Type of Research	**Supporting Material**
Definitions	Provide explanations of words or concepts that your listeners need to understand
Examples	Provide your listeners with illustrations, parallel cases, or representations of a larger group
Statistics	Provide your listeners with numerical data that are used to analyze, interpret, or explain ideas in your speech
Quotes	Provide your listeners with insight from experts in the field or people who have had firsthand experience with the subject matter

When it comes to selecting supporting material for your presentations, remember to include a variety. A statistic revealing that your customer base has declined by 25% is powerful, but supporting that stat with an example from a customer who left is stronger because it adds human interest.

Strategies for Informing With Excellence

When designing an informative speech, or any speech for that matter, you should include all the steps outlined in Chapters 11, 12, and 13. Begin by making certain that the general purpose of the speech is to inform. Develop a clear, specific purpose. Analyze your audience and the context carefully, and be certain that your introductions and conclusions incorporate all the components we discuss in Chapter 12. Develop a clear, easy-to-follow organizational structure with smooth transitions. Follow all the rules for effective supporting aids and delivery with professional excellence (see Chapter 13).

Beyond the all-important basics of any successful speech, you need to take into account some additional variables when speaking to inform. First, make certain that you are informing, not persuading. If you begin to incorporate your emotions and your point of view, you have stopped being objective. The range of topics for informative speeches is infinite. You can inform on people, places, things, new products, old products, history, events, process, corporate visions, governmental relations, and concepts from ancient religions to postmodernism. Some of these topics can be controversial. But remember, although your point of view on a controversial issue may be valuable and interesting, it should not be included in an informative speech.

Second, pay careful attention to your audience's level of knowledge and understanding when doing your audience analysis. You do not want to design a speech that informs them about things they already know. It is a waste of your time and their time. By the same token, if your audience has only a basic knowledge of information about a topic and you design your speech as if they are experts, they will not be able to comprehend the information.

Third, as noted earlier in the chapter, try to incorporate a variety of supporting material, such as definitions, examples, statistics, and quotes. This will make certain you appeal to all types of listeners and will make your speech more memorable.

SPEAKING TO PERSUADE

When giving a persuasive speech, you are acting an as advocate or making an argument. Your role is to advocate for or against something. As noted earlier, you will be trying to persuade the audience either simply to agree or disagree with an idea (passive agreement) or to take some sort of action (active agreement or a call to action). Unlike the informative speaker, the persuasive speaker is subjective, influenced, or affected by individual emotions, biases, or points of view.

Aristotle discussed the three persuasive appeals noted earlier in relationship to persuasive presentations. Let's explore each in relationship to your persuasive speeches.

Again, ethos refers to your credibility as a presenter as well as the credibility of the information shared in your presentation. To present with professional excellence, you must demonstrate credibility and help your audience believe you and the information or argument you are presenting. O'Keefe (1990) found that the more credibility you have with an audience, the more you will be able to persuade them. This may be the case, but the sad truth is that most of the messages you hear all day, every day, are void of any type of credibility. Advertisements make claims that come from "leading scientists," but the scientists are never named. People running for high-ranking political offices throw facts, quotes, and figures around in debates. The information each side presents often contradicts the other side, yet sources are lacking. To speak with professional excellence, you must rise above this common shortcoming and make sure you establish credibility. Remember to be extremely careful when using the internet to conduct research. Tools for Professional Excellence 11.1 offers criteria for evaluating websites.

How do you establish credibility in a persuasive speech? Just as you would in an informative speech, make certain the audience is aware of your expertise and knowledge on the subject matter. Additionally, cite your sources and make certain the sources are credible. When persuading, it is also important to establish common ground with your audience. That is, show how you have a shared interest, concern, or background. If your audience believes that you share their attitude toward a topic, it increases your ability to persuade them (McCroskey & Teven, 1999; O'Keefe, 1990; Plantin, 2012).

Logos, as you should recall, refers to the organizational structure and the supporting information found in your speeches. When developing a persuasive presentation, think of yourself as an attorney making an argument. You're building a case with your presentation. In Chapter 12, we will discuss ways to organize your persuasive speeches.

Types of Reasoning

In addition to these organizational patterns, effective persuasive speeches incorporate clear reasoning that guides the listener through the speaker's argument. Types of reasoning include inductive, causal, deductive, analogical, and cognitive dissonance.

Inductive Reasoning

Inductive reasoning involves building an argument by using individual examples, pieces of information, or cases, and then pulling them together to make a generalization or come to a conclusion. For example, Yesina got bad service at Store X. Samesh got bad service at Store X. Ming got bad service at Store X. The generalization or conclusion is that Store X gives bad service. The obvious question that you must ask yourself when using inductive reasoning is how many examples or cases are needed to make a generalization. Unfortunately, the answer is that it depends. Each situation must be considered individually. But if your audience does not think you have enough cases to support your generalization, you will not be able to persuade them.

Causal Reasoning

Causal reasoning, more commonly known as the cause-and-effect relationship, is a type of inductive reasoning. When developing this type of argument, you must demonstrate that certain events or factors (causes) produced, or in some cases prevented, a certain result (the effect). When using causal reasoning, you must be certain that your causes do indeed produce the effect; therefore, your evidence must be credible. Furthermore, you must determine if the cause in your argument is the only cause. In most situations, it will not be the only cause. Therefore, you are wise to make mention of the other causes in your speech and explain why this cause, your cause, should be the focus.

YOUR COMMUNICATION INTERACTION

Stop, Look, and Listen

As you read the informative speech below, consider what features are most effective and what features could be improved.

Background Information

Sheryl Gardner, a senior-level manager, has been asked to speak to a group of management trainees. The speech will take place during one of their training sessions, and Sheryl was told to make it "educational and about communication." Given this information, Sheryl has determined that her general purpose should be to inform; however, *communication* is far too broad to be considered a specific purpose. After analyzing her audience, Sheryl determines that the people in this group will soon be taking over their own departments and should, as a first step, begin developing a communication climate that will foster open communication and teamwork. Since the audience members have already been persuaded that open communication and teamwork are a must in their jobs, Sheryl is simply informing them of the role the communication climate can play in the process.

Introduction

In her book *It's Always Something*, Gilda Radner shares the true story of a dog that was involved in a lawn mower accident. Somehow, a poor little dog was hit by a lawn mower, and the blade cut off her back legs. To complicate matters, the dog was pregnant with puppies. The good news is that both the mother and the puppies were saved. The bad news is that the mother lost her legs. But the little dog did learn to walk again by taking two steps and then pulling her backside, two steps and then pulling her backside. The most interesting part of the story is that when the puppies learned to walk, they all walked just like her!

Attention Step: A compelling story is an excellent way to gain and hold on to your audience's attention.

Establishing Credibility: It is critical that, early on in your presentation, your audience trusts your ability to speak knowingly about your subject.

Creating a Need: Before too much time has passed, your audience should know the goal of your presentation.

Specific Purpose

Preview of Main Points

As Mr. Ruiz mentioned, my name is Sheryl Gardner, and I have been working for this company for more than 20 years. What began as a part-time job for minimum wage has turned into a career in which I am now a top leader in the management team. Today, I am so grateful to have this opportunity to speak with you about the skill I consider to be one of the most important aspects of managing people and the secret to my success—effective communication. The material we will be covering is pretty easy to understand but hard to apply. Why is it so hard to apply? It is hard because we learn how to communicate by emulating others. Just as those puppies learned to walk by emulating what they saw their mother do, we learn to communicate by emulating what we see others do. The problem is that many of us have had poor role models in how to communicate effectively. We have formed bad habits, and now that those patterns are established, they are very hard to change. The good news is that we can change.

We can all become more effective in the art and skill of communication, which is the key to success as a manager. And it all begins with creating a positive communication climate, which is what we will be focusing on today. But before you can create a positive communication climate, you need to know what is meant by the term. *Communication climate* refers to an environment in which communication either thrives or languishes. The communication environment in an organization, like the weather, can be sunny and beautiful (a place where people enjoy working), or it can be like a severe thunderstorm or even a hurricane in some instances, where there is consistently unresolved conflict and employees—from management down—don't trust or support one another. As you know, when attempting to drive in a severe thunderstorm, the storm makes it twice as hard to complete the task at hand and get from Point A to Point B. It's the same in an organization with a poor communication climate. Employees are much less focused, cooperative, and productive due to extraneous factors. And they can't move the company from Point A to Point B.

To establish the healthiest communication climate possible, it's important that you, as a manager, stop, look, and listen.

Stop and take the time to build relationships with your employees. Look at what your employees are doing for the organization. Listen to your employees' ideas and concerns. Let's start by taking a look at the importance of stopping to build relationships with our employees.

Transition Statement: It is important to create signposts (transitions) throughout your presentation to ensure the audience knows when old information has concluded and new information is about to begin.

Body

I. Stop—and take the time to build relationships with your employees.

To better understand the process of building relationships, we need to define two communication terms—*impersonal communication* and *interpersonal communication*. Impersonal communication is when we treat people as though they are objects. Unfortunately, this is the type of communication we often engage in with a cashier or server. We will say, "How are you today?" However, if that person really stopped and told us how they were, we would think it was quite odd. We all know the standard answer is something like "Fine, thank you."

If we are engaging in interpersonal communication, thus building a relationship, we should really want to hear the answer when we ask a question. As managers, we must remember that employees are not chess pieces. These are real people we are moving around.

To develop relationships with your employees, you must be genuine. So the way to connect and build relationships with employees will be different for each of you. The way you do it is to play off your own strengths. Some of you may be good at remembering details about people. So when Xiang tells you about his kid's broken arm, you remember it. And the next time you talk with Xiang, you ask how the arm is doing. Some of you may not be good at that kind of chitchat; so, instead, you can do something else. Maybe you schedule a lunch for the entire team every month and make it a point to sit beside someone different during each luncheon. If that works for you, it is perfect. Maybe you are naturally funny and enjoy joking around with employees. Again, if that is your strength for developing relationships, use it. There is no one right way to do this. You just have to make a commitment to developing relationships and then find a strategy that works for you.

Another vital part of building strong relationships includes the process of looking at or noticing all that our subordinates are doing for the company.

Transition Statement

II. Look—at what employees are doing for the company, and acknowledge it.

Developing relationships will help you become aware of some of the things your team is accomplishing, but to develop a positive communication climate, you must get in the habit of regularly reviewing high performance and success in your team. One way to do this is to develop a habit of asking customers and employees about their experiences with your company. If they had a negative experience, of course work to evaluate the problems. But if they say their experiences are positive, ask them why. Ask them who makes their job easier. Ask them who gave them excellent service. Look at and explore what employees are doing to make this company a success.

Of course, when you see and hear about employees' outstanding efforts, you will feel a sincere appreciation for that effort, but that is not enough. It's vital that you communicate your appreciation. Acknowledging excellent performance is a central component in developing a positive communication climate.

The obvious ways to show appreciation are by recognizing employees' accomplishments publicly. For example, I give a speech at the beginning of every year titled "The Top 10 Reasons Why We Are Great!" The speech highlights everyone's accomplishments for that year. Of course, a simple pat on the back or thank you can be quite effective as well and should be used all year long. Looking at what your employees are doing is a must if you want to develop a positive communication climate.

Transition Statement

III. Listen—to their ideas and concerns.

Now that we've established the importance of stopping to build relationships with our employees and looking at what they are doing for the company, let's talk about the importance of listening to their ideas and concerns.

Bob Jicks of COL Management is part of a team that oversees the daily operations of numerous Imaging Centers, and he has been in management for 11 years. He was quoted as saying,

Sometimes I just need to listen to them, talk with them—because no one understands or represents your company like the person answering the phone or greeting patients at the window. If they feel like they are part of the decision process then they are more likely to be part of the implementation process. I had one of our techs when we were building our new building a few years ago suggest that we make the entrance the same level as the street—parking lot—instead of being a curb or bump. That was a little thing but actually made sense—more importantly—it gave her ownership or buy-in that she felt like she was part of the team. I used to think it was all about the pay—don't get me wrong it helps—but it is really all about the people. Listening to them—"validating" their issues or complaints—sharing and developing goals together—works better than shoving it down their throat.

Listening is also one of Stephen Covey's *Seven Habits of Highly Effective People*. Covey says, "First seek to understand and then to be understood." Highly effective people listen because they know that listening to the other person is the key to building relationships, is the key to understanding what they are doing for the company, and will greatly enhance what they can accomplish as a leader.

We can sometimes unknowingly send messages to our employees that indicate that we aren't listening to them. For example, I was on a committee recently, and our charge was to recommend a speaker to a very important organizational event. The committee spent long hours going over credentials and conducting interviews with potential speakers for the event. When we sent our suggestion to the president of the organization, he ignored the committee and chose someone else. What do you think, through his actions, he communicated to the people on that committee? That he was not listening, perhaps? That he does not value their input, maybe? Things like this hurt the communication climate, motivation, and, ultimately, productivity.

As I stated in the beginning, a lot of this is quite easy to understand but very difficult to apply, because most of us have very well-established communication patterns that do not include listening. If you are preparing your response before the other person stops talking, then you are not listening. If you fail to ask your employees or your clients questions, you are not allowing for listening opportunities. If every idea in the department is yours, you are not listening. Changing bad habits is difficult, but if you make a commitment and stick to it, you can become an effective listener.

Signaling the Conclusion

Summary

Memorable Ending: Finishing your speech by referring back to the attention-getter at the beginning is an excellent way to tie the whole presentation together and increase audience comprehension.

Conclusion

Today we have talked about some ways to create a positive communication climate. We do this by stopping to build relationships with employees, looking at what they are doing for the company, and listening to their ideas and concerns. You now know how to develop a positive communication climate, and by demonstrating these effective communication patterns, you will become a role model for your entire team. Just as those puppies emulated the mother dog, your employees will emulate you. Together, you and your team can make that positive communication climate a reality—you just need to lead the way.

Questions to Consider

1. How would you rate this speech?
2. What features of the speech did you deem effective? Why?
3. What features should have been improved? How would you improve them?

This strategy is known as inoculation. Think of it as the vaccination you get to inoculate you from the flu virus. By exposing your body to a bit of the inactivated virus now, you will not be affected by later exposure. In the case of persuasion, when the speaker points out other possible causes in a cause-and-effect relationship and then explains why they are not as important or relevant, it inoculates the audience from future attempts to persuade them in the other direction.

For example, let's say a hotel manager was trying to persuade her supervisors that the drop in occupancy in her hotel was due to road construction on the highway in front of the hotel. She should mention that tourism is down throughout the United States due to the economy but that the construction is the primary reason for the drop in tourism at her hotel. To build her argument, she could show occupancy drops in other hotels near the highway versus hotels in her town not impacted by the construction.

Deductive Reasoning

Deductive reasoning occurs when the speaker takes general information (premises) and draws a conclusion from that general information. Deductive reasoning is often set up as a syllogism. One famous syllogism is as follows:

All men are mortal. (Major premise)

Socrates is a man. (Minor premise)

Therefore, Socrates is mortal. (Conclusion)

Although the syllogism has been around for a long time, it is still an excellent way to persuade in today's workplace. For example, consider the following persuasive arguments. Americans want to lose weight (major premise). Our new product aids in weight loss (minor premise). Americans will buy our new product (conclusion). Nursing is a major in high demand (major premise). University W wants to offer majors in high demand (minor premise). Therefore, University W should offer nursing as a major (conclusion). To use deductive reasoning effectively, you must make certain that your major and minor premises are accurate and that you convince the audience to accept those premises in the body of your speech.

Analogical Reasoning

Analogical reasoning is simply reasoning from an analogy. In other words, it involves making an argument by comparing two cases. When you use analogical reasoning, the cases must be comparable. Remember that, although two cases or situations may be very similar, they are never identical. To remedy this situation, we once again suggest using inoculation. You should point out the differences and minimize them. Recently, a small-business owner argued in front of the city council that the town should not support a smoking ban in restaurants and bars. She believed that decisions about smoking should be left to the individual business owners. She based his argument on an analogy comparing the restriction of civil liberties that this ban represented with the limitation of civil liberties when the Nazis first came to power in Germany. She stressed that a ban on smoking was among the Nazis' new anti-tobacco laws when they came into power. She also pointed out that she wasn't trying to compare those that supported the ban to Nazis but that the restrictions were similar. Her argument was partially persuasive because she was a nonsmoker who had made the choice as a business owner not to allow smoking in her establishment.

TABLE 11.2 ■ Tools for Professional Excellence Assessing Internet Sources

Is this site credible? Yes, by looking at the following: The domain.gov is an indicator of an official government site.
The Banner: This indicates that the page is a part of the official site for Missouri governor Michael L. Parson.
The Text: The information in the text includes various dates and basic pieces of biographical information in a factual manner. However, the text also says the governor "strengthened 2nd Amendment rights" and passed legislation to "guarantee all Missourians the right to farm and ranch," which indicates some bias with regard to those topics.
The Date: The page references dates from the last couple of years, which indicates timeliness.

Office of Missouri Governor Mike Parson

To assess the credibility of an internet source, follow these practical tips:

Criteria	Practical Tips
How did you find the page?	● Always check the site if it was found using an online search engine, as noncredible sites are included in searches.
	● If the site was suggested to you by an instructor or a scholar, then it is likely credible.
	● If the site was cited in a journal article or other scholarly article, then it is likely credible.
What is the site's domain?	● Sites that end in .com, .net, or .org should always be checked for credibility.
	● Sites that end in .gov or .edu are usually official, credible sites.
Who is the authority of the page?	● Always be skeptical of any site that does not list any authors.
	● If an author is listed, check for any affiliations with the site, especially if it is related to a specific group or organization.
	● If an author is listed, check for any credentials to ensure that they are a credible expert on the site's topic.
Is the information accurate and objective?	● Always check to see if the author provides citations to support the information shared, or links to other credible sites with the same information.
	● If possible, cross-reference the author's information with other credible sources to ensure the site's accuracy.
	● Unless it is meant to be an opinion piece, be wary of any site that includes an obvious bias in the writing.
Is the page current?	● Always check to see when a site was published. Be wary if no publication date is included.
	● Check to see if there is an updated version of the site with more current, accurate information.
	● Make sure any outside pages that the site links to are current, as well.
Does the page function well?	● Be wary if the site is difficult to navigate, or if the page is difficult to access on a second visit.
	● Check to see if the site has a search bar or index to access other pages.

Source: Adapted from University Library, University of Illinois at Urbana-Champaign. (2018). *Evaluate your sources.* https://www.library.illinois.edu/ugl/howdoi/evaluate_sources/

Cognitive Dissonance

Cognitive dissonance is another useful tool for persuading an audience. Although it is not one of the standard forms of reasoning, it is well worth mentioning. This theory, developed by researcher Leon Festinger (1957), states that when a person holds two ideas that contradict each other, it creates mental noise or cognitive dissonance in that person's mind. This results in a feeling of discomfort for the person, so they look for ways to reduce the contradiction. If you develop an argument that creates cognitive dissonance and then offer a solution that reduces the contradiction, you are likely to have made a successful persuasive argument.

For example, Paul works for a nonprofit organization that helps veterans with disabilities. In his speeches, he reminds the audience of the deep gratitude they feel for all veterans, especially those who have been disabled in battle. He then asks them what they have done to show their gratitude. If they have not done anything to show their gratitude, they feel cognitive dissonance. He then provides them with an opportunity to express their gratitude by donating time or money to his organization. Most audience members are happy to give because it relieves their discomfort.

Pathos

The final type of persuasive appeal (after ethos and logos) is pathos—a term that refers to emotional appeal. Because informative speeches are objective, emotional appeals should not be present in informative speeches. However, pathos is very powerful, and it does play an important role when persuading with professional excellence. But beware—a presentation that has strong pathos but lacks ethos or logos or both is not effective. Far too many presenters rely solely on emotional appeal. In the moment, they may move an audience, but in the long run, the lack of credibility and logic make for a poor presentation. To achieve professional excellence as a presenter, you must include all three appeals (ethos, logos, and pathos) in your presentations.

You might be thinking, "How can I incorporate emotional appeal into my presentation?" One way is with the use of language. Selecting words that have a strong emotional connotation—or implied meaning—can be powerful. Incorporating into your presentation research that has strong emotional appeal is another tool.

Pathos also has a place in informative presentations. Selecting language and supporting material with emotional appeal can help an audience relate to the topic and remember an informative message. In the same way, pathos in a persuasive message can move an audience to action.

Strategies for Persuading With Excellence

When designing a persuasive speech, you should include all the steps outlined in Chapters 11, 12, and 13. Begin by making certain that the general purpose of the speech is to persuade. Develop a clear, specific purpose. Analyze your audience and the context carefully. Be certain that your introductions and conclusions incorporate the appropriate components we discuss in Chapter 12. Develop a clear, easy-to-follow organizational structure with smooth transitions. Follow all the rules for effective supporting aids and delivery with professional excellence (see Chapter 13).

You may be thinking, "Wait a minute, didn't I just read that paragraph earlier in this chapter?" Yes, you did. But the basic components of an effective speech, informative or persuasive, are worth repeating. As we explained earlier, these basics are often overlooked by so-called professionals. You must be certain to include them in all your speeches so that you can speak with professional excellence.

Beyond the basics, you should be aware of a few additional facts when persuading (see Table 11.3). First, your entire speech should be persuasive. In other words, an informative speech with a persuasive conclusion does not rise to the level of excellence. If the audience does not know what

TABLE 11.3 ■ **Action Items.** Skills for Informing and Persuading		
Skill	Strategy	Application
Gain interest	Capture and hold the attention of your audience.	Begin a presentation with an alarming statistic, the use of a prop, or a compelling story.
Spark motivation	Establish a receptive attitude from the audience.	Connect your line of reasoning with an already well-known and accepted piece of information.
Finish strong	Leave a lasting impression on the audience that will keep them thinking after the presentation is over.	Finish with a powerful image, an inspirational quote, or a message that inspires a call to action.

you are persuading them to do or believe until the end of the speech, you have given a weak persuasive speech, at best. Your speech should be organized as an argument. The use of persuasive appeals should be prevalent throughout the speech and not saved for the end.

Step Back and Reflect

Second, although you can and should be subjective in a persuasive speech, your opinion is not enough to persuade an audience. After all, "because I think so" or "because I said so" is not among Aristotle's persuasive appeals. Within your speech, you must develop a clear argument, supported by solid logical appeals and credible evidence, such as definitions, examples, statistics, and quotes.

Third, when analyzing your audience, you must assess the target audience. Think of the target audience as the people on the fence. Some people already agree with you or are already engaging in the action you are trying to persuade them toward. They don't need to be persuaded. Another group—we hope a very small one—may never be persuaded. Your speech should be aimed toward the remaining individuals. A sample of a fully developed persuasive speech is provided in Chapter 12.

Your audience will find it helpful to review statistics presented in a format that's easy to read and understand. Avoid overloading your audience with too much technical information.

iStockphoto/alvarez

KEYS TO EXCELLENCE IN PROFESSIONAL PRESENTATIONS

Although many students will not become public orators in their careers, most jobs require some amount of public speaking. Using the KEYS strategy (see Figure 11.1) can help you become effective in all your public speaking experiences. The first step, *know yourself*, involves knowing your strengths and weaknesses and how to use them to your advantage. Be aware of your shortcomings and try to minimize them, and pay particularly close attention to your nonverbal communication. Most people don't realize they are using distracting body language because it is unconscious; practice your speaking skills and learn to use positive nonverbal communication.

EVALUATE THE PROFESSIONAL CONTEXT

No Raises

As you evaluate the passage below, consider whether this behavior is appropriate for this professional context.

Rose is a supervisor for Child Protective Services. The new budget was just announced for her department. Last year, the budget was flat and no one got a pay raise, so hopes were high that this year would be different. Unfortunately, additional budget cuts translated to another year without raises. Employee morale was clearly lowered by this news. Rose realized she needed to address this issue. She called her team together and gave the following speech:

We do not have easy jobs. In fact, I would argue that we have one of the toughest jobs there is. It's not easy to see the pain and abuse we witness day after day. It's not easy to go home and relax when your heart has been ripped out at work. And it's sure not easy to endure all this when you feel as though you have been slapped in the face by your employer, who is not even willing to give you the raises you have earned. So today, I don't want to make excuses about budget cuts. I just want to share with you a story that helps me handle my anger and keep my morale up in times such as these.

Almost 20 years ago, I was called in to investigate a case of abuse. The situation was not unique. Both parents had drug problems, and the stepfather was abusing both the mother and the children. At one point, I had to physically pull the three boys away from their mother, who was screaming for her babies, while the oldest boy, Samuel, spit in my face. I had to see the fear in the boys' faces as they were placed with strangers, and I wondered if it was all worth it. About a year later, I ran into Samuel at a movie theater. At first, I did not recognize him. He looked so much healthier. He told me that his mom had gotten away from her abusive spouse, she had gone to rehab, and she had gotten her boys back. And then, something I will never forget, he said, "I am so sorry I spit on you that day. I think about that all the time. I was so scared that I didn't realize you were the hero who came in and saved us."

I know that each of you can share a similar story. We all have met a Samuel or two in this job—kids who may hate you in the moment but later see you as the hero. The problem is, it isn't easy being a hero. It's not like in the movies, with superpowers and accolades. It's about a lot of hard work and very little recognition. It's not easy being a hero, but for those kids we save from neglect and abuse, our efforts do make a difference. I wish I could give you all the raises you deserve. But I can't. All I can do is let you know that I'm proud to work with such a fine team. And to me, each and every one of you is a hero. I realize that does not pay your mortgage or put gas in your cars, but to the Samuels of the world, it means a whole lot more. It's okay to be angry about your raises, but don't forget why we are here. None of us took this job for the money. We aren't the kind of people who choose the easy life—we have chosen the lives of heroes. It may not be easy, but I believe, I know you believe, and I am certain the Samuels of the world believe that it's worth the sacrifice.

Questions to Consider

1. How did Rose use language and examples for emotional appeal?
2. Did Rose evaluate the professional context effectively? Why or why not?
3. Do you think she was successful at raising morale? Why or why not?

The second step, *evaluate the professional context*, requires you to understand to whom you are presenting. A presentation given to your superiors will most likely be very formal, but if you are presenting to your coworkers, then you might take a more informal tone to put your audience at ease. Know the culture of your organization, and tailor your presentations to meet the expected standards.

The third step, *your communication interaction*, involves taking what you have learned in the first two steps and applying it to your presentation. Be aware of your personal presentation style, and be prepared to alter it if the situation calls for it. Also, try to critique the audience's responses during your presentation and make any necessary adjustments or clarifications if it appears necessary.

The final step calls for you to *step back and reflect*. Assess your audience's reaction to your presentation, and get feedback to see if your presentation was effective. Think about the verbal and nonverbal communication you used and decide what communication was positive or negative. You must grow continually as a public speaker, and your presentations will become more effective as you continue to practice.

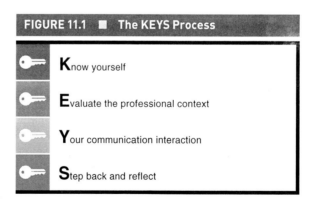

FIGURE 11.1 ■ The KEYS Process

Know yourself

Evaluate the professional context

Your communication interaction

Step back and reflect

EXECUTIVE SUMMARY

Now that you have finished reading this chapter, you should be able to

Discuss the importance of professional excellence in public speaking:

- Just as effective communication skills are essential to your professional success, effective oral communication skills are essential if you want to excel in leadership.

- Product presentations, team huddles, meeting leadership, press conferences, special events, and other forms of oral communication reveal something about you as a professional.

- Presentations serve as a tool to motivate employees and to communicate effectively about business goals.

- Presentational excellence is necessary to achieve professional excellence.

Identify presenting opportunities and purposes:

- The first step in the presentation process is identifying opportunities. Once you have identified the presentation opportunities, you can identify the purpose within them.

- Two types of presentation opportunities are available to leaders. One is a formal presentation, which occurs in a traditional presentation setting. Presenting a sales pitch to clients and giving a progress report at the district meeting are examples of formal presentations.

- The opportunity presentation is identical in preparation and presentation to the formal presentation, but it occurs in a less traditional setting. For instance, many organizations have huddles, during which employees are pulled together to talk.

Design an informative speech:

- Begin by making certain that the general purpose of the speech is to inform. Develop a clear, specific purpose. Analyze your audience and the context carefully.

- Make certain that you are informing, not persuading. If you begin to incorporate your emotions and your point of view, you have stopped being objective.

- Pay careful attention to your audience's level of knowledge and understanding when doing your audience analysis. You do not want to design a speech that informs them about things they already know. It is a waste of your time and their time. By the same token, if your audience has only a basic knowledge of information about a topic and you design your speech as if they are experts, they will not be able to comprehend the information.

- Try to incorporate a variety of supporting material, such as definitions, examples, statistics, and quotes. This will make certain you appeal to all types of listeners and will make your speech more memorable.

Design a persuasive speech:

- To present with professional excellence, you must demonstrate credibility and help your audience believe you and the information or argument you are presenting.

- When persuading, it is also important to establish common ground with your audience. That is, show how you have a shared interest, concern, or background. If your audience believes that you share their attitude toward a topic, it increases your ability to persuade them.

- Begin by making certain that the general purpose of the speech is to persuade. Develop a clear, specific purpose. Analyze your audience and the context carefully.

- Develop a clear, easy-to-follow organizational structure with smooth transitions. Follow all the rules for effective supporting aids and delivery with professional excellence.

Apply the KEYS process to develop professional excellence as an informer and a persuader:

- Know yourself. Know your strengths and weaknesses and how to use them to your advantage. Be aware of your shortcomings and try to minimize them, and pay particularly close attention to your nonverbal communication.

- Evaluate the professional context. Understand to whom you are presenting. A presentation given to your superiors will most likely be very formal, but if you are presenting to your coworkers, you might take a more informal tone to put your audience at ease.

- Your communication interaction. Take what you have learned in the first two steps and apply them to your presentation. Be aware of your personal presentation style and be prepared to alter it if the situation calls for it.

- Step back and reflect. Assess your audience's reaction to your presentation, and get feedback to see if your presentation was effective.

EXPLORE

1. Visit the WellSaid! website and access its free resources (www.wellsaid.com/free-resources/). Identify a short video coaching session that was particularly useful for you. List at least one new insight you gained from watching this video that supplements what you have learned in this chapter.

2. Pick a personal favorite speech from any medium. Identify the different phases (introduction, body, conclusion) as well as the transitions used throughout the speech. Identify the best practices and types of information offered based on what we have covered in this chapter.

3. Find and analyze a speech or presentation with significant historical importance. How might the speaker have altered their presentation given the communication technologies available today? Identify two or three different mediums that are available now that would have been significantly useful given the context and subject matter of your selected historical speech.

REVIEW

1. _____ refers to your credibility as a presenter as well as the credibility of the information delivered in your presentation.

2. _____ refers to the words of a presentation in the context of organizational structure and the supporting information.

3. _____ refers to building an argument by using individual examples, pieces of information, or cases, and then pulling them together to make a generalization or come to a conclusion.

4. _____ occurs when the speaker takes general information (premises) and draws a conclusion from that general information.

5. Explain the stance of cognitive dissonance theory.

6. _____ refers to emotional appeal.

7. Establishing _____ refers to showing the audience you have a shared interest, concern, or background.

8. Define inoculation in a persuasive speaking context.

DISCUSSION QUESTIONS

1. Can you think of a time when a presentation would have been a more effective channel for delivering a message than an email or a memo? Why do you think it would have been more effective?

2. Take a moment to think about someone whom you view as an excellent presenter. What are the qualities of this person's verbal and nonverbal communication? Does this speaker incorporate Aristotle's appeals (ethos, logos, and pathos)?

3. Take a moment to think about someone whom you view as a bad presenter. What are the qualities of this person's verbal and nonverbal communication while presenting? Does this speaker neglect to incorporate Aristotle's appeals (ethos, logos, and pathos)?

4. Discuss the qualities of an excellent presentation. In your view, what factors make a presentation memorable?

5. Reflect on an occupation that interests you or one in which you are currently working. What are some situations that might require you to give an informative or persuasive presentation?

ETHICAL CONNECTION

A Case of False Information

As you read this passage and answer the questions, consider how the way you communicate has an ethical dimension.

Travis is a public relations consultant for the local mayor's office. A large part of his job involves advising the mayor's staff on public opinion and assisting in preparing public speeches for the mayor himself. Recently, the city has seen a fierce debate over the state of the city's water system. The majority of the mayor's office (including the mayor) is against appropriating funds to overhaul the city's water system, while many community leaders favor it. Travis and the mayor's office have recently been given an independent study that indicates there will be significant health risks to the population if renovations are not made to the city's antiquated water system; however, the mayor is preparing to deliver a speech that states the exact opposite of the study. Travis faces an ethical dilemma: Should he discredit the mayor's speech and risk losing his job, or say nothing and attempt to dissuade the mayor without revealing that the speech contained false information?

Questions to Consider

1. What ethical rule is the mayor breaking in this example?

2. How could Travis dissuade the mayor from moving forward with this speech?

3. What element of Plato's ethos, pathos, and logos is being violated here?

4. Is there ever a time when omission of a fact would not be unethical in a presentation?

TERMS TO REMEMBER

Review key terms with eFlashcards: **https://edge.sagepub.com/quintanilla5e.**

active agreement (call to action) (p. 285)

analogical reasoning (p. 295)

Aristotle (p. 283)

causal reasoning (p. 291)

cognitive dissonance (p. 296)

common ground (p. 290)

connotation (p. 297)

credibility (p. 287)

deductive reasoning (p. 295)

ethos (p. 287)

formal presentation (p. 284)

general purpose (p. 285)

huddles (p. 284)

impromptu presentation (p. 285)

inductive reasoning (p. 290)

inform (p. 285)

inoculation (p. 294)

logos (p. 288)

objective (p. 287)

opportunity presentation (p. 284)

passive agreement (p. 285)

pathos (p. 297)

persuade (p. 285)

persuasive appeals (p. 287)

Quintilian (p. 287)

specific purpose (p. 286)

types of reasoning (p. 290)

Visit **https://edge.sagepub.com/quintanilla5e** to help you accomplish your coursework goals in an easy-to-use learning environment.

Professionals like Microsoft CEO Satya Nadella carefully prepare for each speaking engagement.
iStockphoto/Jean-Luc Ichard

12 SPEECH DESIGN

After studying this chapter, you should be able to

12.1   Analyze audience and context

12.2   Explain how to gather research for your speeches

12.3   Organize the body of a speech and incorporate effective transitions

12.4   Develop effective introductions

12.5   Develop effective conclusions

12.6   Discuss the role and value of language

12.7   Apply the KEYS process to develop professional excellence in speech design

Delivering a moving speech does not happen without some measure of preparation. Delivery is just one part of the process. You need to step up your presentation's overall quality, from your delivery style to your slide decks. You're unloading a lot of new information on your audience, so try to keep them entertained and engaged. Patel (2017) offers a few ways to help you bring your presentations to the next level:

- **Brevity is awesome.** The most successful speakers in history understood the importance of brevity in presenting their ideas, so do what they've done: Aim for a shorter, punchier speech during your next presentation.

- **Tell stories.** Focus on the core concepts of your presentation and engage your audience with relatable storytelling.

- **Use visuals wisely.** Don't include a ton of graphs and charts in hopes of making your presentation appear more credible.

- **Speak to the audience, not an individual.** It's not uncommon to see presentations made for a single individual—like the bigwig in the room or a small group of influencers attending a larger event.

ANALYZING THE AUDIENCE AND CONTEXT

If you want to present with professional excellence, you must be audience centered. Don't fall into the trap of so many mediocre presenters by focusing all your energy on your nerves or your PowerPoint slides. The best presenters, the best communicators in general, are aware of all the components involved in the communication process, and they pay particular attention to the audience.

When you envision an audience-centered speaker, what images come to mind? Do you picture a seasoned presenter who can adjust or change the message midsentence to suit the audience's mood? For those of you who are beginners, this might seem like an impossible skill, one that you'll never master. You might say to yourself, "There's no way I'm ever going to be able to adjust my presentation in the moment." With enough practice, we are certain you can develop this skill, but being audience centered is about much more than responding to feedback

What are the most common qualities that contribute to excellent presentations when the audience is seated in a large, open space such as the one shown here?

iStockphoto/uschools

during your actual presentation. There are many things you can and should do proactively to become more audience centered. Start by asking a series of questions designed to answer one all-important larger question: "Who is my audience?" This audience analysis will frame your entire presentation, so it must be considered first, last, and during every stage in the design process (see Tools for Professional Excellence 12.1). So far, we have discussed identifying your purpose and analyzing your audience, but neither of these steps occurs in a vacuum. They can't be done effectively without including a context analysis. After all, the context plays an important role in determining the purpose of the presentation. In addition, the context has a huge impact on the audience. Again, you must ask yourself a series of questions to analyze your context (see Tools for Professional Excellence 12.2).

Once you've answered each of the questions about context, ask yourself, "How can I use this knowledge to improve my presentation?" For example, if you know the audience is required to be at your presentation, you may need to work harder to show them why the information is relevant to them. If the audience is standing, you must keep your remarks brief. If you have a large audience, no stage, and flat seating, you may need to rearrange the furniture to help the audience see you, or you may need to walk around. Use the information you learn from your analysis to enhance your presentation.

RESEARCHING

The internet has made researching so easy. All you have to do is type your topic into Google, and bang, there is everything you need to know. In fact, a quick exploration of Wikipedia is really all anyone needs when it comes to research.

Obviously, the preceding paragraph is a joke. At least, we hope you see it as an obvious joke. Sadly, many of our students and even some executives might miss the sarcastic tone intended in that paragraph. According to Hamilton (1996), poor presenters often make the mistake of either relying solely on their own knowledge or relying solely on the internet. Either way, a lack of research results in a poor presentation.

One of the many skills you will learn during your college experience is how to conduct research. As we discussed in Chapter 7, research is the central skill used during the explorer phase of the creative process. Research is also a central skill needed to present with professional excellence. Shortchanging the research process by limiting yourself to a quick Google search or to the report in hand will result in a poor presentation.

TABLE 12.1 ■ Tools for Professional Excellence Who Is My Audience?	
Question Type	**Audience Analysis**
Demographic questions	● What is the general demographic information for this audience (i.e., sex, age, race, ethnicity, job title)?
	● What is the audience's level of knowledge concerning this topic?
Relational questions	● What is my relationship with the audience?
	● What is the audience members' relationship with one another?

Gathering Research

The research you need in order to develop and support your presentation can and should come from a variety of sources. Depending on the topic, you may use internal sources, external sources, or a combination of the two. Internal sources include information that comes from within the organization, such as reports, policies, or interviews with employees or customers. External sources include information that comes from outside the organization, such as from outside agencies, the competition, the government, and the media.

TABLE 12.2 ■ Tools for Professional Excellence What Is the Context?	
To analyze the context of your presentation, answer the questions below:	
Question Type	**Context Analysis**
Physical setting	● Is there a stage?
	● Will I have a podium or a microphone?
	● Is PowerPoint available and can it be projected on a screen?
	● Is the audience sitting or standing?
	● If they are sitting, how comfortable are the chairs?
Attitudinal questions	● Why are they here (required or by choice)?
	● Is the topic of this presentation seen as positive, negative, neutral, or a mix?
	● Will anyone else speak before or after me? If so, what is the nature of their topic(s)?

If you were giving a presentation on improving customer service within your organization, you could find supporting material in a variety of places. You might start with the new policy on customer service that created this presentation opportunity. You might then research past customer satisfaction scores within your organization, as well as data showing how your organization compares with the competition. You might interview some executives about the importance of customer service or ask some employees with outstanding customer service their thoughts on the subject (see Tools for Professional Analysis 12.3). You might find some quotes or examples from organizations or leaders known for their customer service. Remember that you can't begin and end your research with the new policy if you want to present with professional excellence.

Determining What to Include

If you have done your job as a researcher, you will have more information than you need. At this point in the process, you must determine what to include. Ask yourself a few key questions:

- What information does this audience need to know so that they understand this topic or are persuaded by this argument?

- What information is most relevant to this audience?

- What information would be most interesting (new or different) to this audience?

- What information is needed to support my specific purpose effectively?

Research results, statistics, and financial information must be organized with graphics the audience can understand. Avoid information overload when you are presenting on information that involves a variety of sources.

iStockphoto/FluxFactory

Based on your answers to these questions, you can determine which information should be included in your presentation.

Loading a presentation full of data and statistics that have no relevance to the audience and/or the purpose is the mark of a poor speaker. Furthermore, speakers who give examples based on personal experience are deemed more trustworthy by audiences compared with speakers who present other types of support (Collins, 2012; Koballa, 1989). Put simply, personal examples are more persuasive than statistics (Kazoleas, 1993; Metsämäki, 2012).

EVALUATE THE PROFESSIONAL CONTEXT

The Annual Company Barbeque

As you evaluate the passage below, consider whether this behavior is appropriate for this professional context.

Laurence, Avery, and Evan were all asked to say a few words at the annual company barbeque. The barbeque is designed to be a fun celebration that includes all employees, their families, and their friends. This year, there was a lot to celebrate since the company had experienced tremendous growth. The physical setting included a small stage with a microphone, and a field with no chairs. The audience included employees, family members (many of whom were small children), and friends. The audience was happy to be at the event, but for many of them, the speeches were keeping them from the fun.

Laurence did not prepare his comments, because he didn't see this as a formal speaking opportunity. When handed the microphone, he said, "The annual company barbeque is a long-standing tradition here at Company D. So I encourage all of you to keep the tradition alive and well by having a lot of fun here today."

Avery welcomed this speaking opportunity, and she had prepared some remarks. Her speech went as follows:

> To the rest of the world, Company D is made up of all the outstanding employees who are here today. Let's give a round of applause to all Company D employees. [Allow time for applause.] What a team!
>
> Now stop for one moment and look around this crowd. Go on, look around. What do you see? I'll tell you what I see. I see our real team, our complete team. The unprecedented success of Company D did not happen simply because we have a great team at work. It happened because we are supported by a great team when we leave work, a team made of our families and our friends, many of whom are here today. It is this at-home team that understood our long hours this year, helped us unwind, served as our sounding boards, and supported us, allowing us to grow as a company.
>
> This barbeque is merely a small token of appreciation for all that you do—you being employees, family, and friends. Congratulations on an amazing year, thank you once again, and enjoy the 45th Annual Company D Barbeque—you've earned it!

Evan was the last one to speak. Like Avery, he had prepared her remarks. Evan had been with the company for many years, so he decided to take this opportunity to discuss the history of the organization over the past 45 years. He thought to himself, "This barbeque is part of our history, and the company has gone through a lot of changes this year, so some reflection would be nice." His speech was about 25 minutes long.

By the end of the speech, the audience was restless and unhappy.

Questions to Consider

1. How would you rate each speaker?
2. How did the purpose of the event, the physical setting, and the audience factor into your analysis of each speaker's effectiveness?
3. Using the KEYS process, what advice would you give each speaker?

When determining what to include, you must also think about ways to provide variety to keep the audience engaged. A few well-placed, relevant statistics coupled with some examples can really help reinforce a message. According to Walter Fisher (1984), we are all storytelling creatures and like to tell and hear stories about people (this is where human interest comes in). Combining these elements could enhance your presentation. You can also gather useful information by interviewing people who have experience and expertise related to your topic. For tips on preparing for and conducting professional interviews, review Tools for Professional Excellence 12.3.

TABLE 12.3 ■ Tools for Professional Excellence Conducting an Interview	
To prepare and conduct professional interviews, consider the questions below:	
Stage	**Questions**
Before the interview	● What is your purpose? Know why you are conducting the interview and what information you wish to gain. This may require conducting background research prior to the interview.
	● Whom are you interviewing? Based on your purpose, determine whom you need to interview.
	● When and where is your interview? Schedule your interview in advance. Dress in a style that enhances your credibility.
	● How will you conduct the interview? Decide if you will take notes, record the conversation, or both. Develop an interview schedule. Your interview schedule should include all of your questions.
During the interview	● Are you presenting yourself as a professional? Be sure to arrive early and dress in a style that enhances your credibility.
	● Are you following the rules for good etiquette? These rules include greeting the interviewee, reminding them of your purpose, respecting their time, and saying thank you.
	● Did you ask all your questions? Make sure you ask the questions on your interview schedule and any of the follow-up questions you may have.
After the interview	● What information will you use? As soon as the interview is over, review your notes or listen to your tape and decide what information should be included in your speech.

ORGANIZING YOUR PRESENTATION

Now that you've conducted your research and decided what to include, the time has come to get organized. Giving a presentation that's well organized increases the likelihood that your audience will pay attention to, understand, and remember your message.

Organizing the Body

You must develop clear organization within the body of your presentation. Your typical, not-so-memorable speaker will take all the information available and lump it together as three main points. This is simply not acceptable. In the 21st century, it's as easy as the click of a mouse to move information around as you develop the best organizational pattern for your presentation.

It takes very little effort to develop a presentation that people can follow and remember. To excel as a speaker with professional excellence, make a commitment to solid organization. This is a relatively easy process—all you need to do is consider the various organizational formats until you find the one that best fits the presentation.

ETHICAL CONNECTION

Debate Team Dilemma

As you read this passage and answer the questions, consider how the way you communicate has an ethical dimension.

Jafari is a member of his university's debate team, and his school is in the running to win the regional debate competition this year. Unfortunately, Jafari personally disagrees with the side his team has been assigned to debate. The factual information available for the topic favors the opposing team, so Jafari has suggested that the debate team focus on emotional appeals.

The speech he has designed is very effective on emotional appeals, but his facts and rhetoric are almost nonexistent. The team feels that they can win with their presentation style but are cautious about presenting the speech while not acknowledging the facts. The debate topic covers a controversial issue that is going to a vote in local elections, and the team does not want to mislead voters into making an uninformed decision about the issue.

Questions to Consider

1. What is the ethical dilemma facing the debate team?

2. Why is a scarcity of facts damaging to a presentation?

3. What other strategies could Jafari use for his debate besides an emotional appeal?

4. Why are emotional appeals so dangerous when debating a topic?

An organizational pattern often used to persuade in business and professional settings is Monroe's Motivated Sequence. This five-step process, developed in 1935 by Purdue University professor Alan H. Monroe, includes the *attention step*, the *need step*, the *satisfaction step*, the *visualization step*, and the *action step*. The sequence begins with an attention step, in which the speaker engages the audience through the use of attention-getting devices (we discuss these devices in the Introductions section of this chapter). In the needs step, the speaker establishes the problem and thereby the need for a change. During the satisfaction step, the speaker provides a solution for the problem presented. The visualization step increases the audience's desire for the solution by helping them visualize the benefits it will bring. Finally, the action step reinforces the solution with a specific, clear call to action.

If Monroe's Motivated Sequence is not the right organizational pattern for your presentation, consider other common patterns, which include some of the following: chronological, compare–contrast, sequential, spatial, and topical. Tools for Professional Excellence 12.4 provides a definition and example of each format. Consider each format before making your final selection, and ask yourself two simple questions:

● What is the best way to organize this information so that my audience can follow me?

● What is the best way to organize this presentation so that my audience will remember my message?

Using Monroe's Motivated Sequence requires the speaker to get the audience to visualize how things would be if the speaker's solution is implemented. Try incorporating creative language—such as imagery and metaphors, which you will learn about later in this chapter—to successfully get your audience to visualize your solution.

iStockphoto/Cecilie_Arcurs

Developing Transitions

One mark of an excellent presenter is that they provide a clear organizational structure through the use of transitions. What is a transition? A transition is any word or phrase that helps guide the listener from one point to the next.

Let's face it—most audience members are not good listeners. To counter this problem, you must learn to tell them what you are going to say, say it, and then tell them what you said. Why would you want to use so much repetition? Will it bore the audience? We assure you it will not bore them. Instead, it will help them. Bottom line, if you're giving a presentation and you actually want your audience to remember your message, you must repeat yourself. Begin by clearly introducing your topic and specific purpose during the introduction, followed by a preview of your main points. Next, clearly state each main point during the presentation, and state it again in the conclusion. It sounds very mechanical, but it's a formula that works.

Within the body of your presentation, clear transitions must appear between your main points. Let's say you are giving a presentation on hurricane evacuation procedures for your workplace. As you complete your discussion of the first main point and move to the next main point, add an internal summary followed by an internal preview:

> Now that we have looked at how equipment will be protected during the storm [internal summary], let's examine the ways Company X would protect you if such a disaster were to occur [internal preview].

The use of internal previews and summaries helps the audience follow your organizational structure with ease by providing additional reinforcement of your message.

For presentations with more than three main points, internal previews and summaries between each point can be overkill. Instead, use signposts—words or phrases that let the audience know where you are within the presentation. Imagine you're driving down a stretch of unfamiliar road. If you don't see any road signs for a while, you might worry that you have taken a wrong turn. You ask, "Where am I? How much farther do I have to go?" Then a sign appears telling you where you are, and you feel relieved. A signpost does the same thing within a presentation. Signposts are useful both between main points and within main points. Using the hurricane example again, signposts could be used when discussing steps for protecting electronic equipment:

We will take four steps to protect electronic equipment:

First, all data will be backed up in the cloud. [Discuss this subpoint.]

Second, all electronic equipment will be unplugged and wrapped in plastic bags. [Discuss this subpoint.]

Third, all electronic equipment in exterior offices with windows will be moved to interior offices. [Discuss this subpoint.]

Fourth, all electronic equipment in interior offices will be taken off the floor and placed on desks or shelves. [Discuss this subpoint.]

TABLE 12.4 ■ Tools for Professional Excellence Organizational Patterns for Presentations

Pattern	Example

Chronological (arranges information based on progression of time or events)	Disney Films Through the Years
	I. 1930 to 1949
	  a. *Snow White and the Seven Dwarfs*
	  b. *Dumbo*
	  c. *Bambi*
	II. 1950 to 1969
	  a. *Cinderella*
	  b. *Lady and the Tramp*
	  c. *Mary Poppins*

Compare–contrast (arranges information according to how two or more things compare with one another; i.e., how alike or different they are)	Missouri State and Mizzou
	I. Points of comparison
	  a. Educational programs
	  b. Cost of tuition
	II. Points of contrast
	  a. Quality of education
	  b. Geographical location

Sequential (arranges information according to a step-by-step sequence describing a particular process)	How to Make a PB&J
	I. Gather materials
	  a. Peanut butter, jelly, bread
	  b. Knife
	II. Peanut butter
	  a. Use knife to scoop peanut butter
	  b. Spread to one slice of bread
	III. Jelly
	  a. Use knife to scoop jelly
	  b. Spread to one slice of bread

To determine the right organizational pattern for your presentation, consider the formats below:	
Pattern	**Example**

	IV. Assemble sandwich
	   a. Press the two slices of bread together
	   b. Cut the sandwich in half

Spatial (arranges information according to how things fit together in physical space, or in relation to one another)	Tour of Missouri
	
	  I. Springfield
	    a. Downtown Square
	    b. Hammons Field
	
	  II. St. Louis
	    a. The Arch
	    b. St. Louis Zoo

Topical (arranges information according to different subtopics within a larger topic)	Tennis Grand Slam Champions
	
	  I. Men
	    a. Daniil Medvedev
	    b. Dominic Thiem
	    c. Novak Djokovic
	
	  II. Women
	    a. Emma Raducanu
	    b. Naomi Osaka
	    c. Serena Williams

Source: Adapted from "Patterns of Organization," faculty.washington.edu/ezent/impo.htm

INTRODUCTIONS

Although an introduction should have a preview and a conclusion should have a summary, remember that a preview does not equal an introduction, nor does a summary equal a conclusion. Well-developed introductions and conclusions are essential components of excellent presentations. Let's begin by looking at what makes a well-developed introduction.

Presentations characterized by professional excellence always include a solid introduction—the part of the presentation in which you gain attention, introduce the topic, develop credibility, relate the topic to the audience, and preview your main points. When you stand in front of an audience, you should imagine them sitting there with remote controls in their hands. If you don't immediately capture their attention, they will mentally change the channel. Plus, if you don't immediately pull them in, they will start daydreaming about winning the lottery, running through their to-do lists, or thinking about what they should have for lunch. You can never become an excellent speaker if the audience isn't listening to you, so developing your attention-getter is critical.

How do you gain an audience's attention, and how do you really make yourself stand out as a speaker? First, make certain to eliminate any pre-introductions. Do not begin by saying any of the following or any variation of the following:

- Hi, my name is Tiana.

- I am very excited to have this opportunity to talk to you today.

- I am really nervous.

- Today I would like to talk to you about . . . blah . . . blah.

Instead, start off with something that captures the audience's attention. You can start with a story, a quote, a statistic—anything that is going to spark interest. Once you have their attention, then you can introduce yourself and your topic. But in the first few seconds of your presentation, do something that will pull them in so that they won't change the channel. We'll say it one more time: All introductions should begin by gaining the audience's attention.

Similarly, introductions should always end with a preview of your main points. This will help the audience transition from the introduction to the body—and it will also reinforce your message. Therefore, in an introduction, gaining attention should occur first and the preview should occur last, but there is no formula for how the other three components should appear. When it comes to introducing the topic, making the topic relevant to the audience, and developing credibility, you have some flexibility. For example, you could begin with a story that gains attention and begins to develop your credibility. Or you might start with a statistic that draws attention and establishes credibility, and then introduce the topic. Alternatively, you could address each of the components separately.

Regardless of how they appear, make certain all five components are present during the introduction. Remember, being audience centered is necessary if you want to speak with professional excellence. By introducing your topic, you help orient the audience. We've heard countless presentations that have failed to achieve the simple task of introducing the topic—the audience was left guessing as to the exact focus of the presentation. By establishing credibility, you help the audience determine why they should trust you and the information you are presenting. Further, by making the topic relevant to the audience, you help them answer some of the following questions: Why is this information important to me? How is it going to impact me? Why should I pay attention and listen?

Presenting with professional excellence sometimes requires the use of a microphone. Politicians often use microphones to ensure people watching in person and on television can clearly hear them.

iStockphoto/TriggerPhoto

YOUR COMMUNICATION INTERACTION

Presentations at Work

As you read the passage below, consider what would be a more effective communication strategy in this situation.

Beatrice is an elementary school principal who is developing a presentation that she will give at an orientation for new teachers. She has written the following introduction:

> When you decided to become a teacher, I have no doubt someone shared with you the words of the playwright George Bernard Shaw: "He who can, does. He who cannot, teaches." Today, I would like to counter the words of Mr. Shaw with the words of one of the greatest intellects in the history of the human race, Aristotle. Aristotle said, "All who have meditated on the art of governing mankind have been convinced that the fate of empires depends on the education of youth." If Aristotle is correct, and I believe he is, you accepted an extremely important task when you entered this profession and accepted this job. And I am here today to welcome you to the toughest but most important job there is. Welcome to the world of teaching. This next year will be challenging, but I promise it also will be extremely rewarding. Today, in addition to my welcome, I would like to introduce you to the administrative team and discuss three areas of support we will provide to you throughout the year.

Questions to Consider

1. Is Beatrice's introduction effective? Why or why not?
2. Did she include all five required components of an introduction?
3. What changes, if any, do you think she needs to make?

CONCLUSIONS

When you have completed your main points, it's time to move into the conclusion. But keep in mind that if you have any additional points or information to cover, then you are not ready to conclude. Never create a false close—when a speaker signals to the audience that the presentation is concluding but then keeps going by introducing more information. When you tell the audience that you're concluding, you must summarize, drive the point home, and stop talking. If you say "in conclusion" and then continue on with new information and no clear end in sight, the audience will respond negatively. New information belongs in the body of the presentation.

A well-designed conclusion can elevate a presentation from average to excellent, whereas a poor conclusion can make an otherwise excellent presentation fall flat. By keeping a few simple steps in mind, you can easily design an excellent conclusion. These steps include stating that you are concluding, summarizing concisely, and ending with a strong impression.

Let's assume that you are, indeed, ready to conclude. First, you should let the audience know that you are concluding. There are countless ways to mark your move into the conclusion. You can say, "In conclusion," "In summary," "As I close," "I would like to end with," "I would like to close by saying," and so on. Second, after you signal your conclusion, provide a summary. As noted earlier, tell them what you're going to say, say it, and tell them what you said. The conclusion is the time for the "tell them what you said" part. This is critical if you want your audience to remember your message.

Third, end by leaving a strong impression. End with a quote or story, refer back to something you talked about in the beginning, or use a memorable statistic or something else that people will remember. Never end with a statement such as "Well, I guess that's it." Never begin packing up before the applause, and even if you'll be taking questions, avoid ending with the statement "Does anyone have any questions?" Wait for the applause and then move into questions. Following these three simple steps will help you appear polished and will give the presentation a smooth close that will greatly enhance the audience's perception of you as a speaker.

Know Yourself

Being Organized in the Body of the Presentation

As you answer the questions below, think about how this knowledge can help you be a better communicator.

1. Did you clearly follow an organizational pattern?
2. Did you use section transitions and nonverbal transitions to signal to the audience that you were changing points?
3. Did you use internal previews to let the audience know what you would be discussing next? These are similar to the presentation previews in the introduction, but they cover only main body points.
4. Did you use internal summaries to remind the audience of what you just covered?
5. Did you give signposts (e.g., *first, second, to clarify*) as a way to help the audience know where you were in the middle of a main point?

Source: Edwards, Edwards, Wahl, and Myers (2019).

LANGUAGE

As a presenter, you don't want parts of your presentation to have the same qualities you find in a casual conversation. Specifically, your delivery should have a conversational quality to it, while other parts of your presentation, such as the structure or organization, should be more formal than what is found in a typical conversation. So what about language? Should language be formal or informal? When it comes to language as it relates to public speaking, you'll walk a fine line. Your language needs to be more formal than casual conversation but not so formal that you are speaking over your audience's heads.

One easy step you can take to adapt your language to any speaking occasion is to cut out cuss words, slang, texting language, and colloquialisms. Cuss words or curse words, also referred to as swear words, are viewed as obscene expressions. Slang terms are either made-up words or words used to express something other than their formal meaning. For example, *snow* is a slang term when used to refer to cocaine. Using texting language in your presentations would be considered a type of slang. Texting abbreviations (e.g., OMG, TU, BFF) have no place in a presentation. Colloquialisms are like slang terms but are locally or regionally based. As a result, they may be confusing to people from outside the region or could make you seem less credible to a national or global audience. For example, if you're from the northeastern part of the United States, you may use "yous" or "yous guys." If you're from the South, you might say "y'all" or "all

TABLE 12.5　■　Action Items Skills for Speech Design		
Skill	Strategy	Application
Problem-focused learning	Have the audience focus on a problem, not a subject.	At a work meeting, show how your presentation is personally relevant to the well-being of your coworkers.
Immediate relevance and application	Get right to the point of useful information.	Keeping it simple, show your coworkers as soon as possible how to apply a solution.
Experience	Use your and others' wealth of knowledge and experience.	Finish your presentation by opening the floor to additions or alternatives to the issue you have presented.

y'all." Remember to avoid the use of cuss words, slang, texting language, and colloquialisms in your presentations.

This does not mean that when you have a speaking opportunity you should break out the dictionary and thesaurus to find the longest, fanciest words you can. Your expansive vocabulary may make you look smart, but who cares how smart you are if your audience can't understand you? Select words with which your audience is familiar. If you're going to introduce some terms that audience members may not know, define them within your presentation.

Excellent presenters pay close attention to language. Not only do they understand the line between too formal and too informal, but they also understand the power of imagery and repetition. When a speaker uses imagery, they help the audience paint a picture with words. This can be done with the use of metaphor or descriptive terms.

Repetition is also a powerful language device. By repeating a phrase or creating a parallel structure within your presentation, you can create a sense of anticipation for audience members. Think about the first time you hear a new song. What do you remember when the song is over? More than likely, you remember the chorus because it's repeated. As you listen to the song, you anticipate the chorus after each verse, and it gets stuck in your head. Advertisers use this same technique when trying to get you to remember a product. They repeat a catchphrase or jingle that you will remember. By using repetition or a parallel structure, you can unify a presentation and reinforce the message for each member of the audience.

KEYS TO EXCELLENCE IN SPEECH DESIGN

Think back to the beginning of the chapter and the advice given by Patel (2017). Remember that your speech needs to be audience oriented, but it also needs to be tailored to your personal strengths. The first step, *know yourself*, requires that you know both yourself and your topic, and how your audience can relate to that topic. A speech given in front of your peers in a classroom should sound different than a speech given in a business setting, even if you are covering the same topic. Research your audience, and tailor your speech to address their expectations.

The next step, *evaluate the professional context*, involves knowing the culture of your audience. Is your audience made up mostly of young college students, or older professional businesspeople? Always ensure that you have a general idea of the makeup of your audience, and prepare your speech in a way that can answer almost everybody's concerns about your presentation.

PERSUASIVE SPEECH

Background Information

The following speech will be delivered by a manager, William Orr, to his team. The ABC Company is offering employee training programs on customer service to all employees. The training is not mandatory, but William believes that his team would benefit greatly from taking part in the training. Please review William's speech. Note his use of Monroe's Motivated Sequence, an organizational pattern shown to be effective when attempting to move an audience to action. Also pay attention to his use of transitions and the components of his introduction and conclusion.

Excellent Customer Service Benefits Us All

Introduction

After being introduced, William moves behind the podium and stands there for one minute without saying anything.

Did that seem like a long time? Well, in reality, that was only one minute—one little minute. But it probably seemed like a lot longer to you. You have all experienced bad service, haven't you? We know exactly how it feels to be that waiting customer. You know that one minute seems like an eternity to you when you are the customer who is standing there, waiting to be acknowledged or served. But have you ever left a customer waiting? Even for a minute? I have to admit it—I have. And I didn't think much about it. In fact, until recently, I did not even make the connection that some of my behaviors were leading to bad customer service. Today, I'm here to tell you about some workshops that the ABC Company will offer over the next few weeks. The workshops will be on customer service training. I have attended these workshops, and I know firsthand how beneficial they are. In fact, they have improved my customer service skills tenfold. It is my hope that you'll see these workshops as both important and beneficial for yourself and the team and that you'll sign up to attend. Let's take a moment and discuss how our customers meet our needs. Then we'll discuss some of the problems related to customer service and, finally, how we all benefit when our customers are happy.

Attention Step: Sometimes, less is more. Silence can be a profound tool to gain your audience's attention.

Credibility: Establishing common ground

Credibility: Competence

Specific Purpose

Preview: Remember to give your audience literal cues when transitioning from your introduction to the body of your speech.

Need/Problem Step: Here, a sense of urgency and personal relevance is projected to the audience. Always remember to link what you are saying to the audience personally.

Transition Statement

Solution/Satisfaction

Body

I. Why We Need to Give Excellent Customer Service

To be successful as a company, we must all have good customer relations, because our customers are valuable to us. We need to provide excellent customer service, or we will lose our customers. The bottom line is that, without the customer base, we don't have a company. Without the company, none of us—including you—has a job.

Please don't get me wrong. I am not criticizing your performance. The ABC Company succeeds because of you. You make ABC Company better! But we need our customers to be happy to make it all work. Through these workshops, we are going to learn skills that will aid us in continuing to improve in this area. Even though we are doing a good job, our goal at ABC Company is to strive to get better. It's like in athletics—the champions win by working hard and continually striving to improve for the next game. That doesn't mean they aren't good; it just means they must keep improving to stay at the top. Here, we not only want to be employed, but we want to be successful in what we do. In our game, it is not championship rings; it is bonuses. Strong customer relations will earn each of us, you and me, extra money come bonus time.

Now that we've reviewed how our customers meet our needs, let's look at how these workshops can help us provide better customer service.

II. How to Improve Your Customer Service

The skills and strategies taught during the workshops should help us deal with many of the complexities related to people and, we hope, make your job easier and more enjoyable. For example, one of the topics they will cover is nonverbal communication. The one-minute pause at the beginning is an example of the impact that our nonverbal communication can have on people. According to [SOURCE], 93% of communication effectiveness is determined by our nonverbal cues. So sometimes, we might unintentionally make our customers feel unwelcome in our facility without even meaning to. When is the last time you thought about the way you communicate with customers nonverbally? Could you use some help or insight in this area? Well, these workshops will provide that information.

Another topic the workshops will cover is how our language impacts the listener. Have you ever had a small problem with a customer escalate into a big problem, and you were not sure why? It may have been the difference between saying "you" and saying "I." When there is a potential conflict, you will learn that it's best to start sentences with the word *I*, not *you*, because *you* can put the listener on the defensive and increase the likelihood that the problem will escalate. For example, let's pretend a customer needs assistance filing insurance claims. As our receptionist, Zane, attempts to explain how everything works, the customer continues to ask the same questions over and over, in part because he is attempting to answer his texts at the same time. As this is going on, a line is forming and the other customers are getting upset, so Zane *must* address the problem. Zane *could* say, "You need to stop texting and listen because I can't help you much longer because you are holding up the line." Of course, this is likely to put the customer on the defensive and create additional problems. A better approach is for Zane to say something like "I am having a hard time getting my point across at this time. I would be happy to assist another customer so you can take care of the texting issue. Then we can focus on the forms without the distraction. Which do you prefer to handle first, the texts or the forms?" Of course, there is no perfect solution, but the strategies the workshop teaches will decrease the likelihood of a major conflict.

Another important topic covered in the workshops is how to defuse an upset customer. Sadly, we have all had and will continue to have angry customers. How can this workshop help with that issue? Well, you all know Mark in the Westside office. Mark was telling me about a woman he helped last October. The woman had moved across the United States from Nevada to Florida because of her husband's career. Three months after this dear woman moved, her husband informed her that he wanted a divorce. When she came to Mark's store, the customer had planned to have her phone fixed and then open an account without her husband's name on it. The problem was that she was at a breaking point. When Mark informed her that the tech people had left for the day, she lost it emotionally. The more Mark tried to help her, the more upset she became. The good news is that Mark handled it beautifully. He knew exactly what to do, and he attributed his ability to excel in this situation to the information he learned in the customer service workshops.

Now we've covered a little bit on how our customers meet our needs and how the workshops can assist us in solving many customer-related problems, so we are ready to focus on how we *all* benefit when our customers are happy.

Transition Statement: Remember, emphasize your transitions so that the audience knows they are receiving new information.

III. The Benefits of Improved Customer Service

I was reading that Apple has been rated first on *Fortune* magazine's list of the Top 20 Most Admired Companies. The former CEO and founder of Apple, Steve Jobs, said that he was not easy on his employees. Before he passed away, Jobs explained that he took already great people and pushed them to be even better by coming up with more aggressive visions of how it could be. That is what the ABC Company wants to do for us—for you. You are being offered the resources that will make us even better.

So take a minute and imagine what it could be like. What if you excelled at giving customer service? Even if you see this as one of your strengths, what if you were better? Your current customers would be happy, which always makes coming to work a lot more pleasant. The number of customers would increase, which means larger bonuses. And when those difficult situations come up, and they will inevitably come up, you would have better tools for handling them.

All these benefits are waiting for you, and all you have to do is come after my presentation and sign up. Literally, all you have to do is write down your name. We will take care of the cost and the scheduling. What could be easier?

Action Step
Summary

Conclusion

In conclusion, I have discussed why we need excellent customer service, how you can improve your customer service, and the benefits of improved customer service. I hope you are as excited about the workshops as I am. And the best part is that you don't have to wait, not even one minute, to sign up for this wonderful opportunity. And remember, if we don't care about our customers, they will not care about us!

Memorable Conclusion: Make sure your conclusion reviews the main points of your presentation. You want the audience to remember the overall message, not minute details.

The third step, *your communication interaction*, can be difficult to focus; this step asks you to consistently critique both yourself and the audience. With more practice, this step becomes easier to perform and can help your speeches be more effective with different audiences. Although it is important to focus on delivering your speech correctly, you must also be able to gather feedback for the final task, *step back and reflect*. Think about how you presented your speech to the audience, and decide whether it was an effective method or not. Ask yourself if the same delivery method would work just as well with a culturally different audience. The more you learn to adapt your presentations, the easier it will be to deal with unresponsive or hostile audiences.

Cuss words and profanity can certainly tarnish your presentation. President Joe Biden was caught on a hot mic in January 2022 using a cuss word to describe a journalist (Gregorian & Bronston, 2022). When such occurrences happen, people often focus more on the cussing than they do the speaker's intended message.

iStockphoto/microgen

STEP BACK AND REFLECT

Dr. Jacobs Learns About Audience Analysis

As you read this passage and answer the questions, step back and reflect on what went wrong in this professional situation.

After reviewing enrollment figures, Dr. Jacobs, the vice president of university effectiveness, discovered a way to generate more funds for her institution with only minor changes in scheduling. Dr. Jacobs identified this as a speaking opportunity to persuade the faculty members, who handled scheduling, to make these changes. She set up a meeting with each of the colleges within the university. Since everyone she would be speaking to was a faculty member, she decided to use the same presentation for each audience.

Her first meeting was with the College of Arts and Humanities. She began the presentation with an example. The example came from the College of Science and Technology, but Dr. Jacobs felt that it applied to all colleges. Within the first graph, there was a list of the average salaries for the science and technology faculty. The average for the science and technology faculty was significantly higher than the average salary of the arts and humanities faculty listening to the presentation. The next slide showed the average class size based on college. The class size for the arts and humanities faculty was much larger than that of every other college at the university. Dr. Jacobs went on to explain how to make four scheduling changes, stressing the simplicity of making each change. She ended with a graph that showed how much additional funding would be generated by these changes.

At the conclusion of his presentation, Dr. Jacobs opened for questions. She was surprised by the nature of the questions the audience asked. None of them had to do with the changes he had discussed. Instead, they were all about faculty equity in pay and workload. The audience walked out of the meeting visibly upset. Dr. Jacobs was not sure if they had heard a word she said.

Step Back and Reflect

1. What went wrong?

2. What advice would you give Dr. Jacobs about audience analysis?

3. How can the KEYS process help his situation?

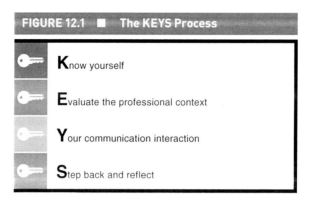

FIGURE 12.1 ■ The KEYS Process

Know yourself

Evaluate the professional context

Your communication interaction

Step back and reflect

EXECUTIVE SUMMARY

Now that you have finished reading this chapter, you should be able to

Analyze audience and context:

- If you want to present with professional excellence, you must be audience centered. The best presenters, the best communicators in general, are aware of all the components involved in the communication process, and they pay particular attention to the audience.

- To become an audience-centered speaker, start by asking a series of questions designed to answer one all-important larger question: "Who is my audience?".

- In addition, the context has a huge impact on the audience. Again, you must ask yourself a series of questions to analyze your context (see Tools for Professional Excellence 12.2).

Explain how to gather research for your speeches:

- The research you need in order to develop and support your presentation can and should come from a variety of sources. Depending on the topic, you may use internal sources, external sources, or a combination of the two.

- Internal sources include information that comes from within the organization, such as reports, policies, or interviews with employees and/or customers.

- External sources include information that comes from outside the organization, such as from outside agencies, the competition, the government, and the media.

- If you have done your job as a researcher, you will have more information than you need. At this point in the process, you must determine what to include.

Organize the body of a speech and incorporate effective transitions:

- You must develop clear organization within the body of your presentation. Your typical, not-so-memorable speaker will take all the information available and lump it together as three main points.

- An organizational pattern often used to persuade in business and professional settings is Monroe's Motivated Sequence. This five-step process, developed in 1935 by Purdue University professor Alan H. Monroe, includes the attention step, the need step, the satisfaction step, the visualization step, and the action step.

- A transition is any word or phrase that helps guide the listener from one point to the next. Within the body of your presentation, clear transitions must appear between your main points. As you complete your discussion of the first main point and move to the next main point, add an internal summary followed by an internal preview.

- For presentations with more than three main points, internal previews and summaries between each point can be overkill. Instead, use signposts—words or phrases that let the audience know where you are within the presentation.

Develop effective introductions:

- Although an introduction should have a preview and a conclusion should have a summary, remember that a preview does not equal an introduction, nor does a summary equal a conclusion. Well-developed introductions and conclusions are essential components of excellent presentations.

- Introductions should always end with a preview of your main points. This will help the audience transition from the introduction to the body—and it will also reinforce your message.

Develop effective conclusions:

- The final part of your presentation is your conclusion. A well-designed conclusion can elevate a presentation from average to excellent, while a poor conclusion can make an otherwise excellent presentation fall flat.

- Once you've verbally moved into the conclusion, you must conclude. Never create a false close—when a speaker signals to the audience that the presentation is concluding but keeps going by introducing more information.

- End by leaving a strong impression. End with a quote or story, refer back to something you talked about in the beginning, or use a memorable statistic or something else people will remember.

Discuss the role and value of language:

- Your language needs to be more formal than casual conversation but not too formal so as to speak over your audience's heads.

- Excellent presenters pay close attention to language. Not only do they understand the line between being too formal and too informal, but they also understand the power of imagery and repetition. When a speaker uses imagery, they help the audience paint a picture with words. This can be done with the use of metaphor or descriptive terms.

- Repetition is also a powerful language device. By repeating a phrase or creating a parallel structure within your presentation, you can create a sense of anticipation for audience members.

Apply the KEYS process to develop professional excellence in speech design:

- Know yourself. Know both yourself and your topic, and how your audience can relate to that topic. A speech given in front of your peers in a classroom should sound different than a speech given in a business setting, even if you are covering the same topic.

- Evaluate the professional context. Always ensure that you have a general idea of the makeup of your audience, and prepare your speech in a way that can answer almost everybody's concerns about your presentation.

- Your communication interaction. Consistently critique both yourself and the audience. With more practice, this step becomes easier to perform and can help your speeches be more effective with different audiences.

- Step back and reflect. Think about how you presented your speech to the audience, and decide whether it was an effective method or not. Ask yourself if the same delivery method would work just as well with a culturally different audience.

EXPLORE

1. Visit Young Entrepreneur on Twitter (@YoungEnt). These young professionals have used speech design to become effective communication professionals. What can you learn from their social media presence?

2. Using a favorite speech or presentation, break down the different pieces of the presentation into a speech design outline. How does it compare with some of the speech designs you have used in class? What new strategies and designs can you apply to your speeches in the future?

3. Find a YouTube video of a global multimedia presentation (e.g., TED Talk, RSA speech). Write a brief summary about how one of your personal speech designs might be altered when tailored to a global audience.

REVIEW

1. _____ include information that comes from within the organization, such as reports, policies, or interviews with employees or customers.

2. _____ include information that comes from outside the organization, such as from outside agencies, the competition, the government, and the media.

3. List the steps of Monroe's Motivated Sequence.

4. A(n) _____ is any word or phrase that helps guide the listener from one point to the next.

5. _____ are words or phrases that let the audience know where you are within the presentation.

6. _____ terms are either made-up words or words used to express something other than their formal meaning.

7. _____ are like slang terms but are locally or regionally based.

8. A(n) _____ occurs when a speaker signals to the audience that the presentation is concluding but keeps going by introducing more information.

DISCUSSION QUESTIONS

1. How would you go about taking an inventory of your audience before presenting? What are some examples of ways to retrieve information about an audience before a presentation?

2. Have you ever seen a speaker make an error when analyzing the audience or context? How did it affect the presentation?

3. How do you typically go about gathering research? Is your method effective? Is it thorough? How could it be improved?

4. Think about someone whom you find to be an excellent speaker. What makes this speaker excellent? How does the speaker structure introductions and conclusions? Does the speaker give attention to language or supporting aids? Are their speeches memorable? Why?

5. Review the organizational patterns discussed in this chapter. Considering this information, what preference do you have related to the way you organize information for a presentation?

TERMS TO REMEMBER

Review key terms with eFlashcards: **https://edge.sagepub.com/quintanilla5e**.

audience analysis (p. 307)

audience-centered speaker (p. 306)

colloquialisms (p. 318)

conclusion (p. 317)

context analysis (p. 307)

cuss words (p. 318)

external sources (p. 308)

false close (p. 317)

imagery (p. 319)

internal preview (p. 313)

internal sources (p. 308)

internal summary (p. 313)

introduction (p. 315)

metaphor (p. 319)

Monroe's Motivated Sequence repetition (p. 312)

research (p. 308)

signposts (p. 313)

slang (p. 318)

texting language (p. 318)

transition (p. 313)

Visit **https://edge.sagepub.com/quintanilla5e** to help you accomplish your coursework goals in an easy-to-use learning environment.

Simon Sinek is known for connecting communication to leadership and employee motivation.

iStockphoto/kasto80

13 DELIVERING A SPEECH WITH PROFESSIONAL EXCELLENCE

After studying this chapter, you should be able to

13.1   Explain how to overcome your fears of public speaking and deliver a presentation with professional excellence

13.2   Explain how to use supporting aids effectively

13.3   Explain the importance of practicing your presentation

13.4   Discuss how to deliver an effective team presentation

13.5   Apply the KEYS process to develop professional excellence in speech delivery

Simon Sinek, the author of *Start With Why*, may be best known for popularizing the concept of *why* in his first TED Talk in 2009. His talk, "How Great Leaders Inspire Action," is listed as the most watched on TED.com as of 2022, with over 58 million views and subtitles in 46 languages (TED, 2022). *360 Live Media* ("Speaking With Power," 2018) provides a few tips for speakers:

- **Practice is Key.** You must be (or appear to be) 100% confident in what you are saying and doing at all times when speaking in front of an audience.

- **Organize Your Speech.** You should prepare your speech as you conduct your research. Creating an outline of your topic as you go will help you avoid going off on a tangent.

- **Be the Alarm Clock.** Listening to someone else speak takes focus. If your presentation is early in the morning, after lunch, at the end of the day, or anywhere in between, your audience may feel sleepy. So walk on that stage with high energy and excitement.

- **Leave Them Intrigued and Motivated.** A good speech will pique the curiosity of the audience, and likely encourage them to change something about themselves. Leave them with a clear and direct call to action connected to your message, followed by a rhetorical question.

Preparing, coaching, maintaining a positive attitude, and visualizing success contribute to presenting with professional excellence.

iStockphoto/Chaay_Tee

DELIVERING A PRESENTATION WITH PROFESSIONAL EXCELLENCE

Why is public speaking dreaded? Do speakers fear their inability to organize information or design an effective introduction? Do they fear conducting research? The truth of the matter is that people don't really fear public speaking; they fear the unknown. As we discussed in Chapter 1, not knowing what to expect and being concerned about what people think of you as a speaker can trigger communication apprehension. Although people have different levels of anxiety when speaking in public, overcoming these fears and honing your skills when delivering a presentation are essential to achieving professional excellence.

The Adrenaline Rush

When you get up to deliver a presentation, you experience an adrenaline rush. The delivery of the presentation requires you to put yourself "out there" in front of an audience, and in the deep recesses of your mind, your body is signaling, "Danger, danger." Now your body must decide to take flight or fight. You may want to take flight and go back to your seat, but you know you have to give the presentation. So your body moves into fight mode and releases lots of adrenaline to help you. Yes, you read that correctly—to help you. Believe it or not, this adrenaline rush is a positive thing. As you practice public speaking, you will learn what responses to expect when you have an adrenaline rush—it will no longer be an unknown. Then you can learn how to handle each response. In the end, you'll be able to use the adrenaline to your advantage by presenting with energy and passion.

In delivering presentations, you will get an opportunity to know yourself. After each presentation, step back and reflect on how you respond to the adrenaline in your system. Learning to understand your responses will help you change the way you think about presentations, which is important, because for some speakers, thinking about the presentation creates more apprehension than does actually giving it (Daly et al., 1995; Yen et al., 2012). Let's review some common responses and some practical ways to handle each of them.

Sweating

What if you sweat? Unfortunately, you can't really control this normal bodily response, so you'll just have to learn how to adjust. To minimize sweating, select clothing that is lightweight and made of natural fibers. Make sure you have access to cold water before and during your presentation. Bring a handkerchief or tissue with you so that you can wipe your brow or dab your lip, if needed. If you're wearing a jacket, leave it on to avoid revealing damp underarms.

Blushing

Just like sweating, blushing is something you can't control. For some of you, your cheeks will get red; for others, it will be your ears. Some of the techniques used to handle sweating may help minimize blushing, but like sweating, it's just something you'll have to learn to live with. However, there's some good news. First, by the time your introduction is over, much of the redness may fade. Second, a little blushing will not be noticed by the audience and is irrelevant to the way people perceive your presentation.

Hands

For some people, the energy created by the adrenaline rush comes out in their hands. If you're lucky, talking with your hands comes naturally. This can be an added benefit for your delivery. Effective hand gestures add visual interest to the speaker and a more dynamic delivery style.

If you do talk with your hands, there are a few things you should do to ensure that this remains a benefit and does not become a distraction. Avoid holding objects such as pens or pointers, and place all beverages beyond the reach of your arms. Nothing is more distracting than accidentally throwing a pen at the audience or knocking a drink all over your notes.

Unfortunately, for some of you, that nervous energy doesn't turn into dynamic hand gestures but, rather, manifests as shaky hands. What should you do if you have shaky hands? Again, don't hold anything. Leave your notes on the podium. If you're not going to use a podium and you need to hold your notes, use index cards. Index paper is thicker and the cards are relatively small, so a little shaking will be far less noticeable.

If you're someone who doesn't talk with your hands, there are a few things you should keep in mind. For example, never put your hands in your pockets. Instead, place your hands comfortably on the podium or allow your arms to hang by your sides.

Feet

For other people, the adrenaline rush will head straight to their feet. You begin your presentation, and suddenly you're overcome by this need to shuffle, bounce, and move. The solution to this problem is simply to walk around. One of the biggest mistakes you can make is boxing yourself into a small space. Squishing yourself behind a podium or in a corner to put the PowerPoint slides center stage is the worst thing you can do to yourself. If you have a lot of nervous energy in your feet and you don't walk around, you will feel like a caged animal. When you're speaking, you have control of the room, so exercise that control while walking around. Slowly and deliberately walk from one side of the room to the other, and maintain eye contact with the entire audience during the presentation.

Vocal Quality

To develop yourself as a presenter with an outstanding delivery style, you will have to master several vocal qualities, each of which can be affected by the rush of adrenaline. Sometimes, nervous energy can translate into a shaky or cracking voice. Just like sweating and blushing, there's not a lot you can do about this. Fortunately, chances are the only person who will notice the change in your voice is you. Furthermore, the effects usually lessen or disappear altogether by the end of the introduction.

Volume is another factor to consider. For some of you, nervousness will result in a quiet presentation. To overcome this problem, you simply need to set your volume dial and focus on projecting. When you begin speaking, focus on an audience member in the back corner of the room and project your voice to that person—and maintain this volume throughout the presentation.

For many speakers, nervousness will cause an increase in speaking rate. The good news is that a rate slightly faster than average may actually be preferred. However, for those of you who are already "fast talkers," this rate increase can make it difficult for the audience to listen to and absorb your presentation. To counter this, take a few deep breaths before beginning your presentation. Deliberate breathing not only will slow your rate of speech but also will help reduce your nervousness in general. Taking sips of water may also be helpful. It will allow you

Presenting a message that motivates employees to work hard and get the job done requires professional excellence.

iStockphoto/fizkes

a moment to slow your pace and check your breathing. It will also aid in reducing dry mouth, which can accompany a quick speaking rate.

Vocal Fillers

One of the most common signs of nervousness is the use of vocal fillers. These occur when the speaker should pause but instead fills the silence. Fillers include sounds such as "umm" and "aah." Words such as *and* and *like* are also commonly used as fillers. Becoming aware of the fact that you're using vocal fillers can be all it takes to reduce them. If you suffer from an overuse of vocal fillers, be certain to prepare your presentation at least one week in advance of the speaking event. Run through the outline a few times each day to increase your familiarity with the material and your comfort level with pauses.

Eye Contact

This might be surprising to you, but making eye contact with your audience is one of the best ways to reduce nervousness. You may find it difficult to take the standard public speaking advice, which is to imagine the audience members in their underwear. Most speakers never succeed in doing that. Unfortunately, many speakers do succeed in imagining their audience as an angry mob waiting to throw rotten tomatoes. Rest assured, this will not be the case. Most audiences are supportive, friendly, and initially interested. Making eye contact with your audience and working to communicate with them in the same way you would communicate with a friend during a conversation is a quick way to reduce nervousness, increase credibility, and establish a positive rapport.

Clothing

Your appearance is part of your nonverbal communication, so it's part of your delivery. Presenting yourself in a way that enhances your credibility and professionalism is important if you want the audience to trust the information you're presenting or to be persuaded by your message. Unfortunately, many speakers don't think about their appearance until it's too late. As a result, their choice of clothing increases nervousness instead of adding to their credibility. The trick is to make your clothing work for you. For example, a few pieces of jewelry, such as a watch or small earrings, are fine. By contrast, wearing dangling bracelets that clank together every time you move your hands is distracting for both you and the audience. As noted earlier, wear clothing that decreases sweating, but make sure you're still appropriately covered. Brand-new shoes may look nice, but if they cause blisters, they will negatively affect your overall performance. Take time to think about the impact your clothing will have on your presentation.

Sense of Play

After teaching public speaking for a combined 30 years and listening to thousands of speeches, we can say with certainty that the most important thing you can do to handle the anxiety created by public speaking is to treat the experience with a sense of play. Let's look at the reality of the situation. Typically, you'll speak to an audience for between 5 and 30 minutes. Is 30 minutes really worth all that worrying? What if you faint? What if you have a wardrobe malfunction? What if you spill your drink on your notes? What if you bump the table over and the podium hits you in the head, knocking you to the ground? Chances are none of these things will happen. Instead, any problems you face will be minor.

But truth be told, all these things have happened to us, and we still continue to love speaking in public. Why? Are we deranged? No, we have learned to treat public speaking with a sense of play. If something small doesn't go according to plan, we realize that, for the most part, no one but us will notice. If we make a bigger mistake, such as spilling a drink, we acknowledge it, laugh it off, and then move forward. Yes, we are embarrassed, but that's life, and it has little impact on the audience.

Public speaking is an extremely valuable skill and one you should work to master. Prior to giving any speech, you should do your research, design an audience-centered message, and practice. In the moment when you are delivering the speech, you have to learn to roll with it. The adrenaline rush will affect you in some way, shape, or form. Begin to determine your responses to the rush, and develop strategies to overcome or accept those responses. Never give public speaking more power over your life than it deserves. It's okay if it makes you a little nervous, but never let it stand between you and an opportunity to express yourself as a leader.

Presenting From an Outline

There is no one right way to deliver a presentation. Each of you will have differences in your speaking styles that will add unique elements to your presentations. Although delivery styles vary, all speakers should strive for a delivery style that has a   , which includes an extemporaneous speaking style and good eye contact. The ultimate goal is to have your delivery enhance, rather than distract from, the overall impression.

Speaking from an outline is one simple way to increase the conversational quality of your presentation. There are many benefits to using an outline. You will not write a presentation, but you will design your presentation. This means that you should not write out your presentation word for word and read it aloud. Speaking from a manuscript is very difficult. Only the most skilled speakers can manage to do it and still maintain a conversational style. When speakers try to deliver their presentations from a manuscript, the result is usually a horrible delivery with the speaker reading the presentation to the audience. No one enjoys having a presentation read to them. It's called public speaking and not public reading for a reason. Having an outline, as opposed to a manuscript, eliminates the possibility of reading the presentation.

On the flip side, having no outline often results in speakers committing their presentations to memory, resulting in a monotone speaking style that's guaranteed to ruin a well-designed presentation. An outline helps the speaker follow the presentation design while still maintaining the freedom to deliver it in a slightly different fashion each time. This doesn't mean you should get up in front of the audience and wing it. You must practice the presentation so that your specific purpose and presentation design remain the same—but your exact choice of words can vary slightly, helping you maintain an extemporaneous speaking style.

What if I lose my place? What if I go blank? Beginning speakers inevitably will ask one or both of these questions when the notion of speaking from an outline is discussed. First, it's far easier to lose your place in a manuscript than in an outline. Second, it's far easier to blank out when trying to recite a presentation from memory than when speaking from an outline. If you find yourself at a loss for words for a moment, a little water will help. Simply pick up the glass or bottle, take a sip, and simultaneously find your place. No one in the audience will even notice.

As noted earlier, although you're not writing out a manuscript or memorizing every word, you should still prepare. There are going to be occasions when you have to give an impromptu presentation, but those situations are rare. Begin by preparing a detailed practice outline, known as your speaking notes. As you become more familiar with your presentation, streamline it into a speaking outline. According to Leech (1992), a speaking outline is less detailed than your speaking notes (see Figure 13.1).

FIGURE 13.1 ■ Presentation Outline Template

Introduction

- Attention-getter
- Introduce topic and specific purpose
- Establish credibility
- Relate topic directly to the audience
- Preview main points

Body

- Main point
  - Definition
  - Supporting example

[Transition: Internal summary; internal preview]

- Main point
  - Supporting graph
  - Relevant statistic

Conclusion

- Restate specific purpose
- Summarize main points
- Memorable ending

EVALUATE THE PROFESSIONAL CONTEXT

Orange Juice and Presentations Don't Mix

As you evaluate the passage below, consider whether this behavior is appropriate for this professional context.

Arianna had just begun her new position as a trainer. She loved presenting and had plenty of experience. One of her first audiences was the assembly-line team. Since their shift started early, her training sessions began at 5 a.m. This was early for Arianna, so she was not hungry when she woke up. Still, she wanted something healthy in her stomach, so she grabbed a big glass of orange juice.

As she began her presentation, some odd things began to happen. First, her lip began to sweat, and then she started to see spots. Neither of these things had ever happened to her before when giving a presentation. She decided to finish her point quickly and then give the group a break. Unfortunately, before she could break, her ears began to ring. Then she heard someone say, "She is turning green." She woke up a few minutes later. She had fainted.

The next day, she went to the doctor and found out she was hypoglycemic. The orange juice, which is pure fruit sugar, on her empty stomach had caused her to faint. She was relieved to learn what was wrong, but she still had a problem: She had to go back and finish the training. She was humiliated. How could she go back? Then she remembered something she had learned in school—treat the situation with a sense of play.

How did her audience respond? Did they "boo" her out of the room? Did they request a new trainer? Of course not; they were very supportive. They were happy that she was fine. They even joked about how they recommended her trainings to all their coworkers because there were extra-long breaks during the fainting spells. Arianna went on to have a long and successful career as a trainer.

Questions to Consider

1. How would you have responded if you were in the audience?
2. What would you have done if you were in Arianna's position?
3. Have you ever had an embarrassing public speaking moment? How did you handle it?
4. How can the KEYS process help you survive situations like Arianna's?

Source: Edwards, Edwards, Wahl, and Myers (2016).

POWERPOINT AND OTHER SUPPORTING AIDS

The world is high tech. As audience members, we've become used to seeing visually stimulating images come at us faster than we can blink and to hearing sounds from state-of-the-art audio systems in our theaters, homes, and cars. It is no wonder, then, that a lonely presenter in front of an audience can seem a bit boring. Don't misunderstand; a speaker with an audience-centered message and a dynamic delivery style can still captivate an audience without supporting aids (tools used by a speaker to help support the audience's interest in and understanding of the presentation), but utilizing them can bring many benefits.

When we ask students what they dislike about public speaking, two common responses are "I don't like everyone looking at me" and "I'm afraid I will be boring." Using supporting aids can help with these problems. When a supporting aid is displayed, the audience will split their attention between you and the aid, which can help reduce some of your anxiety. In addition, supporting aids provide another layer to your presentations that can enhance interest. It's boring to hear someone recite the steps for CPR during the annual refresher course. Most people would find it far more interesting to watch someone go through those steps. You may catch your audience's attention if you tell them about the dangers of failing to wash their hands, but you are far more likely to hold their interest if you show them an illustration of some common germs found in restaurants, hospitals, or educational settings.

A well-designed supporting aid also helps the audience by increasing understanding, enhancing retention, and facilitating listening. Telling an audience how to dress for success is helpful, but showing them visuals of how the attire should (or should not) look will further increase their level of understanding. For audience members who are visual learners, seeing key points, demonstrations, or other supporting materials is essential for their understanding. In addition, every time you repeat your message, you increase retention. It is said that a

TABLE 13.1 ■ Action Items. Skills for Speech Delivery

Skill	Strategy	Application
Speech structure	Have a logical order (introduction, body, conclusion).	Structure your speech the way you would write an instruction manual (e.g., to fix a bike).
Body language	Practice body language that conveys casualness and confidence.	Smile, make eye contact, and move around a bit. Use gestures to animate your words.
Audience interaction	Build a positive rapport with your audience.	Get the audience involved by asking questions and employing humor (if appropriate).

picture is worth a thousand words. Indeed, this seems to be the case when it comes to public speaking. According to Nickerson (1980), our memory of pictures is extremely accurate, and Hishitani (1991) found that this is especially true when the image is vivid. Further, a well-designed PowerPoint or Prezi presentation can also facilitate listening.

Presentation aids used in business seminars similar to the one shown here can make or break professional excellence. What problems do you notice in this speaker's use of supporting aids?

istockphoto/NA/PHOTOS.com

Think back to a time when you were in class and the professor's organization was difficult to follow—not the professor in this class, of course. It may have seemed as though they were jumping around from point to point. What did you do? If you were like most students, you simply stopped listening. If your audience can't follow your organizational structure, chances are they will stop listening. However, if you develop a clear organizational structure that is reinforced by an effectively designed PowerPoint presentation, you'll be providing them with a clear guide throughout your presentation. Since supporting aids increase understanding, enhance retention, and facilitate listening, they also help shorten meetings (Antonoff, 1990; Cicala et al., 2012).

Should I Use Supporting Aids?

As stated previously, you can give a quality presentation without supporting aids. In fact, if not used properly, a supporting aid can negatively impact a presentation. To determine whether or not you should use a supporting aid, consider the following questions:

- Will the aid enhance rather than distract from my presentation?

- Will the aid increase the audience's understanding of the material?

- Will the aid increase the audience's interest in the topic?

- Will the aid reinforce my message, thereby increasing retention?

- Will the aid enhance my credibility?

- Does the aid have a professional appearance or sound quality?

- Do I have the time needed to prepare and practice with this aid?

If you answered yes to all these questions, you should incorporate the supporting aid.

Types of Supporting Aids

Supporting aids may be used throughout a presentation, but they should be used strategically. Supporting aids include presentation slide shows; video clips; audio clips; graphs, charts, illustrations, and photos; objects and models; and demonstrations.

Presentation Slide Shows

When you create a presentation slide show, you should consider the various software options available. Two of the most common technologies are PowerPoint and Prezi. PowerPoint slides and Prezi frames should be designed in a uniform manner. Backgrounds, font, font size, and transitions that are consistent create a better flow of information and concepts, producing a simple yet effective presentation.

PowerPoint. PowerPoint software enables you to develop a slide show to go along with your presentation. There are other software programs with similar capabilities, but PowerPoint is the most commonly used software for the development of presentation slides. PowerPoint has at times been discussed in derogatory terms over the years: "PowerPoint is evil!" (Tufte, 2003), PowerPoint is "the growing electronic menace" (Jaffe, 2000), or PowerPoint is PowerPointless. However, PowerPoint continues to stand the test of time.

What's wrong with PowerPoint? Nothing, when it is used correctly. In fact, it can be a wonderful tool. The problem is that most of the time it is used incorrectly. Many speakers make the mistake of using PowerPoint as a crutch. PowerPoint is a supporting aid; it's not the whole presentation. Speakers get so caught up with making their PowerPoint slides that they fail to truly develop their presentations. As a result, the speaker becomes a talking head reading slides to the audience.

Your PowerPoint slides are not your speaking notes. When you use PowerPoint, you still need a speaking outline. That outline can be in your hands or on a podium and can even be the computer screen if the laptop is in front of you. Regardless of what you use, your notes need to be in front of you, not behind you. If you turn to read the slides, you will be continually turning your back on the audience. Reading slides and turning your back on the audience are signs of a poor speaker.

When designing your PowerPoint slides, use the same background on each slide. The presentation should be consistent in color and pattern throughout. Remember that each slide should have a limited amount of text; it's better to have more slides with less text on each slide (see Tools for Professional Excellence 13.2). Keep reminding yourself that your slides are a supporting aid, not your speaking notes. You don't have to include an entire part of your presentation on the slides. Instead, include key words or phrases. When slides contain complete sentences or entire paragraphs, the audience usually doesn't see anything but a bunch of text, because nothing stands out. Follow the KISS acronym when designing your slides: Keep It Simple, Speaker.

In addition to limiting your text, limit the bells and whistles. You want your PowerPoint presentation to have a professional appearance, so avoid bold or wild backgrounds, cute pictures, sound effects, and odd fonts. Also, make sure there's enough contrast between the slide's background color and the font color you use for text.

In most instances, the timing feature (with which slides are set to advance automatically at a certain pace) is not recommended because it doesn't leave the speaker any room for error. The extemporaneous delivery is the best style of delivery, and when the timing feature in the slide show software is used, it almost forces the speaker to memorize the presentation.

If you're using technology, always make sure it's available or bring it with you. With that said, make certain you know how to use it properly. You should never use supporting aids of any type if you can't practice with them in advance. A good rule to follow is to arrive at your speaking event early and check to see if everything is working properly. If equipment fails for any reason, you must be prepared to deliver your presentation anyway. Always be ready to speak without your supporting aid. Also, remember that just because the technology works on one computer does not necessarily mean it will work on another. The technology should be checked on the computer that will be used for the actual presentation, and it should be checked ahead of time so that problems can be resolved before the presentation begins.

Advanced presentation software features can, of course, be impressive and add a lot of impact to a presentation, but the inclusion of video or audio clips, website hyperlinks, and the like increases the chances that technical problems will occur. Make sure the video or audio clips are on the hard drive, the desktop, cloud storage, or a flash drive so they work properly. Another problem can occur if files are not saved correctly. If, for example, someone has developed a slide show using PowerPoint 2019 within Office 365 and the computer that's being used for the presentation is running PowerPoint 2007, the slide show will not work on that computer unless the file has been saved as the older file type.

Just as you practice what you will say during the presentation, it's also recommended that you practice with the technology. Proficiency with technology can enhance credibility, but technical problems can cause an otherwise smooth presentation to lose momentum quickly. Plus, practicing with the technology should help you feel more comfortable and confident in front of the audience, increasing the likelihood that you'll deliver a peak performance. Bottom line, you should be able to deliver your presentation without PowerPoint. It's merely a supporting aid to enhance your presentation; PowerPoint should never and can never replace you.

Prezi. Prezi is cloud-based presentation software for people on the go. The software is accessible through the Prezi.com website. Prezi allows you to customize presentations that automatically sync with your phone, tablet, and laptop. To use this tool, all you need to do is create a username and password to keep everything in sync; you can use the software for free, although paying an annual fee gives you access to additional features.

TABLE 13.2 ■ Tools for Professional Excellence

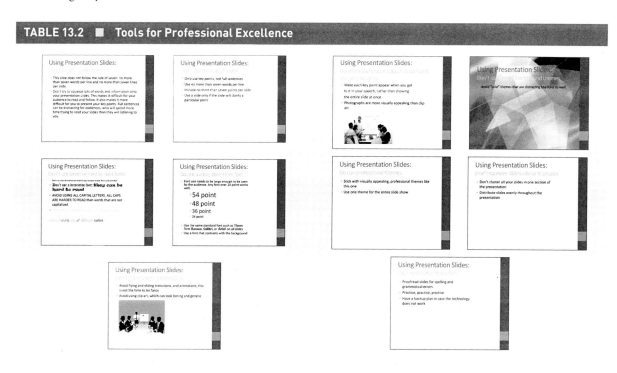

As with all visual aids, you should not rely too heavily on Prezi. The technology is a supporting aid that helps you to create effective and consistent presentations. Keeping this in mind, you should place only key points and ideas on Prezi frames. Although the technology enables you to incorporate music, photographs, PDFs, Excel spreadsheets, and a variety of fonts, remember that presentations should be professional and simple. All the dos and don'ts discussed in relationship to PowerPoint apply to Prezi as well.

Cloud-based software creates an environment that easily lends itself to teamwork. Prezi includes a cocreate feature, which allows for individuals on a team to collaborate, edit, and review presentations simultaneously. The transformation tool feature allows for individuals to produce and manipulate objects within the Prezi frame. Furthermore, team members are able to contribute and present ideas to other individuals instantaneously.

Video Clips

Video clips can add excitement to any presentation. You can use a computer with a projector to show clips from sources such as YouTube and Netflix. If you're going to show a clip from YouTube or some other internet source, remember to pull it up in advance. If you're planning to incorporate PowerPoint into your presentation, it's always best to save these clips directly in the presentation. If not, save them in a separate file. You should never make your audience wait while you search the internet for a clip. Doing so will offset many of the benefits of using video clips as supporting aids.

Audio Clips

There are occasions when audio clips may be a necessary part of the presentation. As with video clips, make certain that the clip is cued in advance. Save the clips directly in your PowerPoint presentation if you can. If not, save them in a separate file, but never waste the audience's time searching for them during your presentation. When bringing your own equipment, it's advisable to make sure your speakers are adequate for the room size; bring along an extension cord just in case.

STEP BACK AND REFLECT

Holly, the Corporate Trainer and Comedian

As you read this passage and answer the questions, step back and reflect on what went wrong in this professional situation.

Holly was asked by the executive office to make the company privacy presentation fun. Holly welcomed the opportunity since she had an interest in adult stand-up comedy. As an attention-getter, she showed the training classes a YouTube clip of one of her stand-up routines that included profanity and several controversial jokes. After all, Holly had good rapport with fellow employees and many friends at work, and she didn't think anyone would be offended by her humor. The first two training classes loved the session, but several members of the third class were offended and filed complaints with the main office.

Step Back and Reflect

1. What went wrong?

2. Have you observed a presentation in which the presenter, like Holly, used a video clip, an audio clip, a graph, or an image in a professional context that included profanity or content that you viewed as offensive?

3. Can a speaker present sensitive information or "R-rated" content and still be professional?

4. Consider a presenter who believes in the right to express themselves freely. Is it unethical to judge a presenter who is simply trying to make a point?

5. Does a presenter have an ethical responsibility to warn the audience if profanity or adult content will be presented? Why? Why not?

6. How could the KEYS process help in this situation?

Graphs, Charts, Illustrations, and Photos

You have four main options for displaying supporting aids: graphs, charts, illustrations, and photos (see Figures 13.2 and 13.3). First, you can copy them directly into your PowerPoint presentation. If you're planning to use PowerPoint, this is by far the easiest method. Second, if you're not using PowerPoint, you can still save the supporting aids in a file or as a PowerPoint slide and then display them at the appropriate time in your presentation. Finally, you can make a poster that incorporates your graphs, charts, illustrations, or photos—these items can be displayed on a tripod or flip chart.

Objects and Models

Other useful supporting aids for increasing both understanding and interest are objects and models. When incorporating objects into your presentation, make certain they are large enough for the entire audience to see. If not, it's better to photograph the object and then incorporate the photo into your PowerPoint presentation. If you want to pass around an object, think twice. Passing things around while you are speaking can be very distracting for listeners and for you.

Objects can also include models that range from scaled-down versions of oil rigs to miniature buildings to enlarged atoms. As with any object, make sure the models are large enough for the entire audience to see. Models can include people who help you conduct demonstrations during your presentation (e.g., dance moves, techniques). Volunteers and assistants are discussed in more detail in the following section on demonstrations.

Demonstrations

Many professional occasions will call for you to give a process presentation (also known as a demonstration or how-to presentation). Effective demonstrations should include supporting aids. In fact, demonstrations often incorporate many of the other types of supporting aids noted earlier. When used correctly, they result in an entertaining, memorable presentation. When used incorrectly, however, they can result in disaster.

If you plan to use a demonstration, the first step is to determine who should perform the demo. If you're illustrating the steps involved in self-defense, it may be difficult for you to perform the demonstration and maintain effective delivery. If the demonstration hinders your eye contact or causes you to become out of breath, use an assistant. Using an assistant is different from using a volunteer. You can't practice with a volunteer, so it's better to use an assistant who can practice the presentation with you in advance.

Remember, when used properly, supporting aids can enhance professional excellence. When used improperly, they can do far more harm than good. Take the time to plan and practice with your supporting aids as you prep for any professional presentation. The KEYS process will help you develop supporting aids with professional excellence.

FIGURE 13.2 ■ Types of Graphs

Pie chart

Who uses social media when searching for jobs?

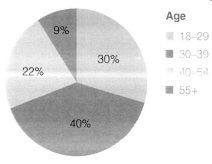

Bar graph

Most popular social networks for job seekers and recruiters

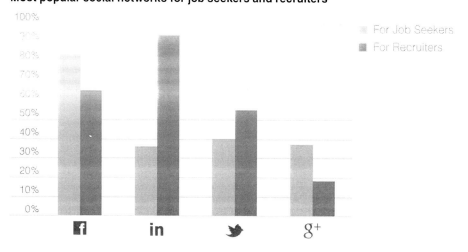

Line graph

Percentage of American adults who use the Internet, by age

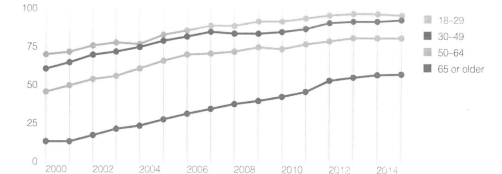

Source: Adapted from http://web.jobvite.com/rs/jobvite/images/2014%20Job%20Seeker%20Survey.pdf

Source: Adapted from http://web.jobvite.com/rs/jobvite/images/2014%20Job%20Seeker%20Survey.pdf

Source: Adapted from Pew Research Center, "Americans' Internet Access: 2000-2015" June 26, 2015. Retrieved from http://www.pewinternet.org/2015/06/26/americans-internet-access-2000-2015/

FIGURE 13.3 ■ **Sample Illustration**

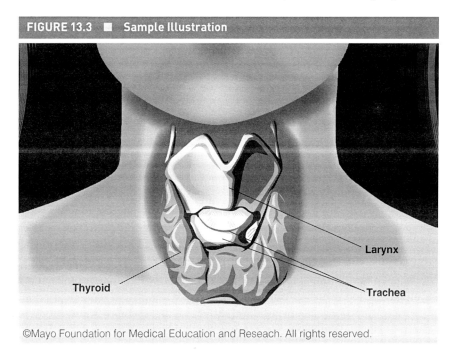

Larynx

Thyroid

Trachea

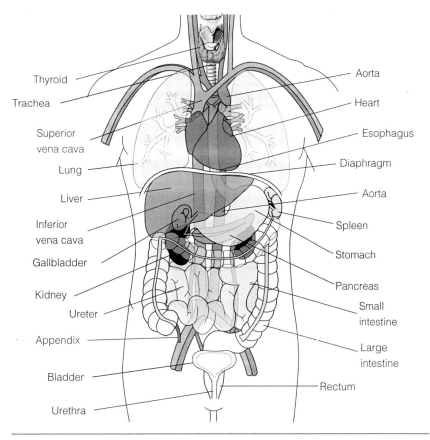

Thyroid

Trachea

Superior
vena cava

Lung

Liver

Inferior
vena cava

Gallbladder

Kidney

Ureter

Appendix

Bladder

Urethra

Aorta

Heart

Esophagus

Diaphragm

Aorta

Spleen

Stomach

Pancreas

Small
intestine

Large
intestine

Rectum

Source: http://www.riversideonline.com/source/images/image_popup/thyroid.jpg

Source: http://www.merck.com/media/mmhe2/figures/MMHE_01_001_02_eps.gif

PRACTICE MAKES PERFECT

How do you enter the ranks of excellence? As with any other skill, to excel in presenting, you must practice and hone your technique. Use all the information provided in this chapter as you develop your presentation, and then practice.

There may be times on the job when you have little notice about a speaking opportunity, but most of the time you will have fair warning, which you should use to your advantage.

Once you feel confident in your presentation design, allow others to hear your presentation, request their honest feedback, and listen openly to their comments. When recruiting this practice audience, be selective. Avoid selecting people who are not willing to be critical. You can't improve if all your practice audience says is "good job." An honest practice audience can help you determine if your presentation is effective. Gaining this audience's point of view prior to the presentation is vital. As Keysar and Henley (2002) found, speakers tend to overestimate their effectiveness (determined by whether or not the listener understood the message). Similarly, Campbell et al. (2001) found that speakers, as compared with members of the audience (peers and instructors), overestimate the importance of visual aids and underestimate the importance of content and delivery. T. Smith and Bainbridge (2006) recommend using a practice audience near in size to your actual audience as a means to increase confidence. If you want to emerge as one of those rare speakers who presents with professional excellence, you must practice.

ETHICAL CONNECTION

Jessica and Shane's Group Presentation Issue

As you read this passage and answer the questions, consider how the way you communicate has an ethical dimension.

Jessica is a communication student who is working in a group on her class's final presentation. The final project involves a group presentation, with the entire group being graded on the final product. Jessica has discovered that one of her team members, Shane, has been plagiarizing his portion of the project. If Jessica informs her professor, Shane will be kicked out of the class and possibly barred from the university. If the plagiarism is exposed after the group presents, however, Jessica could end up failing the class right before her expected graduation. Shane is close to graduating as well, and Jessica is nervous about getting one of her classmates expelled from school so close to the end of his academic training. However, there are only two days left before the project is due, and it is unlikely Shane could completely redo his portion of the project in that time.

Questions to Consider

1. What is the ethical issue facing both Jessica and Shane right now?

2. Why is plagiarism in a presentation such a major ethical issue?

3. How would you approach a professor about this issue?

4. Are there any options Jessica could consider that would not involve Shane's being removed from the class?

While flip charts are not very commonly used these days, they can still be a good option if you will be speaking in an environment with limited technology.

iStockphoto/fizkes

TEAM PRESENTATIONS

Since many speeches in business and professional settings happen in teams, developing your own skills may not be enough to ensure professional excellence as a public speaker. Fortunately, the principles for effective individual presentations are the same for group presentations.

Think of the group presentation as one big speech. As such, it should begin like any other effective presentation. For example, it should have a developed introduction, and the introduction should begin with an attention-getting device. The speaker also should establish credibility, relate the topic to the audience, mention the specific purpose for the entire presentation, and preview the main points of the group presentation as a whole.

When it comes to researching and designing the body of the presentation, the group must work together. For a group presentation, having all group members work in conjunction and prepare thoroughly prior to the presentation is vital for success. The key ideas in the presentation should be broken down into main points and discussed in a manner that is easy to follow. It's important to determine the content, the speaking order, and the amount of time for each speaker. All speakers must work together to avoid significant overlap in content during the presentation. Furthermore, all speakers must work together to guarantee a clearly organized presentation with developed transitions between speakers and their content areas.

When it comes to developing the organization of the presentation, there are several options. The first option is to have one person function as the organizer. The organizer will present the introduction, provide the transitions between the other speakers and their content areas, and give the conclusion. In this option, the organizer doesn't give one of the content-area speeches but, rather, remains solely in the organizing role. A second option is to have the organizer give the introduction and the conclusion, while the speakers provide the transitions between each speech. It is perfectly acceptable for each speaker to introduce the next as long as everyone presenting knows how the transitions will work, when they will speak, and generally what they will say prior to the speech. Another option is to have one person give the introduction, each speaker provide the transition into the speaker that follows, and someone else give the conclusion. Regardless of which option your team selects, the entire presentation must have a clearly defined introduction and conclusion with fully developed transitions between speakers.

KNOW YOURSELF

Quick Guide to Your First Presentation

As you read the guide below, think about how this knowledge can help you be a better communicator.

1. Know your introduction so you can deliver it clearly and passionately.
2. Keep the body of your presentation organized. Writing a clear outline and following it will help you to appear credible and to stay on task.
3. Look for a variety of sources to help you inform or persuade your audience.
4. Use transitions to signal changes in thought during your presentation.
5. End the conclusion strong to leave a lasting impression on the audience.
6. Enjoy the presentation experience. Smile when giving your presentation (if it is appropriate for the topic), and your audience will smile back.

Source: Edwards, Edwards, Wahl, and Myers (2019).

Poorly designed and delivered presentations are common in the business world. In this photo, the speaker made the common mistake of giving the audience members a handout. Does the audience seem to be paying attention to the speaker?

iStockphoto/stockfour

As each new speaker presents their portion of the presentation, they must include the components of an effective presentation. Each speaker must have a clear introduction and conclusion. Each speaker must have clear organization. The use of supporting aids must also be handled by the entire group during planning. For example, if PowerPoint is used, all the slides must have the same look, background, and font. They should also be saved as one large file so that the audience doesn't have to wait as speakers transition from one PowerPoint presentation to the next.

For the presentation to look professional and polished, both planning and practice must occur as a team. Teams that fail to plan together or don't run through the presentation as a group often stumble and bumble in front of the audience. Team members must also be aware of how they are acting during the entire presentation. Nothing looks worse than a team member who appears distracted or uninterested when the rest of the team is presenting. If you apply everything you've learned about professional excellence to group presentations, you will have all the tools you need for success.

KEYS TO EXCELLENCE IN DELIVERING A SPEECH

At the beginning of the chapter, we talked about Simon Sinek and his popular TED Talk, "How Great Leaders Inspire Action." The skills he used can be tied directly to the KEYS process we have followed throughout this text. During the first step, *know yourself*, he knows that in order to be a good leader, he has to bring inspirations to his employees so that the whole team can work together smoothly and go further. Make sure you know what your role is when delivering a speech.

For the next step, *evaluate the professional context*, Sinek used an example of why Steve Jobs succeeded in his business. Jobs knew he was pitching a very advanced piece of technology to a general public that is not always very tech savvy. He tied an expensive piece of technology to everyday life and tailored his speeches so that they would appeal to the largest possible number of consumers. He appealed to both the technology buffs and the technology impaired, which resulted in wildly successful products. Make sure you understand the context of your speech and audience so that you can deliver an effective presentation.

Designing a team presentation can be a difficult task. Communicate your expectations up front and try to establish a team vision and overall presentation goal.

iStockphoto/Cecilie_Arcurs

YOUR COMMUNICATION INTERACTION

Team Presentation

As you read the team presentation below, consider what features are most effective and what features could be improved.

Roxanne Huerta: Holistic Health: Proactively taking care of the whole *person*. That is our mission. That is what we do for our *patients*, because Holistic Health is an organization that is dedicated to living out its mission. But let's look at those words again. It does not say "the whole patient"; it says "the whole person." What's the difference? [Dramatic pause] Our mission extends to everyone who walks through our doors, which includes more than our patients. It includes you, our employees.

Relate to Audience: In the introduction, always try to relate your topic immediately to your audience.

Good morning, everyone, and welcome to the first day of your healthier life. My name is Roxanne Huerta, and I have worked for Holistic Health for the past 25 years, serving as a human resources executive for the past 9 years. It was in my role as an HR exec to learn about a holistic corporate wellness program, aimed not at patients but at employees. We have tested this program in our California offices, and the results were amazing. So today, I would like to introduce you to our new corporate wellness program. This program is divided into three areas: nutritional, physical, and spiritual. And I have with me today the individuals who will be heading each of these areas. They will be discussing with you the importance of each area to your life, as well as previewing the various tools and resources that will be available to you as part of this program. So without further ado, let me introduce Nicole Boswell, our nutritional expert.

Nicole Boswell: Two little words. Two little words are destroying the health of our nation. Two little words jolt us full of energy but then leave us drained and depleted. Two little words make us fat but leave us nutritionally starved. What are these two little words? *Processed foods.*

Clear Theme: Here, you see the theme of the speech is clearly conveyed to the audience.

Sure, we all know that processed food is bad for us, but the temptation to eat it is very powerful. Look around our work environment. In our cafeteria, we served french fries and fish sticks yesterday—two highly processed foods. For snacks, we have vending machines full of processed junk. But not anymore.

Good morning, everyone. My name is Nicole Boswell, and I have worked as a licensed dietician at Holistic Health for 7 years. And I am here to let you know that nutritious can be delicious. But beyond that, it can be just as quick and inexpensive as processed food.

Look at Margaret over there. She is doubting me. Well, Margaret, I don't blame you for doubting me, because most of us lack the tools needed to make delicious, quick, and inexpensive food that is good for us. So over the next 6 months, as part of this wellness program, we are going to do two things.

First, we are going to change all the food served in the cafeteria to meet the criteria of delicious, quick, inexpensive, and nutritious. We are also going to provide you with a shopping list, a cost breakdown, and the recipes for the dishes we serve. We will also be offering cooking classes twice a month to help you further. That way, you can have a healthy meal at work and then make that healthy meal at home. In addition, we will be restocking our vending machines with healthy snacks.

The second thing we are going to do is provide one-on-one nutritional consulting for free to anyone who is interested. We will go over your current diet and lifestyle and help you reach the health goals you set for yourself. The consultations happen during your work day, so you do not have to take time out of your personal life. They are free, they are confidential, and they will be designed to fit you and your life.

So today, I have given you a brief overview of the nutritional part of this program. I look forward to eating nutritional, delicious lunches with you in the cafeteria and talking with you one on one during our nutritional consulting sessions. We are going to replace those two little words, *processed foods*, with two very different words, *delicious* and *nutritious.*

Solution Statement: Now, the speaker has offered a solution to the problem previously mentioned.

Roxanne: Thank you, Nicole, for that overview of nutrition. I am going to sign up for my consultation as soon as our presentation is over. Now that we have learned about the nutritional component of this wellness program, let's turn our attention to the physical component. Coach Amy Peoples is here to tell us more.

Amy Peoples: [Blows a whistle] Drop and give me 20! Just kidding. Hello, folks. My name is Amy Peoples, and for the past 17 years I have worked as a personal trainer and a fitness coach. In this role, I have learned that most people have a "drop and give me 20" image in their heads when it comes to exercise. They see exercise as work, not as play. The good news is that with this wellness program, we are going to change that image. You are going to learn to reconnect with that kid inside yourself and have some fun by joining the Fun Fit Program. Let me give you an overview.

Here at Holistic Health, we have a state-of-the-art workout facility that you could not use—until now, that is. Starting today, all employees will be able to use our facilities free of charge. In addition, we will be sponsoring a host of fun activities that you can sign up for free of charge. For example, we are going to start an intramural kickball league. We are going to offer beginning dance lessons in ballet, tap, ballroom, and hip-hop. Every day we have a class called "Recess," in which you can take part in a variety of games and activities you loved as a kid. We will be sponsoring a walking club with a host of rewards you can earn. In addition, we have money set aside for activities that you all request. If you want yoga, fencing, or karate, we can do it. The goal is to get you moving while you are having fun.

The best part is that you can do this for 30 minutes every day on company time. Yes, you heard me right, play and get paid. It kind of makes you a professional athlete, right?!

In closing, I just want to reiterate that exercise should be fun, it can be fun, and it will be fun. All you have to do is sign up for something that interests you. Life is too short to miss out on the fun.

Roxanne: Thank you, Amy, for informing us about the physical activity and fun that is now available to us. Now I would like to ask our final speaker, Dr. Dawn Colbert, to talk to us about the spiritual component of this wellness program.

Dawn Colbert: According to Willa Cather, "Happiness is to be dissolved into something completely great." Here at Holistic Health, we have no intention of defining what spirituality means to you. Instead, what we want to do is help you find the time to dissolve into something completely great as a way to feed your spirit. My name is Dawn Colbert, and I am the founder of Holistic Health. For the past 30 years, I have worked as both a medical doctor and the president of this company. My life is full of abundance and blessings, but nothing has ever made me feel more rewarded than serving others. I love this wellness program for many, many reasons. Like our organization, it is dedicated to holistic health. But the thing that really sold me on this program over others is the spiritual component that centers on serving others. I would like to explain that component to you.

Starting today, you will each be allotted 1 hour per week to volunteer at the organization of your choice. This hour will be part of your 40 work hours, and you will be paid for this hour. The organization you volunteer for is up to you. You can volunteer at your child's school, the local food bank, your place of worship, a nursing home, or the animal shelter. It is completely your choice. All we ask is that you select a location or a cause that is meaningful to you. Select something that you find completely great, a cause into which you can dissolve and find happiness.

By implementing this wellness program, I am hoping to make a difference in your life by allowing you time to make a difference in the lives of others. As Harriet Naylor said, "Volunteering can be an exciting, growing, enjoyable experience. It is truly gratifying to serve a cause, practice your ideals, work with people, solve problems, see benefits, and know you had a hand in them."

Attention Step: Now the speaker has given the audience a call to action.

Roxanne: Thank you, Dr. Colbert. Well, today, everyone, you were introduced to our new corporate wellness program. You have been given an overview of each of its components—namely, nutritional, physical, and spiritual. All the speakers will be available to answer additional questions following this presentation, and we hope you have a lot of questions, because we hope you all plan to take part in this program. Holistic Health is not just a name on the door; it is a way of life, for our patients and now for each of us.

Questions to Consider

1. How are the individual speeches linked to form a cohesive unit? Do the speakers present a unified voice? Why or why not?
2. How are the introductions and conclusions handled in each speech and for the overall team presentation?
3. How does the team incorporate transitions?

During the third step, *your communication interaction*, Sinek explores how leaders should cooperate with their employees. Whether you are delivering an informative speech or a persuasive speech, your goal should be to keep your audience riveted by your presentation.

The final task, *step back and reflect*, encompasses everything we have discussed about Sinek's successful speech. We see not just what an effective business leader he is but also how great he is at orating. As you reflect on your own speeches, ask yourself if you moved your audience to action; in a business environment, ask if your speech demonstrated professional excellence and motivated the people around you to take action.

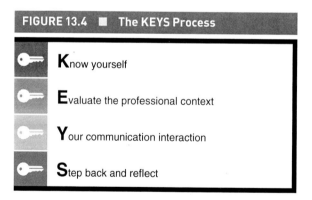

FIGURE 13.4 ■ The KEYS Process

Know yourself

Evaluate the professional context

Your communication interaction

Step back and reflect

EXECUTIVE SUMMARY

Now that you have finished reading this chapter, you should be able to

Explain how to overcome your fears of public speaking and deliver a presentation with professional excellence:

- When you get up to deliver a presentation, you will have an adrenaline rush. The delivery of the presentation requires you to put yourself "out there" in front of an audience, and in the deep recesses of your mind, your body is signaling, "Danger, danger."

- As you practice public speaking, you will learn what responses to expect when you have an adrenaline rush—they will no longer be an unknown. Then you can learn how to handle each response. In the end, you'll be able to use the adrenaline to your advantage by presenting with energy and passion.

Explain how to use supporting aids effectively:

- When a supporting aid is displayed, the audience will split their attention between you and the aid, which can help reduce some of your anxiety. In addition, supporting aids provide another layer to your presentations that can enhance interest.

- A well-designed supporting aid also helps the audience by increasing understanding, enhancing retention, and facilitating listening.

- For audience members who are visual learners, seeing key points, demonstrations, or other supporting materials is essential for their understanding. In addition, every time you repeat your message, you increase retention.

Explain the importance of practicing your presentation:

- An honest practice audience can help you determine if your presentation is effective.

- Speakers tend to overestimate their effectiveness, making the need for honest practice audience feedback very important.

- Speakers tend to overestimate the importance of visual aids and underestimate the importance of content and delivery.

- If you want to emerge as one of those rare speakers who presents with professional excellence, you must practice.

Discuss how to deliver an effective team presentation:

- Think of the group presentation as one big speech. As such, it should begin like any other effective presentation.

- When it comes to researching and designing the body of the presentation, the group must work together. For a group presentation, having all group members work in conjunction and prepare thoroughly prior to the presentation is vital for success.

- As each new speaker presents their portion of the presentation, they must include the components of an effective presentation. Each speaker must have a clear introduction and conclusion. Each speaker must have clear organization. The use of supporting aids must also be handled by the entire group during planning.

- For the presentation to look professional and polished, both planning and practice must occur as a team. Teams that fail to plan together or don't run through the presentation as a group often stumble and bumble in front of the audience.

Apply the KEYS process to develop professional excellence in speech delivery:

- Know yourself. Make sure you know what your role is when delivering a speech.

- Evaluate the professional context. Make sure you understand the context of your speech and audience so that you can deliver an effective speech.

- Your communication interaction. Whether you are delivering an informative speech or a persuasive speech, your goal should be to keep your audience riveted by your presentation.

- Step back and reflect. As you reflect on your own speeches, ask yourself if you moved your audience to action; in a business environment, ask if your speech demonstrated professional excellence and motivated the people around you to take action.

EXPLORE

1. Visit YouTube and watch Amanda Gormon deliver a poem at President Joe Biden's 2021 inauguration. What speech delivery skills did she use to make her presentation exceptional?

2. Identify an election (federal, state, or local) for which a debate was broadcast. Analyze how the different speakers were able to adapt their messages based on the moderators' questions and their opponents' answers. Who won the debate, in your opinion? What delivery skills did the candidates use to communicate effectively on the fly?

REVIEW

1. _____ occur(s) when the speaker should pause but instead fills the silence ("umm," "ahh").

2. Identify the speaking quality that includes an extemporaneous speaking style and good eye contact.

3. _____ are tools used by a speaker to help support the audience's interest in and understanding of the presentation.

4. The _____ of a presentation will present the introduction, provide the transitions between the other speakers and their content areas, and give the conclusion.

5. _____ refers to the loudness of your voice delivery.

6. How quickly you deliver your words to the audience is defined as the _____.

7. For _____, seeing key points, demonstrations, or other supporting materials is essential to their understanding.

8. Nothing looks worse than a _____ who appears distracted or uninterested when the rest of the team is presenting.

DISCUSSION QUESTIONS

1. Have you ever seen a speaker reading a speech? What was your impression of that speaker? How did you feel as an audience member?

2. When a professor presents a PowerPoint slide that is loaded with text, how do you, as a listener, respond?

3. Think about the speeches you have given in the past. How much time did you spend practicing the speech? Do you think it was an adequate amount of time? Why or why not?

4. Have you ever given a team presentation? Did the team members develop their presentations as a team or as individuals? Was your overall presentation cohesive?

5. How do you respond to the adrenaline rush that accompanies your public speaking? What can you do to overcome or deal with these responses?

TERMS TO REMEMBER

Review key terms with eFlashcards: **https://edge.sagepub.com/quintanilla5e**.

adrenaline rush (p. 331)	retention (p. 336)
conversational quality (p. 334)	speaking outline (p. 335)
delivery (p. 331)	speaking rate (p. 332)
eye contact (p. 333)	supporting aids (p. 336)
manuscript (p. 334)	visual learners (p. 336)
monotone (p. 334)	vocal fillers (p. 333)
organizer (p. 345)	volume (p. 332)

Visit **https://edge.sagepub.com/quintanilla5e** to help you accomplish your coursework goals in an easy-to-use learning environment.

SURVIVING IN THE WORKPLACE

A positive work–life balance can lead to greater professional and personal satisfaction.

14 WORK–LIFE BALANCE

CHAPTER OBJECTIVES

After studying this chapter, you should be able to

14.1   Define work-life balance and discuss its impact on professional excellence

14.2   Identify the triggers to imbalance

14.3   Develop strategies for achieving work–life balance

14.4   Apply the KEYS approach to achieve professional excellence regarding work–life balance

You may have asked yourself, "How do I balance my workload between school, work, and family?" "How can I find the time to meet up with my friends this week?" or "I have an exam in two days, but I'm working late tonight and tomorrow night—so when can I squeeze in time to study?" We have some bad news: The same imbalance that many of you are experiencing as you take this course will continue to challenge you as you transition into your professional career. The good news is that part of developing professional excellence includes developing strategies for achieving work–life balance. Stahl (2017) offers a few tips on how to keep the balance between life and work:

- **Learn how to let go of things.** Trying to be perfect and be everything to everyone only ensures failure. Learn how to say "no" when it's warranted.

- **Establish boundaries at work, and stick to them.** Technological advances enable employers to offer flexible work environments, but these technological advances also mean employees are accessible 24 hours a day. Sit down with your boss and discuss what the expectations are of you, and set boundaries on things like your availability outside of work to take calls and emails and how often, if ever, you're able to work overtime.

- **Prioritize your time.** At the end of every day, do a brief assessment of your daily activities. How did you spend your time? Which parts of your day were most and least productive? Are there activities or people in your day that don't seem to add anything?

- **Ask for help.** We are more productive and happier in our lives when we have a strong support system around us. So reach out to your network, and ask a coworker to help you pick up some slack on an overdue project. But always make sure that when the tide turns, you're willing to pick up slack for those in your support system when they need it, too.

THE IMPORTANCE OF WORK–LIFE BALANCE

In previous chapters, we applied the KEYS process to a variety of important aspects of business and professional communication. Those chapters focused on beginning communication principles for entering the workplace, developing in the workplace, and excelling in the workplace. Welcome to survival. In this chapter, we focus on the importance of work–life balance, the triggers that cause imbalance, and strategies for achieving work–life balance. Our goal, then, is to invite you to think about things that are important to people beyond work.

Take a moment to reflect on the most important people in your life (we emphasize people, *not* material possessions or money). You're likely thinking of your family—parents, siblings, spouse or partner—and friends. Now, think about your job getting in the way of your personal relationships and family. What if you didn't have time to spend with your daughter on her birthday because you had to work? What if you felt as though you couldn't take off work, even for one day, because there was simply too much to do? How would you feel if your work life completely dominated your personal life? Many of you have no doubt heard other people say the following: "My job really stinks," "I don't have a life," "All I do is work," or "I'm so behind at work, and the emails keep coming in." Let's face it—sometimes your inbox is simply too full. On top of your world of work, you have bills to pay, pets to care for, kids to feed, games to watch, and people to love. Combine the intensity of your personal life with the intensity of work life, and you have one big vacuum draining away your energy! We're not attempting to paint a completely dark picture of your professional life, nor do we want to discourage you from focusing on or developing your career. Instead, our goal is to encourage you to know yourself and to think about the challenges that people across industries encounter. Further, be aware of challenges such as stress, burnout, information overload, and difficult clients, which can hinder communication.

Achieving work–life balance is important for the following reasons: (1) Imbalance between your work life and your personal life can negatively influence the way you communicate, (2) work–life balance fosters meaningful and successful relationships at home and at work, and (3) work–life balance is necessary to sustain professional excellence. The KEYS process is central to connecting work–life balance with professional excellence, helping you *survive in the workplace.*

Work–Life Balance Defined

Scholars sometimes refer to work–life balance as work–family balance. *Life* is a more general reference to the self outside of work, while *family* refers to a collective group of people (e.g., spouses, children, partners) with whom the professional resides outside of work. We approach the topic of work–life balance by comparing the time people are at the job or completing job-related tasks (work) with the time that people are not working (life).

For many people, personal life is connected to family, whereas others think of it as private experience, leisure time, or downtime separate from work. The line or division between work and life is referred to as a   . Put simply, there's a boundary or line between work and personal and family time. The assumption is that if professionals have a boundary between work and personal life, then balance is the result. However, communication scholar Erika Kirby and colleagues (Kirby et al., 2003) explain that the problem of "boundaries" in work–life management stems from the concept that there are "separate spheres." This distinction assumes the presence of two different spaces of experience and action (Ba', 2011; Bailyn, 1993; Buzzanell, 1994; Medved & Kirby, 2005; Mumby & Putnam, 1992). But in reality, our lives can't be divided neatly into two parts. For example, your sick child does not suddenly recover between the hours of 9 and 5 so that you can go to work with no concerns about your family. Nor does your family say, "Don't worry about spending the holidays with us; we know Christmas is your busiest season at work. We don't really care if we see you." This boundary metaphor has an additional shortcoming. It tends to favor the organization, placing work first and in the position of "managing" employees' personal lives (Ferguson et al., 2012; Kirby & Harter, 2001).

To get more of a handle on this interesting topic, let's begin with some definitions. The definition of family is highly complex and controversial (Coontz, 2000; Glavin & Schieman, 2012; Wahl et al., 2005). We consider family to be all people in a household, which consists of a minimum of two members related biologically, or through adoption, marriage, civil union, or partnership—one of those people being the householder, who owns or rents the residence. Family is about people who share something relationally, mentally, physically, psychologically, economically, or spiritually with one another. Families are arranged in various structures (e.g., blended or intact), characteristics (e.g., healthy or dysfunctional), and systems (e.g., open or closed) across the family life cycle (e.g., married with no children, married with three teenagers; Braithwaite & Baxter, 2006). Indeed, families are diverse across populations.

Work is defined as an "instrument of activity intended to provide goods and services to support life" (Edwards & Rothbard, 2000, p. 179). Further, as Edwards and Rothbard (2000) explain, "work typically entails members in a market or employing organization that compensates the worker for his or her contributions." But for most of us, work is more than merely a means to receive compensation. Work plays an important role in our lives, significantly affecting self-concept and well-being (Martin, 2012; Morris & Madsen, 2007; Schor, 1998).

Another term important to this discussion is *community*—a geographic space identified as a place to work toward a good life (e.g., health, safety, well-being). The term *community* has a number of historical uses—for example, developing a place with boundaries that identifies a neighborhood and thus marks who lives inside and who lives outside or, more ideologically, a coming together in social communion (Bellah et al., 1985; Young & Schieman, 2012).

The most common notion seems to be that communities are identified as groups of interdependent people who discuss actions and share practices and have a concern for the common good. As many of you make decisions about where to live and work, the term *community* helps you understand life and leisure outside of work. To attract the best candidates, companies often talk up the community where the company is located. For example, "Most of our employees live in The Woodlands—it's just a short commute from Houston with some nice housing options, great shopping, and excellent schools." The term *community* is also informative to ethnic minorities, people with disabilities, and LGBTQIA+ working professionals. Indeed, people want to work and live in communities where they feel safe and included.

As you learned in Chapter 5, people often face challenges in the workplace as a result of their identities. It is important for people to work and live in inclusive communities where they are safe.

iStockphoto/Kosamtu

Although this topic is defined inconsistently despite vast scholarly inquiry (Drago, 2007; Glavin & Schieman, 2012), work–life balance is the "accomplishment of role-related expectations that are negotiated and shared between an individual and his or her role-related partners in the work and family [life] domains" (Grzywacz & Carlson, 2007, p. 458). Now that you have a better understanding of the important terms included in the work–life balance topic, let's take a look at why this is important for you as a professional and for the organization.

Why do you need to understand work–life balance? If you are like the vast majority of American workers, you will struggle to find a functional, productive balance between your work and your life. Let's look at some facts. First of all, a majority of couples with children under the age of 18 are both employed (a number that has continued to grow), 45% of U.S. workers are caregivers in some capacity (and the number of professionals providing eldercare to loved ones will continue to grow), and a majority of working professionals in the United States report difficulty balancing work and family life (Drago, 2007; Glavin & Schieman, 2012; Sammer, 2020). Research also suggests that the absence of work–life balance, usually defined in terms of increased family conflict, may be detrimental to personal health and organizational performance (Byrne, 2005; Glavin & Schieman, 2012; Grzywacz & Carlson, 2007). Put simply, work–life balance affects individual lives and the whole organization.

What happens when working professionals feel a sense of balance between their work and personal lives? Does the organization benefit? In fact, indicators of balance have been connected with better employee commitment, job satisfaction, and professional engagement (T. Allen et al., 2000; Yuille et al., 2012). By contrast, when balance is missing, employees are more prone to quit, abuse sick leave, and perform poorly on the job. As a result, work–life balance is at the core of good business practices today, leading organizations to develop a culture that supports the balance of work and individual life (Drago, 2007; Grzywacz & Carlson, 2007; Vidal et al., 2012). Let's take a more detailed look at the individual benefits and then the organizational benefits of work–life balance.

Individual Benefits

What's in it for you? What are the individual benefits of striving for and achieving this balance? If you fail to develop strategies for achieving balance, work time will attempt to colonize your personal time, leaving you with feelings of imbalance, stress, and burnout (Cameron, 2011; Deetz, 1992; Kirby et al., 2003; Rapoport & Bailyn, 1996; Schor, 1992, 1998). Burnout— chronic exhaustion from persistent workload, decreased motivation, and apathy toward work— has a number of causes (Leiter et al., 2007; Morales et al., 2012). As a professional striving for balance, be aware of the causes of burnout:

- Doing the same type of work with little variation, especially if this work seems meaningless

- Giving a great deal personally and not getting back much in the way of appreciation or other positive responses

- Lacking a sense of accomplishment and meaning in your work

- Being under constant and strong pressure to produce, perform, and meet deadlines— many of which may be unrealistic

- Working with difficult people

- Conflict and tension among staff, an absence of support from colleagues, and an abundance of criticism

- Lack of trust between supervisors and associates, creating conflict rather than teamwork toward commonly valued goals

- Not having opportunities for personal expression or for taking initiative in trying new approaches; a situation in which experimentation, change, and innovations not only are not valued but are actively discouraged

- Having unrealistic demands on your time and energy

- Having jobs that are both personally and unprofessionally taxing without much opportunity for supervision, continued education, or other forms of training

- Unresolved personal conflicts beyond the job situation, such as marital tensions, chronic health problems, or financial problems

When individuals in any given industry have a sense of work–life balance or feel that their organization at least takes an interest in their personal life outside of work, some of the major problems for individuals, such as burnout, can be prevented (Leiter et al., 2007; Snyder, 2012).

Many professionals, including many top business executives, report that finding the right balance between work and personal life is difficult (Golden & Geisler, 2007; Snyder, 2012). In cases where there is a balance, however, a number of individual benefits result (see Figure 14.1). These individual employee benefits of work–life balance also have implications related to both personal and organizational health. Simply put, this creates a win–win situation where employees feel supported and more in control of their stress at home and at work, leading to more confidence, loyalty, and better relationships with leadership and management.

FIGURE 14.1 ■ Individual Benefits of Work–Life Balance

Employees are happier at work and at home when they

- Have greater control of their working lives.
- Have the time to focus more on life outside of work.
- Don't bring problems from home to work and vice versa.
- Are shown loyalty and commitment.
- Have improved self-esteem, health, concentration, and confidence.
- Have better relations with management.
- Feel a greater responsibility and sense of ownership.

Source: Byrne (2005).

Organizational Benefits

What's in it for the organization? What are the organizational benefits of having a balanced workforce? Many organizational leaders and human resource professionals are striving to change their work culture by implementing training programs to motivate their workforce and make them feel happy so that they'll continue to produce and perform (Morris & Madsen, 2007; Tews et al., 2012). Work–life balance is challenging for organizations due to mergers, downsizing, changes in government regulations and policies, the complex nature of work and family roles, the expansion and use of technology, the increase in dual-income marriages, the increased number of women entering the workforce, and increases in job-related stress and its impact on employee health and wellness (McDonald & Hite, 2008; Tews et al., 2012). As a result of these challenges, many organizations today have a problem with employee retention—getting employees to continue working for the same company. Due to employee attrition—the loss or turnover of employees to other jobs and industries perceived as having healthier workplace cultures (e.g., employee focused, best places to work)—organizations are focused on the satisfaction of their workforces as much as on the customers and clients they serve, and work–life balance is at the core of this effort (Dex & Bond, 2005; Drago, 2007; Tews et al., 2012). For organizations that foster employee work–life balance, there are a number of benefits (see Figure 14.2).

STEP BACK AND REFLECT

Jarrett and Kim's Story

As you read this passage and answer the questions, step back and reflect on what went wrong in this professional situation.

Six weeks ago, Jarrett and Kim had twins. It was a time of great joy and great stress. Jarrett, a medical resident, had been sleep-deprived from working long hours, even before the twins arrived. Now he was so tired that he began to fear he might make a mistake. He felt his only recourse was to sleep in the break room between shifts so that his sleep would not be interrupted by the twins' crying. Kim's maternity leave was over, and she had to return to work.

Physically, she was in no shape to serve as the superstar employee she had been. A difficult pregnancy and an emergency C-section had left her drained. Trying to care for and nurse twins with little help from her spouse had depleted what few reserves she had left. But the physical issues were nothing compared with the emotional issues. Kim had always considered herself a career woman. She wanted kids, but predelivery, she was certain that by 6 weeks she would be more than ready to get back to work. That did not prove to be the case. The thought of placing her twins in day care left her in tears. She wanted to be at home with her babies. She did not want to go back to work. But they could not afford their house, their cars, and Jarrett's student loan payments without her income.

Step Back and Reflect

1. What went wrong?

2. Do you think that working moms and working dads share the workload on the home front? What impact does this balance or imbalance have on each party?

3. How could Kim and Jarrett use the KEYS approach to improve their communication interaction?

TRIGGERS TO IMBALANCE

What factors contribute to imbalance between work and life? What experiences do professionals have that promote imbalance? We define imbalance triggers as experiences (e.g., conflict, aggression, overload, negativity) that cause professionals to feel drained, used, abused, and unhappy. In the sections that follow, we describe the following imbalance triggers: personality types, difficult people in the workplace, technologically blurred lines, and life demands.

Stress and burnout affect your mood and attitude at work and at home, and while working from home continues to grow in popularity, it can sometimes be difficult to find a healthy work–life balance when working from home.

iStockphoto/Charday Penn

FIGURE 14.2 ■ Organizational Benefits of Work–Life Balance

For employers, having a more motivated, productive, and less stressed workforce results in

- Maximized available labor.
- Reduced costs.
- Retaining valued employees.
- The reputation of being an employer of choice.
- Reduced absenteeism.
- Increased productivity.
- Attracting a wider range of candidates, such as older, part-time workers.
- Making employees feel valued.

Source: Byrne (2005).

Personality Types

Earlier, we defined imbalance triggers as experiences. So are we saying that personality type is an experience? No, of course we aren't. However, your personality type can lend itself to many of the experiences that cause imbalance. The categorization of personality types is extensive and varies with insights ranging from Jung to Myers-Briggs. For our purposes, let's keep it simple and focus on the two classic personality types: Type A and Type B.

Competition and high performance demands exist in most professions.

iStockphoto/staticnak1983

Know Yourself

Work Time and Personal Time

As you read the index below and answer the questions, think about how this knowledge can help you achieve a better work–life balance.

Directions: Beside each statement, place either A for "Agree," B for "Sometimes," or C for "Disagree" as it relates to your experience.

1. At the moment, because the job demands it, I usually work long hours.
2. There isn't much time to socialize or relax with my partner or family in the week.
3. I have to take work home most evenings.
4. I often work late or on weekends to deal with paperwork without interruptions.
5. Relaxing and forgetting about work issues is hard to do.
6. I worry about the effect of work stress on my health.
7. My relationship with my partner is suffering because of the pressure or long hours of my work.
8. My family is missing out on my input, either because I don't see enough of them or because I am too tired.
9. Finding time for hobbies, for leisure activities, or to maintain friendships and extended family relationships is difficult.
10. I would like to reduce my working hours and stress levels but feel I have no control over the current situation.

Results:	
If you wrote all or mostly As	You may already be under considerable stress from your lack of work–life balance. Over time, your productivity could suffer, along with relationships, your health, and long-term employability. As an individual, start to address your own needs so that you become more effective. At work, try to promote better work–life balance to the advantage of the whole workplace.

If you wrote all or mostly *B*s	You are not entirely happy with your work–life balance but in a good position not to let the situation get out of control. By encouraging your organization to adopt a work–life strategy, you can help create an enhanced working environment that will benefit you, the organization, and colleagues at all levels.
If you wrote all or mostly *C*s	You have set your own priorities in work–life balance, making them work for you. As well as the benefits to you and your family, your organization is getting more from you. Show leadership by encouraging a culture that respects work–life balance for all and takes into account the fact that individuals have differing demands at various stages of the life cycle. When people have a sense of control over their work–life balance, they can be more productive and committed to their work and better prepared to manage the demands of today's rapidly changing workplace.

How did you do? For true professional excellence, you should strive for mostly *C*s. Take some time to explore your sources of imbalance, stress, and burnout.

If you did record some *A*s, what can you do to eliminate the imbalance in the future?

Source: Quiz from Daniels, L., & McCarraher, L. (2000). The work–life manual: Gaining a competitive edge by balancing the demands of employees' work and home lives. Industrial Society.

According to Friedman and Rosenman (1974), who studied the relationship between personality type and heart disease, if you have a Type A personality, you are highly competitive, are often seen as driven, are focused on time and deadlines, can be aggressive, and find it difficult to relax. Type As can be described as high-achieving, workaholic stress junkies (Evans et al., 2012; Friedman, 1996). By contrast, if you're a Type B individual, you are laid back, are easygoing, and don't find it difficult to relax. Still other individuals, known as Type AB, are a mix of the two personality types.

Given these definitions, it's not surprising that Type A individuals struggle to find balance between work and life. After all, to maintain the competitive edge and be high-achieving in a world full of people who breathe, eat, and sleep work, you must forget about balance and tip the scale in favor of work, right? Fortunately, this is not the case. As we discuss in the Life Demands section of this chapter, Type As also benefit from work–life balance. Put simply, if you're a Type A personality, you must recognize that you'll have a tendency to live your life out of balance. This does not mean there's something wrong with you. There's nothing wrong with your personality. In fact, most great leaders demonstrate Type A personalities. The workplace and the world need high-achieving individuals—you just need to remember to prioritize things other than work. Therefore, you must actively follow the strategies we outline later in this chapter to help avoid living the life of a workaholic stress junkie and to allow yourself to live life with professional excellence.

As for you Type Bs, don't think you're safe from imbalance. The Type B trait can lend itself to experiences such as procrastination, which can result in as much imbalance as being a workaholic. The Type A stays at work late because she wants to get ahead or make the report perfect. The Type B stays at work late because he didn't pay attention to deadlines and now he has a project that is far from complete and due in the morning. Either way, both people will be at work late experiencing stress, and neither one has good work–life balance.

The Impact of Difficult People on Work–Life Balance

Personality type can also influence the way you deal with difficult people in the workplace. For example, the Type A employee may end up doing all the work of departmental slackers because they cannot stand to wait until the last minute. The Type B leader's laid-back personality may cause them to allow a slacker to get away with doing next to nothing, which they and the rest of the team then have to make up for. Either way, failing to address these difficult people creates more work for leaders and functional employees. The resulting workload imbalance can bleed into one's nonwork time. In Chapter 10, we discussed difficult people as related to leadership and building a team. Because this is such an important and common issue in the workplace, we would like to reexamine it as it relates to work–life balance. To do this, we focus on three specific situations involving difficult people: angry customers and clients, workplace bullying, and workplace mobbing.

Angry Customers and Clients

As we established in Chapter 6, communicating effectively with customers, clients, or potential business contacts is essential in professional contexts. All organizations have customers or clients, and you must excel in communicating with these individuals. At the same time, customers or clients who expect and demand excellent service can sometimes cross the line by acting rude and uncivil. According to a popular saying, "the customer is always right." Do you think this is always true? What about customers who disrespect working professionals in every situation? Working as communication consultants, we have heard professionals across industries tell stories about angry customers and clients. These stories are usually filled with questions about what to do and how to act in these hostile situations. What can professionals do when customers totally lose control? How do you know when the line has been crossed? Indeed, customer service can be extremely difficult when listening, conflict management, and problem-solving skills are ineffective.

Most of the research in this area has focused on how employee communication skills (e.g., politeness, smiling, positive attitude, eye contact) can optimize customer satisfaction (Avey et al., 2008; Evanschitzky et al., 2012; Pugh, 2001). In addition to performance demands for communication excellence, employees have to help the organization recover from service and product failure, respond to customer complaints, apologize for mistakes, and the like. The emotional and psychological demands, especially when dealing with angry customer outbursts, have a negative impact on employees. Thus, dealing with angry customers can serve as an imbalance trigger, leading to staff absenteeism, lack of commitment, burnout, stress, and turnover (Dallimore et al., 2007; Morales et al., 2012). Not only are employees negatively affected, but organizations face decreased customer satisfaction, product quality, and profit.

How can organizations address the negative impact of difficult customers on employees? Managers should consider employee development opportunities (e.g., corporate wellness programs, training activities) to help manage the risk (Dallimore et al., 2007; Kelly et al., 2007; Ritchie, 2012). Now that we've considered the challenges of customer service demands, let's take a look at some sources of imbalance from your fellow employees and coworkers.

Workplace Bullying

Bullying at work can have both a direct and an indirect influence on organizational productivity, as well as a direct impact on your work–life balance. The notion of bullying in the workplace might sound a bit dramatic, but if you encounter a bully in the future (if you haven't already), you'll know what hit you! In fact, bullying in the workplace takes place more often than you might think—the frequency and form of bullying in "professional" environments is alarming and often goes unreported or unnoticed or is swept under the rug (Harvey et al., 2007; Harvey et al., 2006). Further, bullying is more devastating and stressful than all other sources of work-related stress combined. *Workplace bullying* is defined as repeated acts and practices that are directed intentionally or unconsciously and that cause embarrassment, humiliation, and stress. Bullying negatively influences job performance, causes an unhealthy work environment, and leads employees to spend their time away from work trying to figure out how to survive or cope with the abuse at work (Harvey et al., 2007; Harvey et al., 2006; Sandvik & Tracy, 2012).

What does workplace bullying look like? How can you better understand the types of bullying behavior? Let's take a look at the following seven categories provided by workplace bullying experts (Harvey et al., 2006):

- "Calling out" a target in public for being different or because they are not part of the "in-group"

- Using people as scapegoats to draw attention to the victims or to reduce attention on the bully for a failure of the group; the scapegoat's status seems to face more of a threat than the bully's

- Someone with more power or a higher position in the organization sexually harassing coworkers

- Increasing workload and pressure to perform with unrealistic deadlines and the like (e.g., "Get this project done in two weeks or you're fired.")

- Targeting an individual, preventing access to opportunities, withholding information, or physically or socially isolating an individual

- Failing to give credit to individuals who deserve recognition, setting up workers to fail, and overemphasizing failures

- Inflicting physical abuse on or causing harm to the targeted individual or group

On top of the examples listed above, our reliance on instant messaging tools like Slack has created an environment in virtual spaces where employees sometimes engage in bullying behavior (Schiffer, 2019). Remember that tone is difficult to convey in text-based communication, so always be mindful of what you are saying when messaging coworkers so you don't come across as unfriendly.

What kind of negative impact does workplace bullying have on employees and the organization? First, workplace bullies can have a huge impact on the day-to-day, task-oriented performance of employees. They can destroy employees' motivation, damage employees' attitudes about work, and make it impossible for employees to focus on completing tasks (Khan & Khan, 2012; Tracy et al., 2006). Second, productive employees who are committed to the organization and have a positive attitude will tend not to go the extra mile out of fear that the bully will sabotage their best efforts. Bullies tend to extinguish the stars and go-to people, preventing them from helping lead the organization toward positive change and excellence goals. Third, organizational change is difficult since the bully is fighting off all the positive agents for change in the organization; the only demands met are those of the bully. Finally, workplace bullies act as organizational cancer, eventually killing the entire business. Does any of the preceding information about workplace bullying ring true in your experience? How would you strive for balance if you encountered a bully in the workplace? What would you do as a leader or manager to prevent bullying (see Tools for Professional Excellence 14.1)?

How victims talk about workplace bullying is important to explore. To get a richer understanding of the impact of workplace bullying, review in Table 14.1 the painful metaphors associated with this behavior.

Workplace Mobbing

If reading about workplace bullying as an imbalance trigger was not enough, there's more. Another imbalance trigger important to your study of work–life balance is workplace mobbing—"the nonsexual harassment of a coworker by a group of other workers or other members of an organization designed to secure the removal from the organization of the one who is targeted" (Duffy & Sperry, 2007, p. 398). Duffy and Sperry (2007) explain that mobbing "results in the humiliation, devaluation, discrediting, degradation, loss of professional reputation, and, usually, the removal of the target from the organization."

Bullying and incivility at work can cause stress and burnout for anyone. How would you handle a bully at work?

iStockphoto/Credit: mediaphotos

TABLE 14.1 ■ Tools for Professional Excellence. How Can the Negative Consequences of Bullying Be Addressed?	
To address bullying in your workplace, take note of these prevention tips:	
Type of Issue	Prevention Tips
Environmental issues	● Objective determination of the present organizational climate and the employees' perspective on bullying activity levels and severity in the organization
	● Assessment of present formal standard operating procedures relative to dysfunctional bullying activities in the organization
	● Identification of the specific location of bullying activities in the organizational cultures across all departments, locations, or managers
	● Development of training directed specifically at countering bullying activities that should be provided to bullies as well as the personnel in the departments or locations that have been identified as having a higher incidence of bullying activities
	● Assessment of management's past actions relative to bullying activities within the organization in a given period of time
	● Continuous monitoring of bullying policies, processes, and procedures to ensure their successful implementation and updating

(Continued)

TABLE 14.1 ■ Tools for Professional Excellence (*Continued*)

To address bullying in your workplace, take note of these prevention tips:

Type of Issue	Prevention Tips
Issues with existing and potential bullies	● Put selection processes in place to reduce the likelihood of hiring bullies (e.g., behavioral interviewing) ● Restructure the bully's job requirements to reduce their direct contact with vulnerable groups or individuals in the organization ● Assign additional training and awareness coaching to the identified bully based on their past behaviors and the resulting impact on the victims and observers of bullying events ● Redesign the job to reduce the bully's supervision responsibilities and increase the nonpersonnel dimensions of their position ● Provide professional counseling for the bully to allow them to gain insights into the impact of their behaviors as well as the impact on the victim and observers ● Have the willingness and authority to terminate chronic bullies from the organization
Issues with bullied individuals	● Complete an assessment of the victim's self-esteem dimensions (e.g., cognitive, emotional, achievement, character, and physical) and develop training, counseling, and mentoring to address perceived shortcomings in the victim's self-image ● Develop a support mechanism for those in the organization who are potential targets of bullies to help preempt the bully's attacks ● Establish a review mechanism that the victim can use without fear of retaliation ● Provide programs to victims and potential victims that demonstrate the options open to them relative to bullying activities ● Have the willingness to support the potential victim before, during, and after a bullying event ● Give the victim the opportunity to be relocated in the organization to reduce direct supervision of or contact with the documented bully

Source: Harvey, M. G., Heames, J. T., Richey, R. G., & Leopard, M. (2006). Bullying: From the playground to the boardroom. *Journal of Leadership and Organizational Studies, 12*(4). http://jlo.sagepub.com/cgi/content/abstract/12/4/1.

TABLE 14.2 ■ What Does Workplace Bullying Feel Like?

Category	Themes and Examples
Bullying process as . . .	*Game or battle*: Bullies "play dirty" and "make their own rules." *Nightmare*: "It's the Matrix. We live in two different worlds." *Water torture*: It is a "hammering away," "drumbeat," or "pressure screw." *Noxious substance*: "It just kind of drips on down, just festers." He would "feed us a whole line of garbage."
The bully as . . .	*Narcissistic dictator or royalty*: "A tyrant runs things around here." *Two-faced actor*: Bullies put on "a good show for the boss," or they would "be real sweet one time one day, and the next day . . . very evil, conniving." *Evil or demon*: Bullies are "evil," "devils," "witches," "demons," and "Jekyll and Hyde."

Category	Themes and Examples
The target as . . .	*Enslaved*: "You're a personal servant to the owner and his will." "He considers you his property."
	Prisoner: "I feel like I'm doing time." "I felt like I had a prison record."
	Child: "I felt like a little girl." It "is like having an abusive parent."
	Heartbroken lover: "My heart was broken." I felt "sad, confused, unworthy, and broken-hearted."

Adapted from Tracy, S. J., Lutgen-Sandvik, P., & Alberts, J. K. (2006). Nightmares, demons, and slaves: Exploring the painful metaphors of workplace bullying. *Management Communication Quarterly, 20*(2), 148–185.

As with workplace bullying, you might be inclined to think of workplace mobbing as extreme or dramatic. Does this really happen? How often does workplace mobbing occur? Workplace mobbing first received attention in Europe but has emerged as a subject of increasing attention in the United States and Canada (Duffy & Sperry, 2012; Westhues, 2005; 2006). Victims of mobbing are typically accomplished professionals who exemplify commitment, honesty, integrity, intelligence, innovation, and competence (Duffy & Sperry, 2007; 2012). Instances of workplace mobbing continue to grow in the United States. You might be wondering how workplace mobbing is different from bullying. Mobbing is "a group attack on a worker," whereas bullying is "an attack by a single individual" (Duffy & Sperry, 2007, p. 398).

As this image suggests, mobbing in the workplace can certainly make people feel alone.

iStockphoto/MangoStar_Studio

What does workplace mobbing look like? How can you better understand the types of mobbing behavior? There are, in fact, five phases that usually occur in workplace mobbing. The five phases that follow have been identified by professional counselors who worked with mobbing victims in two clinical cases (Duffy & Sperry, 2007, 2012; Ferris, 2004; Leymann & Gustaffson, 1996):

Phase 1: The triggering event. An event occurs that leads an employee to stand out as different or not part of the in-crowd due to high performance or disagreement with the status quo.

Phase 2: Aggressive acts and psychological assaults against the victim. A mob forms and begins to punish the target by cutting them out of professional decisions. The victim is given low-ranking assignments and a difficult work schedule. The mob begins to gossip and spread rumors that the victim is a problem.

Phase 3: Active involvement of the administration. Leaders are alerted to the target and the situation. The administration comes in and raises questions about the victim. They tend to side with the mob because a majority of distrust and dissatisfaction with the victim is expressed. The mob is asked questions about the victim, such as "Are they collegial?" "Do you trust them?" "Are they disgruntled?"

Phase 4: Labeling of the victim. The victim is given an official label (e.g., noncollegial, difficult to work with, not a team player) by the administration and the mob.

Phase 5: Expulsion. The victim has it so bad that they quit or are eventually fired.

Regardless of whether you must deal with angry customers, bullies, mobs, or the array of difficult people discussed previously in this book (e.g., slackers, people who love drama, etc.), dealing with a difficult person in the workplace is a trigger for work–life imbalance.

Technologically Blurred Boundaries

Pam: My boss is driving me crazy.
Julie: What did she do now?
Pam: She is completely overloading me with projects, and she has no boundaries.
Julie: What do you mean?
Pam: There's nothing I can do since she's my boss! Since she gave us all new smartphones and laptops to start the new quarter, she sends text messages constantly and expects us to reply to work-related email late at night. The other night, she sent numerous emails starting at 11:00 p.m. and continuing until 4:30 a.m.!

What does this brief conversation between Pam and Julie reveal? Clearly, Pam is having a problem dealing with a difficult boss who does not understand work–life boundaries. Unfortunately, Pam is not alone. Mobile information and communications technologies (ICTs) such as work smartphones may harm work–life boundaries and also serve as tools for managing them (Eikhof, 2012; Golden & Geisler, 2007). Indeed, technology helps professionals be more productive and stay connected with clients, respond quickly, accomplish tasks despite geographic distance, travel with tons of data, maintain maintain and coordinate shared calendars, and more. Yet some people believe that email systems and other forms of communication technology—created to help us manage our time more efficiently—have actually increased our work-related tasks and maintenance (Ballard, 2008; Eikhof, 2012). Take a moment to think about your own use of technology. Does your use of technology help or hinder work–life boundary management?

Working late or at home on professional projects can open the door for your personal life to take a hit.

iStockphoto/Phiromya Intawongpan

Life Demands

The term *work–life* is a bit misleading. After all, your work is a part of your life, and your life away from the job is full of nonemployment-related work. The term *work–life* is really meant to capture the competing demands placed on the 21st century employee. This book provides you with a host of skills and strategies that will help you handle work demands with professional excellence. So it seems only fair that we turn our attention for a moment to some life demands, such as household and family responsibilities, as well as health responsibilities.

Household and Family Responsibilities

Whether you live alone or with a houseful of people and pets, your household must be maintained. This requires keeping up with housework, yard work, grocery shopping, paying the bills, and more.

As noted earlier, a majority of couples with children under the age of 18 are both employed, and 45% of U.S. workers are caregivers in some capacity (Drago, 2007; Glavin & Schieman, 2012; Sammer, 2020). This means that on top of the duties noted above, you'll probably need to find time to take your elderly parents to the grocery store and medical appointments. You'll have to use your time away from the office to coach soccer and chauffeur your children to and from ballet, piano, and karate lessons. Of course, your dog will also need to go for a walk. If you live in an apartment, make that two or three walks.

Evaluate the Professional Context

Although caring for your home, children, parents, and pets may be a labor of love, it's still very demanding and stressful, with the majority of the stress falling on women. In fact, when women entered the workforce, all their former duties in the home and for the family didn't disappear. Instead, they were moved into a second shift of work (Hochschild, 1989). When women increased their financial contribution, men didn't necessarily increase their domestic contribution (Goldstein, 2000; Greenstein, 1996; Risman & Godwin, 2001; Wood, 2003). In fact, some professional women report that husbands not only fail to do their fair share of housework; they actually add to the amount of housework that needs to be done!

When it comes to caring for elderly parents, that responsibility also tends to fall on daughters more often than sons. According to Wood (1994), the responsibility of caring for aging parents and aging in-laws falls predominantly on women. Since wives take on more than husbands, and daughters take on more than sons, it is not surprising to learn that mothers tend to take on more of the parenting duties than fathers. Some of it is necessary. After all, fathers can't get pregnant or nurse. Nevertheless, fathers are indeed very important, and the demands on working fathers are intense—but the demands placed on working mothers can be downright exhausting.

In recent years, part-time employment has become the new "ideal" for working mothers, with about 1 in 5 women working part time for noneconomic reasons (e.g., childcare, health problems) (Dunn, 2018). This preference for working part time, though, may not be enough for some families, as increased economic pressures have forced some mothers to seek full-time employment, or at least to express the desire to work full time to be able to provide for their families (W. Wang, 2013). The definition of the "ideal" working situation for women also depends on socioeconomic and marital status, as these factors significantly affect the extent to which women have to provide for their families (W. Wang, 2013) (see Figure 14.3 for exact figures).

Establishing activities such as spending time with friends or your pets can help manage stress and provide some sense of leisure time away from work.

iStockphoto/MightyPics

Certainly, some women work outside of the home because they find their jobs fulfilling and rewarding, while some women work to achieve a higher standard of living for themselves and their families. However, not all women have a choice when it comes to working outside of the home. Increased divorce rates and economic necessity due to higher costs of living are also cited as reasons mothers work outside of the home (Pew Research Center, 2007).

FIGURE 14.3 ■ Work Grows Less Attractive to Moms

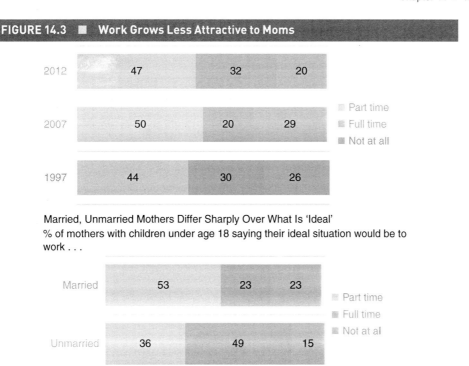

Married, Unmarried Mothers Differ Sharply Over What Is 'Ideal'
% of mothers with children under age 18 saying their ideal situation would be to work . . .

Note: Based on mothers with children under age 18.

Source: W. Wang (2013).

Household and family demands affect men as well. The following stories of Jackson, Joel, and Wesley capture some of the demands and pressures placed on men.

Jackson was a successful partner in a law firm. His firm was profitable, and everyone earned a good salary. But for some of the partners, good was not good enough. There was a move to increase the number of clients and the profile of the firm to increase revenue. Jackson opposed the change because it would mean more time in the office and less time with his family. When Jackson voiced his concerns, the other partners accused him of not being a team player.

When Joel's son was born, he and his spouse decided that one of them should stay home with the child. Joel was thrilled for the opportunity and enjoyed every moment he spent caring for his son and his home. Yet, when Joel's son entered kindergarten and he decided to go back to work, he was shocked at the negative response he got from potential employers when they learned he had "wasted five years playing Mr. Mom."

Wesley is a teacher. He loves teaching, and he's very good at it. The problem is that he doesn't earn the same high-level salaries as his male friends and family members. Wesley often feels like a poor provider because he can't afford an expensive house or expensive gifts for his spouse and children. Although his family has never complained, he feels as though it's his job to provide, and he's concerned that he's not providing enough.

Although the demands vary in type and intensity, both parents and caregivers have to juggle household demands, family demands, and work demands. Unfortunately, living demanding lives takes a toll on your health.

Health Responsibilities

For men, work-related stress and the negative habits that accompany a stressful lifestyle have long been known to have a detrimental impact on health. As the number of women in the workplace has increased, so too have the health risks that accompany work-related stress and a life lived out of balance.

Do you really need to worry about the impact of work and work–life balance on your health? Should your employer worry about your health and your stress level? After all, what's wrong with a little stress? A little stress every once in a while may not be harmful, but prolonged stress and daily stress is very dangerous. Stress is commonly linked to headaches, stomachaches, short temper, depression, and anxiety. See Figure 14.4 for a more extensive list of stress-related problems.

FIGURE 14.4 ■ Health Problems Linked With Stress

Trouble sleeping	Depression
Headaches	Anxiety
Constipation	Skin problems (such as hives)
Diarrhea	Hyperthyroidism
Irritability	Obesity
Lack of energy	Ulcers
Anger	Weight gain or loss
Sadness	Heart disease
Lack of concentration	High blood pressure
Hair loss	Irritable bowel syndrome
Tooth and gum disease	Diabetes
Cancer (possibly)	Neck and/or back pain
Tension	Less sexual desire
Increased asthma flare-ups	Sexual dysfunction
Stomach cramping	Difficulty getting pregnant
Stomach bloating	Obsessive-compulsive disorder
Increased arthritis flare-ups	Anxiety disorder

Source: Adapted from the Office of Women's Health (2018) and Scott (2007).

The link between work–life balance, stress, and health can create a vicious cycle. Let's look at obesity as an illustration of how this works. Obesity is one of the health problems linked to stress and is a growing problem in the United States (see Figure 14.5). Drake was very active and fit in high school, but as his 10-year class reunion approached, he became aware of the negative impact his work had had on his health. During law school, Drake had to study all the time. As a result, he stopped playing sports for fun and rarely made it to the gym. Now Drake is a successful attorney, which requires him to work long hours, including on weekends. This leaves no time for exercise, and his hectic schedule often allows him little time to prepare or eat a healthy meal. Instead, Drake grabs a burger or hits the vending machine for his meals. Because of the stress on the job and the lack of downtime needed to unwind, Drake often has headaches, backaches, and sleepless nights. All this has resulted in what Drake calls the 50-pound spare tire he is carrying around his middle. Drake knows that his weight increases his chances of a heart attack. He also knows that all the stress negatively impacts his performance on the job. But he does not know how to change his current lifestyle. What can he do? Drake is like millions of other Americans. He has no work–life balance, and he lacks the communication strategies that can help him obtain that balance.

Lunch breaks are often rushed, and many of today's professionals are pressured to accomplish numerous tasks in a short amount of time. Some remote workers also face dietary struggles as the structure of daily lunch routines you find in many office environments do not exist in the same way when working from home (Litovsky, 2020).

iStockphoto/FreshSplash

STRATEGIES FOR BALANCE

We recognize that balancing the challenges of work with your personal and family life will not be easy. However, striving for balance will promote better communication at work and at home. Remember, part of professional excellence is getting to know yourself to understand how the sources of imbalance are influencing your communication and well-being. Furthermore, many of the strategies that can help you obtain balance are communication strategies. It is through effective communication that you find work–life balance, and once you have found that balance, it will improve your communication.

In the sections that follow, we review some strategies for developing work–life balance: knowing yourself, developing emotional intelligence, learning time-management skills, using technology as a tool for balance, and taking a vacation.

Knowing Yourself

The first step in developing work–life balance is determining the priorities in your life and then assessing how much time you devote to each priority. Take inventory of how many hours you spend on various tasks and responsibilities each day. How do you manage your life? Many of you may realize that there is too much going on. Even if you're coping, you still may not have work–life balance. Where do you spend most of your time? Is this where you want to spend most of your time? No doubt, friends and family are important to you, but how much time do they get? What about your health? How much time do you spend exercising so that you can unwind and relieve your stress? Knowing yourself means evaluating where you want to spend your time

FIGURE 14.5   ■   Prevalence of Self-Reported Obesity Among U.S. Adults

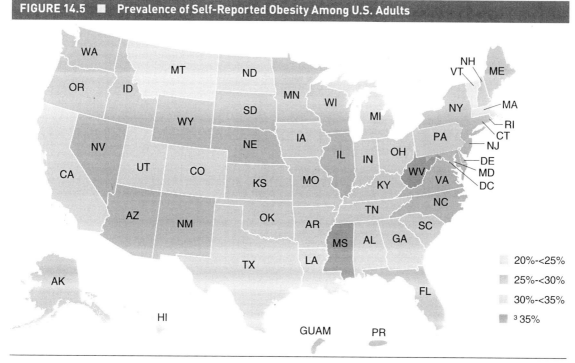

Legend:
- 20%–<25%
- 25%–<30%
- 30%–<35%
- ³ 35%

Source: Centers for Disease Control and Prevention. (2013). Adult obesity prevalence maps. http://www.cdc.gov/obesity/data/prevalence- maps.html

(priorities) as compared with where you actually spend your time (reality). For true work–life balance, your priorities and your reality should line up.

To do this, you must also know your personality type. So are you a Type A or a Type B? If you are a Type A, you must learn the art of saying no. If you are a Type B, you need to become a proactive communicator versus a reactive communicator.

One of the first words you learned to say was "no.". At age 2, it was probably your favorite word, but for adults, it is a difficult word for Type As to say. You may have trouble giving up control, you may think you can do it better, the task may sound appealing to you, or you may believe you can indeed do it all. Regardless of the reason you fail to say no, by repeatedly saying yes, you fill your plate so full that you become overworked, overstressed, angry, ill, or all of the above. If saying no is difficult for you, reframe your thinking. Learn to say yes to your priorities, which means you must turn down nonpriorities. Make a list of your priorities and your future goals. When you are asked to take on another task, buy yourself some time to think by saying something like "I will need to check my calendar." "Let me confer with my team." or "I will need to discuss this with my boss." If the task lines up with your priorities and if you have time to complete the task during your regular work hours, then accept. If not, learn to say no tactfully but firmly. You might say, "I am afraid that will not be possible." "Thank you for considering me, but I must pass." or "Although it's a wonderful opportunity, I cannot accept at this time." Then stop talking. Do not allow the other party to pull you into a debate about how much time you have or how much you are needed. Just repeat your answer again: "As I said, it's a wonderful opportunity, but I cannot accept at this time."

Type B individuals must learn to function as proactive communicators, not reactive communicators. Since Type B individuals tend to be more laid back and less focused on time and deadlines, they may have a tendency to ignore small problems until they become big problems, or they may allow poor time management to affect the quality of their work. As a proactive communicator, you must implement many of the strategies discussed earlier in the text. For example, as a leader, develop agendas for all meetings to keep yourself on task, set up meetings to lay out expectations for employee performance before there's a problem, hold regular meetings to give and receive feedback, hold employees accountable, confront difficult employees, and develop your time-management skills (which we discuss later in this chapter). All these strategies will help you to stay on task, to decrease stress in the workplace, and to achieve professional excellence.

Learning to say no and learning to be proactive benefit everyone, regardless of personality type. The important thing to remember is that if you're going to achieve work–life balance, you must begin by knowing yourself.

Developing Emotional Intelligence

To achieve work–life balance, you also must develop emotional intelligence—your ability to monitor your own and others' feelings and emotions, to discriminate among them, and to use this information to guide your thinking and actions (Angelidis & Ibrahim, 2012; Engelberg & Sjoberg, 2004; O'Sullivan, 2005; Salovey & Mayer, 1990). The concept of emotional intelligence was initiated in the psychology discipline and clearly informs business and professional communication (Angelidis & Ibrahim, 2012; Morand, 2001). People striving for work–life balance and professional excellence often consult popular books on the topic (Bradberry & Greaves, 2005; Chang et al., 2012; Goleman, 1995).

Professionals who exercise emotional intelligence are more balanced in that they know their own emotions and attempt to understand the emotions of others. In addition, emotional intelligence encourages you to use your emotions to plan flexibly, to think creatively, and to motivate you to accomplish goals and solve problems (Chang et al., 2012; Mayer & Salovey, 1993; Morand, 2001). By learning to manage your emotions when you're dealing with stress caused by difficult people, deadlines, information overload, or a whole host of other triggers, you'll be able to address the issue at hand and then move on. The stress, worry, and so on won't bleed into other areas of either your work or your life. Do you have a grasp on your own emotions and how they influence your communication? How perceptive are you of emotions in other people? As a means to better understand emotional intelligence, let's explore one emotion in more detail—anger.

TABLE 14.3 ■ Action Items. Policies for Work–Life Balance		
Policy	**Strategy**	**Application**
Flex time	Permit employees to work nontraditional hours.	Allow 9:00 a.m.–1:00 p.m. shifts and 4:00 p.m.–8:00 p.m. shifts.
Job sharing	Allow workers to collaborate to compensate for vacation time or leave.	Give two workers the ability to work on a project in case one employee needs time off for personal reasons.
Telecommuting	Let employees work from home.	Allow employees to have a Zoom meeting from home instead of going to the office.

Understanding Anger

Many, if not all, of the imbalance triggers described in this chapter can cause a professional to experience anger. *Anger* is defined as an emotional state that varies in intensity from mild irritation to intense fury and rage, a feeling of keen displeasure for what we regard as a wrong toward ourselves or others (Parlamis, 2012; Thomas, 1998). Anger is known as a secondary emotion. In other words, anger occurs as a response to a situation or another emotion. Maybe a coworker embarrasses you, which in turn causes you to feel anger. For many people, anger is viewed as something that shouldn't be expressed or felt, but it's important to realize that anger is a normal human emotion.

In general, people become angry when they encounter a *real* or *perceived* threat to themselves (e.g., bullies, mobs, difficult customers). Similar to our discussion of the causes of or triggers to imbalance, there are also triggers to anger. *External triggers* to anger are things going on in your environment at work and at home, usually stimulated by others. *Internal triggers* to anger are concerns and frustrations you have about past, current, and future events or a general negativity toward yourself (e.g., "I'm really angry at myself for not making that change sooner.").

Something at some point in time is going to cause you to experience anger in a business and professional setting. The trigger source may very well be directly from a coworker or client. Perhaps your anger will be triggered by something going on in your personal life. No matter the source, it's critical for you to avoid the following counterproductive expressions of anger (Callahan, 1999):

- Repressing (swallowing) or denying your anger

- Anger by projecting it onto the wrong target

- Using alcohol, drugs, or other potentially harmful distractions for understanding and expressing your feelings

- Treating depression—which may be anger turned inward—solely as depression

- Confusing anger with the desire for revenge

ETHICAL CONNECTION

Too Much Work

As you read this passage and answer the questions, consider how the way you communicate has an ethical dimension.

Jackie is the vice president of a large petrochemical company. She enjoys her work and her position, but the demands on her time are quite severe. Jackie typically works 60 hours a week, and with a new business merger looming, it looks as though she will be working even more now. Jackie's wife has voiced her concern about her work schedule, and she expects to give birth to their first child within the month. Jackie is worried that with her new work demands she will not be able to give her wife and baby the attention they need. Her company has already indicated that she will need to work long hours for the foreseeable future, and her position is in jeopardy if she takes a personal leave of absence. Jackie has other job options available, but she could not expect the same high-ranking position (and pay) that she enjoys at her current job.

Questions to Consider

1. What is the ethical dilemma facing Jackie?

2. What impact do Jackie's family obligations have on her professional career?

3. Why is achieving work–life balance a critical factor when entering a professional field?

4. Are there any other options Jackie could explore before finding new employment?

Releasing Anger in Healthy Ways

Have you ever felt as though it was impossible to manage all the responsibilities between school, friends, family, and work? Take a moment to reflect on activities or practices for managing anger, especially in business and professional situations. Below is a list of strategies for releasing anger in healthy ways:

- Admit that you're angry. Honesty is crucial. You also need to be free of judgmental reactions to your anger. Remember, anger is a normal feeling. Swallowing or repressing anger can be dangerous.

- Identify the reason for your anger. Ask, "What situation or event is making me angry?" Clarify your position. What is the problem? What is the real issue behind your angry feelings?

- Ask what you want to accomplish with your anger. Anger tells us that something is bothering us. What needs to be done to correct the problem?

- Talk it out. Discuss the problem with a trusted friend or qualified professional. This helps you see if your emotion is "current" anger or "old" anger. If you think you have a lot of unexpressed anger from the past, begin to explore the issue gently.

- Practice relaxation techniques. Deep breathing and other relaxation techniques can help you release anger and tension from your body.

- Use physical exercise to get your anger out. You can often alleviate angry emotions through physical activity, such as a long walk, yard work, or whatever outlet you choose.

- Speak up when you feel angry or shortly afterward. If possible, express your anger to the person with whom you are concerned. Using "I" statements can help you express anger in a reasonable manner when an issue or concern is important to you (e.g., "I feel angry when you fail to complete your part of the project by the assigned deadline."). Then let go of the anger. Don't dwell on hurt feelings.

You'll no doubt have to deal with anger, as well as a host of other emotions, in the workplace. It's up to you to know yourself so that you can recognize those emotions and assess how they are influencing your communication. Part of communicating with professional excellence requires you to lay out expectations and standards of professionalism and hold people accountable when they fail to maintain those expectations and standards. It's best to confront the difficult people or situations that are creating anger and stress in your workplace. Use "I" statements to express your emotions, develop healthy strategies for releasing emotions, and fire people if you must.

Crime dramas like *Law & Order: Special Victims Unit* often highlight the intensity of police work. Christopher Meloni as Detective Elliot Stabler deals with anger and stress associated with murder investigations. As you study work–life balance and ways to manage anger and stress, remember to prepare for the long work hours and emotionality that might be part of certain jobs in your future.

Will Hart/NBCUniversal/Getty Images

If you don't have the power to fire a bully, say no to unrealistic demands, or refuse service to an out-of-control customer, find a new place to work.

Developing Time-Management Skills

Part of striving for balance involves taking control of how you manage your time. In fact, management and business scholars have found that many working professionals have such a difficult time managing the work–life boundary that some give up and are prone to misbehave by engaging in personal activities at work (Bull & Brown, 2012; D'Abate, 2005). To avoid this unprofessional practice, let's take a serious look at how to manage time effectively. You must identify the —things you don't feel as though you have any control over (e.g., things you are required to attend, such as meetings, or people to whom you are required to talk). In addition, identify internal time wasters—more personal internal things brought on by mindset, motivation, and bad habits. Business consultants and leadership coaches offer a variety of time-management strategies for professionals (see Tools for Professional Excellence 14.2).

Review the time-management strategies provided. What strategies stand out to you? Part of striving for balance and professional excellence involves identifying time-management strategies that make sense for you. Do you have a problem with time management? Take a look at Tools for Professional Excellence 14.3 and think about some methods for prioritizing your time that can help you achieve professional excellence. Perhaps technology is the answer. As you reflect on time management, let's transition into the final section of this chapter, which explores the influence of technology on work–life boundary management.

Using Technology to Maintain Balance

As noted earlier, new mobile information and communications technologies (ICTs) such as smartphones and tablets may harm work–life boundaries. However, there are many strategies you can use to help keep a healthy work–life balance (see Tools for Professional Excellence 14.2).

TABLE 14.4 ■ Tools for Professional Excellence. Effective Time-Management Skills for Work–Life Balance

To help achieve work–life balance, consider the time-management tips below:

Key Points	Strategies
Value your time.	● Change your focus: Instead of thinking about how much time you don't have, think about the time you do have and what you can reasonably get done within that time.
	● Think about the time you have as soon as you sit down to work, so as to minimize the amount of time you may spend procrastinating.
	● Treat your time as a commodity: Setting a specific time to end your workday will help you get things done in the allotted window of time, and help you avoid working later than you planned.
Eliminate distractions.	● If you find yourself procrastinating, ask yourself why: Is there something about your workload you want to avoid? Identifying the motivation behind your procrastination can help you overcome it.
	● Don't be afraid to turn off outside communication, such as email or social media, from time to time. Often, these can distract you from the task at hand, even if they are being used for work purposes.
Conduct a time audit.	● Keep track of what your time is devoted to each day for one week.
	● Look at the results of the audit: What areas could use more time devoted to them? What areas could use less?
	● Make a short list of things you consider time well spent, and ask yourself how often you do them.
	● A time audit can help you clearly see what aspects of your life act as time drains, and what aspects deserve more time devoted to them.
Break up your time.	● Reorganizing your workload into smaller time frames can help you focus on the task at hand, and avoid getting overwhelmed.
	● Take small breaks in between tasks to relax and recharge.
	● Take longer breaks during times when work is banned, such as in the evening or on weekends.

Source: Booth, F. (2014, August 28). 30 time management tips for work–life balance. *Forbes.* http://www.forbes.com/sites/francesbooth/2014/08/28/30-time-management-tips/

Taking a Vacation

Vacation may not seem like a relevant topic in a text on communication, but let us assure you that taking vacation time will make you a better communicator, and you will need to use several communication strategies if you plan to enjoy a true vacation. Culturally, people in the United States are not very good at taking vacations. Some countries have minimum requirements for vacation time off. For example, workers in Finland, France, Germany, Norway, and Sweden must be given at least 5 to 6 weeks of vacation time. By contrast, there is no minimum amount of vacation time in the United States.

When looking at these vacation statistics, your first instinct may be to blame employers. Surely, the reason people in the United States take fewer vacation days is because they *have* fewer vacations days, right? Wrong. About 37% of U.S. workers don't use all of their allowed vacation time (Carsen, 2019). So even when they have vacation days, U.S. employees often don't use them. Some reasons for this include the following:

- The need to schedule vacation time in advance (13%)

- The ability to get money back for unused vacation days (12%)

- The feeling that work is life, making it too hard to get away (10%)

Source: Harris Interactive (2008).

TABLE 14.5 ■ **Tools for Professional Excellence.** Prioritizing Your Time	
To prioritize your work tasks, consider these practical tips:	
Category	**Practical Tips**
Important and urgent	These are tasks for which you have to make time. Continually asking yourself "What's important now?" will lead to a manageable number of tasks. Everything you have to do should not go in this category. Remember, these are your high-priority tasks.
Important but not urgent	Tasks in this category are typically "preventative" in nature. For example, spending time with your staff ensures that things are going well and that they're happy. It can also apply to planning, organizing, and starting tasks that will later become important and urgent.
Not important but urgent	Usually, interruptions, some phone calls, and emails fall into this category. They need to be dealt with in an "urgent" way to establish their significance and make a decision on how they need to be dealt with. This category is usually associated with someone else's priorities.
Not important and not urgent	These are tasks that should be done in "slack" periods: some emails, some phone calls, filing, and other busy work. This may also be time when you catch up with colleagues and engage in work-related reading or professional development.

Source: Adapted from Byrne, U. (2008). If you want something done, ask a busy person. *Business Information Review, 25,* 190–196; and Covey, S. R. (2003). *The 7 habits of highly effective people personal workbook.* Fireside.

The COVID-19 pandemic only worsened the trend of American workers not taking advantage of all of their allowed time off work; in 2020, 92% of workers indicated they either canceled, postponed, or didn't book a vacation due to the pandemic (Dickler, 2020). Unfortunately, many companies have policies that require all or a percentage of unused time off to be forfeited at the end of the year, so many employees in 2020 lost their time off altogether. Given the problems resulting from stress, discussed earlier in this chapter, the need to unwind seems clear. In fact, many nations require employees to take a minimum amount of vacation time. In other words, taking a vacation is required. Unfortunately, the United States is not one of those nations, even though 40% of U.S. adults reported working more than 40 hours a week (Harris Interactive, 2008).

Why would employers require a minimum amount of vacation time? Maybe it's because vacation time increases job satisfaction, morale, and productivity (Harris Interactive, 2008). As we discussed earlier, it also helps reduce stress and burnout.

Whether you're looking for an entry-level position or a position as the CEO, be aware of the organization's attitude about vacation time. If you're offered a position with a company that allows or encourages its employees to work to the point of burnout, then you should pass and wait for a better offer. If you're in a leadership position in your organization, you must work to develop an organizational culture that encourages employees to take vacations. Talk to employees about when they plan to take time off. This will allow you to keep the organization running smoothly even when key players are gone. This will also help prevent employees from failing to schedule time in advance and then losing the time as a result. If you notice an employee is stressed, encourage them to take some time off to recharge. Most important, you need to be a role model. Take your vacation time so that employees know it's okay for them to do the same.

When you or any member of your team goes on vacation, set a "Do Not Disturb" policy. Taking calls, checking emails, and conducting meetings via videoconference while in a tropical paradise is not a vacation. You are still plugged in, so you cannot truly relax and rejuvenate. You must unplug completely. This will be difficult, as the technological boundaries between work and vacation are increasingly becoming blurred. If you're taking a vacation, tell everyone that you will not be taking your cell phone (even if you do take it along, leave it turned off). If an emergency occurs, your office can track you down through the hotel. This will reduce the number of so-called emergencies. The same goes for your laptop. Tell your team that you will not be checking your voicemails or emails. Change your voice message and set up an email auto-reply message to tell people you are gone and when you will return. Then stick to your word and don't check in.

KEYS TO EXCELLENCE WITH WORK–LIFE BALANCE

At the beginning of the chapter, we examined several tips to increase satisfaction with your work–life balance. One of the tips involved setting your own rules. By examining the first key, *know yourself*, it should be clear that your first step is to do a reflexive assessment about what makes you happy in relation to time both at and away from your job. Think about times when stress from work has interfered with your family, social, or personal time. When you find yourself becoming overwhelmed by work, think critically about steps you can take to create more personal time for yourself.

Professionals who are out of balance or burned out may find it difficult to relax. In our consulting practice, we have heard many professionals talk about how they feel guilty if they take any time away from work-related projects.

iStockphoto/Moyo Studio

The second step, *evaluate the professional context*, tasks you with assessing how (and if) your company or organization can accommodate you. One of the tips at the beginning of the chapter recommended stepping away from email, but in certain professions, this is not feasible. Clearly, there is no one-size-fits-all approach to work–life balance, so be sure to explore other ways your company can provide a healthy separation between work and personal life. If it is possible, working from home can be very effective for achieving work–life balance, but make sure you understand the culture of your company before suggesting such an arrangement.

The third step, *your communication interaction*, offers several innovative ideas to be productive in your personal time. New technology allows people from around the globe to meet, brainstorm, and work together, eliminating the need for lengthy business trips and time away from home. Find out if some of your collaborative work can take place away from the office via a smartphone, tablet, or personal computer.

The final step, *step back and reflect*, asks you to determine if both you and your employer are happy with your work–life balance. If your company is flexible and you are creative, you shouldn't have too much trouble creating a system that keeps both your personal life and your professional career in a healthy state.

CHRISTINA'S EXPERIENCE WITH TELECOMMUTING

As you evaluate the passage below, consider whether this behavior is appropriate for this professional context.

Christina thought that her use of technology was going to help her work–life balance. Christina had three children ranging in age from 4 to 10. When she was given the option to work from home, she was thrilled—her dream had come true. She would no longer have to drive back and forth through rush-hour traffic. Her children would no longer have to go to the latchkey program after school. She could set her own hours—as long as everything was completed by the preset deadlines. Yet Christina's dream quickly turned into a nightmare. For example, because she was "home" all day, her partner would ask her to run errands for them because they had to be at work, her neighbor would drop by to chat, and her friends would insist that she meet them for lunch since she was "free." As for her children, they had a difficult time understanding that their mom was working even though she was in the house. When they arrived home at 3:00 p.m., there was a constant demand for her help or attention. As a result, Christina found herself working until the wee hours of the morning trying to get her projects completed. Work life and home life had blurred into one big blob, which included absolutely no downtime for Christina.

Questions to Consider

1. What advice would you give Christina?
2. Do you think her situation is common?
3. Would you have difficulty working from home? Why or why not?
4. Is the professional context different for employees working from home? Why or why not?
5. How could the KEYS process help Christina's situation?

Do you ever feel completely overwhelmed by all the demands on your time? How do you handle the stress? What have you learned in this chapter that could help you better manage work–life balance?

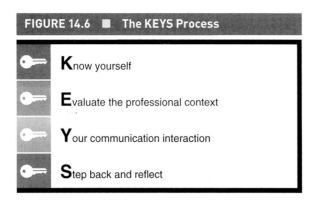

FIGURE 14.6 ■ The KEYS Process

Know yourself

Evaluate the professional context

Your communication interaction

Step back and reflect

EXECUTIVE SUMMARY

Now that you have finished reading this chapter, you should be able to

Define work–life balance and discuss its impact on professional excellence:

- Achieving work–life balance is important for the following reasons: (1) Imbalance between your work life and your personal life can negatively influence the way you communicate, (2) work–life balance fosters meaningful and successful relationships at home and at work, and (3) work–life balance must be present to sustain professional excellence.

- If you fail to develop strategies for achieving balance, work time will attempt to colonize your personal time, leaving you with feelings of imbalance, stress, and burnout.

- Employees are happier at work and at home when they have greater control of their working lives; have the time to focus more on life outside of work; don't bring problems from home to work and vice versa; are shown loyalty and commitment; have improved self-esteem, health, concentration, and confidence; have better relations with management; and feel a greater responsibility and sense of ownership.

- For employers, having a more motivated, productive, and less stressed workforce results in maximized available labor; reduced costs; retention of valued employees; the reputation of being an employer of choice; reduced absenteeism; increased productivity; the ability to attract a wider range of candidates, such as older, part-time workers; and a workforce that feels valued.

- Scholars sometimes refer to work–life balance as work–family balance. *Life* is a more general reference to the self outside of work, whereas *family* refers to a collective group of people (e.g., spouses, children, partners) with whom the professional resides outside of work.

- Work–life balance is the "accomplishment of role-related expectations that are negotiated and shared between an individual and their role-related partners in the work and family [life] domains" (Grzywacz & Carlson, 2007, p. 458).

Identify the triggers to imbalance:

- Imbalance triggers are experiences (e.g., conflict, aggression, overload, negativity) that cause professionals to feel drained, used, abused, and unhappy.

- External triggers to anger are things going on in your environment at work and at home, usually stimulated by others.

- Internal triggers to anger are concerns and frustrations you have about past, current, and future events or a general negativity toward yourself.

Develop strategies for achieving work–life balance:

- Striving for balance will promote better communication at work and at home. Part of professional excellence is getting to know yourself to understand how the sources of imbalance are influencing your communication and well-being.

- The first step in developing work–life balance is determining the priorities in your life and then assessing how much time you devote to each one.

- You also must develop emotional intelligence—your ability to monitor your own and others' feelings and emotions, to discriminate among them, and to use this information to guide your thinking and actions.

- Part of striving for balance involves taking control of how you manage your time. In fact, management and business scholars have found that many working professionals have such a difficult time managing the work–life boundary that some give up and are prone to misbehave by engaging in personal activities at work.

Apply the KEYS approach to achieve professional excellence regarding work–life balance:

- Know yourself. Determine if you want to achieve professional excellence, and know that part of that entails improving your work–life balance.

- Evaluate the professional context. Become more audience centered and aware of how you come across to other people when you experience stress and burnout. Become more mindful of how your communication can be influenced by your anger.

- Your communication interaction. Be a more professional communicator in that you manage your emotions and make better choices even when you are stressed out due to managing numerous challenges in your life. Start to think before reacting, and be much more mindful of how your overload can negatively affect your communication.

- Step back and reflect. Become more reflective of your workload and how it influences communication in your personal and professional lives and your overall health.

EXPLORE

1. Find an online resource or social media account related to your professional work field. Find out what other professionals in your field are doing to maintain an optimal work–life balance. Websites such as Reddit and LinkedIn have specialized groups that allow you to engage with other members of your profession and communicate positive work–life balance strategies.

2. Visit the website for WorkLifeBalance.com—under the Knowledge Center tab, review some of the case studies concerning work–life balance. Can any of these examples relate to your personal work experience? Reflect on how the solutions offered could be applied to your work environment.

3. Communicate with your coworkers to discover if there is a mutually shared hobby within your office. If there is, see how this hobby could be incorporated with the next team-building meeting or exercise.

REVIEW

1. A(n) _____ is the line or division between work and life.

2. _____ is an instrument of activity intended to provide goods and services to support life.

3. Define *work–life balance*.

4. _____ refers to the chronic exhaustion from persistent workload, decreased motivation, and apathy toward work.

5. Employee _____ is the loss or turnover of employees to other jobs and industries perceived as having healthier workplace cultures.

6. _____ is the nonsexual harassment of a coworker by a group of other workers or other members of an organization designed to secure the removal from the organization of the one who is targeted.

7. List two examples of information and communications technologies (ICTs).

8. Define *emotional intelligence*.

DISCUSSION QUESTIONS

1. Discuss a time when you felt burned out or overloaded. How did you respond? How did burnout influence your communication with other people?

2. Have you ever experienced or observed bullying? How did you respond to the bullying? As a professional, what steps would you take to address workplace bullying?

3. How do you manage stress and emotions such as anger? What strategies do you have, if any, that work for you?

4. Can the risks and health consequences (for individuals and organizations) associated with difficult customers and coworkers be alleviated with employee education and training? What experiences have you had, if any, concerning training or education related to uncivil workplace behavior?

5. Do you use ICTs to manage time between your school, work, and family life? Do these devices help you achieve balance? If so, what technologies work for you? If not, what traditional life organizers do you recommend?

YOUR COMMUNICATION INTERACTION

Rachel's Work–Life Balance

As you read the passage below, consider what would be a more effective communication strategy in this situation.

Rachel recently returned to work after delivering her second child. Although she was more than ready to get back to her job, Rachel has discovered that balancing her responsibilities at work and at home is even more difficult than before. Always the overachiever, though,

Rachel does not let on just how stressful her life has become. One day at work, Rachel's boss mentions that she needs to put together a team to handle a high-profile account. Having had plenty of experience as a team leader and as the most seasoned employee in the meeting, Rachel immediately volunteers to head the team. Her boss hesitates, and then suggests that she sit this one out. When Rachel asks why, her boss hesitates once more, and then says that she just had another baby, she has too much on her plate, and he does not want to take any risks with the account. Before Rachel can formulate a response, her boss indicates that the conversation is over, and moves on with the meeting. Later in the day, Rachel overhears the newly formed team begin work on the account. After listening in on the meeting for a while, Rachel begins to feel frustrated and angry at being passed over.

Questions to Consider

1. Are Rachel's feelings at the end of the scenario justified? Why or why not?
2. What, if anything, could Rachel's boss have done differently when not choosing her for the team?
3. If you were one of Rachel's coworkers, how could you help her out after the meeting?
4. If you were Rachel, what would you do next?

TERMS TO REMEMBER

Review key terms with eFlashcards: **https://edge.sagepub.com/quintanilla5e.**

anger (p. 380)

balance (p. 359)

boundary (p. 359)

burnout (p. 361)

community (p. 360)

emotional intelligence (p. 379)

employee attrition (p. 363)

employee retention (p. 363)

external time wasters (p. 382)

external triggers (p. 380)

family (p. 359)

imbalance triggers (p. 363)

information and communications technologies (ICTs) (p. 372)

internal time wasters (p. 382)

internal triggers (p. 380)

work (p. 360)

work–life balance (p. 361)

workplace bullying (p. 367)

workplace mobbing (p. 369)

Visit **https://edge.sagepub.com/quintanilla5e** to help you accomplish your coursework goals in an easy-to-use learning environment.

EPILOGUE

COMMUNICATION IS WORK

In November 2001, we became friends and colleagues who share a passion for applying communication research and competencies across contexts. Our careers have been spent teaching communication in higher education, working as communication consultants in corporate environments, and communicating professionally as university presidents or as college deans. In many ways, communication defines our lives. Still, we too must continually remind ourselves that communication is work. No matter how many successes we have or challenges we overcome in our own professional and personal lives, we must work to maintain communication excellence.

We both believe that communication is a foundation of business and professional excellence—and that is the driving theme of this text, which we hope resonates with you in whatever professional and personal stage you're currently experiencing. As you look back on the topics you studied in this course and look into the future, it's natural for you to think, "What do I do now? Will I know when I've arrived? Am I still doing a good job?" While most of your time spent reading this book, studying for exams, and completing projects is integral to striving for business and professional excellence, we must emphasize that much more is left on the horizon that goes beyond what we have presented in this textbook.

We want to emphasize that communication is a constant process, something that must be at the center of both your professional life and your personal life. Thus, as you move forward, remember that communication is not a destination you reach, leading you to cheer, "I'm done and have arrived." The focus must be more of constant energy from moment to moment, not just at work but also at home. This constant presence of communication in your life may make you feel as though you are continually trying to become something or someone else—but the good news is that constant communication presence and self-awareness is what excellence is all about. Remember that communication can be a form of labor (work) that takes effort, structure, persistence, quality, and frustration.

Beyond our view of communication as work, we want to emphasize that, just like your personal family, your professional family can be both functional and dysfunctional. Many of our own professional experiences have been filled with joy, civility, dignity, and respect—and these are ideal in human relationships. In contrast, we also have experienced firsthand while working as consultants across professional contexts situations in which frontline employees, shift leaders, general managers, and corporate executives suffered from utter chaos, uncivil communication, uncertainty, information overload, and burnout in the workplace. Our former client Mitch, president and CEO of a large health care system in the United States, said, "Everything professionally [at work] is going well, but I'm losing my family. The stress and work demands have taken over my family. . . . I think Stacey and I are moving toward divorce." Another professional, Robert, who works in the petrochemical industry, describes the stress of company downsizing: "We [the employees] don't know what to expect here at the plant on a day-to-day basis. . . . There are so many people losing their jobs, and the folks in the executive office don't communicate with us. . . . We are completely in the dark . . . and don't know if we will have jobs tomorrow or the next day." Throughout this text, we have provided you with the tools to overcome the challenges faced by Mitch and Robert—to move beyond dysfunctional environments and excel with professional excellence.

We hope that the KEYS process presented in this text will serve as a constant reminder that evaluating your own communication across professional contexts should be at the core of everything—and remember that excellence should feel never-ending, like a journey without a finish line. The conversation about the quality, ethicality, and emotionality of communication across contexts has started. What goals will you set for yourself? How will you respond in good times and in bad? What will be your role? The journey (and the work) continues.

REFERENCES

23 best Gregg Popovich quotes on coaching and teamwork. (2017, September 27). *Spongecoach.* http://www.spongecoach.com/top-gregg-popovich-quotes/

Adams, K., & Galanes, G. J. (2009). *Communicating in small groups: Applications and skills* (7th ed.). McGraw-Hill.

Adler, R. B., & Proctor, R. F., II. (2007). *Looking out/looking in* (12th ed.). Thomson/Wadsworth.

Alarcon, G. M. (2011). A Meta-analysis of burnout with job demands, resources, and attitudes. *Journal of Vocational Behavior, 79,* 549–562.

Albrecht, K. (1992). *The only thing that matters: Bringing the power of the customer into the center of your business.* HarperBusiness.

Ali, A., & Gulzar, A. (2012). Impact of emotional intelligence competencies on impression creation: Exploring the mediating role of impression management skills. *International Journal of Economics and Management Sciences, 1*(6), 29–34.

Allen, G. (2002). *Supervision: A hyperlink book.* http://telecollege.dccccd.edu/

Allen, T. D., Herst, D. E., Bruck, C. S., & Sutton, M. (2000). Consequences associated with work-to-family conflict: A review and agenda for future research. *Journal of Occupational Health Psychology, 5,* 278–308.

Andersen, P. A., Guerrero, L. K., & Jones, S. M. (2006). Nonverbal behavior in intimate interactions and intimate relationships. In V. Manusov & M. L. Patterson (Eds.), *The SAGE handbook of nonverbal communication* (pp. 259–277). SAGE.

Angelidis, J., & Ibrahim, N. A. (2012). The impact of emotional intelligence on the ethical judgment of managers. *Journal of Business Ethics, 99*(1), 111–119.

Antonoff, M. (1990, July 27). Presentations that persuade. *Personal Computing, 14,* 62–68.

Argyle, M. (1988). *Bodily communication.* Methuen.

Arlat, J., Kalbarczyk, Z., & Nanya, T. (2012). Nanocomputing: Small devices, large dependability challenges. *Security and Privacy, 10*(1), 69–72.

Armour, S. (2005, July 19). Your appearance can affect the size of your paycheck. *USA Today.* www.usatoday.com/money/workplace/2005-07-19-bias-usat_x.htm

Arruda, W. (2017, September 8). *Surprising advice from some of the best public speakers out there.* Forbes. https://www.forbes.com/sites/williamarruda/2017/09/08/surprising-public-speaking-advice-from-some-of-the-best-public-speakers/#ca94502102bd

Aslam, S. (2022, February 22). *Twitter by the numbers: Status, demographic and fun facts.* Omnicore, https://www.omnicoreagency.com/twitter-statistics/

Avery, D. R., & Ruggs, E. N. (2020, July 14). *Confronting the uncomfortable reality of workplace discrimination.* MIT Slogan Management Review. https://sloanreview.mit.edu/article/confronting-the-uncomfortable-reality-of-workplace-discrimination/

Avey, J. B., Wernsing, T. A., & Luthans, F. (2008). Can positive employees help positive organizational change? Impact of psychological capital and emotions on relevant attitudes and behaviors. *Journal of Applied Behavioral Science, 44,* 48–70.

Ba', S. (2011). Symbolic boundaries: Integration and separation of work and family life. *Community, Work and Family, 14*(3), 317–334.

Babad, E., Avni-Babad, D., & Rosenthal, R. (2003). Teachers' brief nonverbal behaviors in defined instructional situations can predict students' evaluations. *Journal of Educational Psychology, 95,* 553–563.

Bailyn, L. (1993). *Breaking the mold: Women, men, and time in the new corporate world.* Free Press.

Ballard, D. I. (2008). The experience of time at work. In L. K. Guerrero & M. L. Hecht (Eds.), *The nonverbal communication reader: Classic and contemporary readings* (3rd ed., pp. 258–269). Waveland.

Banks, G. C., Whelpley, C. E., Oh, I.-S., & Shin, K. (2012). (How) are emotionally exhausted employees harmful? *International Journal of Stress Management, 19,* 198–216. http://dx.doi.org/10.1037/a0029249

Baratta, M. (2015, May 14). *4 tips for writing compelling press releases.* PR Daily. www.prdaily.com/Main/Articles/18562.aspx?utm_content=buffercb504&utm_medium=social&utm_source=twitter.com&utm_campaign=buffer

Barbuto, J. E., & Gifford, G. T. (2012). Motivation and leader-member exchange: Evidence counter to similarity attraction theory. *International Journal of Leadership Studies, 7*(1), 18–28.

Barker, L., & Watson, K. (2000). *Listen up.* St. Martin's Press.

Barley, S. R., Meyerson, D. E., & Grodal, S. (2011). E-mail as a source and symbol of stress. *Journal of Organization Science, 22*(4), 897–906.

Barrett, J. (2018, March 1). *Dicks Sporting Goods is no longer selling AR-15 assault rifles and millennials are listening.* GROWCO. https://www.inc.com/jeff-barrett/dicks-sporting-good-is-no-longer-selling-ar-15-assault-rifles-its-a-powerful-lesson-in-brand-voice.html

Bass, A. N. (2010). From business dining to public speaking: Tips for acquiring professional presence and its role in the business curricula. *American Journal of Business Education, 3*(2), 57–64.

Beatty, M. J. (1988). Situational and predispositional correlates of public speaking anxiety. *Communication Education, 37,* 28–38.

Bell, M. P., Özbilgin, M. F., Beauregard, T. A., & Sürgevil, O. (2011). Voice, silence, and diversity in 21st century organizations: Strategies for inclusion of gay, lesbian, bisexual, and transgender employees. *Human Resource Management, 50*(1), 131–146.

Bellah, R., Madsen, R., Sullivan, W. M., Swidler, A., & Tipton, S. M. (1985). *Habits of the heart: Individualism and commitment in American life.* University of California Press.

Benne, K., & Sheats, P. (1948). Functional roles of group members. *Journal of Social Issues, 4,* 41–49.

Bergman, M. E., Watrous-Rodriguez, K. M., & Chalkley, K. M. (2008). Identity and language: Contributions to and consequences of speaking Spanish in the workplace. *Hispanic Journal of Behavioral Science, 30,* 40–68.

Bernstein, A. J. (2001). *Emotional vampires: Dealing with people who drain you dry.* McGraw Hill.

Bhunia, A., & Das, S. A. (2012). Explore the impact of workplace spirituality on motivations for earnings management: An empirical analysis. *International Journal of Scientific and Research Publications, 2*(2), 194–201.

Biggiero, L., Sammarra, A., & Dandi, R. (2012). The effect of e-mail use and adoption on organizational participation: The case of a public administration. *Human Systems Management, 29*(1), 27–39.

Bingham, S. G. (1991). Communication strategies for managing sexual harassment in organizations: Understanding message options and their effects. *Journal of Applied Communication Research, 19,* 88–115.

Birdwhistell, R. L. (1970). *Kinesics and context.* University of Pennsylvania Press.

Blake, R. R., & Mouton, J. S. (1964). *The managerial grid.* Gulf.

Blake, R. R., & Mouton, J. S. (1978). *The new managerial grid.* Gulf.

Bly, R. W. (1999). *The encyclopedia of business letters, fax memos, and e-mail.* Career Press.

Boerner, S., Schäffner, M., & Gebert, D. (2012). The complementarity of team meetings and cross-functional communication: Empirical evidence from new services development teams. *Journal of Leadership & Organizational Studies, 19*(2), 1–11.

Bok, S. (1989). *Secrets: On the ethics of concealment and revelation.* Vintage Books.

Bok, S. (1999). *Lying: Moral choice in public and private life.* Vintage.

Bolman, L. G., & Deal, T. E. (1997). *Reframing organizations: Artistry, choice and leadership* (2nd ed.). Jossey-Bass.

Bort, J. (2014, December 9). The 14 best tech companies to work for. *Business Insider.* www.businessinsider.com/the-14-best-tech-companies-to-work-for-2014-12?op=1

Bradberry, T., & Greaves, J. (2005). *The emotional intelligence quick book.* Simon & Schuster.

Braithwaite, D. O. (1990). From majority to minority: An analysis of cultural change from ablebodied to disabled. *International Journal of Intercultural Relations, 14,* 465–483.

Braithwaite, D. O. (1996). "I am a person first": Different perspectives on the communication of persons with disabilities. In E. B. Ray (Ed.), *Communication and disenfranchisement: Social health issues and implications* (pp. 257–272). Erlbaum.

Braithwaite, D. O., & Baxter, L. A. (Eds.). (2006). *Engaging theories in family communication: Multiple perspectives.* SAGE.

Braithwaite, D. O., & Braithwaite, C. A. (2009). "Which is my good leg?" Cultural communication of persons with disabilities. In L. W. Samovar, R. Porter, & E. R. McDaniel (Eds.), *Intercultural communication: A reader* (9th ed., pp. 207–218). Wadsworth.

Braithwaite, D. O., & Thompson, T. L. (2000). *Handbook of communication and people with disabilities: Research and application.* Erlbaum.

Breeze, H. (2013, June 28). *Microsoft leads tech firms on best workplace in Europe list.* Channel Web. www.channelweb.co.uk/crn-uk/news/2278286/microsoft-leads-tech-firms-on-best-workplace-in-europe-list

Bremner, S. (2012). Socialization and the acquisition of professional discourse: A case study in the PR industry. *Written Communication, 29*(1), 7–32.

Briody, E., Pester, T. M., & Trotter, R. (2012). A story's impact on organizational-culture change. *Journal of Organizational Change Management, 25*(1), 67–87.

Brownell, J. (1994). Teaching listening: Some thoughts on behavioral approaches. *Business Communication Quarterly, 57,* 19–24.

Brownell, J. (1996). *Listening: Attitudes, principles, and skills.* Allyn & Bacon.

Bruneau, T. (2012). Chronemics: Time-binding and the construction of personal time. *A Review of General Semantics, 69*(1), 72–92.

Bryant, A., & Sharer, K. (2021). *Are you really listening?* Havard Business Review. https://hbr.org/2021/03/are-you-really-listening

Bull, M., & Brown, T. (2012). Change communication: The impact on satisfaction with alternative workplace strategies. *Facilities, 30*(3), 135–151.

Burgoon, J. K., & Jones, S. B. (1976). Toward a theory of personal space expectations and their violations. *Human Communication Research, 2,* 131–146.

Burkard, A. W., Boticki, M. A., & Madson, M. B. (2002). Workplace discrimination, prejudice, and diversity measurement: A review of instrumentation. *Journal of Career Assessment, 10,* 343–361.

Buzzanell, P. M. (1994). Gaining a voice: Feminist organizational communication theorizing. *Management Communication Quarterly, 7,* 339–389.

Buzzanell, P. M. (1999). Tensions and burdens in employment interviewing processes: Perspectives of non-dominant group applicants. *Journal of Business Communication, 36*, 134–162.

By, R. T., Burnes, B., & Oswick, C. (2012). Change management: Leadership, values and ethics. *Journal of Change Management, 12*(1), 1–5.

Byrne, U. (2005). Work-life balance: Why are we all talking about it? *Business Information Review, 22*, 53–59.

Byrne, U. (2008). If you want something done, ask a busy person. *Business Information Review, 25*, 190–196.

Byron, K., & Baldridge, D. C. (2007). E-mail recipients' impressions of senders' likeability: The interactive effect of nonverbal cues and recipients' personality. *Journal of Business Communication, 44*, 137–160.

Callahan, B. N. (1999). *Grief counseling: A manual for social workers.* Love.

Cameron, S. (2011). *Handbook on the economics of leisure.* Edward Elgar.

Campbell, K. S., Mothersbaugh, D. L., Brammer, C., & Taylor, T. (2001). Peer versus self assessment of oral business presentation performance. *Business Communication Quarterly, 64*, 23–43.

Carsen, J. (2019, July 24). *Study: 37% of workers don't use up all of their PTO.* HR Dive. https://www.hrdive.com/news/study-37-of-workers-dont-use-up-all-of-their-pto/559114/

Carter, S. (1996). *Integrity.* Basic Books.

Cavico, F. J., Muffler, S. C., & Mujtaba, B. G. (2012). Sexual orientation and gender identity discrimination in the American workplace: Legal and ethical considerations. *International Journal of Humanities and Social Science, 2*(1), 1–20.

Chang, J. W., Sy, T., & Choi, J. N. (2012). Team emotional intelligence and performance interactive dynamics between leaders and members. *Small Group Research, 43*(1), 75–104.

Chen, C. Y., Pedersen, S., & Murphy, K. L. (2012). The influence of perceived information overload on student participation and knowledge construction in computer-mediated communication. *Instructional Science, 40*(2), 325–349.

Chen, X. H., Zhao, K., Liu, X., & Wu, D. (2012). Improve employees' job satisfaction and innovation performance using conflict management. *International Journal of Conflict Management, 23*(2), 23–33.

Chesebro, J. D., & McCroskey, J. C. (2001). The relationship of teacher clarity and immediacy with student state receiver apprehension, affect, and cognitive learning. *Communication Education, 50*, 59–68.

Cho, V., & Hung, H. (2011). The effectiveness of short message service for communication with concerns of privacy protection and conflict avoidance. *Journal of Computer-Mediated Communication, 16*(2), 250–270.

Choy, S. C., & Oo, P. S. (2012). Reflective thinking and teaching practices: A precursor for incorporating critical thinking into the classroom? *International Journal of Instruction, 5*(1), 167–182.

Christian, J., Porter, L. W., & Moffit, G. (2006). Workplace diversity and group relations: An overview. *Group Process and Intergroup Relations, 9*, 459–466.

Cicala, J. E., Smith, R. K., & Bush, A. J. (2012). What makes sales presentations effective: A buyer-seller perspective. *Journal of Business and Industrial Marketing, 27*(2), 78–88.

Clare, J., & Danilovic, V. (2012). Reputation for resolve, interests, and conflict. *Conflict Management and Peace Science, 29*(1), 3–27.

Clarke, J. T. (1989). Lawyer-client relations. *Journal of Professional Services Marketing, 5*, 101–104.

Cohen, S. (2017, January 10). *Gary Kelly defies gravity at Southwest Airlines: Meet a CEO with a stellar personal brand.* Huffington Post. https://www.huffingtonpost.com/stacey-cohen/gary-kelly-defies-gravity_b_13942660.html?ncid=engmodushpmg00000003

Coldewey, D. (2014, May 28). *"Time to be candid": Google admits lack of workplace diversity.* NBC News. www.nbcnews.com/tech/tech-news/time-be-candid-google-admits-lack-workplace-diversity-n116866

Collins, P. (2012). *The art of speeches and presentations.* Wiley.

Conrad, D., & Newberry, R. (2011). 24 business communication skills: Attitudes of human resource managers versus business educators. *American Communication Journal, 13*(1), 4–23.

Coontz, S. (2000). Historical perspectives on family studies. *Journal of Marriage and the Family, 62*, 283–297.

Couch, D., & Liamputtong, P. (2008). Online dating and mating: The use of the internet to meet sexual partners. *Qualitative Health Research, 18*, 269–279.

Covey, S. R. (2003). *The 7 habits of highly effective people personal workbook.* Fireside.

Cowan, K. (2011, December 15). *Twitter etiquette: The rules.* The Guardian. www.theguardian.com/culture-professionals-network/culture-professionals-blog/2011/dec/15/twitter-rules-etiquette

Cozzetto, D. A., & Pedeliski, T. B. (1996). Privacy and the workplace. *Review of Public Personnel Administration, 16*, 21–31.

Crockett, R. O. (2011, March 14). Listening is critical in today's multicultural workplace. *Harvard Business Review Blog Network.* blogs.hbr.org/cs/2011/03/shhh_listening_is_critical_in.html

Crosby, O. (2000). Employment interviewing: Seizing the opportunity and the job. *Occupational Outlook Quarterly, 44*, 14–21.

D'Abate, C. P. (2005). Working hard or hardly working: A study of individuals engaging in personal business on the job. *Human Relations, 58*, 1009–1032.

Dallimore, K. S., Sparks, B. A., & Butcher, K. (2007). The influence of angry customer outbursts on service providers' facial displays and affective states. *Journal of Service Research, 10*, 78–92.

Daly, J. A., Vangelisti, A. L., & Weber, D. J. (1995). Speech anxiety affects how people prepare speeches: A protocol analysis of the preparation process of speakers. *Communication Monographs, 62*, 383–397.

Daniels, L., & McCarraher, L. (2000). *The work-life manual.* Industrial Society.

Deetz, S. A. (1992). *Democracy in an age of colonization.* State University of New York Press.

DeGroot, M. G., & Motowidlo, S. J. (1999). Why visual and vocal interview cues can affect interviewers' judgments and predict job performance. *Journal of Applied Psychology, 84*, 986–993.

Den Hartog, D. N., & Belschak, F. D. (2012). When does transformational leadership enhance employee proactive behavior? The role of autonomy and role breadth self-efficacy. *Journal of Applied Psychology, 97*(1), 194–202.

Deshpande, A. (2012). Workplace spirituality, organizational learning capabilities and mass customization: An integrated framework. *International Journal of Business and Management, 7*(5), 3–18.

Dewey, J. (1910). *How we think.* D. C. Heath.

Dex, S., & Bond, S. (2005). Measuring work-life balance and its covariates. *Work, Employment, and Society, 19,* 627–637.

Diaz, I., Chiaburu, D. S., Zimmerman, R. D., & Boswell, W. R. (2012). Communication technology: Pros and cons of constant connection to work. *Journal of Vocational Behavior, 80*, 500–508.

Dickler, J. (2020, December 31). *The year is over and workers left almost all of their vacation days on the table.* CNBC. https://www.cnbc.com/2020/12/31/this-is-what-happens-to-all-those-vacation-days-that-never-got-used.html

Diffle, W., & Landau, S. (2007). *Privacy on the line: The politics of wiretapping and encryption.* MIT Press.

Dillard, J., & Segrin, C. (1987). *Intimate relationships in organizations: Relational types, illicitness, and power.* Paper presented at the annual conference of the International Communication Association, Montreal, Canada.

Dillard, J. P., Solomon, D. H., & Palmer, M. T. (1999). Structuring the concept of relational communication. *Communication Monographs, 66,* 49–65.

Dipboye, R. L. (1992). *Selection interviews: Process perspective.* South-Western.

Dishman, L. (2012, October 10). *How Target's CEO inspires teamwork at a massive scale.* Fast Company. www.fastcompany.com/30019

88/how-targets-ceo-inspires-teamwork-massive-scale

Dorio, M., & Axelrod, A. (2000). *The complete idiots guide to the perfect interview.* Alpha.

Dougherty, D. S. (2001). Sexual harassment as [dys]functional process: A feminist standpoint analysis. *Journal of Applied Communication Research, 29,* 372–402.

Doyle, T. A. (1998). *Allyn & Bacon quick guide to the Internet for speech communication.* Allyn & Bacon.

Drago, R. (2007). *Striking a balance: Work, family, and life.* Dollars & Sense.

Driscoll, K., & Wiebe, E. (2007). Technical spirituality at work: Jacques Ellul on workplace spirituality. *Journal of Management Inquiry, 16*, 333–348.

Duck, S. W. (1994). *Meaningful relationships.* SAGE.

Duck, S. W. (2007). *Human relationships* (4th ed.). SAGE.

Duffy, K., & Nicoll, A. (2021, December 10). *Better.com's CEO is 'taking time off effective immediately' after firing 900 employees on Zoom.* Business Insider. https://www.businessinsider.com/better-ceo-takes-leave-fires-900-employees-zoom-2021-12

Duffy, M., & Sperry, L. (2007). Workplace mobbing: Individual and family health consequences. *Family Journal: Counseling and Therapy for Couples and Families, 15,* 398–404.

Duffy, M., & Sperry, L. (2012). *Mobbing: Causes, consequences and solutions.* Oxford University Press.

Dunn, M. (2018). *Who chooses part-time work and why?* Bureau of Labor Statistics. https://www.bls.gov/opub/mlr/2018/article/pdf/who-chooses-part-time-work-and-why.pdf

Eadie, W. F. (2009). In plain sight: Gay and lesbian communication and culture. In L. W. Samovar, R. Porter, & E. R. McDaniel (Eds.), *Intercultural communication: A reader* (9th ed., pp. 219–231). Wadsworth.

Edwards, A., Edwards, C., Wahl, S. T., & Myers, S. (2019). *The communication age: Connecting and engaging* (3rd ed.). SAGE.

Edwards, C., Edwards, A., Qing, Q., & Wahl, S. T. (2007). The influence of computer-mediated word-of-mouth communication on student perceptions of instructors and attitudes toward learning course content. *Communication Education, 56*, 255–277.

Edwards, J. R., & Rothbard, N. P. (2000). Mechanisms linking work and family: Clarifying the relationship between work and family constructs. *Academy of Management Review, 25*, 178–199.

Eikhof, D. R. (2012). A double-edged sword: Twenty-first century workplace trends and gender equality. *Gender in Management: An International Journal, 27*(1), 7–22.

Eisenberg, E., Goodall, H. L., Jr., & Trethewey, A. (2007). *Organizational communication: Balancing creativity and constraint* (5th ed.). Bedford/St Martin's.

Ekman, P. (1965). Communication through nonverbal behavior: A source of information about an interpersonal relationship. In S. S. Tomkins & C. E. Izard (Eds.), *Affect, cognition, and personality* (pp. 390–442). Springer.

Ekman, P., & Friesen, W. V. (1969a). Nonverbal leakage and clues to deception. *Psychiatry, 32*, 88–106.

Ekman, P., & Friesen, W. V. (1969b). The repertoire of nonverbal behavior: Categories, origins, usage, and coding. *Semiotica, 1*, 49–98.

Engelberg, E., & Sjoberg, L. (2004). Emotional intelligence, affect intensity, and social adjustment. *Personality and Individual Differences, 37*, 533–542.

Equal Employment Opportunity Commission. (2004). Guidelines on discrimination because of sex. *Federal Register, 45*, 74676–74677.

Evans, G. W., Becker, F. D., Zahn, A., Keesee, A. M., & Bilotta, E. (2012). Capturing the ecology of workplace stress with cumulative risk assessment. *Environment and Behavior, 44*(1), 136–154.

Evans-Reber, K. (2021, November 10). *How to meet Gen Z's workplace expectations.* Forbes. https://www.forbes.com/sites/forbeshumanresourcescouncil/2021/11/10/how-to-meet-gen-zsworkplace-expectations/?sh= 750b0f4b74ff

Evanschitzky, H., Sharma, A., & Prykop, C. (2012). The role of the sales employee in securing customer satisfaction. *European Journal of Marketing*, *46*(3), 489–508.

Farrington, R. (2021, August 26). *More companies are offering college tuition benefits to their employees*. Forbes. https://www.forbes.com/sites/robertfarrington/2021/08/26/more-companies-are-offering-college-tuition-benefits-to-their-employees/?sh=650dbb932fba

Ferguson, M., Carlson, D., Zivnuska, S., & Whitten, D. (2012). Support at work and home: The path to satisfaction through balance. *Journal of Vocational Behavior*, *80*(2), 299–307.

Ferré-Sadurní, L., & Bromwich, J. E. (2021, November 11). *Andrew Cuomo is charged in sexual misconduct complaint*. The New York Times. https://www.nytimes.com/2021/10/28/nyregion/cuomo-forcible-touching-complaint.html

Ferris, P. (2004). A preliminary typology of organizational response to allegations of workplace bullying: See no evil, hear no evil, speak no evil. *British Journal of Guidance and Counseling*, *32*, 389–395.

Festinger, L. (1957). *A theory of cognitive dissonance*. Stanford University Press.

Fiedler, F. E. (1997). Situational control and a dynamic theory of leadership. In K. Grint (Ed.), *Leadership: Classical, contemporary, and critical approaches*. Oxford University Press.

Fiedler, F. E., & Garcia, J. E. (1987). *New approaches to effective leadership*. Wiley.

Finder, A. (2006, June 11). For some, online persona undermines a resume. *New York Times*, p. 11.

Fine, M. G. (1996). Cultural diversity in the workplace: The state of the field. *Journal of Business Communication*, *33*, 485–502.

Fisher, R., Ury, W., & Patton, B. (1991). *Getting to yes: Negotiating agreement without giving in* (2nd ed.). Penguin Books.

Fisher, W. R. (1984). Narration as human communication paradigm: The case of public moral argument. *Communication Monographs*, *51*, 1–22.

Fleming, P. (2007). Sexuality, power, and resistance in the workplace. *Organization Studies*, *28*, 230–256.

Flynn, N. (2006a). *Blog rules: A business guide to managing policy, public relations, and legal issues*. AMACOM.

Flynn, N. (2006b). *E-mail management: 50 tips for keeping your inbox under control*. Thomson Course Technology.

Flynn, N. (2009). *The e-policy handbook: Rules and best practices to safely manage your company's email, blogs, social networking, and other electronic communication tools* (2nd ed.). AMACOM.

Flynn, N., & Flynn, T. (2003). *Writing effective e-mail: Improving your electronic communication*. Thomson Course Technology.

Foley, G. N., & Gentile, J. P. (2010). Nonverbal communication in psychotherapy. *Psychiatry (Edgmont)*, *7*(6), 38–44.

Ford, C. E., & Stickle, T. (2012). Securing recipiency in workplace meetings: Multimodal practices. *Discourse Studies*, *14*(1), 11–30.

Fortune. (2021). *Fortune 100 best companies to work for: 2021*. https://fortune.com/best-companies/2021/

Foste, E. A., & Botero, I. C. (2012). Personal reputation: Effects of upward communication on impressions about new employees. *Management Communication Quarterly*, *26*(1), 48–73.

Freiberg, K., & Freiberg, J. (1996). *NUTS! Southwest Airlines' crazy recipe for business and personal success*. Bard.

French, J. R. P., & Raven, B. (1968). The bases of power. In D. Cartwright & A. Zander (Eds.), *Group dynamics* (pp. 601–623). Harper & Row.

Friedman, M. (1996). *Type A behavior: Its diagnosis and treatment*. Plenum.

Friedman, M., & Rosenman, R. H. (1974). *Type A behavior and your heart*. Knopf.

Fryer, B. (2009, November 5). Is listening an endangered skill? *Harvard Business Review Blog Network*. blogs.hbr.

org/hbr/hbreditors/2009/11/is_listening_an_endangered_ski.html

Fulk, J., & Mani, S. (1986). Distortion of communication in hierarchical relationships. In M. L. McLaughlin (Ed.), *Communication yearbook*, (Vol. 9, pp. 483–510). SAGE.

Gabbott, M., & Hogg, G. (2000). An empirical investigation of the impact of non-verbal communication on service evaluation. *European Journal of Marketing*, *34*, 384–399.

Galliard, B. M., Myers, K. K., & Seibold, D. R. (2010). Organizational assimilation: A multidimensional reconceptualization and measure. *Management Communication Quarterly*, *24*, 552–578.

Genova, G. L. (2009). No place to play: Current employee privacy rights in social networking sites. *Business Communication Quarterly*, *72*, 97–101.

Gibbs, M., Hewing, P., Hulbert, J., Ramsey, D., & Smith, A. (1985). How to teach effective listening skills in a basic communication class: Teaching methodology and concepts committee. *Business Communication Quarterly*, *48*, 30–33.

Gilbert, J., Carr-Ruffino, N., Ivancevich, J. M., & Konopaske, R. (2012). Toxic versus cooperative behaviors at work: The role of organizational culture and leadership in creating community-centered organizations. *International Journal of Leadership Studies*, *7*(1), 29–47.

Gillett, R. (2017, December 6). *The 50 best places to work in 2018, according to employees*. Business Insider. https://www.businessinsider.com/best-places-to-work-2018-2017-12

Glavin, P., & Schieman, S. (2012). Work-family role blurring and work-family conflict: The moderating influence of job resources and job demands. *Work and Occupations*, *39*(1), 71–98.

Goffman, E. (1971). *Relations in public: Microstudies of the public order*. Harper Colophon.

Golden, A. G., & Geisler, C. (2007). Work-life boundary management and the personal digital assistant. *Human Relations*, *60*, 519–551.

Goldstein, A. (2000, February 27). *Breadwinning wives alter marriage equation.* Washington Post, p. A1.

Goleman, D. (1995). *Emotional intelligence.* Bantam.

Goodall, H. L. (1991). *Living in the rock n roll mystery.* Southern Illinois University Press.

Gosselin, P., Gilles, K., & Dore, F. Y. (1995). Components and recognition of facial expression in the communication of emotion by actors. *Journal of Personality and Social Psychology, 68,* 83–96.

Gouran, D. S. (1990). *Making decisions in groups: Choices and consequences.* Prospectus Waveland. (Original work published in 1982)

Gouran, D. S., & Hirokawa, R. Y. (1996). Functional theory and communication in decision-making and problem-solving groups. In R. Y. Hirokawa & M. S. Poole (Eds.), *Communication and group decision-making,* (2nd ed., pp. 55–80). SAGE.

Graham, S., Santos, D., & Vanderplank, R. (2008). Listening comprehension and strategy use: A longitudinal exploration. *System, 36,* 52–68.

Gray, F. E. (2010). Specific oral communication skills desired in new accountancy graduates. *Business Communication Quarterly, 73*(1), 40–67.

Gray, K. (2011). You're hired! Practical tips and techniques for the confident interview. *Legal Information Management, 11*(1), 69–71.

Greenstein, T. (1996). Husband's participation in domestic labor: The interactive effect of wives' and husbands' domestic ideologies. *Journal of Marriage and the Family, 58,* 585–595.

Gregorian, D., & Bronston, S. (2022, January 24). *Biden caught cursing about Fox News reporter on a hot mic.* NBC News. https://www.nbcnews.com/politics/joe-biden/biden-caught-cursing-about-fox-news-reporter-hot-mic-n1287956

Grzywacz, J. G., & Carlson, D. S. (2007). Conceptualizing work-family balance: Implications for practice and research. *Advances in Developing Human Resources, 9,* 455–471.

Gudykunst, W. B. (2004). *Bridging differences* (4th ed.). SAGE.

Gueguen, N., & Jacob, C. (2002). Direct look versus evasive glance and compliance with a request. *Journal of Social Psychology, 142,* 393–397.

Guerin, L., & DelPo, A. (2015). *Create your own employee handbook* (pp. 201–203). NOLO Press.

Haas, J. W., & Arnold, C. (1995). An examination of the role of listening in judgments of communication competence in co-workers. *Journal of Business Communication, 32,* 123–139.

Hackman, J. R. (2012). From causes to conditions in group research. *Journal of Organizational Behavior, 33*(3), 428–444.

Haden, J. (2016, June 20). *27 most common job interview questions and answers.* Inc. https://www.inc.com/jeff-haden/27-most-common-job-interview-questions-and-answers.html

Hall, E. T. (1959). *The silent language.* Doubleday.

Hall, E. T. (1963). A system for the notation of proxemic behavior. *American Anthropology, 65,* 1003–1026.

Hall, E. T. (1966). *The hidden dimension.* Doubleday.

Hamilton, C. (1996). *Essentials of public speaking.* Wadsworth.

Hancock, S. (1999). How to learn more by studying less. *Management Services, 43,* 20–22.

Hansen, R. (n.d.). *Salary negotiation do's and don'ts for job seekers.* https://www.livecareer.com/career/advice/jobs/salary-dos-donts

Hansen, R. (n.d.). *Top tips for how to ace your online video job interview.* Quintessential Careers. www.quintcareers.com/acing_online_video_interview.html

Harris Interactive. (2008). *Expedia.com: 2007 International Vacation Deprivation Survey Results.* https://media.expedia.com/media/content/expus/graphics/promos/vacations/Expedia_International_Vacation_Deprivation_Survey_Results_2007.pdf

Harris, P., & Sachau, D. (2005). Is cleanliness next to godliness? The role of housekeeping in impression formation. *Environment and Behavior, 37,* 81–99.

Harrison, R. P., & Crouch, W. W. (1975). Nonverbal communication: Theory and research. In G. J. Hanneman & W. J. McEwen (Eds.), *Communication and behavior* (pp. 76–97). Addison-Wesley.

Harrison, T. (1985). Communication and participative decision-making: An exploratory study. *Personnel Psychology, 38,* 93–116.

Hartmans, A. (2021, August 2). *Wall Street has a new uniform now that the pandemic has destroyed formal dress codes.* Business Insider. https://www.businessinsider.com/wall-street-workers-wearing-lululemon-pants-untuckit-shirts-2021-8

Harvard University. (2022). *Dress for success.* Harvard University. https://ocs.fas.harvard.edu/dress-success.

Harvey, M. G., Buckley, M. R., Heames, J. T., Zinko, R., Brouer, R. L., & Ferris, G. R. (2007). A bully as an archetypal destructive leader. *Journal of Leadership and Organizational Studies, 14,* 117–129.

Harvey, M. G., Heames, J. T., Richey, R. G., & Leopard, M. (2006). Bullying: From the playground to the boardroom [Electronic version]. *Journal of Leadership and Organizational Studies, 12,* 1–11.

Hellweg, S. (1987). Organizational grapevine: A state of the art review. In B. Dervin & M. Voight (Eds.), *Progress in the communication sciences* (Vol. 8, pp. 213–230). Ablex.

Hermes, J. J. (2008, April 25). *Colleges create Facebook-style social networks to reach alumni.* Chronicle of Higher Education, p. A18.

Hersey, P., & Blanchard, K. H. (1977). *The management of organizational behavior: Utilizing human resources* (3rd ed.). Prentice Hall.

Heslin, R. (1974, May). *Steps toward a taxonomy of touching.* Paper presented at the meeting of the Midwestern Psychological Association, Chicago.

Hewett, B., & Robidoux, C. (2010). *Virtual collaborative writing in the workplace: Computer-mediated communication technologies and processes.* IGI Global.

Hicks, R., & Hicks, K. (1999). *Boomers, X-ers, and other strangers*. Tyndale House.

Highet, G. (1989). *The art of teaching*. Random House.

Hill, C. J., & Garner, S. J. (1991). Factors influencing physician choice. *Hospital and Health Services Administration*, *36*, 491–504.

Hinkle, L. L. (2001). Perceptions of supervisor nonverbal immediacy, vocalics, and subordinate liking. *Communication Research Reports*, *18*, 128–136.

Hishitani, S. (1991). Vividness of image and retrieval time. *Perceptions and Motor Skills*, *73*, 115–123.

Hlemstra, K. M. (1999). Shake my hand: Making the right first impression in business with nonverbal communications. *Business Communication Quarterly*, *62*, 71–74.

Hochschild, A. (with A. Machung). (1989). *The second shift: Working parents and the revolution at home*, Viking/Penguin.

Houtenville, A., & Kalargyrou, V. (2012). People with disabilities: Employers' perspectives on recruitment practices, strategies, and challenges in leisure and hospitality. *Cornell Hospitality Quarterly*, *53*(1), 40–52.

Huffcutt, A. I. (2010). From science to practice: Seven principles for conducting employment interviews. *Applied H.R.M. Research*, *12*(1), 121–136.

Hult, C. A., & Huckin, T. N. (1999). *The new century handbook*. Allyn & Bacon.

Ivy, D. K., & Wahl, S. T. (2019). *Nonverbal communication for a lifetime* (3rd ed.). Kendall Hunt.

Jablin, F. (1979). Superior-subordinate communication: The state of the art. *Psychological Bulletin*, *86*, 1201–1222.

Jablin, F. (1987). Organizational entry, assimilation, and exit. In F. Jablin, L. Putnam, K. Roberts, & L. Porter (Eds.), *Handbook of organizational communication*, (pp. 679–740). SAGE.

Jackson, H. (2005). Sitting comfortably? Then let's talk! *Psychologist*, *18*, 691.

Jafari, J., & Way, W. (1994). Multicultural strategies in tourism. *Cornell Hotel and Restaurant Administration Quarterly*, *35*, 72–80.

Jaffe, G. (2000, April 26). *What's your point, Lieutenant? Just cut to the pie charts: The Pentagon declares war on electronic slide shows that make briefings a pain*. Wall Street Journal, p. A1.

Jalongo, M. R. (2008). *Learning to listen, listening to learn*. National Association for the Education of Young Children.

Jang, C. Y., & Stefanone, M. A. (2011). Non-directed self-disclosure in the blogosphere. *Information, Communication and Society*, *14*(7), 1039–1059.

Janis, I. L. (1982). *Groupthink* (Rev. ed.). Houghton Mifflin.

Janis, I. L. (1989). *Crucial decisions: Leadership in policymaking and crisis management*. Free Press.

Japp, P. M., Meister, M., & Japp, D. K. (2005). *Communication ethics, media, and popular culture*. Peter Lang.

Jeffries, S. (2014, November 7). *Ten tips for a better work-life balance*. The Guardian. www.theguardian.com/life andstyle/2014/nov/07/ten-tips-for-a -better-work-life-balance

Johannesen, R. L., Valde, K. S., & Whedbee, K. E. (2008). *Ethics in human communication* (6th ed.). Waveland.

Johnson, T. (2012). *Negotiating salary 101: Tactics for better compensation*. Women for Hire. http://womenforhire. com/negotiating_salary_benefits/ negotiating_salary_101_tactics_for_ better_compensation/

Jones, S. E., & LeBaron, C. D. (2002). Research on the relationship between verbal and nonverbal communication: Emerging integrations. *Journal of Communication*, *52*, 499–523.

Jovin, E. (2007). *E-mail etiquette for business professionals*. Syntaxis.

Judge, T. A., Higgins, C. A., & Cable, D. M. (2000). The employment interview: A review of recent research and recommendations for future research. *Human Resource Management Review*, *10*, 383–406.

Kals, E., & Jiranek, P. (2012). Organizational justice. *Justice and Conflicts*, *4*, 219–235.

Karanges, E., Johnston, K., Beatson, A. & Lings, I. (2015). The influence of internal communication on employee engagement: A pilot study. *Public Relations Review*, *41*(1), 129–131.

Karl, K., & Peluchette, J. (2006). How does workplace fun impact employee perceptions of customer service quality? *Journal of Leadership and Organizational Studies*, *13*, 1–13.

Katzenbach, J. R., & Smith, D. K. (1993). *The wisdom of teams: Creating the high performance organization*. Harvard Business School Press.

Kauffeld, S., & Lehmann-Willenbrock, N. (2011). Meetings matter: Effects of team meetings on team and organizational success. *Small Group Research*, *43*(2), 130–158.

Kazoleas, D. C. (1993, Winter). A comparison of persuasive effectiveness of qualitative versus quantitative evidence: A test of explanatory hypothesis. *Communication Quarterly*, *41*, 40–50.

Kelleher, Z., & Hall, H. (2005). Response to risk: Experts and end-user perspectives on email security, and the role of the business information professional in policy development. *Business Information Review*, *22*, 46–52.

Kellogg Murray, J. (2021, March 29). *Jobs in diversity, inclusion and belonging have risen 123% since May—here's how to get one*. Indeed, https://www.indeed. com/career-advice/finding-a-job/ diversity-inclusion-and-belonging- jobs-rise

Kelly, J. (2021, August 11). *New policy requires diversity on corporate boards for Nasdaq-listed companies*. Forbes. https: //www.forbes.com/sites/ jackkelly/2021/08/11/new-policy- requires-diversity-on-corporate- boards-for-nasdaq-listed-companies/? sh=325d3d311abe

Kelly, P., Allender, S., & Calquhoun, D. (2007). New work ethics? The corporate athlete's back end index and organizational performance. *Organization*, *14*, 267–285.

Kent, S. *Dick's Sporting Goods to stop selling assault-style rifles immediately*. NJ.com. http://www.nj.com/news/ index.ssf/2018/02/dicks_sporting_ goods_to_stop_selling_assault-style.html

Key, J. (2012). *Journey towards professionalism: Straight talk for today's generation.* Universe.

Keys, K. (2017, April 4). *Seven tips to make your press release search-friendly.* Forbes. https://www.forbes.com/sites/forbesagencycouncil/2017/04/04/seven-tips-to-make-your-press-release-search-friendly/#7f9ed19e308f

Keysar, B., & Henley, A. S. (2002). Speakers' overestimation of their effectiveness. *Psychological Science, 13,* 207–213.

Keyton, J., & Beck, S. J. (2010). Examining emotional communication: Laughter in jury deliberations. *Small Group Research, 41,* 386–407.

Khan, A., & Khan, R. (2012). Understanding and managing workplace bullying. *Industrial and Commercial Training, 44*(2), 85–89.

Khan, F., & Khan, M. E. (2012). Achieving success through effective business communication. *Information and Knowledge Management, 2,* 46–50.

Kibby, M. D. (2005). Email forwardables: Folklore in the age of the Internet. *New Media and Society, 7,* 770–790.

Kinlaw, D. C. (1991). *Developing superior work teams: Building quality and the competitive edge.* Lexington Books.

Kirby, E. L., Golden, A. G., Medved, C. E., Jorgenson, J., & Buzzanell, P. M. (2003). An organizational communication challenge to the discourse of work and family research: From problematics to empowerment. In P. J. Kalbfleisch (Ed.), *Communication yearbook 27* (pp. 1–44). Erlbaum.

Kirby, E. L., & Harter, L. M. (2001). Discourses of diversity and the quality of work life: The character and costs of the managerial metaphor. *Management Communication Quarterly, 15,* 121–127.

Kirkhaug, R. (2010). Charisma or group belonging as antecedents of employee work effort? *Journal of Business Ethics, 96*(4), 647–656.

Kleinke, C. L. (1986). Gaze and eye contact: A research review. *Psychological Bulletin, 100,* 78–100.

Knapp, M. L., & Hall, J. A. (2006). *Nonverbal communication in human interaction* (6th ed.). Thomson/Wadsworth.

Knapp, M. L., & Hall, J. A. (2009). *Nonverbal communication in human interaction.* Wadsworth.

Koballa, T. R., Jr. (1989). Persuading teachers to reexamine the innovative elementary science programs of yesterday: The effect of anecdotal versus data-summary communications. *Journal of Research in Science Teaching, 23,* 437–449.

Konop, J. (2014, June 18). *10 job interview questions you should ask.* Forbes. www.forbes.com/sites/nextavenue/2014/06/18/10-job-interview-questions-you-should-ask/

Konrad, A. M., Moore, M. E., Doherty, A. J., Ng, E. S. W., & Breward, K. (2012). Vocational status and perceived well-being of workers with disabilities. *Equality, Diversity and Inclusion: An International Journal, 31*(2), 100–123.

Krapels, R. H. (2000). Communication training in two companies. *Business Communication Quarterly, 63,* 104–110.

Kress, G. L., & Schar, M. (2012). Teamology—the art and science of design team formation. In H. Plattner, C. Meinel, & L. Leifer (Eds.), *Design thinking research: Studying co-creation in practice,* (pp. 189–209). Springer.

Kuntz, J. R. C., & Gomes, J. F. S. (2012). Transformational change in organizations: A self-regulation approach. *Journal of Organizational Change Management, 25*(1), 143–162.

Kupritz, V., & Hillsman, T. (2011). The impact of the physical environment on supervisory communication skills transfer. *Journal of Business Communication, 48*(2), 148–185.

Langan, K. (2012). Training millennials: A practical and theoretical approach. *References Services Review, 40*(1), 24–48.

Laplante, D., & Ambady, N. (2003). On how things are said: Voice tone, voice intensity, verbal content, and perceptions of politeness. *Journal of Language and Social Psychology, 22,* 434–442.

Lavan, I. (2002). NLP in business—Or more than a trip to the zoo. *Industrial and Commercial Training, 34,* 182–188.

Lawson, H. M., & Leck, K. (2006). Dynamics of Internet dating. *Social Science Computer Review, 24,* 189–208.

Leech, T. (1992). *How to prepare, stage, and deliver winning presentations* (2nd ed.). AMACOM.

Lehrer, V. (1998). Vital speeches of the day. *Journalism, 57,* 139–143.

Leigh, T. W., & Summers, J. O. (2002). An initial evaluation of industrial buyers' impressions of salespersons' nonverbal cues. *Journal of Personal Selling and Sales Management, 22,* 41–54.

Leiter, M. P., Day, A. L., Harvie, P., & Shaughnessy, K. (2007). Personal and organizational knowledge transfer: Implications for worklife engagement. *Human Relations, 60,* 259–283.

Leswing, K. (2021, October 18). *Apple listened to its most loyal customers and fixed its laptop problems from the last five years.* CNBC. https://www.cnbc.com/2021/10/18/apple-new-macbook-pros-fix-laptop-problems-from-the-last-five-years-.html

Levi, D. (2011). *Group dynamics for teams.* SAGE.

Lewis, J. S., & Geroy, G. D. (2000). Employee spirituality in the workplace: A cross-cultural view for the management of spiritual employees. *Journal of Management Education, 24,* 682–694.

Leymann, H., & Gustaffson, A. (1996). Mobbing at work and the development of post traumatic stress disorders. *European Journal of Work and Organizational Psychology, 5,* 251–275.

Li, N., Jackson, M. H., & Trees, A. R. (2008). Relating online: Managing dialectical contradictions in massively multiplayer online role-playing game relationships. *Games and Culture, 3,* 76–97.

Lindsell-Roberts, S. (2004). *Strategic business letters and e-mail.* Houghton Mifflin.

Litovsky, P. (2020, October 20). *How to implement healthy eating while working remotely.* Forbes. https://www.forbes.com/sites/forbesbusinesscouncil/2020/10/20/how-to-implement-healthy-eating-while-working-remotely/?sh=1367de6d6941

Liu, J. (2021, October 6). *These 10 companies have the happiest employees—here's why.* CNET, https://www.cnbc.com/2021/10/06/comparably-top-10-companies-with-the-happiest-employees-in-2021.html

Livingston, R. (2020, October). *How to promote racial equity in the workplace.* Harvard Business Review. https://hbr.org/2020/09/how-to-promote-racial-equity-in-the-workplace

Locher, M. A. (2010). Introduction: Politeness and impoliteness in computer-mediated communication. *Journal of Politeness Research, 6*(1), 1–5.

Locke, E., & Latham, G. (1984). *Goal setting: A motivational technique that really works!* Prentice Hall.

Lohmann, A., Arriaga, X. B., & Goodfriend, W. (2003). Close relationships and placemaking: Do objects in a couple's home reflect couplehood? *Personal Relationships, 10*, 437–449.

Louët, S. (2012, January 27). Your voice: Your passport to authority. *Science.* sciencecareers.sciencemag.org/career_magazine/previous_issues/articles/2012_01_27/caredit.a1200010

Lumsden, G., & Lumsden, D. (1997). *Communicating in groups and teams: Sharing leadership* (2nd ed.). Wadsworth.

Mann, R. D. (1959). A review of the relationship between personality and performance in small groups. *Psychological Bulletin, 66*(4), 241–270.

Manning, G. L., & Reece, B. (1989). *Selling today: An extension of the marketing concept.* Allyn & Bacon.

Martin, M. (2012). *Happiness and the good life.* Oxford University Press.

Martin, W. B. (1986). Defining what quality service is for you. *Cornell Hotel and Restaurant Administration Quarterly, 26*, 32–39.

Marulanda-Carter, L., & Jackson, T. W. (2012). Effects of e-mail addiction and interruptions on employees. *Journal of Systems and Information Technology, 14*(1), 82–94.

Maslow, A. (1965). *Eupsychian management.* R. D. Irwin.

Mathenge, G. D. (2011). Ethical considerations in human resource management in Kenya: Theory and practice. *Public Policy and Administration Research, 1*(4), 8–20.

Mayer, J., & Salovey, P. (1993). The intelligence of emotional intelligence. *Intelligence, 17*, 433–442.

McCroskey, J. C. (1982). Oral communication apprehension: A reconceptualization. In M. Burgoon (Ed.), *Communication yearbook 6* (pp. 136–170). SAGE.

McCroskey, J. C. (1984). The communication apprehension perspective. In J. A. Daly & J. C. McCroskey (Eds.), *Avoiding communication: Shyness, reticence, and communication apprehension* (pp. 13–38). SAGE.

McCroskey, J. C., & Teven, J. (1999). Goodwill: A reexamination of the construct and its measurement. *Communication Monographs, 66*, 90–103.

McDaniel, E. R., Samovar, L. A., & Porter, R. E. (2009). Understanding intercultural communication: The working principles. In L. W. Samovar, R. Porter, & E. R. McDaniel (Eds.), *Intercultural communication: A reader* (9th ed., pp. 6–17). Wadsworth.

McDermott, E. (2006). Surviving in dangerous places: Lesbian identity performances in the workplace, social class, and psychological health. *Feminism and Psychology, 16*, 193–211.

McDonald, K. S., & Hite, L. M. (2008). The next generation of career success: Implications for HRD. *Advances in Developing Human Resources, 10*, 86–103.

McGregor, D. (1960). *The human side of enterprise.* McGraw Hill.

McKnight, M. R. (1995). The nature of people skills. *Journal of Management Education, 19*, 190–204.

Medved, C. E., & Kirby, E. L. (2005). Family CEOs: A feminist analysis of corporate mothering discourses. *Management Communication Quarterly, 18*, 435–478.

Mehrabian, A. (1981). *Silent messages: Implicit communication of emotions and attitudes.* Wadsworth.

Metsämäki, M. (2012). Persuasive discourse in EFL debate. *Theory and Practice in Language Studies, 2*(2), 205–213.

Mitroff, I., & Kilmann, R. (1975). Stories managers tell: A new tool for organizational problem solving. *Management Review, 64*, 18–28.

Moe, N. B., Dingsøyr, T., & Dybå, T. (2010). A teamwork model for understanding an agile team: A case study of a scrum project. *Information and Software Technology, 52*(5), 480–491.

Molloy, J. T. (1988). *New dress for success.* Warner Books Edition.

Molloy, J. T. (1996). *New women's dress for success.* Warner Books Edition.

Monster. (2021). *The future of work: 2021 global outlook. Monster Worldwide, Inc.* https://media.newjobs.com/cms/content30/images/Future-of-Work_2021-Global-Outlook.report.pdf

Morales, M., Piero, J. M., Rodriguez, I., & Bliese, P. D. (2012). Perceived collective burnout: A multilevel explanation of burnout. *Anxiety, Stress and Coping: An International Journal, 25*(1), 43–61.

Morand, D. A. (2001). The emotional intelligence of managers: Assessing the construct of validity of a nonverbal measure of "people skills." *Journal of Business and Psychology, 16*, 21–33.

Morasch, L. J. (2004). *I hear you talking, but I don't understand you: Medical jargon and clear communication.* Molina Healthcare and California Academy of Family Physicians.

Morris, D. (1985). *Body watching.* Crown.

Morris, M. L., & Madsen, S. R. (2007). Advancing work-life integration in individuals, organizations, and communities. *Advances in Developing Human Resources, 9*, 439–454.

Muir, C. (1996). Workplace readiness for communicating diversity. *Journal of Business Communication, 33*, 475–484.

Mumby, D. K., & Putnam, L. L. (1992). The politics of emotion: A feminist reading of bounded rationality. *Academy of Management Review, 17*, 465–486.

Myers, K. K., & McPhee, R. D. (2006). Influences on member assimilation in workgroups in high-reliability organizations: A multilevel analysis. *Human Communication Research, 32*, 440–468.

Myers, S. A., & Anderson, C. M. (2008). *The fundamentals of small group communication.* SAGE.

Nelson, D., & Heeney, W. (1984). Directed listening: A model for administrative communication. *National Association of Secondary School Principals, 68,* 124–129.

Nichols, R. G., & Stevens, L. A. (1957, September). *Listening to people.* Harvard Business Review, https://doi.org/hbr.org/1957/09/listening-to-people/ar/1

Nickerson, R. S. (1980). Short-term memory for complex meaningful visual configurations: Demonstration of capacity. *Canadian Journal of Psychology, 19,* 155–160.

Nitin, A. B., Shamra, S. M., Kumar, K., Aggarwal, A., Goyal, S., Choudhary, K., Chawla, K., Jain, K., & Bhasin, M. (2012). Classification of flames in computer-mediated communications. *International Journal of Computer Applications, 14*(6), 1–6.

Nixon, J., & West, J. (1989). Listening: Vital to communication. *Business Communication Quarterly, 52,* 15–18.

Nolan, M. J. (1975). The relationship between verbal and nonverbal communication. In G. J. Hanneman & W. J. McEwen (Eds.), *Communication and behavior* (pp. 98–119). Addison-Wesley.

O'Connor, E. S. (1993). People skills as a discipline, pedagogy, and set of standard practices. *Journal of Management Education, 17,* 218–227.

O'Keefe, D. J. (1990). *Persuasion: Theory and research,* SAGE.

O'Sullivan, M. (2005). Emotional intelligence and deception detection: Why most people can't "read" others, but a few can. In R. E. Riggio & R. S. Feldman (Eds.), *Applications of nonverbal communication* (pp. 215–253). Erlbaum.

Office of Women's Health. (2018, May 17). *Stress and your health.* h ttps://www.womenshealth.gov/mental-health/good-mental-health/stress-and-your-health

Okoro, E., & Washington, M. (2011). Communicating in a multicultural classroom: A study of students' nonverbal behavior and attitudes toward faculty attire. *Journal of College Teaching and Learning, 8*(7), 27–38.

Okoro, E. A., & Washington, M. C. (2012). Workforce diversity and organizational communication: Analysis of human capital performance and productivity. *Journal of Diversity Management, 7*(1), 57–62.

Parlamis, J. D. (2012). Venting as emotion regulation: The influence of venting responses and respondent identity on anger and emotional tone. *International Journal of Conflict Management, 23*(1), 77–96.

Patel, S. (2017, March 27). *6 ways to take your next presentation to the next level.* Entrepreneur. https://www.entrepreneur.com/article/287146

Patterson, K., Grenny, J., McMillan, R., & Switzler, A. (2005). *Crucial confrontations: Tools for resolving broken promises, violated expectations, and bad behavior.* McGraw Hill.

Pearce, W. B., Cronen, V. E., & Conklin, F. (1979). On what to look at when analyzing communication: A hierarchical model of actors' meanings. *Communication, 4,* 195–220.

Peluchette, J. V., Karl, K., & Rust, K. (2006). Dressing to impress: Beliefs and attitudes regarding workplace attire. *Journal of Business and Psychology, 21,* 45–63.

Peters, T. (1987). *Thriving on chaos.* Knopf.

Peterson, D. R. (1992). Interpersonal relationships as a link between person and environment. In W. B. Walsh, K. H. Craik, & R. H. Price (Eds.), *Person-environment psychology: Models and perspectives* (pp. 127–155). Erlbaum.

Petronio, S. (2000). *Balancing the secrets of private disclosures.* Erlbaum.

Petronio, S. (2002). *Boundaries of privacy: Dialectics of disclosure.* State University of New York Press.

Petronio, S. (2007). Translational research endeavors and the practices of communication privacy management. *Journal of Applied Communication Research, 35,* 218–222.

Pew Research Center. (2007, July 12). *Fewer mothers prefer full-time work: From 1997 to 2007.* http://www.pewsocialtrends.org/2007/07/12/fewer-mothers-prefer-full-time-work/

Pickholz, M. G., & Zimmerman, P. (2002). Litigation in the current environment. *CPA Journal, 72,* 62–63.

Piercy, C. W., & Underhill, G. R. (2020). Expectations of technology use during meetings: An experimental test of manager policy, device use, and task-acknowledgment. *Mobile Media & Communication, 9*(1), 78–102.

Plantin, C. (2012). Persuasion or alignment? *Argumentation, 26*(1), 83–97.

Posthuma, R. A. (2012). Conflict management and emotions. *International Journal of Conflict Management, 23*(1), 4–5.

Powell, G. (2012). Six ways of seeing the elephant: The intersection of sex, gender, and leadership. *Gender in Management: An International Journal, 27*(2), 119–141.

Press-Reynolds, K. (2021, September 21). *Nascar, Tinder, and Tampax used a TikTok creator's ugly logo redesigns for their profile pictures.* Business Insider. https://www.businessinsider.in/thelife/news/nascar-tinder-and-tampax-used-a-tiktok-creators-ugly-logo-redesigns-for-their-profile-pictures/articleshow/86383234.cms

Pugh, D. (2001). Service with a smile: Emotional contagion in the service encounter. *Academy of Management Journal, 44,* 1018–1027.

Quintanilla, K., & Mallard, J. (2008). Understanding the role of communication bravado: An important issue for trainers/ teachers. *Texas Speech Communication Journal, 33,* 44–49.

Quiroz-Gutierrez, M. (2021, June 2). *The top 20 Fortune 500 cmopanies on diversity and incusion.* Fortune. https://fortune.com/2021/06/02/fortune-500-companies-diversity-inclusion-numbers-refinitiv-measure-up/

Ramsey, R., & Sohi, R. (1997). Listening to your customers: The impact of perceived salesperson listening behavior on relationship qutcomes. *SpringerLink, 25,* 127. https://doi.org/10.1007/BF02894348

Rapoport, R., & Bailyn, L. (1996). *Rethinking life and work: Toward a better future*. Ford Foundation.

Redfield, R. (1953). *The primitive world and its transformation*. Cornell University Press.

Regenbogen, C., Schneider, D. A., Gur, R. E., Schneider, F., Habel, U., & Kellermann, T. (2012). Multimodal human communication-targeting facial expressions, speech content and prosody. *NeuroImage, 60*, 2346–2356.

Reid, A. (2014, September 2). *3 brands that prove listening to customers is key to company comebacks*. Fast Company. w ww.fastcompany.com/3035054/hit-the -ground-running/3-brands-that-prove -listening-to-customers-is-key-to-company-comeback

Rezab, J. (2015, March 15). *Facebook is in the middle of the biggest media shift since the internet*. Forbes. www.forbes.com/ sites/janrezab/2015/05/15/facebook-is-in-the-middle-of-the-biggest-media-shift-since-the-internet/

Rhoads, M. (2010). Face-to-face and computer-mediated communication: What does theory tell us and what have we learned so far? *Journal of Planning Literature, 25*(2), 111–122.

Richmond, V. P., McCroskey, J. C., & Johnson, A. E. (2003). Development of the Nonverbal Immediacy Scale (NIS): Measures of self-and other-perceived nonverbal immediacy. *Communication Quarterly, 51*, 502–515.

Riggio, R. E. (2005). Business applications of nonverbal communication. In R. E. Riggio & R. S. Feldman (Eds.), *Applications of nonverbal communication* (pp. 119–138). Erlbaum.

Riley, P., & Eisenberg, E. (1992). *The ACE model of management*. Unpublished working paper, University of Southern California.

Risman, B., & Godwin, S. (2001). Twentieth-century changes in economic work and family. In D. Vannoy (Ed.), *Gender mosaics* (pp. 134–144). Roxbury.

Ritchie, L. (2012). Negotiating power through communication: Using an employee participation intervention to construct a discursive space for debate.

Journal of Communication Management, 16(1), 95–107.

Roach, K. D. (1997). Effects of graduate teaching assistant attire on student learning, misbehaviors, and ratings of instruction. *Communication Quarterly, 45*, 125–141.

Roberts, J. A., & Wasieleski, D. M. (2012). Moral reasoning in computer-based task environments: Exploring the interplay between cognitive and technological factors on individuals' propensity to break rules. *Journal of Business Ethics, 106*, 1–22.

Robinson, E. J., & Robinson, W. P. (1982). The advancement of children's verbal referential communication skills: The role of metacognitive guidance. *International Journal of Behavioral Development, 5*, 329–355.

Rosener, J. B. (1997). Sexual static. In K. Grint (Ed.), Leadership: Classical, contemporary, and critical approaches. Oxford University Press.

Ruetzler, T., Taylor, J., Reynolds, D., Baker, W., & Killen, C. (2012). What is professional attire today? A conjoint analysis of personal presentation attributes. *International Journal of Hospitality Management, 31*(3), 937–943.

Rule, J. B. (2007). *Privacy in peril: How we are sacrificing a fundamental right in exchange for security and convenience*. Oxford University Press.

Ryan, R. (2021, February 9). *Want to be noticed by recruiters? Try this resume strategy to get through the applicant tracking system*. Forbes. https://ww w.forbes.com/sites/robinryan/2021 /02/09/resume-keywords-and-the -applicant-tracking-system-atswhat-you-need-to-know/?sh=61ef1c74bcc3

Sadler, P. (1997). *Leadership*. Kogan.

Sakdiyakorn, M., Golubovskaya, M., & Solnet, D. (2021). Understanding Generation Z through collective consciousness: Impacts for hospitality work and employment. *International Journal of Hospitality Management, 94*.

Salovey, P., & Mayer, J. (1990). Emotional intelligence. *Imagination, Cognition, and Personality, 9*, 185–211.

Sammer, J. (2020). *Improving the lives of employee caregivers makes business sense*. Society of Human Resource Management. https://www.shrm.org/ resourcesandtools/hr-topics/benefits/ pages/improving-lives-of-employee-caregivers-makes-business-sense.aspx

Samovar, L., Porter, R. E., & McDaniel, E. R. (2007). *Communication between cultures* (6th ed.). Wadsworth.

Sampson, E. (1995). First impressions: The power of personal style. *Library Management, 16*, 25–29.

Samsung. (2021, November 8). *Samsung Home Appliances ranked highest in customer satisfaction by 2021 ACSI survey*. Samsung. https://news.samsung.com/ us/samsung-home-appliances-ranked -highest-customer-satisfaction-2021 -acsi-survey/

Sanders, C. R. (2020, November 10). Historically Black colleges and universities are remaking American politics. *The Washington Post*. https://www.was hingtonpost.com/outlook/2020/11/10/ historically-black-colleges-universities -are-remaking-american-politics/

Sandvik, P. L., & Tracy, S. J. (2012). Answering five key questions about workplace bullying: How communication scholarship provides thought leadership for transforming abuse at work. *Management Communication Quarterly, 26*(1), 3–47.

Savolainen, R. (2007). Filtering and withdrawing: Strategies for coping with information overload in everyday contexts. *Journal of Information Science, 33*, 611–621.

Scarduzio, J. A., & Geist-Martin, P. (2010). Accounting for victimization: Male professors' ideological positioning in stories of sexual harassment. *Management Communication Quarterly, 24*(3), 419–445.

Schein, E. (1992). *Organizational culture and leadership* (2nd ed.). Jossey Bass.

Schiffer, Z. (2019, December 5). *Emotional baggage*. The Verge. https:// www.theverge.com/2019/12/5/ 20995453/away-luggage-ceo-stephkorey-toxic-work-environment-travel-inclusion

Schiller, S. Z., & Mandviwalla, M. (2007). Virtual team research: An analysis of theory use and framework for theory appropriation. *Small Group Research, 38*, 12–59.

Schor, J. B. (1992). *The overworked American: The unexpected decline of leisure.* Basic.

Schor, J. B. (1998). *The overspent American: Why we buy what we don't need.* Basic Books.

Scott, E. (2007). *Stress: How it affects your body and how you can stay healthier.* stress.about.com/od/stresshealth/a/stresshealth.htm

Shaw, M. E. (1981). *Group dynamics: The psychology of small group behavior* (3rd ed.). McGraw-Hill.

Sheriff, A., & Ravishankar, G. (2012). The techniques and rationale of e-surveillance practices in organizations. *International Journal of Multidisciplinary Research, 2*(2), 281–290.

Shipley, D., & Schwalbe, W. (2008). *Send: Why people email so badly and how to do it better.* Knopf.

Shirey, M. R. (2012). Group think, organizational strategy, and change. *Journal of Nursing Administration, 42*(2), 67–71.

Shivaram, D. (2021, July 31). *Across federal workforce, people with disabilities see need for more representation.* NPR. https://www.npr.org/2021/07/31/1020746037/disability-access-representation-ada

Shoichet, C. E. (2021, February 28). *Read the full text of Jane Fonda's powerful speech at the Golden Globes.* CNN. https://www.cnn.com/2021/02/28/entertainment/jane-fonda-golden-globes-speech-full-text-trnd/index.html

Simon, L. S., Judge, T. A., & Halvorsen-Ganepola, M. D. (2010). In good company? A multi-study, multi-level investigation of the effects of coworker relationships on employee well-being. *Journal of Vocational Behavior, 76*, 534–546.

Slovensky, R., & Ross, W. H. (2012). Should human resource managers use social media to screen job applicants?

Managerial and legal issues in the USA. *Info, 14*(1), 55–69.

Smith, J. (2013, August 13). *How to give a great speech.* Forbes. www.forbes.com/sites/jacquelynsmith/2013/08/13/how-to-give-a-great-speech-3/

Smith, J. (2014, July 1). 7 excellent ways to start a presentation. *Business Insider.* www.businessinsider.com/excellent-ways-to-start-a-presentation-2014-7?op=1

Smith, T. E., & Bainbridge, A. (2006). Get real: Does practicing speeches before an audience improve performance? *Communication Quarterly, 54*, 111–125.

Snyder, J. (2012). Extending the empathic communication model of burnout: Incorporating individual differences to learn more about workplace emotion, communicative responsiveness, and burnout. *Communication Quarterly, 60*(1), 122–142.

Solove, D. J. (2008). *Understanding privacy.* Harvard University Press.

Sorenson, S. (2017, April 4). *Teamwork is what separates the good from great companies.* Huffington Post. https://www.huffingtonpost.com/entry/teamwork-is-what-separates-the-good-from-great-companies_us_58e3c783e4b09deecf0e1a88?ncid=engmodushpmg00000003

Speaking with power: Tips on giving an unforgettable speech. (2018, February 1). *360 Live Media.* https://360livemedia.com/2018/02/01/speaking-with-power-tips-on-giving-an-unforgettable-speech/

Spitzberg, B. H. (2006). Preliminary development of a model and measure of computer-mediated communication (CMC) competence. *Journal of Computer-Mediated Communication, 11*(2), 629–666.

Stahl, A. (2017, March 30). *5 secrets to achieving work-life balance.* Forbes. https://www.forbes.com/sites/ashleystahl/2017/03/30/5-secrets-to-achieving-work-life-balance/#4c668fca3bba

Stamou, A. G., Maroniti, K. S., & Dinas, K. D. (2012). Representing "traditional" and "progressive" women in Greek television: The role of

"feminine"/"masculine" speech styles in the mediation of gender identity construction. *Women's Studies International Forum, 35*, 38–52.

Staples, S. D., & Webster, J. (2007). Exploring traditional and virtual team members' "best practices": A social cognitive theory perspective. *Small Group Research, 38*, 60–97.

Stengel, J. R., Dixon, A., & Allen, C. (2003, November). *Listening begins at home.* Harvard Business Review. hbr.org/2003/11/listening-begins-at-home/ar/1

Stogdill, R. M. (1948). Personal factors associated with leadership: A survey of the literature. *Journal of Psychology, 25*, 35–71.

Stout, M. (2005). *The sociopath next door.* Broadway.

Supan, D. (2017, November 14). *How to use emoticons, memes and GIFs in social media marketing without embarrassing yourself.* https://www.semrush.com/blog/how-to-use-emoticons-memes-and-gifs-in-social-media-marketing/

Sypher, B., Bostrom, R., & Seibert, J. (1989). Listening, communication abilities, and success at work. *Journal of Business Communication, 26*, 293–303.

Tamaki, J. (1991, October 10). *Sexual harassment in the workplace.* Los Angeles Times, p. D2.

Tannen, D. (1990). *You just don't understand: Women and men in conversation.* HarperCollins.

Tannen, D. (1998). *The argument culture: Stopping America's war of words.* Ballantine.

Tayeb, Z. (2021, August 8). *After this CEO raised his company's minimum wage to $70,000, he said the number of babies born to staff each year grew 10-fold and revenue soared.* Business Insider, https://www.businessinsider.com/gravity-payments-dan-price-ceo-raise-minimum-wage-revenue-2021-8

Taylor, B., & Conrad, C. (1992). Narratives of sexual harassment: Organizational dimensions. *Journal of Applied Communication Research, 20*, 401–418.

TED. (2022). *The 10 most popular TEDx talks*. TED. https://www.ted.com/play lists/180/the_10_most_popular_tedx _talks

Teece, D. J. (2010). Business models, business strategy and innovation. *Long Range Planning*, *43*, 172–194.

Tews, M., Michel, J. W., & Bartlett, A. (2012). The fundamental role of workplace fun in applicant attraction. *Journal of Leadership and Organizational Studies*, *19*(1), 105–114.

Thomas, M. (2021, July 26). *After hours emails are worse than you think*. Forbes. https://www.forbes.com/sites/mau rathomas/2021/07/26/after-hours-emails-are-worse-than-you-think/?sh =280afcf66420

Thomas, S. P. (1998). *Transforming nurses' anger and pain*. Springer.

Thompson, B. (2008). Characteristics of parent-teacher e-mail communication. *Communication Education*, *57*, 201–223.

Thoroughgood, N., Sawyer, K., & Webster, J. (2020, April). *Creating a trans-inclusive workplace*. Harvard Business Review. https://hbr.org/2020/03/creating-a-trans-inclusive-workplace

Ting-Toomey, S. (1990). *A face negotiation perspective communicating for peace*. SAGE.

Totenberg, N. (2020, June 15). *Supreme Court delivers major victory to LGBTQ employees*. NPR. https://w ww.npr.org/2020/06/15/86349884 8/supreme-court-delivers-major-victory-to-lgbtq-employees

Tracy, S. J., Lutgen-Sandvik, P., & Alberts, J. K. (2006). Nightmares, demons, and slaves: Exploring the painful metaphors of workplace bullying. *Management Communication Quarterly*, *20*, 148–185.

Travers, N. L. (2012). Academic perspectives on college-level learning: Implications for workplace learning. *Journal of Workplace Learning*, *24*(2), 105–118.

Trenerry, B., & Paradies, Y. (2012). Organizational assessment: An overlooked approach to managing diversity and addressing racism in the workplace. *Journal of Diversity Management*, *7*(1), 11–26.

Tuckman, B. W., & Jensen, M. C. (1977). Stages of small group development revisited. *Group and Organizational Studies*, *2*, 419–427.

Tufte, E. (2003, September). *PowerPoint is evil! Wired*. www.wired.com/wired/arc hive/11.09/ppt2.html

Turak, A. (2012, March 2). *10 leadership lessons from the IBM executive school*. Forbes. www.forbes.com/sites/augustturak/2012/03/02/10-leadership-lessons-from-the-ibm-executive-school/

Twitter. (2018). Our company. about.twit ter.com/company

U.S. Bureau of Labor Statistics. (2010). *Occupational outlook handbook*. U.S. Department of Labor.

Vallotton, C., & Ayoub, C. (2009). Symbols build communication and thought: The role of gestures and words in the development of engagement skill and social-emotional concepts during toddlerhood. *Social Development*, *19*, 601–626.

Vanevenhoven, J., Delaney-Klinger, K., Winkel, D., & Wagner, R. (2011). How to get in the "first pile". *American Journal of Business Education*, *4*(8), 19–24.

Varlander, S. (2012). Individual flexibility in the workplace: A spatial perspective. *Journal of Applied Behavioral Science*, *48*(1), 33–61.

Vidal, M. E., Leiva, D. C., & Navarro, J. G. (2012). Gaps between managers. *International Journal of Human Resource Management*, *23*(4), 645–661.

Von Oech, R. (1983). *A whack on the side of the head*. Warner.

Von Oech, R. (1986). *A kick in the seat of the pants*. HarperPerennial.

Vorakulpipat, C., Visoottiviseth, V., & Siwamogsatham, S. (2012). Polite sender: A resource-saving spam e-mail countermeasure based on sender responsibilities and recipient justifications. *Computers and Security*, *31*(3), 286–298.

Wahl, S. T., McBride, M. C., & Schrodt, P. (2005). Becoming "point and click" parents: A case study of communication and online adoption. *Journal of Family Communication*, *5*, 279–294.

Wahl, S. T., & Scholl, J. C. (2014). *Communication and culture in your life*, Kendall Hunt.

Wahl, S., & Simmons, J. (2018). *Intercultural communication in your life*. Kendall Hunt.

Waldeck, J., Seibold, D., & Flanagin, A. (2005). Organizational assimilation and technology use. *Communication Monographs*, *72*, 161–183.

Walther, J. B., Loh, T., & Granka, L. (2005). Let me count the ways: The interchange of verbal and nonverbal cues in computer-mediated and face-to-face affinity. *Journal of Language and Social Psychology*, *24*, 36–65.

Wang, W. (2013, August 19). *Mothers and work: What's "ideal"? Pew Research Center*. www.pewresearch.org/fact-tank/2013/08/19/mothers-and-work-whats-ideal/

Wang, Z., David, P., Srivastava, J., Powers, S., Brady, C., D'Angelo, J., & Moreland, J. (2012). Behavioral performance and visual attention in communication multitasking: A comparison between instant messaging and online voice chat. *Computers in Human Behavior*, *28*(3), 968–975.

Watkins-Allen, M., Coopman, S. J., Hart, J. L., & Walker, K. L. (2007). Workplace surveillance and managing privacy boundaries. *Management Communication Quarterly*, *21*, 172–200.

Watson, K., & Barker, L. (1995). *Listening styles profile*. Pfeiffer.

Watson-Manheim, M. B., Chudoba, K. M., & Crowston, K. (2012). Perceived discontinuities and constructed continuities in virtual work. *Info Systems*, *22*(1), 29–52.

Watzlawick, P., Beavin, J., & Jackson, D. (1967). *Pragmatics of human communication*. Norton.

Welch, M. (2012). Appropriateness and acceptability: Employee perspectives of internal communication. *Public Relations Review*, *38*(2), 246–254.

West, M. A. (2012). *Effective teamwork*. Wiley.

Westhues, K. (2005). *Workplace mobbing in the academe: Reports from twenty universities*. Edwin Mellen.

Westhues, K. (2006). *The envy of excellence: Administrative mobbing of high achieving professors.* Edwin Mellen.

Wheeless, L. R. (1975). An investigation of receiver apprehension and social context dimensions of communication apprehension. *Speech Teacher, 24,* 261–268.

Wheeless, L. R., Preiss, R. W., & Gayle, B. M. (1997). Receiver apprehension, informational receptivity, and cognitive processing. In J. A. Daly, J. C. McCroskey, J. Ayres, T. Hopf, & D. M. Ayres (Eds.), *Avoiding communication: Shyness, reticence, and communication apprehension* (pp. 151–187). Hampton Press.

Wisse, B., & Rus, D. (2012). Leader self-concept and self-interested behavior. *Journal of Personnel Psychology, 11*(1), 40–48.

Wollman, D. (2008, March). Get ahead: Don't be an email ass. *Laptop,* pp. 120–121.

Wood, J. T. (1994). *Who cares: Women, care, and culture.* Southern Illinois University Press.

Wood, J. T. (2003). *Gendered Lives: Communication, gender, and culture* (5th ed.). Wadsworth/Thomson Learning.

Wood, J. T. (2009). *Communication in our lives* (5th ed.). Wadsworth.

Wood, J. T. (2015). *Gendered lives* (11th ed.). Cengage.

Wright, B., Moynihan, D., & Pandey, S. (2012). Pulling the levers: Transformational leadership, public service motivation, and mission valence. *Public Administration Review, 72*(2), 206–215.

Wright, K. (2004). On-line relational maintenance strategies and perceptions of partners with exclusively Internet-based and primarily Internet-based relationships. *Communication Studies, 55,* 239–253.

Wright, P. (1996). *Managerial leadership.* Routledge.

Yahr, E. (2021, August 31). *'Jeopardy!' severs ties with executive producer Mike Richards after podcast controversy.* The Washington Post. https://www.washingtonpost.com/arts-entertainment/2021/08/31/mike-richards-out-jeopardy-producer/

Yate, M. (2020, September 22). *8 behavioral skills for increased job security.* Society of Human Resources Management. https://www.shrm.org/resourcesandtools/hr-topics/organizational-and-employee-development/career-advice/pages/8-behavioral-skills-for-increased-job-security.aspx

Yee, N., Bailenson, J. N., Urbanek, M., Chang, F., & Merget, D. (2008). The unbearable likeness of being digital: The persistence of nonverbal social norms in online virtual environments. In L. K. Guerrero & M. L. Hecht (Eds.), *The nonverbal communication reader: Classic and contemporary readings* (3rd ed., pp. 203–208). Waveland.

Yen, J. Y., Yen, C. F., Chen, C. S., Wang, P. W., Chang, Y. H., & Ko, C. H. (2012). Social anxiety in online and real-life interaction and their associated factors. *Cyberpsychology, Behavior, and Social Networking, 15*(1), 7–12.

Young Entrepreneur Council. (2013, March 14). 13 tips for delivering a memorable keynote speech. *Small Business Trends.* smallbiztrends.com/2013/03/13-public-speaking-tips.html

Young, M., & Schieman, S. (2012). When hard times take a toll: The distressing consequences of economic hardship and life events within the family-work interface. *Journal of Health and Social Behavior, 53*(1), 84–98.

Young, S., Kelsey, D., & Lancaster, A. (2011). Predicted outcome value of e-mail communication: Factors that foster professional relational development between students and teachers. *Communication Education, 60*(4), 371–388.

Yuille, C., Change, A., Gudmundsson, A., & Sawang, S. (2012). The role of life friendly policies on employees. *Journal of Management and Organization, 18*(1), 53–63.

Zakrzewski, C., & Albergotti, R. (2021, October 11). *The education of Frances Haugen: How the Facebook whistleblower learned to use data as a weapon from years in tech.* The Washington Post. https://www.washingtonpost.com/technology/2021/10/11/facebook-whistleblower-frances-haugen/

Zhou, Q., Hirst, G., & Shipton, H. (2011). Context matters: Combined influence of participation and intellectual stimulation on the promotion focus–employee creativity relationship. *Journal of Organizational Behavior.* https://doi.org/10.1002/job.779

Zhu, C. (2012). Student satisfaction, performance, and knowledge construction in online collaborative learning. *Educational Technology and Society, 15*(1), 127–136.

GLOSSARY

accent. A person's pronunciation of various words in a language

action-oriented listeners. Characterized by direct, concise, error-free communication that is used to negotiate and accomplish a goal

active agreement (call to action). Persuading the audience to take some sort of action analogical reasoning

active listener. One who is fully engaged in the role of listener, making sense of the message and then verifying the accuracy of sense making

adapters. Gestures we use to release tension

adrenaline rush. A physiological process that occurs when adrenaline enters the body; often results in nervous behavior and anxiety for a speaker

advocacy. A strategy for communicating with a supervisor in which the employee evaluates the supervisor's needs and preferences and then develops a message, an argument, or a proposal that lines up with those needs and preferences

_____. Facial expressions and gestures that display emotion

agenda. A guide or an overview of the topics that will be covered during the meeting

_____. Reasoning from an analogy; making an argument by comparing two cases

anger. An emotional state that varies in intensity from mild irritation to intense fury and rage; a feeling of keen displeasure for what we regard as a wrong toward ourselves or others

annual feedback trap. Saving all feedback, both positive and negative, for discussion during an employee's annual performance appraisal

Aristotle. Greek philosopher, author of *The Art of Rhetoric*, student of Plato, and teacher of Alexander the Great

artifacts. Temporary embellishments (e.g., jewelry, sunglasses, perfume) or objects characteristic of a particular culture or institution (e.g., furniture, buildings, technology, artwork, logos) that provide information—both good and bad—about personalities, attitudes, group affiliation, and organizational membership

artist. One of the four roles in innovative problem solving; puts ideas together in new ways

assimilation process. The adjustment period and "settling in" that's common for anyone starting a new job

audience analysis. Asking a series of questions designed to enhance the speaker's understanding of the listeners

audience-based communication apprehen-____. Explains a person's fear of speaking to certain people or groups

_____. A speaker who thinks about the audience during every step of the presentation design and delivery process

authoritative. A leadership style in which the leader makes all the decisions with little input from the team

awards and honors. A résumé section that lists relevant awards and honors received by the job seeker

balance. When there's equal time divided between work and personal life

behavioral questions. A type of interviewing question that asks job seekers to explain how they have handled past situations and how they would handle hypothetical situations

bias. Any assumption we make or attitude we have about a person, an issue, or a topic before we have heard all the facts

birthright. A position of power passed on from parent to child; monarchies are based on birthright

boundary. The line or division between work and life

bully. A type of difficult person characterized by a bad temper; uses aggression and anger to get his or her way

burnout. Chronic exhaustion from persistent workload, decreased motivation, and apathy toward work

business letter. Used to address formal matters in professional communication including cover letters, information sent to customers, announcements about business events, and the like

career exploration. A part of the exploring stage of the job-seeking process; requires job seekers to research opportunities and careers in their majors that correspond with their desires, goals, and priorities

_____. A student services department located on most college and university campuses whose mission is to help students identify careers, find internships, and prepare for employment; may also be referred to as career services, career placements, career development, or career counseling

causal reasoning. A type of inductive reasoning, more commonly known as the cause-and-effect relationship

_____. The means by which messages are sent

charisma. Includes characteristics such as magnetic charm, allure, and an almost supernatural or magical ability to appeal to followers

chronemics. The study of time as communication

cisgender. individuals whose gender identity aligns with the sex they were assigned at birth

coach. The role of the team member with the designated leadership title; duties include calling the meetings, setting the agenda, and facilitating the discussion

codes. Categories of nonverbal communication

coercive power. Derived from one's ability to control another person's behavior with negative reinforcement

cognitive dissonance. A theory, developed by Leon Festinger (1957), positing that when a person has two ideas that contradict each other, it creates mental noise or cognitive dissonance; a useful persuasive strategy

colloquialisms. Slang terms that are locally or regionally based

common ground. Showing the audience how you have a shared interest, concern, or background

communication apprehension. An individual's level of fear or anxiety associated with either real or anticipated communication with another person or persons

Having a positive view of one's own communication when, in reality, it is bad, leading to conflict and hurt feelings in others

communication network. A group of individuals who regularly share a line of communication; can be either formal or informal

Communication Privacy Management. Theory developed by Sandra Petronio that describes how people establish rules about privacy and manage privacy using spatial metaphors

communication rules. Shared understanding of what communication means and what constitutes appropriate communication given the context

community. A geographic space identified as a place to work toward a good life (e.g., health, safety, well-being)

compromise. A lose–lose approach to decision making in which parties blend and concede parts of their individual solutions

computer-mediated communication (CMC). Human communication that occurs through some form of technology

conclusion. The end of a presentation; should include a concluding statement, a summary of the specific purpose and main points, and a strong final impression

conflict. A necessary part of team problem solving and innovative thinking; can be productive and positive if handled properly

connection power. Based on one's connection to people in positions of power or access to a strong support system

connotation. The feelings or emotions that a word implies

consensus. A win–win approach to decision making that occurs when a solution or an agreement that all team members can support is reached

constitutive rules. Rules that define what communication means by prompting us to count certain kinds of communication

contact information. The part of a résumé that includes the job seeker's name, mailing address, phone number, and email address

The information being discussed; descriptive information such as the time of a meeting, a project due date, or the names of coworkers assigned to a team

content-oriented listeners. Characterized by an interest in intellectual challenge, complex information, and a desire to evaluate information carefully before forming judgments and opinions

context. The location, space, and occasion where communication occurs

context analysis. Asking a series of questions designed to enhance the speaker's understanding of the speaking situation

context-based communication apprehension. Describes a fear of communicating in certain contexts, for example, a fear of public speaking

Contingency Theory. A situational leadership theory developed by Fiedler; requires leaders to assess the situation by examining three factors: the leader–follower relationship, the task structure, and the position power

conversational listening. Listening exemplified by the speaking role shifting from one person to another with some degree of frequency

conversational quality. Presenting in a style similar to that used in casual conversation; known as an extemporaneous speaking style

corporate blog. A web log used to improve internal communication at work or for external marketing and public relations

cover letters. One-page letters that accompany the résumé; include the job seeker's interest in a specific position, overview of qualifications, and desire for an interview

credibility. The believability of the speaker and/or the information being presented

criteria. The standard used to make a decision

critical listening. Requires the listener to evaluate the information being sent; may also require some sort of oral or written feedback

The level of knowledge a person has about others who are different in some way in comparison with himself or herself

cultural diversity awareness. Being aware of diversity that's present in any working or social environment

cultural rituals. Practices, behaviors, celebrations, and traditions common to people, organizations, and institutions

culture. The rules of living and functioning in society

cuss words. Also referred to as curse or swear words; viewed as obscene expressions; should not appear in a presentation

customer relations. The interaction between employees or representatives of an organization or business and the people the organization sells to or serves; also known as customer service

customized résumé. A résumé tailored to each position to which the job seeker applies; a concise, audience-centered version of the generic résumé

decision by the leader. Decision-making approach in which members advise the leader, who then makes the ultimate decision

decision making. A step in the problem-solving process in which the team chooses among a set of alternatives

decode. When we make meaning out of verbal and nonverbal cues others send

deductive reasoning. Occurs when the speaker takes general information (premises) and draws a conclusion from that general information

deintensification. When we reduce the intensity of a facial expression connected to a certain emotion

delivery. The nonverbal component of public speaking; ideally consists of good eye contact and a conversational speaking style

democratic. Leadership style in which the leader follows the will of the people, or at least the majority of the people, with decisions often made through voting

                    The functional team role that ensures dissenting points of view are discussed

dialect. Pronunciation, vocabulary, and syntax variations in a language

                  The act of excluding or denying people of products, rights, and services based on their race, ethnicity, religion, gender, age, sexual orientation, or disability

disguising conversation. Making statements about something to see how other people react

distracter. A type of difficult person characterized by a communication style full of tangents

downsizing letter. Used to inform other businesses about skilled employees

available for employment due to company downsizing (e.g., layoffs, fired employees)

dyads. Two people communicating

education. A résumé section that highlights a job seeker's educational background; should not include high school information

electronic aggression. A form of aggressive communication in which people interacting on professional topics are filled with emotionality

electronic bulletin board. An online service to which anyone, not just a subscriber, can obtain access to read postings

electronic résumés. Résumés that will be submitted to employers electronically via the internet; formatting is extremely important when designing electronic résumés

email dialogues. Exchanges of messages about a particular topic using email, professional blog space, and other electronic tools to encourage participation that will ideally lead to new ideas, strategic planning, and sound decision-making

email flame. A hostile message that is blunt, rude, insensitive, or obscene

                  Virus alerts, chain letters, stories disguised as warnings, petitions or calls for help, jokes, pictures, and the like

emblems. Specific, widely understood meanings in a given culture that can substitute for a word or phrase

emotional intelligence. Your ability to monitor your own and others' feelings and emotions, to discriminate among them, and to use this information to guide your thinking and actions

empathetic listening. The ability to pay full attention to another person, void of critique, and to express sensitivity to the sender's nonverbal behavior

employee attrition. The loss or turnover of employees to other jobs and industries perceived as having healthier workplace culture

employee retention. Getting employees to continue working for the same company

employee reviews. A form of written communication used in business and professional settings to provide feedback to employees about how they are performing on the job

employment experience. A résumé section that includes information on past employment positions, such as name of organization, dates of employment, location of organization, and possibly duties; also can be titled "Work History" or "Work/Employment History"

encode. Use of verbal and nonverbal cues to help others understand what we mean

environment. Constructed or natural surroundings that influence your communicative decisions, attitude, and mood

ethical considerations. The variety of factors important for us to consider in any scenario in which we're making a decision, conducting an evaluation, or making a selection

ethical dilemmas. Situations that do not seem to present clear choices between right and wrong or good and evil

ethics. The discussion, determination, and deliberation processes that attempt to decide what is right or wrong, what others should or should not do, and what is considered appropriate in our individual, communal, and professional lives

ethnicity. A social group that may be joined together by factors such as shared history, shared identity, shared geography, or shared culture

ethos. The credibility of the speaker and the information presented in the presentation; one of Aristotle's three forms of rhetoric

evaluating. The logical assessment of the value of the message

expert power. Derived from one's superior expertise in a specific field

explorer. One of the four roles in innovative problem solving; seeks out new information

exploring stage. The first stage of the job-seeking process, which includes self-exploration and career exploration external communication plan. A plan that focuses on communicating information about the organization or business to citizens or employees' families outside any given business

external customers. The people or entities that an organization serves or provides products to and that are external to the company

external noise. Outside distractions that interfere with the message, such as audible talking during a meeting, ruffling of papers, or a cell phone going off in the next cubicle

external sources. Include information that comes from outside the organization, such as from outside agencies, the competition, the government, and the media

external time wasters. Things you don't feel as though you have any control over (e.g., things you are required to attend, such as meetings, or people to whom you are required to talk)

external triggers. Things going on in your environment at work and at home, usually stimulated by others

eye contact. When a speaker looks at the audience while speaking; effective means for reducing nervousness

face-saving action. Verbal and non-verbal communication that honors and maintains the other person's sense of self-respect in a given situation

face-to-face interviews. An interview format in which all parties are in the same room

false close. When speakers tell the audience they are concluding and then present new information

false empowerment. Occurs when a leader acts as if he or she plans to involve the group in the decision-making process and then makes his or her own decision regardless of the input received from the group

family. People in a household, which consists of a minimum of two members related by blood, adoption, marriage, civil union, or partnership—one of them being the householder, who owns or rents the residence

feedback. Information or messages communicated between sender and receiver

fight. One of three modes of conflict resolution; requires you to engage in some type of confrontation; a win–lose approach to problem-solving

flight. One of three modes of conflict resolution; occurs when you choose not to engage or deal with a conflict; a lose–lose approach to problem-solving

formal communication network. The official lines of communication and reporting structure prescribed by the organizational chart

formal presentation. A public speaking opportunity that occurs in a traditional speaking setting, such as presenting a sales pitch to clients or a progress report at the district meeting

friendship/warmth touch. The type of touch people use to show platonic affection toward each other

functional/professional touch. The type of touch that typically takes place within the context of a professional relationship and is low in intimacy

gatekeeping. When subordinates pass some, but not all, of the information on to the supervisor

gender. cultural and involves a person's internal concept of oneself as female, male, a blend of both, or neither

gender nonbinary. their gender identity does not fit within a traditional gender binary of male and female

general distortion. When a superior is given a message that the subordinate has changed or altered to serve his or her own purposes

general language. Characterized by vague descriptions that can be interpreted in a variety of ways by the recipient

general purpose. The overall goal of a presentation, to either inform or persuade

generic résumé. A list of all the information a job seeker may wish to include in a customized résumé

globalization. A process that brings each of us into greater contact with the rest of the world and gives our daily lives an increasingly international orientation

Goal Setting Theory. A motivational theory in which a leader and a team member develop the goal(s) for the team member together

grammar. Attention to the rules of language, such as appropriate use of complete sentences, punctuation, transitions, organization, spacing, paragraphs, and format

grapevine. Regularly occurring lines of communication that exist within an organization but are not prescribed by the organizational chart; also known as the informal communication network

group. Three or more individuals who are working toward a common goal or share a common purpose

groupthink. The tendency of highly cohesive groups to suspend critical thinking and make faulty decisions

grump. A type of difficult person characterized by a negative attitude

haptics. The study of touch and human contact

hearing. Your physical ability to detect sounds

hobbies and interests. A section that appears on some job seekers' résumés; not recommended

huddles. Short meetings in which employees are pulled together to share information; often occur at the beginning or end of the day

human communication. The process of making sense of the world and sharing that sense with others by creating meaning through the use of verbal and nonverbal messages

HURIER model. A six-step listening process: Hearing, Understanding, Remembering, Interpreting, Evaluating, and Responding

illegal questions. Interview questions that violate the Civil Rights Act of 1964, Title VII, by asking questions regarding race, color, religion, sex, national origin, disability, or age when hiring or promoting employees

illustrators. Gestures that complement, enhance, or substitute for the verbal message

imagery. Painting a picture or image with one's words

imbalance triggers. Experiences (e.g., conflict, aggression, overload, negativity) that cause professionals to feel drained, used, abused, and unhappy

impression management. Directing the formation of an impression, a perception, or a view that others have of you

impromptu presentation. Delivering a presentation with very limited, if any, preparation

indirect questioning. Asking questions in a roundabout way to retrieve information that will make you more competitive, help you make better choices, and help you survive in an organization

inductive reasoning. Building an argument by using individual examples, pieces of information, or cases, and pulling them together to make a generalization or conclusion

inform. The general purpose of presentations in which the speaker presents the facts, acting as a teacher relaying information

informal communication network. Regularly occurring lines of communication that exist within an organization but are not prescribed by the organizational chart; also known as the grapevine

informational listening. Listening that allows you to focus on the content of the message in order to acquire knowledge

information and communications technologies (ICTs). Mobile digital devices such as personal digital assistants and smartphones that may harm work–life boundaries and also serve as tools for managing them

information overload. When information, requests for feedback, new projects, responses to questions, phone calls, and required online classes for work, on top of attending to loved ones, children,

pets, and other family matters, leave you stressed and feeling as though things are spinning out of control

ingratiation. A strategy for communicating with a supervisor in which the employee acts warm and friendly toward him or her

inoculation. When a speaker points out information that could hurt a persuasive argument and explains why it is not important or relevant, in an attempt to minimize its impact in the future

intensification. Expression that exaggerates how we feel about something

interests. The needs and concerns underlying each position

internal communication plan. A plan that focuses on communication taking place inside the daily operations of any given business

internal customer. An employee who needs services or products from other parts of the organization to complete his or her work

internal noise. Internal conditions or distractions that interfere with the message

internal preview. The preview of an idea or a main point found within the body of a presentation

internal sources. Include information that comes from within the organization, such as reports, policies, or interviews with employees and/or customers

internal summary. The summary of an idea or a main point found within the body of a presentation

internal time wasters. More personal internal things brought on by mindset, motivation, and bad habits

internal triggers. Concerns and frustrations you have about past, current, and future events or a general negativity toward yourself (e.g., "I'm really angry at myself for not making that change sooner")

internet. An excellent tool for locating employment opportunities and researching potential employers

internship. An on-the-job learning opportunity for students; can be paid, unpaid, or for college credit

interpersonal communication. The cocreation of meaning as people interact

interpreting. Making sense of verbal and nonverbal codes to assign meaning to the information received

intimacy. Characterized by feelings of closeness and trust that you share with other people

introduction. The start of a presentation; should include five components: gain attention, introduce the topic, develop credibility, relate the topic to the audience, and preview the main points

jargon. The terminology or language of a given field or profession

job fairs. Events in which multiple employers come together to recruit potential employees; held both on college campuses and in the community

job seeker. Any person trying to gain employment (although job seekers are commonly referred to as interviewees, the job-seeking process includes much more than the interviewing stage)

job-seeking process. Six stages involved in finding employment: exploring, researching, applying, interviewing, following up, and negotiating

job title. The name associated with each position in an organization; intended to designate duties and status

judge. One of the four roles in innovative problem-solving; evaluates possible solutions and then selects

kinesics. General term for the study of human movement, gestures, and posture

laissez-faire. Leadership style in which the team makes the decisions with little input from the leader; French expression meaning "allow to do"

language barriers. When people trying to communicate do not share a common language

lead. The person who is accountable for a given task

leadership. A dynamic relationship based on mutual influence and common purpose between leaders and collaborators, in which both are moved to higher levels of motivation and moral development as they affect real, intended change

leadership functions. Include influencing and guiding followers, as well as being innovative and creating a vision for future direction

legitimate power. Derived from one's position of authority

listening. Receiving verbal and nonverbal messages and then determining meaning from those messages

listserv. A computer service that facilitates discussions by connecting people who share common interests

logos. The logic of the presentation; established through both the organizational structure and the supporting information; one of Aristotle's three forms of rhetoric

love/intimacy touch. Highly personal and intimate touch used to communicate affection

managerial functions. Include being in charge of and responsible for various goals and functions in an organization, as well as supervising subordinates

managerial grid. A situational leadership theory developed by Robert Blake and Jane Mouton; includes five managerial styles: impoverished, country club, authoritative, middle-of-the-road, and team

manuscript. A speaking text written out word for word; speakers should avoid using manuscripts

masking. Hiding an expression connected to a felt emotion and replacing it with an expression more appropriate to the situation

meeting environment. Includes both the time a meeting is held and its location; considered a part of the communication

meetingthink. The suspension of critical thinking due to common variables such as false empowerment, overload, or poorly run meetings

memo. Short for memorandum; typically a short note or update distributed in business

message. The information or feedback that is communicated

message overload. Receiving too much information at once, making it difficult to stay focused on the primary message being communicated

metaphor. A literary device in which the speaker uses comparison

misspellings. Mistakes in spelling

mock interviews. A practice run done prior to an interview to help job seekers anticipate questions, script answers, and lessen nervousness

monotone. A vocal quality that has only one pitch; a lack of vocal variety in a speaker's voice

Monroe's Motivated Sequence repetition. The five-step process, developed in 1935 by Purdue University professor Alan H. Monroe, includes the attention step, the need step, the satisfaction step, the visualization step, and the action step.

mutual respect. People seeking understanding through the vehicle of open dialogue; attempting to understand others with an open mind leads them to respond with mutual respect and understanding

narratives. Stories we use to come to understand the organizational culture and one another

negotiation. A strategy used by a job seeker if he or she does not believe the salary, working conditions, and/or benefits are satisfactory; involves providing a counteroffer to the initial terms of employment presented by a potential employer

networking notes. A form of thank-you letter used to remind employers of your interview and to convince them that you're the right person for the job

neutralization. The process of using facial expressions to hide how we really feel

noise. External or internal disruption to the context

nonverbal communication. Communication other than written or spoken language that creates meaning for someone

norm. An unwritten rule of behavior

objective. A one- or two-sentence declarative statement about a job seeker's career goals; also, relaying information without being influenced or impacted by emotions or individual point of view, necessary in informative presentations

objective. A one- or two-sentence declarative statement about a job seeker's career goals; also, relaying information without being influenced or impacted by emotions or individual point of view, necessary in informative presentations

oculesics. The study of eye behavior

one-on-one interview. A face-to-face interview that can consist of one interviewer and one interviewee; job seekers may undergo a series of one-on-one interviews

online application. An electronic form used by employers to standardize the information gathered from job seekers; commonly requests information found on a traditional résumé

organic speaking opportunity. A public speaking opportunity that occurs in a less traditional speaking setting, such as during huddles or at the start of meetings

organizational chart. Visual representation of the supervision and reporting structure of a company; outlines the formal communication network

organizational culture. The way an organization operates, the attitudes the employees have, and the overall tone and approach to any given business

organizational values. Specific principles or guidelines such as safety, teamwork, integrity, or ownership that are typically outlined in support of any given organizational mission or goal

organizer. Member of a team presentation who provides the introduction, conclusion, and transitions to the presentation

overload. Occurs when group members have so much on their plates that they cannot truly concentrate on and engage in a meeting

overtalker. Group member who dominates conversations, occasionally leading the discussion

overt questioning. The practice of asking a direct question about what you want to know

panel interview. An interviewing format that includes more than one interviewer, multiple interviewees, or both

paraphrase. Restating or summarizing what is communicated to clarify meaning and check understanding

passive agreement. Persuading the audience simply to agree or disagree with an idea

passive listener. One who simply receives a message without giving feedback or verifying understanding of the message

pathos. The emotional appeal; one of Aristotle's three forms of rhetoric

patient. A type of difficult person who treats coworkers and sometimes even supervisors as counselors; brings personal problems to work and discusses them on company time

perception process. Characterized by demonstrating concern for others' emotions and interests, finding common ground, and responding to the emotional states of human behavior

perception checking. Asking others if one's perception or sense of understanding is correct or incorrect

performance appraisal. Formal evaluation that often involves an interview and a written summary of the employee's strengths and weaknesses on the job

performance improvement plan. A specific and clear strategy for improving employee performance; should be derived from two-way communication

persuade. The general purpose of presentations in which the speaker advocates for something or against something

persuasive appeals. Developed by Aristotle—ethos, logos, and pathos

phishing. Sending authentic-looking but fraudulent emails designed to steal sensitive personal information

physical appearance. The ways our bodies and overall appearance nonverbally communicate to others and impact our view of ourselves in everyday life

planning documents. Forms of written communication usually presented with maps and other visual designs to lay out a broader vision of where the company is going and what specific strategies will be used in the near future

position. A demand that includes each person's solution to the problem

presentational listening. Listening that takes place in situations where a clear role of speaking and listening functions is prescribed

press releases. Forms of written communication used to send messages to a variety of media organizations, including newspaper, radio, television, and internet

private employment agencies. For-profit organizations, also known as headhunters, that help job seekers find jobs and help employers find qualified workers for a fee

press release. A form of written communication similar to a press release that emphasizes an organization's commitment to safety and compliance

problem-solving. Generating quality alternatives from which to select, selecting the best alternative, and then working to implement that choice

process directives. Descriptions of new policies/procedures and changes to those already in place

professional associations. Organizations designed to facilitate networking and educational opportunities for professionals in a given field or industry by sponsoring meetings and conferences

professional etiquette. Displaying the behaviors of social etiquette and good manners in a professional setting

professional excellence. Being recognized for your skills as a communicator, serving as a role model to those around you, recognizing your strengths and developing your weaknesses, being audience centered, understanding the context, and possessing the ability to adapt and continually improve

proposals. Forms of written communication used in many business and professional settings to propose products and services to potential clients

proxemics. How people create and use space and distance, as well as how they behave to protect and defend that space

public image. The impression you give or present to others both verbally and nonverbally

qualitative data. Characterized by actual words, phrases, responses to open-ended questions, and interviews

quantitative data. Characterized by numbers, percentages, statistics, and surveys

questions. Requests made to learn information or clarify understanding

Quintilian. A Roman philosopher and educator

race. The categorization of people based on physical characteristics such as skin color, dimensions of the human face, and hair

receiver. The listener who interprets the message

receiver apprehension. The fear of misinterpreting, inadequately processing, and/or not being able to adjust psychologically to messages sent by others

recommendation letter. A form of written communication used to provide a documented reference for students and professionals

references. Persons who can tell potential employers about a job seeker's experience, knowledge, work ethic, and character

referent power. Given to someone because you want that person to like you

reflection. Listening technique characterized by observing and interpreting verbal and nonverbal cues in order to summarize and restate back to the speaker to clarify content and meaning

Reflective Thinking Process. Problem-solving process developed by John Dewey that includes describing and analyzing the problem, generating possible solutions, evaluating all solutions, deciding on the solution, and planning how to implement the solution

regulative rules. Describe when, how, where, and with whom to talk about certain things; also dictate appropriateness

regulators. Gestures used to control turn-taking in conversations

relational layer. Communication that reveals how you feel about the receiver

relationship roles. Functional roles that help the team maintain positive relationships among members

relevant experience. A résumé section that includes relevant employment history as well as internships, relevant class projects, relevant work with student organizations, or volunteering; often used in place of the "Employment Experience" section by recent college graduates

retrieval. Recalling the message so that it can be acted on

reports. Written communication used to summarize research or assessment findings to inform managers about important issues related to business (e.g., customer service, employee satisfaction, employee morale)

research. Gathering information (e.g., definitions, examples, statistics, testimonies) that aids in the design of the presentation and supports the specific purpose

researching stage. The second stage of the job-seeking process, which comprises two components: researching openings and researching potential employers; requires job seekers to find the right fit as opposed to merely searching for vacancies and applying to anything and everything that is available

responding. Giving some form of a *response* to the message, either verbally or nonverbally

résumé. A snapshot of the job seeker as an employee; highlights skill sets to provide a picture of how the job seeker fits this position and this organization

retention. To remember over a long period of time

reward power. Derived from one's ability to control another person's behavior with positive reinforcement

roadblock to change. A type of difficult person characterized by a dislike and even refusal to carry out changes in his or her duties

role models. People who display behaviors and attitudes that are replicated by others

round robin technique. A communication technique in which team members go around the circle, allowing everyone to share his or her perceptions of the issue; requires members to listen and not interrupt while other team members are speaking

scannable résumés. A résumé that will be submitted to an employer and/or transmitted by the employer via fax or computer scanning; formatting is extremely important when designing scannable résumés

scripting. The process of mentally rehearsing what you will say during the discussion

scripting answers. Answering interview questions using a three-part formula: directly answer the question, back up the answer with a specific example, and tie the answer back to this company and/or this position

self-centered roles. Dysfunctional roles that can interfere with a team's functioning

self-disclose. To share information that people cannot learn about us unless we reveal it to them

self-exploration. Part of the exploring stage of the job-seeking process; requires a job seeker to identify his or her desires, goals, and priorities

semantic information distance. A difference in perception that exists between employees and supervisors over fundamental areas such as organizational issues or basic job duties

sender. The person initiating the exchange

sex. Label (i.e., female or male) a person is assigned at birth based on biological characteristics

sexual arousal. Touches that are extremely intimate

sexual orientation. involves who a person is attracted to romantically, emotionally, and sexually.

shadowing. A learning opportunity for job seekers in which they watch or follow a professional to learn what is involved in a given position or profession

signposts. Words or phrases that indicate the speaker's place in the organizational structure (e.g., *first, second, to clarify*)

situational communication apprehension. Refers to apprehension to communicate in specific sets of circumstances

Situational Leadership Theory. Developed by Hersey and Blanchard; requires leaders to examine task behavior, relationship behavior, and level of maturity/readiness of the followers to select the most effective communication style

skills. Information that must be highlighted on the job seeker's résumé either as a separate section or as part of his or her experiences; may include information about computer knowledge, leadership, communication abilities, language fluency, and more

slacker. A type of difficult person characterized by lack of productivity; finds any excuse not to work

slang. Words that are either made-up or used to express something other than their formal meaning; should not appear in a presentation

sniper. A type of difficult person characterized by sarcastic and inappropriate comments meant to wound those at which they are aimed

social/polite touch. Touch connected to cultural norms, such as hugs or pats on the back; conveying relatively low intimacy within a relationship verbal communication

socialization. The experiences that shape our attitudes, perceptions, emotions, and communication choices

sociopath. A type of difficult person characterized by a lack of conscience and guilt; it is estimated that 1 out of every 25 people is a sociopath

spam. The use of a user's email address for a purpose to which the user didn't agree; junk email sent by "spammers" who obtain email addresses by buying company customer lists or using programs to produce email addresses randomly

speaking outline. A tool used by the speaker when delivering a presentation; more concise and less detailed than the practice outline

speaking rate. The rate of speed at which a speaker talks

specific language. Specific with facts, percentages, conclusions, and recommendations

specific purpose. Declarative sentence telling the listeners what the speaker wants them to understand, know, or believe by the end of the presentation; the equivalent of a thesis statement in an essay

stages of team development. Forming, storming, norming, performing, and adjourning

star. An employee who possesses all the qualities of a team player but also wants to take on extra duties, learn more, and advance his or her career

State employment service. A not-for-profit government agency, sometimes called the Job Service, that helps job seekers find jobs and employers find qualified workers, at no cost to either party summary

status. A person's rank or position in an organization

stereotypes. The way humans use their minds to perceive others as belonging to a social group

strategic planning. The development of a plan that emphasizes goals, initiatives, strategies, and targets utilized to help employees strive for a shared vision and commitment to an organization's core values

subordinate. Employee, typically a lower-status person

summarization. Occurs when an employee summarizes a message in such a way that emphasis is placed on certain aspects of the message

superior. Supervisor or employee, typically a higher-status person

supporting aids. Tools used by a speaker to help support the audience's interest in and understanding of the presentation; visual or audio aids used to enhance a presentation

surveillance. Using observational skills to take stock of any given situation

task roles. Functional roles that help the team complete its tasks and achieve its goals

team. A group in which members share leadership responsibility for creating a team identity, achieving mutually defined goals, and fostering innovative thinking

team player. An employee who completes tasks, gets along with coworkers, and serves customers with a positive attitude; hardworking and dependable

telephone interview. A type of interview conducted over the phone; often used during the early screening phases of the interview process

testing limits. Cutting corners or choosing to avoid a behavior or practice to see how it will influence the outcome

texting language. Expressions or acronyms used when sending instant messages and text messages—for example, LOL (laugh out loud) or TU (thank you); should not be used

thank-you letters. Written communication used to express appreciation to coworkers and clients

Theory X. Management theory based on the underlying assumption that employees are inherently lazy and will avoid

work whenever possible; therefore, workers must be closely supervised and communication should be top down; developed by McGregor

Theory Y. Management theory based on the underlying assumption that employees can be ambitious and self-motivated and that, therefore, supervisors should seek to empower employees and two-way communication is needed; developed by McGregor

third-party questioning. Asking direct questions of people who have had the same experiences as you at a different time

time-oriented listeners. Characterized by an awareness of or desire to be in control of the time constraints of interactions

traditional questions. A type of interviewing question that asks for basic information about the job seeker, such as "Tell me about your strengths and weaknesses"

trait. A distinguishing characteristic or quality that is part of a person's character; traits are often seen as inborn or genetically based

trait communication apprehension. Means that one possesses a "shy trait," for example, tending not to raise a hand in class, avoiding certain social situations, and feeling extremely anxious about giving a professional presentation

transformational leaders. Leaders who articulate a goal or vision to an organization and then inspire followers to make this vision a reality; a change agent

transgender. individuals—or individuals whose gender identity differs from the sex they were assigned at birth

transition. Any word or phrase that helps guide the listener from one point to the next

translation services. Interpretation systems available to assist with language barriers and other communication-related concerns

types of reasoning. Include inductive reasoning, causal reasoning, deductive reasoning, analogical reasoning, and cognitive dissonance

typos. Mistakes in typing

understanding. The process of attaching meaning to the verbal communication, or comprehending the literal meaning of the message

undertalker. Group member who tends to sit silently during meetings, failing to participate or give input

unite. One of three modes of conflict resolution; defines team members as joint problem solvers as opposed to adversaries; a win–win approach to problem-solving

unplugged. The avoidance of checking email, sending text messages, watching television, or answering the phone

upward distortion. The alteration of messages sent from subordinates to supervisors

values. Moral principles or rules that determine ethical behaviors

vampire. A type of difficult person characterized by an appealing personality and a lack of productivity; a type of slacker

videoconference. A type of interview conducted via live video

virtual team. A group of coworkers who use computer-mediated communication to accomplish tasks and professional projects traditionally completed face to face, in order to save on time and travel

visual learners. Audience members who more easily comprehend and remember information presented to them through visual as opposed to audio channels

vocal fillers. Also known as vocalized pauses; occur when the speaker should pause but instead fills the silence;

common fillers include "umm" and "aah" and the words and and like

vocalics. Sometimes referred to as paralanguage; refers to how people use their voices to communicate and express themselves

volume. The loudness or softness of a speaker's voice

voting. A decision-making approach in which team members cast a vote for the solution they find most meritorious; the solution that receives the most votes is implemented

warrior. One of the four roles in innovative problem-solving; develops and carries out the plan

white space. The portion of the résumé that is void of text; balancing text and white space creates visual appeal; also, the unprescribed portions of the organizational chart where the informal communication network develops

white space. The portion of the résumé that is void of text; balancing text and white space creates visual appeal; also, the unprescribed portions of the organizational chart where the informal communication network develops

withholding. The failure of subordinates to pass information on to supervisors

word-of-mouth. A useful tool in the job-seeking process; involves telling everyone the job seeker knows that he or she is job seeking; most effective when the job seeker is specific about the kind of job he or she is seeking

work. Instrument of activity intended to provide goods and services to support life

workforce communication assessment. An inventory or evaluation of the communication practices of an organization (also known as a communication audit)

work–life balance. "Accomplishment of role-related expectations that are negotiated and shared between an individual and his or her role-related partners in the work and family [life] domains" (Grzywacz & Carlson, 2007, p. 458)

workplace bullying. Repeated acts and practices that are directed intentionally or unconsciously and that cause embarrassment, humiliation, and stress

workplace mobbing. The nonsexual harassment of a coworker by a group of other workers or other members of an organization, designed to secure removal from the organization of the one who is targeted

workplace surveillance systems. Efforts to monitor and track employee behavior in terms of the information they access or communicate while at work

worldview. A culture's orientation to supernatural, human, and natural entities in the cosmological universe and other philosophical issues influencing how its members see the world

writing startup sheet. A list of questions that encourage the writer to think about audience, purpose, key issues, and delivery

ABOUT THE AUTHORS

Kelly Quintanilla Miller, formerly Quintanilla (PhD, Pennsylvania State University), is the president and CEO of Texas A&M University-Corpus Christi (TAMUCC). She earned her doctorate in communication in 1994, joining the TAMUCC faculty that same year. During her time at TAMUCC, Dr. Miller was provost and vice president of academic affairs, dean of the College of Liberal Arts, and director of the School of Arts, Media & Communication. She also served as chair for the Department of Communication & Theatre.

Dr. Miller is a professor of communication. She has taught courses in business and professional communication, teamwork and leadership, organizational communication, public relations, and public speaking. Over the years, she has received awards for her teaching, advising, service, and scholarship. She has also worked as an executive coach and as an organizational communication consultant for a variety of industries. Although she loves her career, her greatest love is spending time with her family on the sunny beaches of South Texas.

Shawn T. Wahl (PhD, University of Nebraska, Lincoln) is a professor of communication and dean of the Judith Enyeart Reynolds College of Arts and Letters (RCOAL) at Missouri State University (MSU). Under Dean Wahl's leadership, the college received the largest scholarship gift in MSU history. Dean Wahl served as the co-chair of the MSU Long-Range Plan (LRP). He served as the interim dean of RCOAL from 2017 to 2019 and as the department head of Communication at MSU from 2012 to 2017. Prior to MSU, he served as the department head of Communication, Mass Media, & Theatre at Angelo State University and as the founding director of graduate studies at Texas A&M University, Corpus Christi. Shawn completed the Harvard Management Development Program (MDP) in 2016 and the Harvard Institute for Educational Management (IEM) in 2022. Shawn served as resident of the Central States Communication Association (CSCA) in 2016. He has authored seven books

including *Public Speaking: Essentials for Excellence, Nonverbal Communication for a Lifetime, The Communication Age: Connecting and Engaging, Business and Professional Communication: KEYS for Workplace Excellence, Persuasion in Your Life, Intercultural Communication In Your Life* and *Public Relations Principles: Strategies for Professional Success*. Shawn has published numerous international and national research articles in *Communication Education, Communication Research Reports, Communication Studies, Communication Teacher, Journal of Family Communication*, and the *Basic Communication Course Annual*. Shawn earned the Distinguished Article Award: Instructional Development Division (IDD) National Communication Association (NCA) in 2021. In addition, Shawn has worked across the globe as a corporate trainer, communication consultant, and leadership coach in a variety of industries.

INDEX